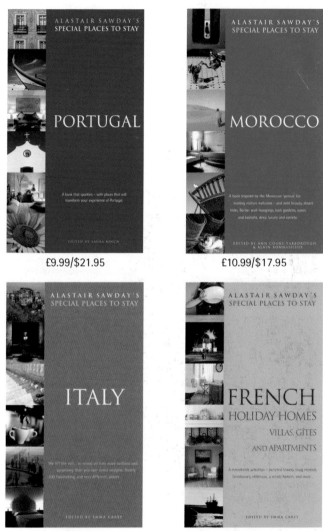

Sixth edition
Copyright © February 2005
Alastair Sawday Publishing Co. Ltd
Published in February 2005
Alastair Sawday Publishing Co. Ltd
The Home Farm Stables,
Barrow Gurney, Bristol BS48 3RW
Tel: +44 (0)1275 464891
Fax: +44 (0)1275 464887
Email: info@specialplacestostay.com
Web: www.specialplacestostay.com

The Globe Pequot Press
P.O. Box 480, Guilford,
Connecticut 06437, USA
Tel: +1 203 458 4500
Fax: +1 203 458 4601
E-mail: info@globepequot.com
Web: www.globepequot.com

Design:
Caroline King

Maps & Mapping:
Bartholomew Mapping, a division of
HarperCollins, Glasgow

Printing:
Pims, UK

UK Distribution:
Penguin UK, 80 Strand, London

US Distribution:
The Globe Pequot Press, Guilford,
Connecticut

A catalogue record for this book is
available from the British Library.

This publication is not included under
licences issued by the Copyright Agency.
No part of this publication may be
used in any form of advertising, sales
promotion or publicity.

**Alastair Sawday has asserted his right
to be identified as the author of this
work.**

ISBN 1-901970-56-6

Printed in UK on Revive Silk: 75% de-inked
post-consumer waste, 25% mill broke and
virgin fibres.

The publishers have made every effort to
ensure the accuracy of the information
in this book at the time of going to
press. However, they cannot accept
any responsibility for any loss, injury
or inconvenience resulting from the
use of information contained therein.

ALASTAIR SAWDAY'S
SPECIAL PLACES TO STAY

SPAIN

Contents

Alastair Sawday Publishing

We began by chance, in 1993, seeking a job for a friend. On my desk was a file: a miscellany of handsome old houses in France, some that could provide a bed, and some a meal, to strangers.

I ran a small travel company at the time, taking people off the beaten track; these places were our 'finds'. No chain hotels for us, no tourist restaurants if we could possibly visit old manor houses, farms and châteaux whose owners would breathe new life into our enthusiasm for France.

So Jane set off with a file under her arm and began to turn it into a book. We were then innocent enough to ignore advice and print 'far too many' – 10,000. We sold them all, in six months – and a publishing company was born.

We exhorted readers to enjoy a 'warm welcome, wooden beams, stone walls, good coffee' and nailed our colours firmly to the mast: 'We are not impressed by TVs, mini-bars and trouser-presses'. We urged people to enjoy simplicity and authenticity and railed against the iniquities of corporate travel. Little has changed.

Although there are now more than 25 of us working out here in our rural idyll, publishing about 20 books, we are holding tightly to our original ethos and gradually developing it. Our first priority is to publish the best books in our field and to nourish a reputation for integrity. It is critically important that readers trust our judgement.

Our next priority is to sell them – fortunately they sell themselves, too, such is their reputation for reliability and for providing travellers with memorable experiences and friendships.

However, publishing and selling books is not enough. It raises other questions: what is our impact on the world around us? How do we treat ourselves and other people? Is not a company just people working together with a shared focus? So we have begun to consider our responses to those questions and thus have generated our Ethical Policy.

There is little intrinsically ethical about publishing travel guides, but there are ways in which we can improve. Firstly, we use recycled paper and seek the most eco-friendly printing methods. Secondly, we are promoting local economies and encouraging good work. We seek beauty and are providing an alternative to the corporate culture that has done so much damage. Thirdly, we celebrate the use of locally-sourced and organic food among our owners and have launched a Fine Breakfast scheme in our British bed & breakfast guides.

But the way we function as a company matters too. We treat each other with respect and affection. An easy-going but demanding office atmosphere seems to work for us. But for these things to survive we need to engage all the staff, so we are split into three teams: the Green team, the Better Business team and the Charitable Trust team.

Each team meets monthly to advise the company. The Green team uses our annual Environmental Audit as a text and monitors progress. The Better Business team ponders ethical issues such as flexible working, time off in lieu/overtime, and other matters that need a deep airing before decisions are made. The Trust team allocates the small sum that the company gives each year to charities, and raises extra money.

A few examples of our approach to company life: we compost our waste, recycle the recyclable, run a shared car to work, run a car on LPG and another on a mix of recycled cooking oil and diesel, operate a communal organic food ordering system, use organic or local food for our own events, take part in Bike to Work day, use a 'green' electricity supplier, partially bank with Triodos

Photo Paul Groom

(the ethical bank in Bristol), have a health insurance scheme that encourages alternative therapies, and sequester our carbon emissions.

Especially exciting for us is an imminent move to our own eco offices; they will conserve energy and use little of it. But I have left to the end any mention of our most tangible effort in the ethical field: our Fragile Earth series of books. There are *The Little Food Book*, *The Little Earth Book* and T*he Little Money Book* – hugely respected and selling solidly – look out for new titles in the Fragile Earth series.

Perhaps the most vital element in our growing Ethical Policy is the sense of engagement that we all have. It is not only stimulating to be trying to do the right thing, but it is an important perspective for us all at work. And that can only help us to continue to produce beautiful books.

Alastair Sawday

Acknowledgements

The vastnesses of Spain have exhausted many an intrepid traveller; others have taken their time to wander slowly across the landscape - perhaps on a donkey or a horse. Jose Navarro, our intrepid editor, had no such luxury. He was in a hurry, but he took care to create a strong base camp in a village to the north of Zaragoza. From there he directed his team of inspectors (Guy, Barry and Rob were stalwart and, like Jose, also took some of the photographs which appear here). He juggled flocks of letters, an effluence of emails and a barrage of enquiries. His job was to put together this new edition, discovering the special places that had opened since the last one and checking out many of the previous entries. It is a huge job and he has done it with integrity and energy.

So, our thanks go to Jose. He works with the spirit of a real traveller - bicycling wherever possible, asking questions and penetrating deep below the skin of everywhere he goes. His one major disappointment this year was the cancellation of the annual transhumance of thousands of sheep across Spain and to pastures new. He was to accompany them. That is the sort of man he is.

Alastair Sawday

Series Editor
Alastair Sawday

Editor
Jose Navarro

Editorial Director
Annie Shillito

Managing Editor
Jackie King

Production Manager
Julia Richardson

Web & IT
Russell Wilkinson, Matt Kenefick

Production
Rachel Coe, Paul Groom,
Allys Williams

Copy Editor Jo Boissevain

Editorial
Maria Serrano, Roanne Finch,
Danielle Williams, Paula Brown,

Sales & Marketing & PR
Siobhán Flynn, Paula Brown,
Sarah Bolton

Accounts
Sheila Clifton, Bridget Bishop,
Christine Buxton, Jenny Purdy,
Sandra Hasell

Writing
Jo Boissevain, Viv Cripps,
Guy Hunter-Watts, Sue Merriman,
Helen Pickles, Hamish Wills

Inspections
Barry Birch, Vanessa Elliott-Smith,
Guy Hunter-Watts, Jose Navarro,
Rob Paterson

Previous Editor Guy Hunter-Watts

'The trouble with many travellers is that they take themselves along.'

Thus wrote Joseph Prescott – and I know what he meant. Horace long ago had similar thoughts: 'They change their skies but not their souls who run across the seas.' But I earnestly hope that such thoughts need not always be true. What of those who go with open minds to far places and stay with the locals?

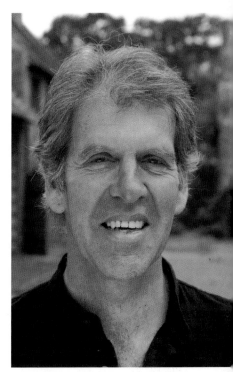

This book enables you to achieve that. I defy you to remain entirely unchanged by your experience with it. It will take you to places where you will learn what it is to be Spanish, to people whose sheer conviviality will inspire you to be more convivial at home. You will taste food that will linger on and remind you to try harder in the kitchen. (You will come home and buy only the best of local ingredients.) You will have conversations of an animation and intensity that you thought only existed on stage. You will, in short, love it – and you will experience it at many levels.

This book has changed bit by bit with every edition. Where once it was hard to find hundreds of places to excite the senses, it is no longer so. There are houses and hotels within these pages that will astonish and delight you for the sheer exuberance of their design and 'Spanishness'. We now need to make very few concessions, for the level of comfort has soared and the range of types of places has grown enormously.

Spain's natural ability to feed our souls and our imaginations has always been powerful; now she does it with panache and confidence. The results are here for you to admire – and enjoy.

Alastair Sawday

Photo Paul Groom

Introduction

WE HOPE IT WILL BRING YOU CLOSER TO THE
SPAIN THAT WE LOVE, A COUNTRY WHOSE
PEOPLE ARE VIBRANT AND SPONTANEOUS...

How we choose our Special Places? I confess that our choices are subjective, almost entirely so. I suspect that most of our inspectors walk into a place and make the sort of rapid judgement that we all make when we meet new people or places. I certainly do. Yet an hour or so spent with an owner who takes a while to unfreeze can change one's mind.

So we select the places that, first and foremost, we like; and that means choosing our inspectors with some care. Jose Navarro, who has put much of this book together, has earned our respect over a long period. (We were initially attracted by the notion of a Spaniard from Zaragoza spending so much time in the Hebrides; he must be just a little unusual, we thought.) We like places that buzz with humanity and individuality, where the smiles spring from a genuine interest in people and where the fabric of the building reflects a real feel for place. We look, too, for a sense of fun.

The horrors of mass tourism remain, but the standards of accommodation are improving massively. There is fierce competition now: new *casas rurales* (country houses) and *hoteles con encanto* (charming hotels) open every week, and new hotelier associations are being set up to encourage good taste and good practice – 'Casonas Asturianas', for example. We have included over 90 new places in this edition, many of which provide not only extraordinary value for money, but also a special experience.

Expect this book to lead you to places that are original, individual and welcoming. We hope it will bring you closer to the Spain that we love, a country whose people are vibrant and spontaneous, incredibly friendly and – yes, the cliché is true – different.

Photo left Posada de Lluc, entry 359
Photo opposite La Almunia del Vallee, entry 319

Introduction

Photo Hotel San Roque, entry 368

There are quite a lot of foreign-run places in this book, for which we make no apology. We don't search them out, but some of them are marvellous places to stay and those we include have a proven track-record of commitment to their adopted land and people. A night or two with people from one's own culture can be a relief to all of us after a long journey.

What to expect

The Spanish 'way of being' is – well – just Spanish. Expect things to happen differently – and long may that be the case. One small scene illustrates the point. Imagine that you are standing at the counter of a bar in, say, the old town of Ronda.

Two working men enter the bar, and one shouts at the barman. "Oiga! Una cerveza," – literally, "Here, give me a beer". The barman doesn't bat an eyelid and a beer is thumped down on the bar: not a 'please' nor a 'thank you' from either party. You might think that the two men are about to come to blows: why else would they be shouting at each other when standing one foot apart? It gradually dawns on you from the smiles and laughter that this is simply a lively discussion and that daggers will not be drawn. Meanwhile, just behind the two men, an unwatched TV screams at full volume. You are both irritated and deafened. So you pluck up courage and ask the barman if he could just turn it down "un poquito". "Of course, amigo", he replies, and turns it off, clearly bemused because he had not even noticed it was switched on.

You cannot judge Spain by your own cultural yardsticks. So in hotels, bars and restaurants be quick to pardon what might at first seem a brash or an abrupt way of being. The Spanish language can be as rich and convoluted as it is economical, almost austere. And don't be surprised or put off by how rarely the words 'please' and 'thank you' are used in daily conversations. No rudeness is meant.

Mañana, mañana

Yes, we all know that the Spanish conception of time can be fairly loose. It makes me think of Salvador Dali's painting of a melting watch dripping from a table onto the floor. Spaniards firmly believe they determine the course of time and not the other way round. You will have to take this on board and relax about time when in Spain. Enjoy all those 'little' things that can make life so enjoyable, with which the Spaniards regularly indulge themselves. The *sobremesa*, the ubiquitous chat over coffee after lunch; a siesta to cope with the rigours of the hot summers; or *el paseo*, the aimless stroll down the main avenue at dusk with no specific purpose in mind.

Standards of living

Spain is not the cheap place to travel that it used to be. Whether this is due to the euro or not, standards have gone up, and so, correspondingly, have prices. While some things, such as petrol and transport, are cheaper than in the UK, others – including accommodation – have become more expensive.

Cheap *menús del día* (set menus) are becoming harder to find. A full trolley at the local supermarket will not be any cheaper than in the UK – apart from the wine and the olive oil, perhaps. Books are definitely more expensive than in the UK. Tickets for the theatre and exhibitions are much more expensive.

Finding the right place for you

We have sought out beautiful homes and hotels throughout Spain. But we have also chosen some good places where the 'charm' factor may, at first glance, be low. But choose your hotel on looks alone and you will miss out on some remarkable places to stay. Don't be too put off by, say, a cavernous-looking and noisy restaurant – the food may be tremendous. Likewise, be prepared to tolerate a 'sugary' taste in decoration. The rooms will be comfortable and come with a reasonable price tag.

Photo Hotel San Gabriel, entry 270

Introduction

We want you to spend your time in places that you will like. We aim to write honest descriptions. Hotels, like people, are never perfect. So read the descriptions carefully!

Maps

Plan your trip by starting with the maps at the front of the book; pages and entry numbers correspond. Many including new dual-carriageways do not appear on the maps. bear in mind that our maps are for guidance and not for detailed route planning, for this you need a proper road map. In Spain you have the toll motorways, and the *autovias*, or dual carriageways. For example, between Zaragoza and Huesca there is an *autovia* which, to all intents and purposes, acts as a motorway, except it's free.

Photo above Mas Fontanelles, entry 185
Photo opposite The Town House, entry 278

A = motorways (usually with a toll)
E = new European nomenclature for motorways or dual carriageways
N = national roads (equivalent of British A roads), some of which have been converted into dual carriageways
For minor roads, each region has its own number system, the letter(s) usually standing for the particular region eg. CV = Commundad Valenciana

Characteristic of most roads in Spain are the km markers – invaluable in remoter areas.

Rooms

We tell you the range of accommodation in single, double, twin, triple and family rooms and suites; in self-catering entries, we mention the number of people who can sleep comfortably (eg. 2-3) in the apartment, cottage or house. Suites may mean rooms big enough to contain a sitting area, or even with an extra room; we do not distinguish between suites and junior suites. Extra beds can often be added for children. Check when booking.

Bathrooms

Do not assume bath and shower rooms are en suite. If it is important to you that they are, ask when booking. In some of the simpler places, a bathroom may be shared.

Introduction

It seems that Spaniards do not fully appreciate the benefits of a long soak in a foaming bath. Hence the plug may be missing from your bathroom. Just in case, pack one of those handy universal bath plugs you can buy.

Children

The majority of Spanish hotels and B&Bs love having families to stay. However, a percentage of our Special Places do not welcome children of all ages: perhaps the hotel is a peaceful couples' retreat, or the grounds contain an unfenced pond. Check important details before booking.

Weddings, conferences and courses

We try to say when a hotel or B&B is a popular wedding or conference place, in any event, it is best to ask if a large party is likely to be present when you book. The same goes for courses. More places are encouraging relaxation or painting breaks (for example) but you may well find your peaceful haven does not turn out to be quite as peaceful as you hoped. Again, pick up the phone and check.

Prices

The prices that we quote for rooms are exclusive of VAT at 7%. When VAT is included we say so. Note that prices are per room not per person, and assume breakfast is included; if it's not, we give the price.

Meal prices are per person. Half-board prices may be quoted per room or per person; if in any doubt, check.

The prices we quote were applicable at the time that this book went to press. We publish every two years so expect prices to be higher if you are using this book towards the end of 2005 or in 2006.

A word about the Balearic & the Canary islands

Expect to pay about 50% more here than in the rest of Spain. We promise that we haven't sought out expensive places – that's just the way it is.

Photo Posada Real La Vadima, entry 153

Symbols

There is an explanation of our symbols on the last page of the book. Use these as a guide, not as a statement of fact.

Opening hours

As a general rule:
Shops open 9am-1.30pm, 4.30/5pm–8/8.30pm Monday-Friday; 9am-1.30pm on Saturdays.

Banks are usually open 8am-3pm, Monday-Friday.

Post Offices generally open at 8.30am and close at 2.30pm, Monday-Friday.

Phones and phone codes

Emergency number 112, wherever you are in Spain.

From Spain to another country: dial 00 then the country code and then the area code without the first 0. eg. Alastair Sawday Publishing in England, from Spain:
Tel: 01275 464891
becomes 00 44 1275 464891.

Within Spain: all nine digits are needed whether intra or inter-provincial.

Calling Spain from another country:
From the USA: 011 34 then the nine-digit number
From the UK: 00 34 then the nine-digit number.

Most mobile numbers begin with 6. This is the best clue as to when you're dialling an (expensive) mobile number.

Buy telephone cards from tobacconists or post offices (coin-operated boxes are few and far between). The cheapest starts at about €6.

Hacienda A large estate; originally a South American term

Hostal Another type of simple inn where food may or may not be served

Hostería A simple inn which often serves food

Hostelería An inn which may or may not serve food

Mas or masía A farmhouse in the north-east of Spain.

Posada Originally a coaching inn, with beds and food available

Palacio A grand mansion

Palacete A slightly less grand version of the above

Pazo A grand country or village manor in Galicia

Venta A simple restaurant, usually in the countryside; some have rooms

Abbreviations

Co – camino = pathway or track
c/ – calle = street
Ctra – carretera = road
s/n – sin número = un-numbered
Avda. – avenida = avenue

Types of properties

Can A farmhouse in Catalonia or the Balearic islands, often isolated.

Casita Cottage or small house.

Casona A grand house in Asturias; many were built by returning émigrés

Cortijo A free-standing farmhouse, generally in the south

Finca A farm; most of those in this book are on working farms

Fonda A simple inn which may or may nor serve food.

Regional spelling of place names

Where there are two official languages (as in Galicia, the Basque country, Valencia and Catalonia) place names will often have two spellings. Orense will be Ourense in Galicia. Lerida will be spelt Lleida on road signs in Catalonia. In the Basque Country, regional spellings usually accompany the Spanish one eg. Vitoria will be signposted Vitoria-Gasteiz. We try to use the ones that you are most likely to see: this may mean one version in the address, another in the directions on how to get there. We have no political agenda!

Photo above La Gándara, entry 136
Photo opposite The Beach House, entry 280

Many Spaniards breakfast on pâtés and olive oil, perhaps with garlic and certainly with tomato in Catalonia. Your hotelier may assume that you prefer a blander, more northern-European offering. So check. Tea tends not to be widely available, and the tea you are offered may have been on the shelves for years; take your favourite brew with you and ask for hot water! Ask for it 'con leche' if you like it with milk or 'con limón' for a slice of lemon. Bars nearly always serve camomile tea (manzanilla) – it can be a useful evening drink because the coffee is very strong.

Lunch and dinner

The daily set meal – *el menú del día* – is normally available at lunch time and occasionally at dinner, when waiters may present you simply with the à la carte menu. But do ask for it; it tends to be great value and will often have fresher ingredients. Many restaurants serve only à la carte at weekends.

Meals

The Spanish eat much later than we do: breakfast often doesn't get going until 9am, lunch is generally eaten from 2pm and dinner rarely served before 8.30pm.

Breakfast

The 'continental' in larger hotels tends to be uninspired: coffee, toast (perhaps cakes), butter and jam. Marmalade is a rare sight and freshly squeezed juice the exception. But few places would object if you were to supplement your meal with your own fruit.

Photo above Villa Soro, entry 61

Tapas and raciones

A tapa is a small plate of hot or cold food served with an aperitif before lunch or dinner: it remains an essential part of eating out in Spain. It could be a plate of olives, anchovies, cheese, spicy chorizo, fried fish... portions vary as does the choice. It is a delicious way to try out local specialities and don't worry if your Spanish is poor – tapas are often laid out along the bar for you to see. If you would like a plateful of any particular tapa then ask for *una ración de queso* (cheese), for example. Many bars will also serve you a half portion – *una media ración*.

Some historians attribute the Spanish 'obsession' with meat to the rationing that followed the Spanish Civil War. The truth is that meat is a ubiquitous element in the Spanish diet. Outside main towns it might be difficult to arrange for vegetarian meals; salads may be the only vegetarian alternative on offer.

Tipping
Leaving a tip is not unusual, but do not feel obliged, particularly when you've just had a few tapas and a couple of drinks in a busy bar. If you are given your change on a small saucer, you could leave a couple of small coins. For lunch or dinner leave 5%-10%. You would rarely be made to feel embarrassed if you don't tip. Taxi drivers don't all expect a tip.

Seasons
Prices given range from low to high season. In most of Spain, high season includes Easter, Christmas, public holidays and the summer.

Photo Hacienda San José, entry 295

Some hotels, especially city hotels, classify weekends as high and weekdays as low.

Public Holidays
Apart from the public holidays nationwide, there is an array of local festivities in the honour of one saint or another in every town and village in Spain. You may find this frustrating – shops and restaurants might be shut – or you may enjoy joining the locals in the celebration. Either way, it may be difficult for you to find out the relevant dates beforehand. As a rule, August tends to be filled with local festivities. National holidays are 1 January, Good Friday, 1 May, Corpus Christi (usually early June), 24 June, 25 July, 12 October, 1 November, 6 December, 8 December, 25 December. In some parts of Spain, 15 August and Easter Monday are also holidays.

Booking

Try to book well ahead if you plan to be in Spain during any of these holidays. August is best avoided unless you are heading somewhere remote. Many hotels will ask you for a credit card number when you book. And remember to let smaller hotels and B&Bs know if you want dinner.

There's a bilingual booking form at the back of the book. Hotels often send back a signed or stamped copy as confirmation – but don't necessarily assume that you are expecting a speedy reply (this can include emails)!

Photo above El Nobo, entry 257
Photo opposite El Jardin Vertical, entry 196

Arrival & registration

Many city hotels will only hold a reservation until the early evening, even though you might have booked months in advance. So ring ahead if you are planning to arrive late.

It remains law that you should register on arrival in a hotel – but hotels have no right to keep your passport, however much they insist. (Similarly they sometimes insist on holding on to identity cards.)

Payment

The most commonly accepted credit cards are Visa, MasterCard and Eurocard. Many smaller places don't take plastic because of high bank charges. But there is nearly always a cash dispenser (ATM) close at hand; again, Visa and MasterCard are the most useful.

Euros

Some Spaniards still refer to the old peseta, particularly if talking about large sums of money. Be prepared to make some calculations in the much loved and lamented peseta (approx. 165 pesetas to €1).

Plugs

Virtually all sockets now have 220/240 AC voltage (usually two-pin). Pack an adaptor if you travel with electrical appliances. Note that telephone plugs are also different from the ones in the UK; you will

Introduction

Public transport

Trains, buses and taxis are cheap in Spain. You meet people, can start a good conversation, and get much more of a feel for the country by travelling this way. Spain has a high-speed rail link (known as AVE – pronounced like ave in Ave María) between Lerida (Lleida) and Cordoba, via Zaragoza and Madrid. Here it splits and one branch goes to Malaga, while the other one reaches Seville. Some regional lines would bring a tear to a rail buff's eye, such as the one between Ronda and Algeciras.

In the north the FEVE company runs several narrow-gauge trains, which usually travel through extraordinary landscapes and have retained the magic and the romance of old railway journeys. You can travel by FEVE trains from Bilbao all the way to El Ferrol, in Galicia, or to Léon. Visit www.feve.es for more info.

Look out for the national coach company if you want to travel by public transport. ENATCAR (Empresa Nacional de Transportes por Carretera) underwent a massive restructuring some years ago and established concessions in every major town. As a result of this it has some of the most comfortable coaches you will find in Europe. And they are relatively cheap. The rarity of roundabouts in the road network

also need an adaptor if you intend to bring your laptop.

Driving

Foreign number plates attract attention so never leave your car with valuables inside. Use a public car park; they are cheap and safe. It is compulsory to have in the car: a spare set of bulbs, a car jack, a spare/emergency wheel, two warning triangles, a visibility jacket – which you must carry at the front, not in the boot – and a basic first aid kit.

Photo above La Corte de Lugás, entry 31
Photo opposite Casa de San Martín, entry 76

and the existence of motorway tolls – which deter drivers from using the faster roads – mean that coach journeys tend to be swift, too.

Subscriptions

Owners pay to appear in this guide. Their fee goes towards the high costs of inspecting and producing an all-colour book. We only include places that we like and find special for one reason or another, so it is not possible to buy – or bribe! – your way in.

Internet

www.specialplacestostay.com has online pages for all the places featured here and from all our other books – around 4,500 places to stay in total. There's a searchable database, a snippet from the write-up and colour photos. New kid on the block is our dedicated UK holiday home web site, www.special-escapes.co.uk.

Disclaimer

We make no clains to pure objectivity in choosing these places. They are here simply because we like them. We try our utmost to get our facts right but we apologise unreservedly if any errors have sneaked in.

We do not check such things as fire alarms, swimming pool security or any other regulations with which owners of properties receiving paying guests should comply. This is the responsibility of the owners.

And finally

Thank you to all those who have taken the time to share your opinions with us. You have helped make this edition of the book even better than the last!

Please let us have your comments; there is a report form at the back of this book. Or email us at *spain@sawdays.co.uk*.

Photo Hospedería Convento de La Parra, entry 199

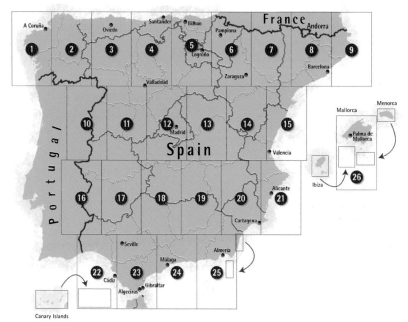

©Bartholomew Ltd, 2004

Please remember: our maps are designed to be used as a guide, not as road maps for navigation.

On the following map pages:
places with self-catering accommodation are marked in red **86**
places with overnight accommodation are marked in blue **84**
places with a mixture are marked with both **85**

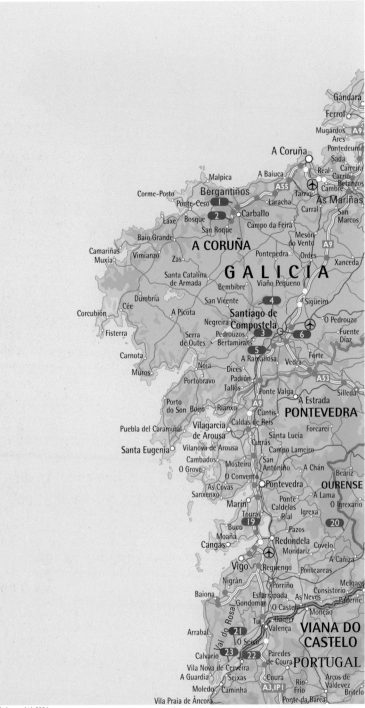

Map 2

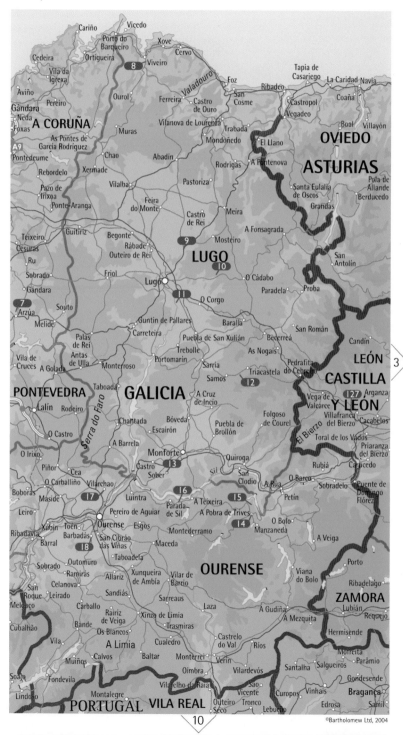

©Bartholomew Ltd, 2004

Map 3

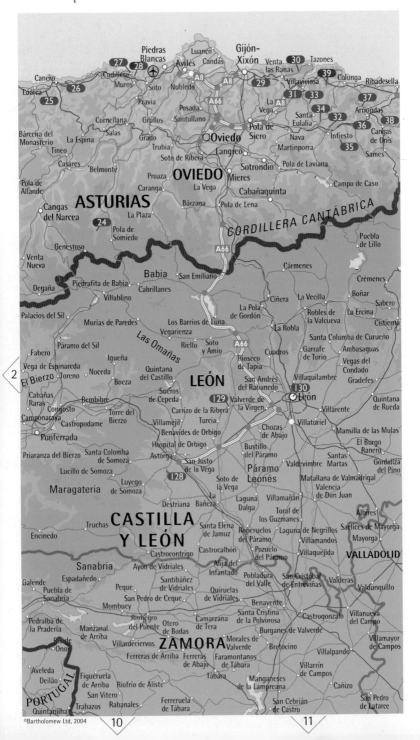

Map 4

31

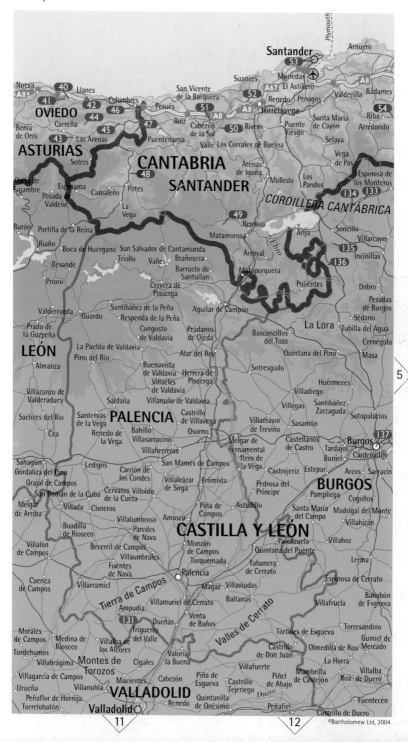

Map 6

33

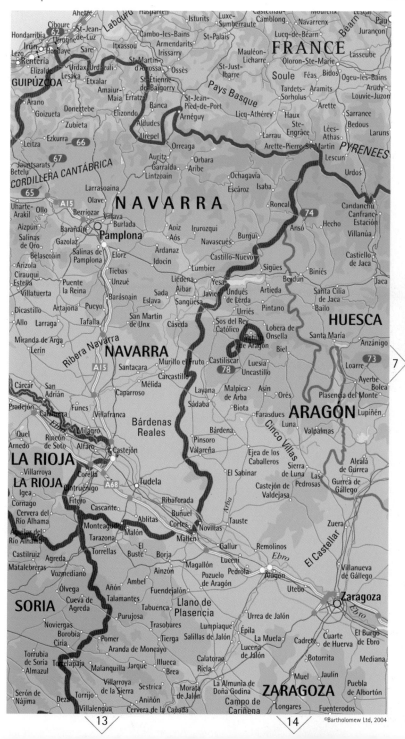

Pau
Mazères-Lezons
Gan
Coarraze
Lestelle
Bétharram St-Pé-de-Bigorre
Arbéost
Laruns
Eaux-Bonnes
Ibos Tarbes
Pontacq
Montaut
Lourdes
Agos-
Vidalos
Aucun Argelès-Gazost
Lavedan Chèze
Cauterets
Cabanac
Aureilhan Bonnefont
Barbazan-
Debat Galan
Bernac-Dessus
Cieutat
Montgaillard
Bagnères-
de-Bigorre Campan
Nébouzan St-Martory
Villeneuve-
de-Rivière A64
Lannemezan St-Gaudens
La Barthe-de-Neste
Hèches
Mauléon-Barousse
Sarrancolin
Bigorre FRANCE
Arreau
La Mongie
Barèges Bordères-Louron
Vielle-Aure
Luz- Luz-St-
Ardiden Sauveur Tramezaïgues
St-Lary-
Soulan
Salies-
du-Salat Fabas
Mane
St-
Lizier
Aspet Árbas St-Giron
Juzet-d'Izaut
Fronsac Engomer
Castillon-en-Couserans
Sost
Cierp-
Gaud
Cier-de-
Luchon
Bagnères-
de-Luchon
Bonac-
Irazein
Sentein
Canejan
Lès Val d'Aran
Bossost
Vielha Arties
Salardu
95

Sallent
de Gállego
Gavarnie
75 Balneario de
Panticosa Huesca
Torla
Biescas
Broto Fanlo
Sarvisé
Navasa Sabiñánigo
Orna de
Gállego Yebra de Basa
Molino de Laguarta
Villobas Secorún
Caldearenas
Aquilué
Arguis
Bolea Nueno
Igriés
Alerre
Fiscal 76
Albella
Gèdre Piau-Engaly

Bielsa
Salinas
de Sín
Puértolas Lafortunada
Laspuña
Boltaña
Ainsa
Morillo
de Monclús
Santa Liestra
y San Quílez
Arcusa
71 Barcabo
Naval
Bierge Alquézar
Adahuesca El
Grado
Benasque
Sahun
Castejón de Sos
Seira
Campo
Condado
Lascuarre
Puente de Montañana
Graus
Benabarre Tolva
La Torre
de Cabdella
Pont de
Suert
Senterada
Sopeira La Pobla de Segur
Arén 93
94
Tremp
Huesca
Sobrarbe 77
Aguas
72 Angüés
Albero Alto Blecua
Vicién Pertusa
Novales
Llanos de la Violada Sesa
Tardienta Grañén Huerto
Torralba Alberuela de Tubo
de Aragón Poleñino
Robres
Alcubierre Lalueza
Lecíñena Canaja
Perdiguera
Farlete
Monegrillo
Villafranca de Ebro
Osera
Fuentes Pina
de Ebro
Mediana Quinto
Gelsa Velilla de Ebro
Sástago
Olvena
Estadilla
Fonz
Peralta
de la Sal
Azanúy
Alcampell
Tamarite
de Litera
Peraltilla Barbastro
Somontano
Berbegal
Peralta
de Alcofea
Castejón
del Puente Monzón
Pueyo de Santa Cruz
Alfántega
Castelflorite
Alcolea
de Cinca
Albalatillo Sena
Ontiñena
Castejón
de Monegros Los Monegros
La Almolda
Valfarta
Candasnos
Bujaraloz Peñalba
ZARAGOZA
Binéfar
Esplús
Albalate de Cinca
Belver
de Cinca
Ballobar
Fraga
Llanos de
Cardiel
Mequinenza
Ebro
Binaced Albelda
La Litera
Alguaire
Alpicat
Segriá
Alcarrás
Soses
Aitona
Serós
La Granja
d'Escarp
Camporrells
Lleida
Alfarràs
Almenar Balaguer
Albesa
Térmens Els Arcs
Almacelles Rosselló
Bell-Lloc
d'Urgell
Torregrossa
Lleida Juneda
A2
Castelldans
L'Albagès
Sarroca de Lleida
El Soleràs Juncosa
Llardecans
Maials
La Granadella
87
La Bisbal de Falset
Cabacés
Fayón Riba-roja Flix Gratallops
Les
Avellanes Noguera
Camarasa
Chalamera
Alcolea
de Cinca
HUESCA
Cinca
Alfoz
ARAGÓN
LLEIDA
CATALUÑA
Àger

Map 8

35

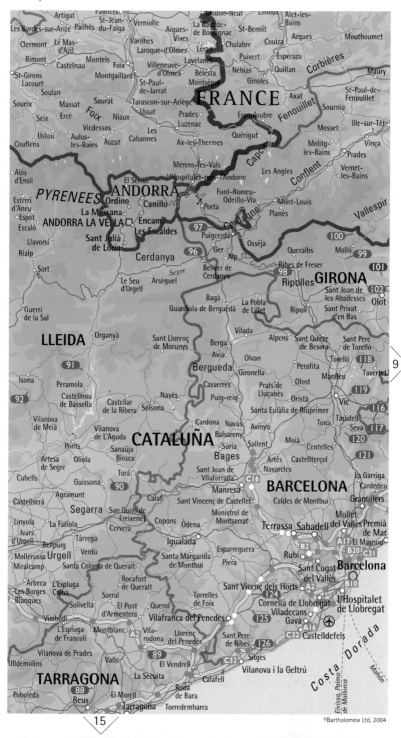

Map 10

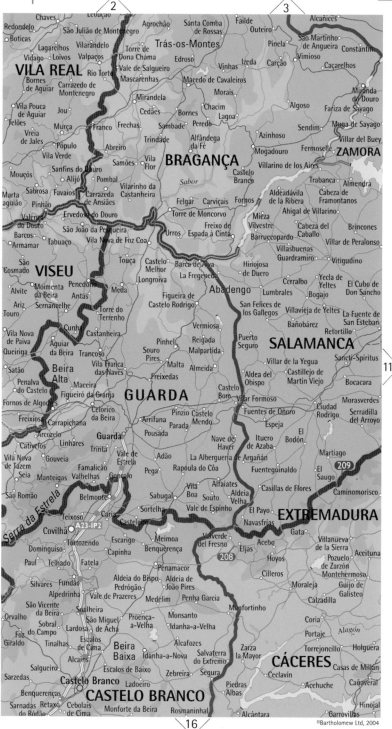

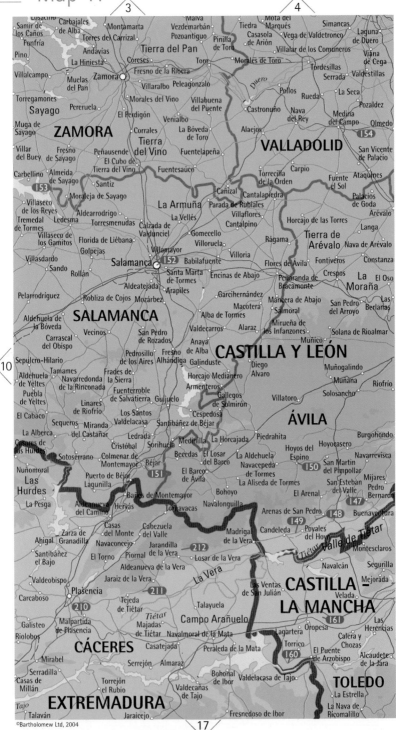

Map 12

39

4 5

VALLADOLID

SORIA

Aldeamayor de San Martin
Canalejas de Peñafiel
Moradillo de Roa
Honrubia de la Cuesta
Fuentecambrón
Montemayor de Pililla
Campaspero
Sacramenia
Maderuelo
Languilla
Campo de San Pedro
Ayllón
Fuentidueña
Valtiendas
Portillo
Olombrada
Liceras
San Miguel de Arroyo
Frumales
Adrados de Bernuy
San Miguel
Boceguillas
Ribota
Mojados
Cuéllar
Hontalbilla
Carrascal del Río
Castillejo de Mesleón
Riaza
Alcazarén
Chañe
Íscar
Fuenterrebollo
Pedrajas de San Esteban
Samboal
Lastras de Cuéllar
Sepúlveda
Olmedo
SEGOVIA
Cantalejo
Cerezo de Abajo
Cantalojas
Coca
Fuentepelayo
Aguilafuente
Rebollo
La Matilla
140
GUADALAJARA
Santiuste de San Juan Bautista
Navalmanzano
Navas de Oro
Aldea Real
142
Turégano
Valverde de los Arroyos
Nava de la Asunción
Mozoncillo
Carbonero El Mayor
141
Robregordo
Bernardos
Torreiglesias
146
Navafría
Montejo de la Sierra
Tamajón
San Cristóbal de la Vega
Armuña
Cantimpalos
143
Braojos
Retiendas
Santa María la Real de Nieva
CASTILLA –
Collado Hermoso
Villavieja del Lozoya
Buitrago del Lozoya
Martín Muñoz de las Posadas
145
Palazuelos de Eresma
Lozoya
Garcillán
144
Lozoyuela
Sangarcía
Segovia
175
174
Matarrubia
Adanero
Marugán
Abades
San Ildefonso
Rascafría
Sanchidrián
Y LEÓN–
Miraflores de la Sierra
Torrelaguna
Uceda
Villanueva de Gómez
Labajos
Otero de Herreros
Viñuelas
Hernansancho
Zarzuela del Monte
MADRID
El Molar
El Casar
A6
Villacastín
Colmenar Viejo
Cardeñosa
Tolbaños
El Espinar
A61
Guadarrama
San Agustín de Guadalix
Torrejón del Rey
Mingorria
Aldeavieja
A6
Collado Villalba
A51
ÁVILA
Las Navas del Marqués
San Lorenzo de El Escorial
El Escorial
Torrelodones
San Sebastián de los Reyes
Algete
Meco
Ávila
Galapagar
MADRID
R2
Alcalá de Henares
13
El Fresno
Tornadizos de Ávila
Navalperal de Pinares
Las Rozas de Madrid
M40
Alcobendas
Torrejón de Ardoz
San Juan de la Nava
El Hoyo de Pinares
Robledo de Chavela
Majadahonda
MADRID
A2
San Fernando de Henares
El Barraco
Cebreros
Navas del Rey
Colmenar del Arroyo
Pozuelo de Alarcón
Coslada
Mejorada del Campo
Navaluenga
El Tiemblo
Chapinería
Boadilla del Monte
Rivas-Vaciamadrid
Campo Real
Burgohondo
San Martín de Valdeiglesias
Villaviciosa de Odón
50
Alcorcón
Casillas
Cadalso de los Vidrios
Villa del Prado
Villamanta
Navalcarnero
Móstoles
Getafe
Arganda
Piedralaves
Sotillo de la Adrada
R5
Humanes de Madrid
Leganés
Morata de Tajuña
Valle de Tiétar
Almorox
Méntrida
Valmojado
Fuenlabrada
Parla
Pinto
San Martín de la Vega
La Torre de Esteban Hambrán
Carranque
Griñón
Valdemoro
Escalona
Santa Cruz del Retamar
Casarrubios del Monte
Illescas
Ciempozuelos
Titulcia
El Real de San Vicente
Nombela
Lominchar
Yuncos
Esquivias
R4
Villaconejos
Colmenar de Oreja
Castillo de Bayuela
Quismondo
Camarena
La Sagra
Borox
Hinojosa de San Vicente
Santa Olalla
Novés
Fuensalida
Villalenga de la Sagra
Añover de Tajo
Aranjuez
Villarrubia de Santiago
El Casar de Escalona
TOLEDO
Rielves
Villaseca de la Sagra
Ocaña
Noblejas
Cazalegas
Torrijos
Bargas
Mocejón
Ciruelos
Mesa de Ocaña
Carmena
Gerindote
Villasequilla de Yepes
Yepes
La Pueblanueva
Cebolla
La Mata
Escalonilla
Burujón
165
162
164
Villamuelas
Huerta de Valdecarábanos
Talavera de la Reina
Malpica de Tajo
El Carpio de Tajo
163
Toledo
La Guardia
San Bartolomé de las Abiertas
La Puebla de Montalbán
Guadamur
Argés
Nambroca
San Martín de Pusa
CASTILLA –
Polán
Layos
Almonacid de Toledo
Villanueva de Bogas
El Romeral
Santa Ana de Pusa
LA MANCHA
Ajofrín
Mascaraque
Tembleque
Los Navalmorales
Gálvez
Mazarambroz
Senseca
Mora
Manzaneque
Torrecilla de la Jara
Cuerva
Orgaz
Turleque
Espinoso del Rey
Los Navalucillos
Navahermosa
Menasalbas
Hontanar
Las Ventas con Peña Aguilera
Los Yébenes
Marjaliza

18

Map 14   41

ZARAGOZA   Campo de Cariñena   Belchite   Vinaceite   Azaila
Calatayud   Azuara
Maluenda   Codos   Encinacorba   Lécera   La Puebla de Híjar
Fuentes   Herrera de   Híjar   Samper de
de Jiloca   Miedes   Villarreal los Navarros Villar de   Calanda
         Montón   de Huerva   los Navarros Moneva
Villafeliche   Villadoz   Albalate de   Desierto
                                               Arzobispo   de Calanda
Acered   Atea   Cucalón   Badenas Blesa Muniesa Alacón   Ariño
      Daroca   Monforte de Moyuela   Cortes   Oliete   Andorra
                     Fonfría   Huesa Plou de Aragón   Alloza   Calanda
      Báguena Burbáguena   del Común   Alcaine   Foz-Calanda
                                               ARAGÓN   Alcorisa
   Tornos   Torrecilla Segura de   Obón   Mas de
                del Rebollar los Baños La Mata de los Olmos   Berge las Matas
Embid   Bello Fuentes- Cálamocha Fuenferrada   Montalbán   Castellote
      Torralba Claras   Martín del Río   Gargallo Molinos
      de Sisones Bañón   Utrillas Escucha Castel Ejulve
Campillo   Caminreal   Cosa   de Cabra
de Dueñas Blancas Monreal   Pancrudo Mezquita Hinojosa   Guadalope
Hombrados   del Campo Rubielos de de Jarque de Jarque   Bordón
   El Pobo Pozuel   la Cérida Rillo Cañada   Villarluengo Olorau
   de Dueñas del Campo Bueña Argente   Vellida   Pitarque   del Rey
Setiles   Villafranca del Campo Visiedo Perales del Camarillas
GUADALAJARA   Villar del Salz Camañas   Alfambra Miravete de   Mirambel
Tordesilos   Ródenas Torrelacarcel   Aguilar de la Sierra Cañada de Cantavieja
Alustante Almohaja Alba Torremocha de Jiloca Orrios Alfambra   Benatanduz
Alcoroches Motos Pozondón Santa Alfambra Escorihuela   Villarroya de Fortanete
Checa Orihuela del Tremedal Eulalia Villarquemado TERUEL Jorcas Allepuz los Pinares
Orea   Celadas Peralejos El Gudar
      Bronchales   Pobo
Noguera   Cuevas Labradas   Cedrillas
Tramacastilla   Cella   Corbalán Alcalá de Valdelinares
   Griegos Albarracín Grea de   la Selva Mosqueruela
Guadalaviar Villar del Cobo Albarracín   El Castellar Cabra
      Royuela Saldón   Teruel   Formiche de Mora Linares
   Terriente   Bezas   Alto Mora de de Mora
Montes   Valdecuenca Villastar   Rubielos Puertomingalvo
Universales Jabaloyas Villel La Puebla de Valverde Valbona Nogueruelas Villahermosa
Huélamo   Cubla   Rubielos Cortes de del Río
Zafrilla Alobras El Tramacastiel Cascante Sarrión de Mora Arenoso Zucaina
Huerta del Tejadillos Cuervo Libros del Río Camareña de Albentosa Millars
Marquesada Salvacañete   Bíndeva la Sierra
Valdemoro-Sierra   VALENCIA Los Olmos   Cirat
            Rincón de Ademuz Manzanera Barracas Fuentes
La Cierva Salinas   Casas Altas Arcos de   de Ayódar
   Cañete del Manzano   las Salinas   Pavias
Valdemorillo Huérguina   Caudiel
de la Sierra Campillos-   Viver Jérica
Pajarón Boniches Paravientos Moya Santa Cruz de Moya Abejuela Bejís   Segorbe
   Pajaroncillo Fuentelespino   Alpuente La Teresa Sacañet Altura
CASTILLA - LA MANCHA de Moya Landete Aliaguilla Yesa   CASTELLÓN Soneja
Carboneras   Titaguas   Alcublas Gátova
de Guadazaón Villar   Higueruelas Villar del
   Arguisuelas del Humo Garaballa   Chelva Arzobispo Olocau
Monteagudo   Tuéjar   Marines
de las Salinas Cardenete CUENCA   Loriguilla Casinos
Yémeda   Sinarcas   Chulilla Valencia Lliria Bétera
Paracuellos Víllora Mira Aliaguilla   Bugarra 195
Almodóvar Enguídanos   VALENCIA   La Pobla
del Pinar   Camporrobles   Chera   de Vallbona
                  Caudete de Utiel   VALENCIA Manises
Campillo de Alto Buey   las Fuentes   Cheste A7
Motilla del Palancar Minglanilla Villargordo San   Siete Chiva
            del Cabriel Antonio Requena Aguas
El Peral Villalpardo   Venta 194   Buñol Godelleta
Iniesta   del Moro   Yátova Turís
   Villarta   La Portera   Monserrat
Villanueva de la Jara El Herrumbl   Los Pedrones Dos Llombai
      Villamalea Cabriel   Aguas Catadau

80   81   15   20   195   194   A7

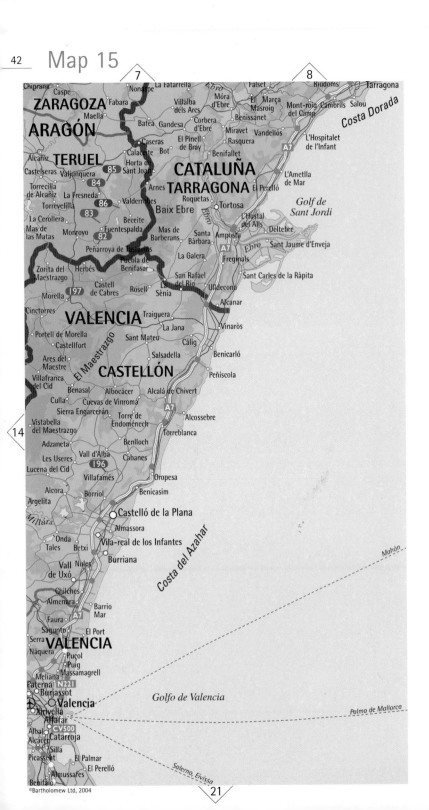

Map 16

43

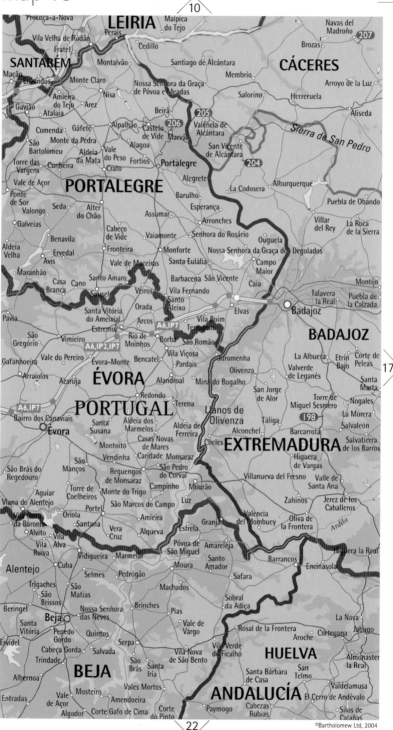

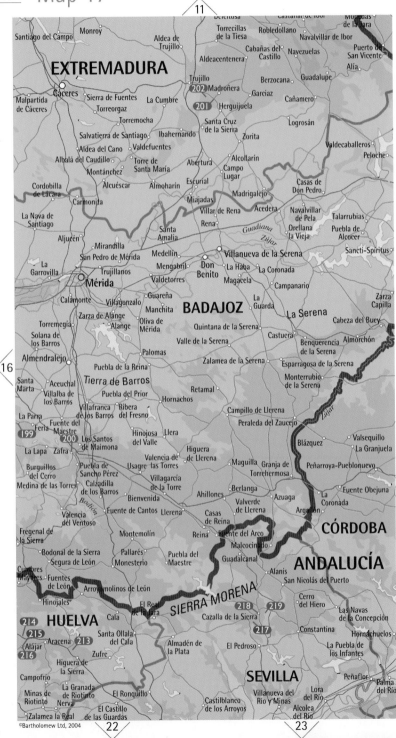

Map 18

45

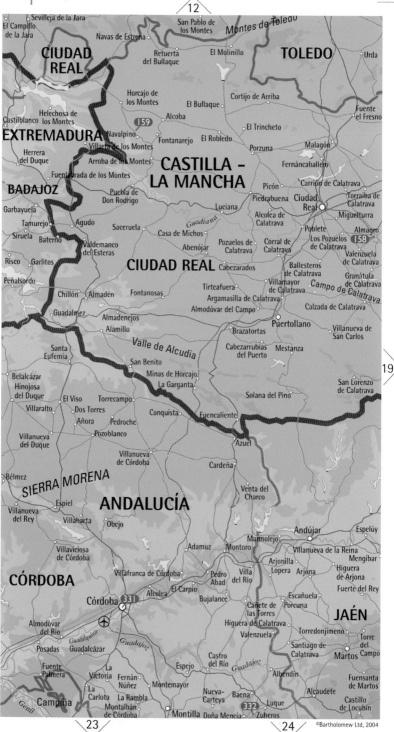

Sevilleja de la Jara
El Campillo de la Jara
Navas de Estrena
San Pablo de los Montes
Montes de Toledo
Retuerta del Bullaque
El Molinillo
CIUDAD REAL
TOLEDO
Urda

Horcajo de los Montes
Cortijo de Arriba
El Bullaque
Fuente el Fresno
Helechosa de los Montes
Castilblanco
Alcoba
159
El Trincheto
EXTREMADURA
Navalpino
Villar de los Montes
Fontanarejo
El Robledo
Porzuna
Malagón
Herrera del Duque
Arroba de los Montes
CASTILLA – LA MANCHA
Fernáncaballero
Fuenlabrada de los Montes
Picón
Carrión de Calatrava
BADAJOZ
Puebla de Don Rodrigo
Piedrabuena
Ciudad Real
Torralba de Calatrava
Garbayuela
Luciana
Alcolea de Calatrava
Miguelturra
Tamurejo
Agudo
Saceruela
Guadiana
Poblete
Almagro
Siruela
Baterno
Casa de Michos
Pozuelos de Calatrava
Corral de Calatrava
Los Pozuelos de Calatrava
158
Risco
Garlitos
Valdemanco del Esteras
Abenójar
CIUDAD REAL
Cabezarados
Ballesteros de Calatrava
Valenzuela de Calatrava
Peñalsordo
Villamayor de Calatrava
Granátula de Calatrava
Chillón
Almadén
Fontanosas
Tirteafuera
Argamasilla de Calatrava
Campo de Calatrava
Guadalmez
Almadenejos
Almodóvar del Campo
Calzada de Calatrava
Alamillo
Brazatortas
Puertollano
Villanueva de San Carlos
Valle de Alcudia
Cabezarrubias del Puerto
Mestanza
Santa Eufemia
San Benito
Belalcázar
Minas de Horcajo
La Garganta
Solana del Pino
San Lorenzo de Calatrava
Hinojosa del Duque
El Viso
Torrecampo
Conquista
Fuencaliente
Villaralto
Dos Torres
Añora
Pedroche
Villanueva del Duque
Pozoblanco
Azuel
Villanueva de Córdoba
Cardeña
Bélmez
SIERRA MORENA
Venta del Charco
Espiel
ANDALUCÍA
Villanueva del Rey
Villaharta
Obejo
Andújar
Espelúy
Marmolejo
Villanueva de la Reina
Villaviciosa de Córdoba
Adamuz
Montoro
Arjonilla
Lopera
Arjona
Mengíbar
Higuera de Arjona
CÓRDOBA
Villafranca de Córdoba
Pedro Abad
Villa del Río
Escañuela
Porcuna
Fuerte del Rey
Córdoba
331
Alcolea
El Carpio
Bujalance
Cañete de las Torres
JAÉN
Almodóvar del Río
Higuera de Calatrava
Torredonjimeno
Torre del Campo
Posadas
Guadalcázar
Guadalquivir
Valenzuela
Santiago de Calatrava
Martos
Fuente Palmera
La Victoria
Fernán Núñez
Espejo
Castro del Río
Guadajoz
Albendín
Fuensanta de Martos
Campiña
La Carlota
Montalbán de Córdoba
La Rambla
Montemayor
Nueva-Carteya
Baena
Luque
Alcaudete
Castillo de Locubín
Genil
Montilla
Doña Mencía
Zuheros
332

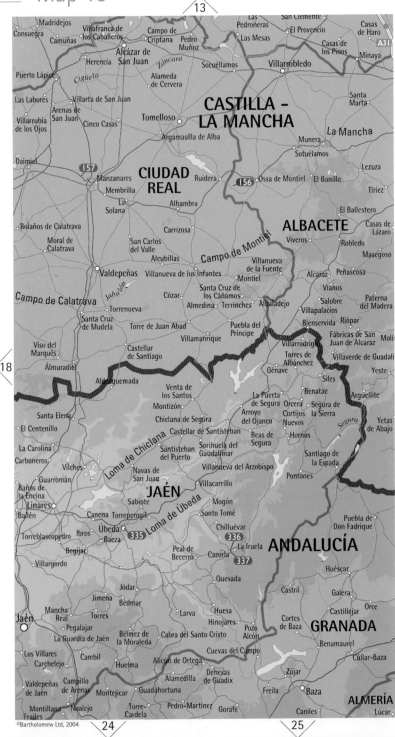

13

Madridejos · Villafranca de los Caballeros · Campo de Criptana · Pedro Muñoz · Las Pedroñeras · San Clemente · El Provencio · Casas de Haro

Consuegra · Cámuñas · Alcázar de San Juan · Las Mesas · Casas de los Pinos · Minaya · A31

Herencia · Záncara · Socuéllamos · Villarróbledo

Puerto Lápice · Ciguela · Alameda de Cervera

Las Labores · Villarta de San Juan · Santa Marta

Arenas de San Juan · Cinco Casas · Tomelloso · CASTILLA – LA MANCHA · La Mancha

Villarrubia de los Ojos · Argamasilla de Alba · Munera · Sotuélamos

Daimiel · 157 · Manzanares · CIUDAD REAL · Ruidera · 156 · Ossa de Montiel · El Bonillo · Lezuza

Membrilla · Alhambra · Tiriez

La Solana · Carrizosa · El Ballestero

Bolaños de Calatrava · San Carlos del Valle · ALBACETE · Casas de Lázaro

Moral de Calatrava · Alcubillas · Campo de Montiel · Viveros · Robledo · Maségoso

Valdepeñas · Villanueva de los Infantes · Villanueva de la Fuente · Alcaraz · Peñascosa

Campo de Calatrava · Jabalón · Cózar · Santa Cruz de los Cáñamos · Montiel · Vianos · Paterna del Madera

Torrenueva · Almedina · Terrinches · Albaladejo · Salobre · Villapalacios

Santa Cruz de Mudela · Torre de Juan Abad · Puebla del Príncipe · Bienservida · Ríopar

Villamanrique · Villarrodrigo · Fábricas de San Juan de Alcaraz · Moli

Viso del Marqués · Castellar de Santiago · Torres de Albánchez · Villaverde de Guadali

Álmuradiel · Génave · Siles · Yeste

18 · Aldeaquemada · Venta de los Santos · La Puerta de Segura · Benatae · Arguellite

Montizón · Orcera · Segura de la Sierra

Santa Elena · Chiclana de Segura · Arroyo del Ojanco · Cortijos Nuevos · Segura · Yetas de Abajo

El Centenillo · Castellar de Santisteban · Beas de Segura · Hornos

La Carolina · Loma de Chiclana · Santisteban del Puerto · Sorihuela del Gaudalímar · Santiago de la Espada

Carboneros · Villanueva del Arzobispo · Pontones

Vílches · Navas de San Juan · Villacarrillo

Guarromán · JAÉN · Mogón

Baños de la Encina · Sabiote · Santo Tomé · Puebla de Don Fadrique

Linares · Canena · Torreperogil · Loma de Úbeda

Bailén · Chilluévar

Torreblascopedro · Ibros · Úbeda · 335 · Baeza · La Iruela · ANDALUCÍA

Begíjar · 336

Villargordo · Peal de Becerro · Cazorla · 337 · Huéscar

Jódar · Quesada · Castril · Galera · Orce

Jimena · Bedmar · Larva · Huesa · Castillejar

Jaén · Mancha Real · Torres · Hinojares · Cortes de Baza · GRANADA

Pegalajar · Bélmez de la Moraleda · Cabra del Santo Cristo · Pozo Alcón · Benamaurel

La Guardia de Jaén · Cuevas del Campo · Cúllar-Baza

Los Villares · Cambil · Alicún de Ortega

Carchelejo · Huelma · Dehesas de Guadix · Zújar

Valdepeñas de Jaén · Campillo de Arenas · Alamedilla · Freila · Baza

Montejícar · Guadahortuna

Montillana · Noalejo · Torre-Cárdela · Pedro-Martínez · Gorafe · Caniles · ALMERÍA · Lúcar

Frailes

©Bartholomew Ltd, 2004 · 24 · 25

Map 20

47

15

Carlet · Alginet · Sueca
L'Alcudia · Algemesi · Cullera
Guadassuar
Alberic · Alzira · Favara
Carcaixent · Tavernes de la Valldigna
Navarrés · Villanueva · Xeraco
Bolbaite · de Castellón
Chella · 193 · Llosa de Ranes
Anna · Xátiva · A7 · Gandia
VALENCIA · Benigánim · Alqueria de · Oliva
Enguera · Canals · la Condesa
Vallada · L'Olleria · 192 · Villalonga · Pego · Ondara · Las Rotas
Moixent- · La Pobla · Castelló · Denia
Mogente · del Duc · de Rugat · 179 · Jávea-Xábia
Ontinyent · Albaida · Planes · 188 · Orba · Pedreguer · Gata de Gorgos
Bocairent · Agullent · 187 · Castell de · Jalón · Teulada
191 · 186 · Muro de Alcoy · Castells · Benissa · Moraira
Banyeres · Cocentaina · 189 · 180 · Callosa · 178 · Calpe
de Mariola · **VALENCIA** · Benasau · d'En Sarrià
Benejama · Alcoy- · Guadalest · La
185 · 190 · Alcoi · Benifallim · 181 · Nucia · Altea
Biar · Onil · Ibi · Sella · L'Alfàs del Pi
Castalla · Relleu · 182
Tibi · Jijona- · A7 · Benidorm
Sax · Kixona · Aguas · Villajoyosa -
da · Petrer · de Busot · La Vila Joíosa
Monóvar · Mutxamel · Campello
Novelda · San Vicente · San Juan de Alicante
del Raspeig · **ALICANTE** · 183 · Alicante-Alacant
Aspe
Hondón de · Los Arenales del Sol
las Nieves
20 · 184 · Elche-Elx · Costa Blanca
Crevillente · Santa Pola
Albatera
Dolores
Cox
Almoradi · Guardamar del Segura
Callosa · Rojales
de Segura
San Miguel · Torrevieja
de Salinas · A37
Pilar de la Horadada
San Pedro del Pinatar
San Javier
MURCIA
Los Alcázares
MURCIA · La Manga del
El Algar · Mar Menor
La Unión · Cabo de
Palos
Escombreras

Eivissa

Sète

Orán

Map 22 49

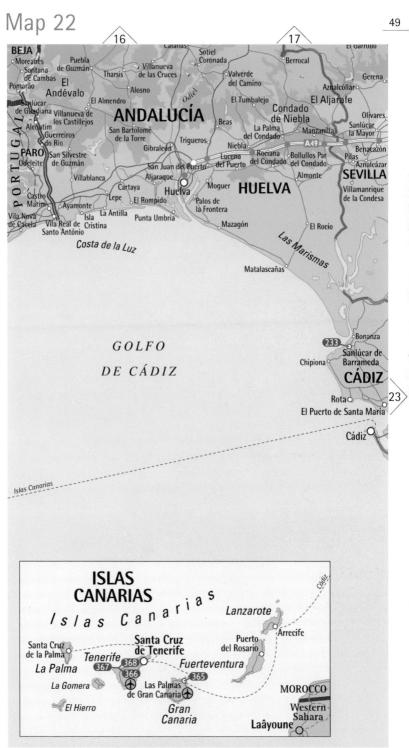

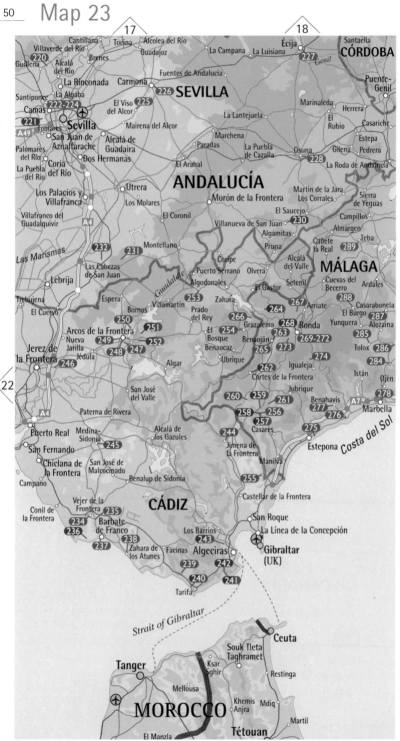

©Bartholomew Ltd, 2004

Map 24

51

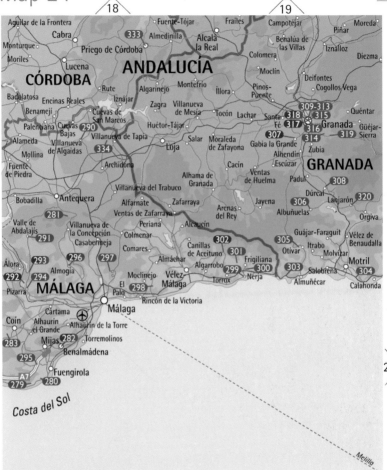

18 19

Aguilar de la Frontera
Cabra
Monturque
Moriles
Lucena
CÓRDOBA
Badolatosa Encinas Reales
Benamejí
Palenciana Cuevas
Bajas
Alameda Villanueva
Mollina de Algaidas
Fuente
de Piedra
Bobadilla Antequera

Priego de Córdoba
Rute Algarinejo
Iznájar
Zagra Villanueva
de Mesía
Cuevas de
San Marcos
Villanueva de Tapia Huétor-Tájar
Archidona

Fuente-Tójar Frailes
333 Almedinilla Alcalá
la Real
Campotéjar
Piñar Moreda
Benalúa de
las Villas Iználloz
Colomera
Moclín Diezma
ANDALUCÍA
Montefrío Íllora Pinos- Deifontes
Puente Cogollos Vega
Tocón Lachar Santa 309-313
Fé 318 315 Quéntar
317 316 Granada Güéjar-
307 314 319 Sierra
Salar Moraleda Gabia la Grande
Loja de Zafayona Alhendín Zubia
Cacín Escúzar GRANADA
Alhama de Padul 308
Granada Ventas
de Huelma Dúrcal
Villanueva del Trabuco Alfarnate Zafarraya Jayena 306 Lanjarón 320
Ventas de Zafarraya Arenas Albuñuelas
del Rey Órgiva
Valle de Villanueva de Periana Alcaucín
Abdalajís la Concepción Colmenar Guájar-Faraguit Vélez de
291 Casabermeja 302 305 Itrabo Benaudalla
Comares Canillas Otívar Molvízar
Álora 293 296 297 de Aceituno 301 303 Motril
292 Almogía Almáchar Algarrobo Frigiliana Salobreña 304
294 Moclinejo Vélez 299 300 Almuñécar Calahonda
Pizarra MÁLAGA El Málaga Torrox Nerja
Palo 298 Rincón de la Victoria

Cártama
Coín Alhaurín Alhaurín de la Torre
el Grande
283 Mijas 282 Torremolinos
295 Benalmádena
A7
279 280 Fuengirola

Costa del Sol

25

Melilla

Málaga

©Bartholomew Ltd, 2004

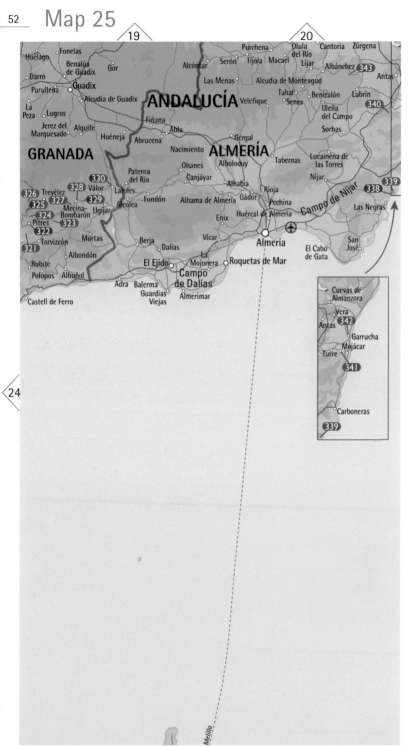

Map 26

53

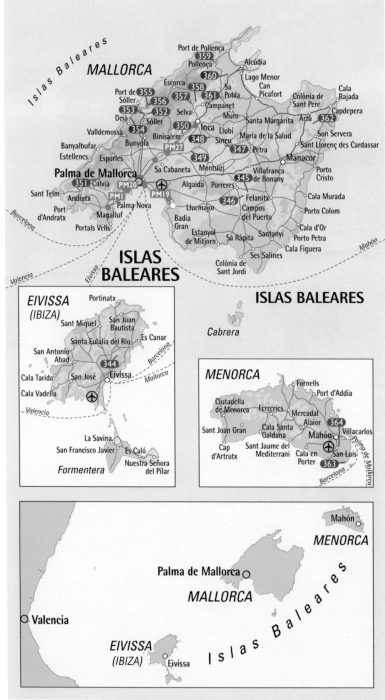

ISLAS BALEARES

Photo Jose Navarro

galicia

Casa Entremuros

Cances Grandes 77, 15107 Carballo, La Coruña

Here are long stretches of fine, sandy beaches, hidden coves and a number of old fishing villages where the seafood is among the best in Spain. Rest awhile at Santiago and Rosa's solid old granite house and B&B – they will enjoy helping you unlock the region's secrets. You approach through the pretty stable yard, with annexe to one side, lawns and flowers. There are four bedrooms, not huge, but handsome, with shining parquet-clad floors, fitted wardrobes, white bedspreads and matching rag rugs, carefully restored antique beds, a modern upholstered chair or two, and good (though somewhat small) bathrooms. There is a large, light-filled lounge with a dresser and a wood-burner in the huge stone *lareira*. Rosa makes fresh fruit juices and gives you local cheeses and honey and cake. No meals apart from breakfast but the popular Casa Elias is only two miles away – you can have a memorable meal there at any time of year. This is a warm, quiet and unassuming place to stay on the wild, indented coastline of the Rías Altas, little known beyond Galicia.

rooms	4 twins/doubles.
price	€42-€52. Singles €36-€44. VAT inc.
meals	Breakfast €4. VAT included. Restaurants nearby.
closed	15 December-15 January.
directions	From Santiago de Compostela, by Alameda, road for 'Hospital General'. On to Carballo, then towards Malpica to Cances; house signed by petrol station.

	Santiago Luaces de La-Herrán
tel	+34 981 757099
fax	+34 981 703877
email	entremuros@finisterrae.com
web	www.casaentremuros.com

Map 1 Entry 1

Pazo de Souto
Lugar de la Torre 1, 15106 Sisamo-Carballo, La Coruña

The fine old manor, lost among fields of maize and wooded glades, was built by a member of the Inquisition in 1672; the inquisitor's safe still lurks in one wall. Later it became a school: José attended as a boy. Now he and young Carlos have one of the best small hotels in this little-known corner of Galicia. The house is dark and wonderfully labyrinthine. The vast sitting room has a *lareira* (inglenook), old-fashioned fauteuils and chunky beams, the dining room is lovely, with a gallery, lighting is subtle and the bar deliciously cosy. Some bedrooms are on the ground floor; a splendid granite staircase leads to more above. Those on the first floor have classic Spanish beds and a certain decadent flair; the smallest and plainest are in the attic. A few rooms have waterbeds; bathroom suites are new. Plenty of locals come for the fresh fish from Malpica – always a good sign. Carlos is eager to please and has impeccable English; it would be hard to find more charming hosts. Fine views from the palm-treed garden – and all the rugged beauty of the north coast. *A Pazos de Galicia hotel.*

rooms	11 twins/doubles.
price	€50-€78. Singles €36-€60.
meals	Lunch/dinner €15; €22 à la carte.
closed	Rarely.
directions	From Santiago C-545 for Santa Comba & Carballo; after 27km through Carballo for Malpica; left 100m after BP petrol station, for Sisamo. Pazo 2.5km beyond, on left after church.

	Carlos Taibo Pombo
tel	+34 981 756065
fax	+34 981 756191
email	reservas@pazodosouto.com
web	www.pazodosouto.com

Map 1 Entry 2

Hotel Casa Rosalía

Soigrexa 19, 15280 Os Anxeles-Brión, La Coruña

Named after Galicia's most famous poetess, the Rosalía was opened for Holy Year in 1993. A reliable and friendly staging post, the hotel is essentially an old granite farmhouse with a modern extension that holds most of the bedrooms. You enter by a rather grand wrought-iron gate, then through to a patio bounded by a series of intimate eating areas – suitably snug for winter dining. Meals are served in the courtyard in summer. The food – mostly regional, with plenty of roasts – is good value and there are often barbecues. Pride of place in the restaurant goes to the ubiquitous *lareira*, the vast inglenook fireplace typical of old Galician farmhouses. These owners, the Román brothers, are attentive English-speaking hosts who often find time for a chat. Most of the bedrooms are smallish, with modern prints, wooden or tiled floors and stained pine furniture; bathrooms are roomy. The décor is hotelly modern, and colours muted; we preferred those in the old part of the building. There's a pool in the garden, and riding can be arranged.

rooms	30 twins/doubles.
price	€38-€58. Singles €28-€45.
meals	Breakfast €4.50. Lunch/dinner €12 set menu; €24 à la carte.
closed	22 December-21 January.
directions	From Santiago, N-550 for Pontevedra. Before leaving city, right on C-543 for Noía. After Bertamirans, hotel signed to left.

	Alberto & Javier Román
tel	+34 981 887580
fax	+34 981 887557
email	romanulloa@interbook.net
web	www.hotelcasarosalia.com

Map 1 Entry 3

Casa Grande do Bachao

Monte Bachao s/n, Sta. Cristina de Fecha, 15898 Santiago de Compostela, La Coruña

In a clearing in a wood… not a gingerbread cottage nor the home of Red Riding Hood's grandmother, but a solid, four-square house. Arrive at the right time of day, and lunch or (latish) dinner will be in full swing, the dining room packed with all ages. The house has been stylishly furnished without eclipsing the original bones of the place. Bedrooms are elegant, simple and distinct. The dining room is huge and light, with a high raftered ceiling, slab-stone floor and the odd sculpture dotted about; as if to emphasise the importance of food, there's a vast stone feeding trough next door. If you like splendid isolation you'll love it here – and you can actually walk to Santiago de Compostela (it's 35km). There are sauna, gym, a library stacked with books on flora and fauna, and bikes for hire. A spot of trout fishing can also be arranged. The setting, with its storybook appeal, will please the children, as will as the telescope, the games room and the swimming pool. And the freedom to explore. Great value. *A Pazos de Galicia Hotel.*

rooms	12: 9 twins/doubles, 2 singles, 1 suite.
price	€45–€75. Singles €36–€60. Suite €67–€112.
meals	Breakfast €7. Lunch/dinner €15 set menu.
closed	Rarely.
directions	From Santiago, CP-0701, Santa Comba road. Pazo signed on right at 11km milepost before village. Follow road for 5km; signed.

	Javier Goyanes
tel	+34 981 194118
fax	+34 981 192028
email	bachao@pazosdegalicia.com

Map 1 Entry 4

Casa Grande de Cornide

Cornide (Calo-Teo), 15886 Santiago de Compostela, La Coruña

This very special B&B 15 minutes from Santiago centre is surrounded by Galician green. Casa Grande may be likened to a good claret: refined, select, worth paying a bit more for. José Ramón and María Jesús are lecturers (he wrote *The Way to Compostela*) and a love of culture is evident throughout their home. It houses a large collection of modern Galician paintings, hundreds of ceramic pots, a huge library and decoration that is a spicy cocktail of old and new: exposed granite, designer lamps, wooden ceilings, and, everywhere, art. A place to come to read, to paint in the beautiful mature garden full of ancient trees – and a surprising number of palms for so far north – and to cycle: bikes are provided free for guests. The studied décor of the lounges and library is mirrored in the bedrooms and suites, some of which are in a separate building. They have all mod cons and the same mix of modern and old; there are books, ornaments, paintings and exquisite little details such as handmade tiles in the bathrooms to create a special feel. "A glorious place," enthused one reader. *A Pazos de Galicia hotel.*

rooms	10: 6 twins/doubles, 4 suites.
price	€75-€85. Singles €60-€65. Suites €85-€100.
meals	Breakfast €7.
closed	November-Easter.
directions	From Santiago, N-550 for Pontevedra. There is a sign for Cornide on that road. At the roundabout, turn left.

María Jesús Castro & José Ramón Ponsa

tel	+34 981 805599
fax	+34 981 805751
email	info@casagrandedecornide.com
web	www.casagrandedecornide.com

Map 1 Entry 5

Casa Hotel As Artes

Travesia de Dos Puertas 2, 15707 Santiago de Compostela, La Coruña

Where would you want to stay when visiting Santiago? As close as possible to the cathedral, of course. Look no further than this delightful small hotel, in the quietest area of a busy city (the bars round the cathedral close at 10pm). It is the creation of two friendly and energetic Galicians, entirely inspired by Carlos's six-month stay in an intimate Parisian hotel. Guest bedrooms look to music and the arts for their leitmotif: choose between Rodin, Dante, Vivaldi, Gaudí, Picasso, Duncan and Chaplin. All are stylishly furnished with new wrought-iron bedsteads on polished parquet, fashionable fabrics, paintings and prints on exposed stone walls; beds have embroidered sheets, bathrooms sport dressing gowns and thick towels. There's a little sauna, too, and physiotherapy on request. It's fantastic value, and what makes it even better is the professionalism of your hosts. Breakfast – fresh orange juice, fruit salad, charcuterie, cakes, several breads – is served at pretty red-clothed tables. The setting is unbeatable: the cathedral two steps away, restaurants outside the door.

rooms	7 twins/doubles.
price	€52–€86.
meals	Breakfast €8.
closed	January.
directions	In Santiago head for Praza do Obradoiro. Rua de San Francisco to left of cathedral. Hotel 50m past cathedral on right. Have a look at their web site for precise location.

	Esther Mateos & Carlos Elizechea
tel	+34 981 555254
fax	+34 981 577823
email	recepcion@asartes.com
web	www.asartes.com

Map 1 Entry 6

Hello

Pazo de Sedor

Castañeda, 15819 Arzua, La Coruña

One of a number of grand Galician *pazos* open to guests, and a delectable place to stay if you're on the road to or from Santiago. It is an imposing, 18th-century country house surrounded by wooded hillsides and fields of maize and cattle. Inside you get a proper sense of its aristocratic past: cavernous rooms and a broad stone staircase between the two floors. Also memorable is the open fireplace that spans an entire wall of the dining room, with bread ovens at each side; an airier second dining room has been created in an outbuilding and has sweeping views. The bedrooms are a treat: high-ceilinged and parquet-floored, they have family antiques (one with interesting Art Deco beds) and embroidered bedcovers. Some come with their own balcony, and all have enough space for an extra bed. Meals are as authentic as the house: all the flavours of Galicia, most of the vegetables home-grown and meats free-range. María is charming, and fills the house with flowers. *A Pazos de Galicia Hotel.*

rooms	7 twins/doubles.
price	€56–€70. Singles €40–€53.
meals	Breakfast €4.50. Dinner €13.
closed	February.
directions	From Lugo N-540, then N-547 for Santiago. 400m past km57 marker, right to Pazo.

Joaquín Saavedra
tel   +34 981 501600
fax   +34 981 501600
email   info@pazodesedor.com
web   www.pazodesedor.com

Map 2 Entry 7

Pazo da Trave

Galdo, 27850 Viveiro, Lugo

Plants scramble over old stone, the garden laps up to the house, vines hang heavy under the trellis, big trees give shade… even the shutters are green. The lovely garden is an integral part of this place – and is peppered with interesting ceramic sculptures. There is also an *horio* – a wooden storage area where food was traditionally stored and meat hung away from the animals. Food is still taken seriously at Pazo da Trave and dinners are a delight, with traditional dishes made from mouthwatering ingredients, served by friendly staff. Beautiful bedrooms have big oak beds, beamed ceilings and art on the walls; children are thoughtfully considered, with small beds and cots. There is a lovely whitewashed beamy sitting room with an open fire – for cosy winter nights – and a gallery on the first floor with a chaise-longue and armchairs so you can gaze over the large garden or dip into a book (there's quite a collection). A sauna, gym and billiard room are further reasons to stay in this friendly, arty and unstuffy hotel. *A Pazos de Galicia hotel.*

rooms	17 twins/doubles, 2 suites.
price	€64–€103. Singles €45–€60. Suite €115–€145.
meals	Breakfast €8. Lunch/dinner €22. Restaurant closed 1–15 November.
closed	Rarely.
directions	From N-642 to Viveiro, C-640, Lugo road. After 2km, Galdo signed to right. Pazo on right after village.

	Alfonso Otero Regal
tel	+34 982 598163
fax	+34 982 598040
email	traveregal@interbook.net
web	www.nosnet.com/trave

Map 2 Entry 8

Casa Grande de Camposo
Camposo 7, 27364 O Corgo, Lugo

Inside and out – a rare, intriguing place. A high stone wall encloses the four-square farmhouse and its grounds, fortifying Casa Grande against the outside world. The stables have been turned into a quirky covered patio – usable in even the wettest Galician weather – and the unfussy garden is a brilliant place for children. The house itself, built in the 1740s by a wealthy farmer, is a fascinating labyrinth of passages, landings and rooms. María Luisa – whose father inherited the place – presides, priding herself on the family atmosphere and the traditional cooking. You'll be welcomed into a softly lit, stone-floored hall, with oak and chestnut beams and a massive traditional open fireplace. Big, airy bedrooms have pretty rugs on shining wooden or terracotta floors, solid original furniture and bright immaculate bathrooms. The village is tiny – 14 inhabitants – and grew up around the house. The area is not yet on the tourist trail and there's plenty to explore: you're within easy reach of the Sierra de los Aucares and the river Miño has monasteries and churches dotted all along its banks.

rooms	8 twins/doubles.
price	€57–€78. Singles €42–€52.
meals	Breakfast €4. Lunch/dinner €18 set menu.
closed	15 January–15 February.
directions	Lugo-Salida A-6, exit 488 (road C-546 to Sarria-Monforte). 10km, then right onto DP-1611 that takes you to house. Follow signs.

	María Luisa Sánchez
tel	+34 982 543800
fax	+34 982 543937
email	camposo@canal21.com
web	www.camposo.com

Map 2 Entry 9

Pazo de Vilabade

Villabade, 27122 Castroverde, Lugo

In a delectably quiet corner of Galicia, on one of the old routes to Santiago, the deeply rural Pazo de Vilabade is worth at least two nights. Behind the sober façade and fine granite entrance of the manor house by the church waits a charming family home. And heirlooms at every turn. In the corridors: statues, a chaise-longue and family portraits above the grandest of stairwells; in the big, airy bedrooms, named after beloved family members, stacks more lovely pieces: old brass or walnut beds (beware old sizes too), dark wardrobes, huge mirrors. Most seductive of all: the lofty breakfast room with its enormous *lareira* (fireplace) and two tables at which you will be served cheeses, homemade cakes and jams and delicious coffee. The heart and soul of it all is Señora Teresa Arana, an entertaining and sprightly lady, so determined to get it right that she studied rural tourism in France before opening her historic house. Meet her — just a few words of English but her French is very good — and share a wonderful home and gardens. "Totally special, a fascinating place," wrote a reader.

rooms	6: 5 twins/doubles, 1 single.
price	€89. Singles €75.
meals	Breakfast €5.20. Good restaurant in Castroverde.
closed	November-May.
directions	From Madrid for La Coruña on A6. Exit onto C-630 to Castroverde. At exit of town left signposted 'Pazo de Villabade'. House 2km beyond by prominent village church.

	Teresa Arana
tel	+34 982 313000
fax	+34 982 312063
email	labraira@teleline.es
web	www.elpazo.com

Map 2 Entry 10

Casa Grande da Fervenza

Ctra. Lugo-Páramo km11, 27163 O Corgo, Lugo

The River Miño laps at the walls of this house and ancient, working mill. Girdled by 18 hectares of magnificent ancient woodland, it's precious enough to have been declared a UNESCO Biosphere Reserve. The Casa, named after the amazing rocky waterfall outside, is both hotel *and* museum – a fascinating one, in perfect working order; ask for a guided tour. The restaurant with glorious open fireplace is in the oldest part and dates from the 17th century, and the menus are based on the sort of food that was around when the building was built… beef and wild boar stew with chestnuts, mushrooms in November. Wines are outstanding, the region's best. After a day on the river (with canoe or *batuxo*) return to quiet, simple, stylish bedrooms in this house where the miller once lived. Restoration has been meticulous in its respect for local tradition and lore, yet there's no stinting on creature comforts. Antiques have been beautifully restored, rugs woven on their looms, there are linen curtains, chestnut beams and floors and hand-painted sinks. Superb. *A Rusticae hotel.*

rooms	9: 8 doubles, 1 suite.
price	€56–€70. Singles €39.20–€49. Suite €80–€100. VAT included.
meals	Breakfast €5. Lunch/dinner €15; €15–€30 à la carte. VAT included.
closed	Rarely.
directions	From Lugo, N-VI for Madrid. After 4km in Conturiz, right by Hotel Torre de Núñez for Páramo for 11km; right at sign for 1km to hotel.

	Modesto Seoane Pérez
tel	+34 982 150610
fax	+34 982 151610
email	info@fervenza.com
web	www.fervenza.com

Map 2 Entry 11

Casa de Labranza Arza

Reigosa-San Cristobo do Real, 27633 Samos, Lugo

Glorious views, a farmhouse-family welcome, the smell of newly baked bread…
this place is special, and you'll feel at home the moment you kick off your mud-
caked boots. The views really *are* something, the 6,000-foot-high peaks strung
together like a dowager's diamonds for all to admire. On a clear day you can see
as far as Portugal. Casa Arza is on the slopes of Monte Oribio and is a working
dairy farm – hence the delicious butter and soft cheeses served at breakfast.
Ramona cooks meat in a wood-fired oven and vegetables straight from the farm,
and the bread is kneaded in an old bread chest and baked daily in the ancient,
stone-built oven. This is back to basics in the best possible sense, and the warmth
of the hospitality the icing on the cake. The slate walls and roof of the Casa are
typical of the area; bedrooms have rafters and exposed stone walls. Beds are
wooden and old, widened to take modern mattresses. Be sure to visit the
Monasterio de Samos nearby – it's the biggest monastic cloister in Spain.

rooms	9 twins/doubles.
price	€35. Singles €30. VAT included.
meals	Breakfast €4. Dinner €10.
closed	Rarely.
directions	From Lugo, N-VI for Ponferrada; C-546 to Sarria-Monforte. Left at Sarria on LU-633 to Samos. Through San Cristobo; signposted to right at end of village. 4km uphill on left, on entering Reigosa.

	Cristina Arza Rio
tel	+34 982 187036
fax	+34 982 187036
email	arza@mundo-r.com

Map 2 Entry 12

Casa Grande de Rosende

27460 Rosende-Sober, Lugo

Sleep deeply in the Bedroom of the Drunkards – so named because of its Goyaesque fresco of lurching figures. This monument to medieval life is full of fascination – from the suits of armour to the vast stone-walled rooms, the setting in former times for many a grand feast. The tower is medieval, the rest is noble 18th century, and several of the bedrooms are stupendously raftered, with furnishings to match. The vibrant personalities of Pauloba and Manuel add to the sense of fun, and Manuel's knowledge of history is worthy of investigation. His grandmother left this, the long-standing family home, to become a celebrated pastry chef in Madrid; she returned to share her knowledge with the locals and Pauloba's fresh almond pudding is alone worth a detour. Now the area is renowned for its pastries and cakes! Guests are invited to sample *aguardiente*, a homemade digestif, in the sitting room before dinner, magnificent with its neo-classical paintings and a piano crowded with family photos. Not the easiest place to find, but worth any number of wrong turns. *A Pazos de Galicia hotel.*

rooms	9: 6 doubles, 3 singles.
price	€47-€59. Singles €29-€36.
meals	Breakfast €5.50. Lunch €19. Dinner €14.
closed	15 December-15 January.
directions	From Orense, N-120 for Monforte. At km50, exit for Canaval. Right at 1st T-junc., following signs for house. Casa Grande 3km down road.

	Manuel Vieítez
tel	+34 982 460627
fax	+34 982 455104
email	rosende@pazosdegalicia.com
web	www.casagrandederosende.com

Map 2 Entry 13

Casa Grande de Trives

c/Marqués de Trives 17, 32780 Pobra de Trives, Orense

This noble village house with its own chapel (mass held every Wednesday) was one of the first to be restored with government help and open to guests; like good claret it has got better and better. Rooms are filled with antique pieces, many exquisitely upholstered or carved, and a very fine restored piano – rained on for years in this once-derelict house – a present from Elizabeth II of Spain. Bedrooms in a separate wing are a quiet delight, big with polished floors and (in some cases) French windows to the gardens. And the garden is huge, straight out of a fairytale, full of shady hidden corners and heaven for kids. There's a lovely sitting room where you can have a quiet drink, and an unforgettable dining room where breakfast is served. Here the richness of the furnishings, the cut flowers and the classical music vie with the homemade cakes, fresh fruits, big pots of coffee and croissants that make their way up from the kitchen via a dumb waiter. Fine bone china adds to the elegance of the meal. A marvellous place and a most gracious and charming welcome from mother and son. *Grand Cru* Galicia!

rooms	9 twins/doubles.
price	€50–€72. Singles €41–€60.
meals	Breakfast €5. Dinner €18 on request only.
closed	Rarely.
directions	From Madrid A-6 for La Coruña. Exit 400 for N-120 for Monforte de Lemos. At km468, branch off for Pobra de T, signed Terra de Trives, then right at lights onto C-536 for Trives. On left in village.

Alfredo Araujo & Adelaida Alvarez Martínez

tel	+34 988 332066
fax	+34 988 332066
email	informacion@casagrandetrives.com
web	www.casagrandetrives.com

Map 2 Entry 14

Pazo Paradela

Carretera Barrio km2, 32780 Puebla de Trives, Orense

Your home for the night: a 17th-century manor house with supreme views to the Galician hills. Your host: delightful Manuel, who speaks superb English. He grew up in the States, dreamed of returning to his native soil, and ended up restoring the imposing old granite house, close to sleepy Trives, that his father bought 30 years before. Manuel's natural generosity is reflected in the renovation; "be proud of your work," is his philosophy. Bedrooms and bathrooms, not large, have been treated to the simple best: chestnut floors and furniture, Portuguese marble, antique mirrors on rustic stone walls. There's central heating for winter, air conditioning for summer, views are long and green and the peace is total. The treats continue at table: in the vast granite-hearthed dining room you may expect homemade honey and jams for breakfast and, for dinner, the best of Galician country cooking and vegetables fresh from the kitchen garden. And there's true hospitality: a *queimada* shared with your hosts, the local hot brandied brew that keeps evil spirits at bay.

rooms	8: 7 twins/doubles, 1 suite.
price	€57-€75. Singles €45. Suite €67. VAT included.
meals	Breakfast €6. Dinner €20. VAT inc.
closed	22 December-2 January.
directions	From León, N-VI to Ponferrada; N-120 into A Rua Petin; C-536 to Trives. Through centre of town, cross bridge, then 1st right; follow signs.

	Manuel Rodríguez Rodríguez
tel	+34 988 330714
fax	+34 988 337001
email	1pa712e1@infonegocio.com

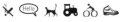

Map 2 Entry 15

Reitoral de Chandrexa

Casalta 6, 32747 Parada do Sil, Orense

The age-old rectory has become a simple farmstead. In it live a young family who abandoned the city to farm, their only aid a plough pulled by Good Boy the donkey. Now they welcome guests too. It's a wonderfully unsophisticated home, this ancient stone house with its pretty carved balcony. Fresh bedrooms have the basics for simple, wholesome comfort – new mattresses and carved bedheads, the minimum of furniture and central heating. Two rooms share a bathroom. There's character, too, from nooks, crannies and good pictures. Best of all is the food, nearly all homemade and home-grown, whether it be bread and butter or yogurt and chestnut honey; let your tastebuds rejoice. It's so good that outsiders pop in for hearty vegetarian dinners (courgette soup, wild mushroom risotto) and plenty of choice, all washed down with your hosts' own wine. Make up for any over-indulgence by an exploration of the nearby river canyon on foot, or help out on the farm. The church bells ring loudly every 15 minutes – but it's amazing how quickly you get get used to them!

rooms	3 doubles.
price	€31–€49.
meals	Breakfast €3. Lunch/dinner €11–€15.
closed	November–February.
directions	From Orense on OU-536 for Trives. At Vilariño towards Parada do Sil; on for 5km towards A Teixeira.

Mercedes Martínez Modroño

tel	+34 988 208099
fax	+34 988 208099
email	chandrexa@inicia.es
web	www.inicia.es/de/chandrexa

Map 2 Entry 16

Casa Grande de Soutullo

Soutullo de Abaixo, 32152 Coles, Orense

Come for charming owners and stylish country living. This was Benito's great-grandfather's house, a pile of stones in 1973; then Gill and Benito nurtured it back to life. From the breezy and beautiful internal courtyard – with unusual stone settee – radiate a series of elegantly raftered galleries and rooms decorated with Gill's paintings and many wonderful antiques. The breakfast room is inviting, its several tables set with white china. Wooden-floored bedrooms are equally good, enhanced with period pieces and lively colours; un-air-conditioned they are naturally cool. Bathrooms have hand-painted washbasins: the attention to detail is a delight. Outside, unkempt grounds though which a 100-year-old tortoise roams, a sun loggia, a serene pool and tennis. Hard to tear yourself away… but do make time for Ortense with its seven-arched bridge, one of the finest in Spain, and its amazing Bishop's Baths. Its three outdoor pools built by the Cardinal Queredo, Japanese stove garden and treatments galore are your passport to heaven, modestly priced. Very special. *A Pazos de Galicia hotel.*

rooms	8 twins/doubles.
price	€77. Singles €61.
meals	Breakfast €6.50. Various restaurants nearby.
closed	Rarely.
directions	From Orense, N-525 for Santiago to Gustei. Take the CP-6 to A Peroxa; first turning on the right to Soutullo de Abaixo.

	Benito Vázquez
tel	+34 988 205611
fax	+34 988 205694
email	pazosoutullo@yahoo.com
web	www.pazosdegalicia.com

Map 2 Entry 17

Pazo Bentraces

Bentraces, 32890 Barbadás, Orense

The granite stones of Bentraces are steeped in history. Built for a bishop, this delectable *palacio* was passed on to a Galician family who in turn sold it on, and on... spot the six different coats of arms. Angeles will unravel the history and tell of the three long years of restoration that have resulted in one of the most elegant manor house hotels in Spain. The plushness of the interiors is barely hinted at by the Florentine façade, or the gardens that lap up to the walls. Push aside the heavy doors and enter a world of marble, parquet and warm colours, books, rugs, antiques and engravings. Anyone with an interest in finery would love it here: the several public rooms, the vast and vibrant kitchen where you breakfast, the bedrooms, which are sumptuous. Come for superb mattresses and fine bed linen, soft bathrobes in marble bathrooms, and suites big enough to hold a cocktail party. Spin off on bikes, discover romanesque chapels and monasteries, visit the galleries of Santiago (an hour's drive), return to a tempting pool. *A Rusticae hotel*

rooms	7: 5 doubles, 2 suites.
price	€100–€110. Singles €80. Suites €140.
meals	Breakfast €10. Dinner €30.
closed	22 December–22 January.
directions	From Orense for Madrid N-525; just past km7 marker, N-540 for Celanova to Bentraces. Here at 'Bar Bentraces', right; house beside church. Ring bell at main gate.

Angeles Peñamaría Cajoto

tel	+34 988 383381
fax	+34 988 383035
email	info@pazodebentraces.com
web	www.pazodebentraces.com

Map 2 Entry 18

Rectoral de Cobres 1729

San Adrian de Cobres, 36142 Vilaboa, Pontevedra

Mussel platforms, fishing boats and the majestic sweep of the de Vigo – a special site! The house was built for a priest in 1729 and has been beautifully renovated by Norwegian architect Randi, who, with husband Juan Carlos, has created this charming small hotel. Relax in the long living room divided by an old stone arch, graced with a delicate Persian carpet and red sofas; dip into a fascinating tome from your multi lingual hosts' library (3,000 books!), take a drink to the terrace with those estuary views. Bedrooms are sensitively designed (one with the disabled or elderly in mind) and reveal an architect's love of clean lines and uncluttered spaces. One double has a sweep of polished parquet, French windows to a balcony (more views) and an entire wall of ancient stone. Gravitate to the bar, where strong Galician beer is served; Juan Carlos may even pick up the guitar or the Gallic pipes and serenade you. The stunning outdoor *horio* (granary) has been converted into a further sitting area: what a place to watch the sun go down. *A Pazos de Galicia hotel.*

rooms	8 twins/doubles.
price	€80–€120.
meals	Breakfast €7.
closed	15 January–15 February.
directions	From Pontevedra, A-9 for Vigo. Exit 146 for Cangas. After toll, left following signs for Vilaboa & Cobres. 2km from junc., at km8 marker, take track on left. 100m from road.

	Juan Carlos Madriñán
tel	+34 986 673810
fax	+34 986 673803
email	info@rectoral.com
web	www.rectoral.com

Map 1 Entry 19

Rectoral de Fofe
Covelo, 36873 Fofe, Pontevedra

Hard to believe this was once a rectory; what is now the 'special' bedroom was once the priest's own. He chose well: from the shuttered windows are wonderful views to the Valle de Tilas. A high vaulted ceiling gives the room an airy quality, while the austerity of the stone walls is softened by a wrought-iron bedstead and rugs on the floor. The other bedrooms are decorated simply and pleasingly in yellow and blue. Some have balconies and one has a platform cantilevered out over the doors reached by a ladder, it would appeal to a child. The old kitchen has been turned into an attractive sitting room, with a beamed ceiling and a fireplace where the oven used to be. Paintings and ceramics look well against the natural stone walls. But you'll want to be outside, making the most of those green valleys and hills. It's deep countryside here and there are some superb walks, as well as bicycles to hire and rivers to fish. You can't go far along the twisting road towards Pontevedra without being stunned by panoramic views of this part of Galicia's ancient, broom-covered granite massif. *A Pazos de Galicia hotel.*

rooms	9: 8 doubles, 1 single.
price	€60–€81. Singles €30–€45.
meals	Breakfast €5. Lunch/dinner €13.50.
closed	Rarely.
directions	From Vigo, A-52 for Madrid. Exit 282 to Paraños. Take service road into village & on to Covelo, through Maceira to Fofe. Hotel on right at village entrance.

	Amador Barcia
tel	+34 986 668750
fax	+34 986 668737
email	fofe@free.recynet.com
web	www.rectoraldefofe.com

Map 1 Entry 20

Os Bravos I

Estas, 36730 Tomiño, Pontevedra

Pluck fresh kiwi, peaches and nectarines for breakfast. Stroll around your walled garden – yes, you will feel proprietorial – before breakfasting on your bedroom balcony with its views to Portugal. Slipped into this unspoilt pocket of Spain, this is a genuine hideaway. Several notches above the average self-catering villa, the sprawling, five-bedroom, colonial-style house combines modernity with Galician charm. Locally-made chestnut furniture, sloping ceilings and splashes of chintz give a hint of 'country' while the modern sofas and owner's bold paintings add panache. The kitchen is so well-equipped you'll want to take it home. Couples or small families will be cosier in the nearby, but screened, stone cottage. Judith (English and the artist) and Karl (half-Galician) are warm, engaging, fun and know all the best beaches, walks and romantic ruins. But often it's just too tempting to do anything but drift around the garden and pool, or perhaps sketch or paint (studio and materials available for budding artists). At night, you'll be hard pushed to hear anything more than the soft plop of an over-ripe peach.

rooms	4 + 2: 4 doubles. 1 cottage for 4, 1 villa for 8-10.
price	€60. Cottage £450 p.w.; villa £750 p.w.; cottage + villa £1,000 p.w. (s/c prices in sterling).
meals	Excellent restaurants nearby.
closed	Rarely.
directions	From Vigo N-550 for Tui. Pass yellow bar, El Paso; next right for Estas; through village for 2km. Os Bravos behind mint-green wall.

Judith Mary Goater & Karl Abreu

tel	+34 986 623337
fax	+34 986 623338
email	huntingfordfarm@farmersweekly.net

Map 1 Entry 21

Hostal Restaurante Asensio

Rua do Tollo 2, 36750 Goian, Pontevedra

At first glance you may wonder how this unprepossessing hostelry earns its place in the pages of this guide. There are two excellent reasons for coming here: one, delightful Dolores ('Loli') and mustachioed Fernando, who lived for many years in the UK and who love receiving English-speaking guests, and two, the food. Fernando's claim that he can satisfy even the most demanding of palates is no idle boast. With the river Mino a hop away and the sea not much further the menu naturally gravitates towards fish: lamprey and elvers are house specials, seafood too – and to accompany it all is a quality-rather-than-quantity wine list; the wine from the village is superb. Good meat dishes are also available. Pink and white tables are crisply laid in the small, pine-clad dining room; the bar area next door is where you breakfast. Bedrooms could be just an afterthought but they're as spruce as can be, not hugely memorable but comfortable and clean; our favourites are the newest ones grafted onto the original building a few years ago.

rooms	6 twins/doubles.
price	€42. Singles €36.
meals	Breakfast €2. Lunch €10. Dinner €30 à la carte.
closed	16 September-16 October.
directions	E-1 Vigo to Tuy; exit at km172 onto N-550 La Guardia & A Guarda. On for 15km. Hostal on left on passing through Goian.

Fernando Asensio

tel	+34 986 620152
fax	+34 986 620152
email	correo@restauranteasensio.com
web	www.restauranteasensio.com

Map 1 Entry 22

Finca Río Miño

Carril 6, Las Eiras, 36760 O Rosal, Pontevedra

It's like being on holiday in two countries at the same time. Portuguese Vila Nova de Cerveira (worth a visit for its Saturday market alone) is 10 minutes by car; on this side of the water, one of the most rugged – and lushest – areas of Spain. And what a position, up on the bank of the Miño with views to the Alto Minho on a clear day. Robin fell in love with Galicia many years ago, returned with Deborah on their 25th wedding anniversary and booked into Finca Río Miño; now they own the whole lovely place. Previous owners Tony and Shirley proudly passed on a small but successful business – two simple, comfortable pine-clad lodges in a verdant garden, and a room in the 350-year-old farmhouse. Plus… a breakfast room, a bar, a pool with a view and an unforgettable terrace with a rambling passion fruit to give shade. One of the big attractions here is the proximity of river and sea, so anyone interested in fishing, kayaking, surfing or white water rafting will be in clover. Hiking, riding and biking too can be arranged – and the purchasing of land should you wish to stay! Let Robin be your expert guide.

rooms	1 + 2: 1 twin. 2 self-catering lodges for 4.
price	€60. Lodges €80–€99.
meals	Breakfast €8. Restaurants nearby, within walking distance.
closed	December-end January.
directions	Vigo E1/A3 to Tui; La Guardia/O Rosal exit onto C550/PO552; bypass Goian; left at Eiras sign just past Adegas Tollodouro; thru' forest to T-junc; right; Finca 100m on left.

Robin & Deborah Winterhalder

tel	+34 986 621107
fax	+34 986 621035
email	info@fincariomino.com
web	www.fincariomino.com

Map 1 Entry 23

Photo Jose Navarro

asturias & cantabria

La Corte

33843 Villar de Vildas, Asturias

Cows are herded down tiny steets: Villar de Vildas is a genuine working village and a delight to visit. Your inn is a 19th-century farmhouse of wood and stone, converted by Adriano to create a small guesthouse and restaurant. You enter via a small courtyard, then up old stone steps to a wooden-floored sitting room. Here are books and photographs (spot your host as a young boy), modern Spanish furniture, a handsome hearth and an exterior gallery that catches the afternoon sun. A wooden spiral staircase leads to five bedrooms; Adriano will help you with your cases. These vary in size and have good bathrooms, new pine furniture and comfy beds; two come with dormer windows so you can gaze at the peaks and the stars from your bed. The studio in the raised granary is huge fun. La Corte is the sort of place where locals pop in for a drink or a meal – and the restaurant is cosy: low-ceilinged, beamed and with basket lamps. There is no sweeter place from which to discover the walks of the Pigüeña valley; on the western flank of the Somiedo Park, where some of the last bears in Europe roam free.

rooms	6 + 1: 5 doubles, 1 studio. 1 self-catering apartment for 4.
price	€60. Studio €60. Apt €95. VAT inc.
meals	Breakfast €3.90. Lunch/dinner €10.
closed	Rarely.
directions	From Oviedo N-634 west. Just before Cornellana, left on AS-15 to Puente de San Martín. Here AS-227 south to Aguasmestas. Here, right to Pigüeña; up via Cores to Villar.

	Adriano Berdasco Fernández
tel	+34 985 763131
fax	+34 985 763117
email	lacorte@somiedorural.com
web	www.somiedorural.com/lacorte

Map 3 Entry 24

Hotel Villa La Argentina

Parque de la Barrera, Villar de Luarca, 33700 Luarca, Asturias

This aristocratic villa was constructed in 1899 by an emigrant who'd made his fortune in South America – hence its name. It was later abandoned, then rediscovered by the González Fernández family who saw in the crumbling stucco a brighter future. Once again it breathes an air of light-hearted elegance and optimism. The breakfast room is parquet-floored and high-ceilinged, with beautiful stained-glass windows; gilt-framed oil paintings, candelabras and tall mirrors add to the lofty feel. The best bedrooms are in harmony with the house and have glorious garden views; most are large with stuccoed and corniced ceilings and king-sized beds. Good mattresses and hydromassage tubs add to the feel-good factor; bathrooms are quirky. La Argentina's low-raftered restaurant is a good place to dine on turbot or steak 'Ultramar', and Antonio and his staff are delightful. After dinner, slip off for a swim or a game of billiards, then wander the Villa's overgrown gardens with their 100-year-old seqoias brought all the way from America. There's also a faded and charming little chapel.

rooms	12: 9 twins/doubles, 3 suites.
price	€51–€81. Suites €81–€102.
meals	Breakfast €6. Lunch/dinner €15 menu; €20 à la carte.
closed	7 Jan–end Feb except 14 Feb.
directions	From Oviedo & Gijón on A-8/N-632 for Avilés. Exit onto N-634 for Luarca. At AGIP petrol station just before Luarca, right on LU-1; follow yellow signs for hotel.

	Antonio González & Marta Cela
tel	+34 985 640102
fax	+34 985 640973
email	villalaargentina@villalaargentina.com
web	www.villalaargentina.com

Map 3 Entry 25

La Torre de Villademoros
Villademoros s/n (Cadavedo), 33788 Valdés, Asturias

In meadowland high above the coast stands this elegant retreat – hike down to undiscovered shingle beaches. Young, smiling Manolo designed La Torre with his brother, and the 18th-century Asturian exterior, with a medieval tower to one side, gives little hint of the delights within. It is intimate, cosy and hugely appealing. Old granite walls, chunky rafters and gleaming wooden or slate floors are the background to sleek sofas and sculpted lighting, while warm colours, modern paintings and an open hearth add depth. Serene bedrooms and private sitting rooms are finished with polished chestnut and pine; bathrooms are rustic-contemporary. Views are grand – over the sea or the lush eucalyptus forests. Dinner is an inexpensive and convivial affair with traditional dishes (stuffed tuna a seasonal delicacy), good wines and delicious desserts. Breakfasts are equally scrumptious – pastries, cakes, crêpes, homemade jams, a cooked breakfast on request – and will set you up for the superb coastal path to Cudillero (return by train). Not easy to find, but well worth the effort. *A Rusticae hotel.*

rooms	10 twins/doubles.
price	€70-€98. Singles €52-€75.
meals	Breakfast €6.50. Dinner €15.
closed	15 November-7 January
directions	From Oviedo, N-632/E-70 for La Coruña; exit for Cadavedo. Through village & into Villademoros. 30m after Villademoros road sign right following signs to hotel.

	Manolo Santullano Méndez
tel	+34 985 645264
fax	+34 985 645265
email	correo@torrevillademoros.com
web	www.torrevillademoros.com

Map 3 Entry 26

La Casona de Pío

c/Riofrío 3, 33150 Cudillero, Asturias

Hard to believe Pío ever had a fish-salting factory here – in this elegant little hotel, one street back from the main square. Cudillero is one of the prettiest fishing villages of the Asturian coast, a huddle of houses around a sheltered cove where you can still watch the catch being landed first thing. La Casona de Pío is one of the area's best fish restaurants and is hard to fault – beautifully presented tables and food, an extraordinarily crafted wooden ceiling, and a chef who knows his stuff. We were ushered through to the kitchen to see all kinds of good things on the go in boiling pots and sizzling pans. Out of season Pío's charming owners will give you a choice of rooms. We might choose no. 104 for its private terrace – or a top-floor room for its light. All the rooms are smart yet cosy, the furniture is of chestnut, there are matching bedcovers and drapes, rugs on gleaming tiled floors and swish bathrooms with hydromassage baths. Picnics can be prepared for walks and other sorties. Excellent value, lovely people.

rooms	11: 10 doubles, 1 suite.
price	€48-€74. Singles €38.60-€59.60 Suite €70.95-€89.55.
meals	Breakfast €6. Lunch/dinner €20 set menu.
closed	9 January-9 February.
directions	From Oviedo, A-66 to Avilés; then on for Luarca. Turn right off road for Cudillero. Hotel in town centre, just off main square.

	Rosario Fernández Martínez
tel	+34 985 591512
fax	+34 985 591519
email	casonadepio@arrakis.es
web	www.arrakis.es/~casonadepio/

Map 3 Entry 27

Casona de la Paca
El Pito, 33150 Cudillero, Asturias

Worth coming here for the breakfasts alone... Asturian cheeses, smoked meats, *torrejas, maranuelas, frixuelos*, doughnuts and crêpes – all superb. The Casona's strawberry-coloured façade and exotic gardens packed with New World species grab the attention on arrival – as was intended. This is one of Asturias's many flamboyant edifices built by emigrant who made their fortune in the Americas, then headed home. Revived from ruin only 15 years ago, the house contains an elegant mix of classic and colonial styles in sympathy with the spirit of the place. There are mahogany and teak in abundance, contemporary fabrics and handmade, Deco-style floor tiles. The conservatory is exquisite, the well-upholstered lounge is a lovely place to read and there are plenty of books in the library. Bedrooms are divided between the main house and the annexe; the Tower Suite is worth the extra for its wraparound terrace. There are also 10 immaculate self-catering studios. Casona de la Paca runs on well-oiled wheels, and the fishing town of Cudillero is delightfully nearby. *A Rusticae hotel.*

rooms	9 + 10: 6 twins/doubles, 1 single, 2 suites. 10 studios for 2.
price	€62-€83. Singles €50-€70. Suites €88-€109. Studios €55-€76.
meals	Breakfast €6.
closed	11 December-January.
directions	From Oviedo/Gijón on A-8/N-632 for La Coruña. After Soto de Barco, right at signs for Cudillero. House on right after approx. 1km.

	Montserrat Abad
tel	+34 985 591303
fax	+34 985 591316
email	hotel@casonadelapaca.com
web	www.casonadelapaca.com

Map 3 Entry 28

Hotel Quinta Duro

Camino de las Quintas 384, 33394 Cabueñes-Gijón, Asturias

The family estate is a haven of greenery and mature trees, girdled by a high stone wall. It and its stately house lie just to the east of Gijón and you overlook the city; though 800m from the main road, you hear nothing but birds. Carlos, a delightfully warm presence, has redecorated house and large veranda and the result is stylish yet homely. Panelled walls and period Portuguese and English furniture show the family's love of quality and detail, and bedrooms are distinguished, one with its own terrace. The bronze statue in the lovely gardens is of Carlos's grandfather who casts a wistful eye on all those who visit – he would surely approve of his grandson giving the house this new lease of life. Breakfasts are excellent and there are two restaurants close by – or head for the lively resort. The beach gets busy, but on the harbour front you'll find two Austurian specialities in abundance: fish and cider. The former comes in varieties distinct to the Cantabrian sea, the latter poured from a bottle held above the waiter's head into a glass held at knee height – huge fun. *Pottery courses available.*

rooms	11 twins/doubles.
price	€80–€111. VAT included.
meals	Restaurants nearby.
closed	Rarely.
directions	From A-8 exit 385 to Gijón, then to Hospital de Cabueñes at 1st & 2nd r'bouts. At r'bout by Jardín Botánico 1st right for Santurio y Cefontes; after 200m left for Santurio. 200m on, right for Deva. 350m on right.

	Carlos Velázquez-Duro
tel	+34 985 330443
fax	+34 985 371890
email	info@hotelquintaduro.com
web	www.hotelquintaduro.com

Map 3 Entry 29

La Quintana de la Foncalada
Argüero, 33314 Villaviciosa, Asturias

Severino welcomes you with unaffected simplicity at this honeysuckle-clad farmhouse in the flat, coastal *mariña* area of Asturias. The shady, breezy front garden is a delight, while the inside of the house is light, bright and simple. Bedrooms have basic furniture and artistic splashes of colour, bathrooms are small; the stable apartment with open fire is the most atmospheric. Make yourself a hot drink in the big, rustic kitchen whenever you like; enjoy the games room – popular with families; find out about the area and its traditions in the guest lounge filled with leaflets and books. Your hosts encourage adults and children to try potting in their new workshop: every plate, lamp and tile in the house is homemade. You may also help with the Asturian ponies and the organic veg patch. Much is home-produced: honey, cheese, juices, cider, jam. Make the most of the delectable beaches nearby, the good eateries and the excursions from La Quintana by bike or pony. Equinophiles should know that Severino has created a museum dedicated to the Asturian pony, the *asturcón*; he also breeds them.

rooms	6 + 1: 6 twins/doubles. 1 apartment.
price	€40-€50. Singles €35-€40. Apartment €70-€90 VAT included.
meals	Breakfast €4. Lunch/dinner €15. VAT included.
closed	Rarely.
directions	A-8 Santander-Oviedo, at exit to Villaviciosa AS-256 for Gijón. Arguero 8km further; follow signs.

	Severino García & Daniela Schmid
tel	+34 985 876365
fax	+34 985 876365
email	foncalada@asturcon-museo.com
web	www.asturcon-museo.com

Map 3 Entry 30

La Corte de Lugás

c/Lugás s/n, 33311 Villaviciosa, Asturias

The road ends at Lugás! Secluded it is, remote even, surrounded by eucalyptus and walnut forests, off the lushly beaten track. The young owners used to own a soft furnishings business, and their new venture is a showcase for their decorative talent. Bedrooms, named after the kings of Asturias, are divided between the 17th-century house (including attic) and the former bakery (where spaces are loftier). They vary in size and theme and there's a stylish rusticity at play: some rooms feel darkly medieval, others bohemian, one has a seaside air; all are bold, eye-catching, simple and luxurious. Some of the wrought-iron furniture was commissioned by local artists, a few beds are country antiques; fabrics are subtle and of fine quality, the attention to detail is superb, and real art adds an original touch. Note that windows tend to be small. Outside, huge lawns and wide-ranging field and forest views. Venture forth to discover the estuary town of Villaviciosa, famous for its migratory birds; return to suave leather armchairs before a fire, and dinner worth waiting for.

rooms	10: 7 twins/doubles, 3 suites.
price	€70–€99. Singles €55–€75. Suites €100–€120.
meals	Breakfast €6. Lunch/dinner €30.
closed	7 January–7 February.
directions	From Villaviciosa towards Infiesto; at km3 marker, left for Lugás. Hotel 2km further.

	Daniel Gonzalez Alvarez
tel	+34 985 890203
fax	+34 985 89 02 03
email	info@lacortedelugas.com
web	www.lacortedelugas.com

Map 3 Entry 31

Palacio de Cutre
33583 Villamayor, Asturias

Javier worked for one of Spain's big hotel chains but is now a firm convert to the 'small is beautiful' school. He and his wife Alejandra have lavished energy and care on this intimate luxurious small, 16th-century hotel. Part of the spirit is captured by the hotel's own literature, written as if all were overseen by the ancient oak that towers over the lovely gardens. In the beautifully decorated bedrooms are flounced and beribboned curtains, lavish cushions, Tiffany-style lamps, antique bedsteads and plush fabrics. The toile de Jouy suite sits under white-painted rafters, the bathrooms are fittingly fabulous. But we give Alejandra herself the final word: she insists that what makes Cutre so special is the cuisine, an innovative mix of traditional Asturian dishes and more elaborate fare, such as duck breast with red peppers. Enjoy breakfast in elegance on rush-seated chairs in the dining room with astonishing views; ham and eggs, tortilla, many different jams. And the lovely old *pueblo* village of Villamayor-Infiesto is just down the road.

rooms	17: 15 twins/doubles, 2 suites.
price	€89–€160. Singles €65–€80. Suites €160–€175.
meals	Breakfast €9.50. Lunch/dinner €35 menu; €45 à la carte.
closed	Christmas (24th, 25th December)
directions	From Santander A-8, exit 326 for Ribadesella. N-634 direction Arriondas. 3km after Sevares right on AS-258 & PI-II to hotel.

	Javier Alvarez Garzo
tel	+34 985 708072
fax	+34 985 708019
email	hotel@palaciodecutre.com
web	www.palaciodecutre.com

Map 3 Entry 32

Casona de Bustiello

Ctra. Infiesto - Villaviciosa s/n, 33535 Infiesto, Asturias

Cave paintings and monasteries, beaches and mountains, towns and tranquillity, all within easy reach of this little hotel on the western edges of the Picos de Europa. Its mix of traditional Asturian and modern architecture gives the house an eccentric look, the shallow roof being dominated by a large, obtrusive dormer window, but enter that room in the attic space and you'll find it delightful, with rosy walls, sloping ceilings and an entertaining mass of beams. The hotel was not long ago converted and the owners have done a great job. All the rooms are painted in warm colours and furnished with confidence and restraint, keeping a cosy, rural feel. From the sitting room, with its big bookcases, a door leads to a long, windowed gallery – a wonderful place to sit and take in the views of the Sierra de Ques. Excellent new stress-busting treatments are on offer, and horse riding for beginners. And if the solitude and wildlife of the mountains appeal, head south-east into the wild magnificence of the Picos de Europa.

rooms	9: 8 twins/doubles, 1 suite.
price	€59-€95. Suite €95-€126.
meals	Breakfast €7. Dinner €17.
closed	Rarely.
directions	From Oviedo, N-634 for Santander. 2km before Infiesto, left on AS-255 for Villaviciosa. On right after 4km.

	Aurora R Huergo
tel	+34 985 710445
fax	+34 985 710760
email	info.hcb@hotelcasonadebustiello.com
web	www.hotelcasonadebustiello.com

Map 3 Entry 33

Finca Troniella

c/Pintueles 33, 33534 Infiesto (Piloña), Asturias

You're deep in the country, the Picos de Europa National Park lies next door and a half-hour walk brings you to the little railway that covers the north coast. Barbara and Bryan had a country farmhouse in Andalucía, then fell for the friendly, unspoilt hamlet of Pintueles and this 18th-century farmhouse... whose roof fell in the moment the purchase was complete! That was four years ago; now your holiday house is beautifully intact. Chestnut, oak, antique pine... Troniella is an irresistibly woody wonderland, particularly its huge sitting room, where stout timbers rise to support even stouter beams. From here, doors open onto a typically Asturian porch – a place for reading, dreaming and soaking up the silence of this birdsonged valley. Bedrooms are rustic, fuss-free and roomy, with chestnut floors, generous beds and good furniture, the result of some enthusiastic antique collecting. Bathrooms have bags of character – one with floor tiles dating from the Spanish Civil War and a big roll-top bath, the other with its own balcony... just hope that any post-shower air-drying doesn't frighten the natives!

rooms	House for 8.
price	€150 per night.
meals	Self-catering. Restaurants 6km.
closed	Rarely.
directions	Santander A-8 exit 326 onto N-634 for Arriondas. Pass Infiesto, right for Villaviciosa; immed. right for Pintueles. After 3.5km 1st right at entrance of village; on for 300m. Right at fork; 100m.

	Barbara Emery & Bryan Holloway
tel	+34 985 711270
email	info@casatroniella.com
web	www.casatroniella.com

Map 3 Entry 34

Los Cuetos

Santianes s/n, 33537 Infiesto, Asturias

The newly rebuilt 16th-century farmhouse has a commanding position and uninterrupted views – best appreciated from its covered gallery. All is warm and friendly inside and blends serenely with the majestic setting. Furnishings are smartly stylish with well-matched fabrics, rugs on tiled floors, pictures, plants – plastic and real – and porcelain figurines. Seila, a 'hands on' hostess, is happy in the kitchen cooking breakfast, or creating one of her special fish dishes for dinner. The sweeping curved staircase takes you up to the first floor where that great galleried window lets the light in; there's a sizeable sitting room and five regal guest rooms. Each one is themed, well-lit and furnished with good-looking repro furniture and rugs. Central heating and air conditioning add to the comfort; Les Mimoses with its sparkling jacuzzi occupies an entire wing. In the gardens, a lazy swing and a pool-with-a-view, tennis, racquets and a marquee with a great round table that spins. The old *horreo* (a granary on stilts) is listed and striking. And the glorious Redes Parque Natural is no distance at all.

rooms	5 twins/doubles.
price	€50–€85. VAT included.
meals	Breakfast €4. Dinner €12.
closed	Rarely.
directions	From Santander A-8 junc. 326; N-634 for Arriondas. There, on towards Infiesto. Enter village & left for Lozana on PI-III. Los Cuetos on right after 1.5km; large black entrance gate.

Seila Sánchez Barro

tel	+34 985 710656
fax	+34 985 710874
email	loscuetos@loscuetos.com
web	www.loscuetos.com

Map 3 Entry 35

Hotel Palacete Real

c/El Caneyu s/n, Villamayor, 33583 Piloña, Asturias

Alfredo started the Palacete Real in order "to relax". He was working too hard in Tenerife and missed his homeland. The result is this small but memorable hotel. Originally a private mansion (it sports the Alvarez-Nava coat of arms and has a decidedly aristocratic air) its rooms are rather splendid. A massive, gleaming wooden staircase, solid beams and stained-glass windows give a medieval touch – but, as the date over the door clearly states, it was built in 1922. The bedrooms are all different, vividly coloured and magnificent. Vast beds – mostly from Toledo – range from elegantly draped four-posters to wrought-iron-and-porcelain or elaborately carved and wooden. An abundance of marble, gleaming chrome and solid wood gives the bathrooms a pristine, prosperous look. If you've booked the high-ceilinged tower suite, you can lie in bed and watch the stars come out over the hills. Windows let into each of the four walls give all-round views over the village and the countryside. In front of the house is a formal, landscaped garden: definitely for admiring, not for playing in.

rooms	9: 8 twins/doubles, 1 suite.
price	€85–€95. Suite €195.
meals	Lunch/dinner €28 set menu; €30 à la carte.
closed	Rarely.
directions	From Oviedo A-8 towards Santander. At km356 marker turn for Villamayor (signposted Lieres-Arriondas), on N-634. Through & before you come out of village, hotel on right.

	Alfredo López & Dora Valledor
tel	+34 985 702970
fax	+34 985 707282
email	info@palacetereal.com
web	www.palacetereal.com

Map 3 Entry 36

Hotel Posada del Valle

Collia, 33549 Arriondas, Asturias

After two years of searching the hills and valleys of Asturias, Nigel and Joann Burch found the home of their dreams – a century-old farmhouse just inland from the rugged north coast, with sensational views to mountain, hill and meadow. (Find a seat in the green, hillside garden and gaze.) Now they are nurturing new life from the soil – they are a fully registered organic farm – while running this small and beguiling hotel. The apple orchard has been planted, the flock graze the hillside, the menu celebrates the best of things local, and you will delight in this sensitive conversion. Bedrooms are seductive affairs with shutters and old beams, polished wooden floors, exposed stone, colourful modern fabrics and matching colour-washed walls. There's a stylishly uncluttered living room with an open brick fire, and a dining room with glorious views. You are close to the soaring Picos, the little-known sandy beaches of the Cantabrian coast and some of the most exceptional wildlife in Europe. And there's loads of info on the best local rambles available from Nigel and Joann. Great value.

rooms	12 twins/doubles.
price	€54-€75. Singles €42-€52.
meals	Breakfast €6.50. Dinner €17.50.
closed	15 October-31 March.
directions	N-634 Arriondas; AS-260 for Mirador del Fito. After 1km, right for Collia. Through village (don't turn to Ribadesella). Hotel 300m on left after village.

	Nigel & Joann Burch
tel	+34 985 841157
fax	+34 985 841559
email	hotel@posadadelvalle.com
web	www.posadadelvalle.com

Map 3 Entry 37

Hotel Aultre Naray

Peruyes, 33547 Cangas de Onis, Asturias

Amid the greenest green, beneath the highest peaks of the Cuera Sierra, one of the most exquisite places to stay in Asturias. The town's grand *casonas* date from a time when returning emigrants invested the gains of overseas adventures in fine, deliberately ostentatious homes. The transition from grand home to fine hotel has been a natural progression at Aultre Naray; the name comes from a medieval motto meaning, 'I'll have no other'. The hotel continues to flourish under new ownership and the mood remains warm, relaxed and comfortable. Designer prints, fabric and furniture have been married with the rustic core elements of beam and stone walls. No expense was spared to get things just right – how often do you get the chance to sleep beneath a Dior duvet? We marginally preferred the attic rooms, but all are memorable. It is a treat to breakfast on the terrace in the English-style garden, with a choice of crêpes, homemade cakes – or eggs and bacon! – to accompany the heavenly views. And there are lots of good places to eat nearby. *A Rusticae hotel*

rooms	10: 9 twins/doubles, 1 suite.
price	€67-€95. Singles €57-€80. Suite €77-€105.
meals	Breakfast €3.95-€8. Lunch/dinner approx. €20 à la carte.
closed	November-March weekends only.
directions	From Oviedo for Santander on m'way, then N-634. After passing Arriondas at km335 marker, right for Peruyes. Climb for 1km; hotel on left just before village.

	Maxi Suarez & Teresa Barreiro
tel	+34 985 840808
fax	+34 985 840848
email	aultre@aultrenaray.com
web	www.aultrenaray.com

Map 3 Entry 38

El Correntiu
c/Sardalla 42, 33560 Ribadesella, Asturias

It's must be the swishest grain silo in Spain. Set in nine acres, it stands to one side of the Asturian farmhouse – a stunning renovation. It is stylishly simple: a crisp use of wood, ochre tones to impart warmth, discreet lighting to give character, lots of space. There are three apartments in all, each with its own kitchen garden – pick to your heart's content. There is also an abundance of kiwi, avocado and citrus trees: in this micro-climate everything thrives. Inside, a feast for the eye – chunky rafters, chestnut floors, country furniture, bright cushions – and all you need: books, games, linen, towels. If you're a traditionalist you may prefer the little cottage nearby, just as beautifully equipped. A stream babbles by: *escorentia* means 'place that collects rain water'. It's a long, steep walk down to the lovely fishing village of Ribadesella at the mouth of the Sella, and the beaches are magnificent. Your hosts couldn't be nicer and keep rare Xalda sheep. María Luisa, who speaks very good English, can supply you with eggs and milk fresh from the farm. An irresistible place.

rooms	3 apartments for 2; 1 cottage for 4.
price	Apts €50–€75. Cottage €75–€100.
meals	Self-catering.
closed	Rarely.
directions	From Santander A-8/N-632. At Ribadesella N-632 for Gijón. Immediately after bridge, left for Cuevas & Sardalla. From here, 2km to El Correntiu.

	María Luisa Bravo & Jose Luis Valdés
tel	+34 985 861436
email	elcorrentiu@fade.es
web	www.elcorrentiu.com

Map 3 Entry 39

La Montaña Mágica
El Allende, 33508 Llanes, Asturias

Wedged between beaches and the mighty Picos mountains, the hill-perched farmstead has a privileged position and the approach is sensational. Ecologically-minded Carlos, who has his own tree-planting programme, has sensitively restored the old ruins, and the finish is rustic and cheerful. Warm colours and robust furniture in walnut and oak mingle beautifully with stonework and rafters. The reception leads to a log-fired sitting room and library, and a map room for walkers – just what you need in trekking country. The riding too is superb. There are six lovely suites in this part of the house, some split-level with huge woodburning stoves, all with a modern alpine feel. Words cannot do justice to some of the views... ask for a room facing south. A second large building has good, well-insulated, pine-finished rooms with big bathrooms – clean, practical, bright. The dining room stands on its own beside the old *horreo* (granary), now converted into a children's playroom. Lunches and dinners are great value, there's a small bar where you can enjoy a digestif, and Carlos and his staff are wonderful.

rooms	16: 10 twins/doubles, 6 suites.
price	€48–€67. Suites €68–€88.
meals	Breakfast €4.60. Lunch/dinner €12.
closed	Rarely.
directions	From Santander W on E-70/N-634. Past Llanes; at km307 right for Celorio; AS-263 to Posada. Here left on AS-115 for Cabrales to La Herreria. At Allende right over bridge; right, following signs; 3km.

	Carlos Bueno & Pilar Pando
tel	+34 985 925176
fax	+34 985 925780
email	magica@llanes.as
web	www.lamontanamagica.com

Map 4 Entry 40

La Posada del Babel
La Pereda s/n, 33509 Llanes, Asturias

Demure, quaint, unobtrusive it is not. But what a sensation for the eye. The cool lines, bold colours and extravagant glass of the three buildings that dot these lawns are a modernist's dream. Designed with an architect's attention to detail, it has views from within as exciting as those from without: floor to ceiling windows look onto undulating lawns and meadows while the foothills of the Cuera rise behind. White walls, bursts of cobalt blue, polished tiles, understated furnishings, sleek lighting. (Lucas and Blanca are from Madrid, and it shows.) The open-plan design of the dining and drawing rooms is languorous, large and washed with the light; shade your eyes and you might wonder if you're inside or out. Breakfast on homemade breads, pastries, local fruit and cheeses. In the evening, the dining room takes on a cool elegasnce. Blanca and Lucas are inventive cooks, giving modern twists to the local Asturian cuisine. Gentle and knowledgeable, they will also point you to the best local walking, riding or fishing. Or you might prefer simply to unwind in these unusually beautiful spaces.

rooms	12: 10 twins/doubles, 2 suites.
price	€72-94. Suite €112-125.
meals	Breakfast €7.50. Dinner €25.
closed	November-February.
directions	A-8 m'way exit for Llanes; right for La Pereda. Over railway tracks & left at village. Posada is 300m down road (signposted).

Lucas Cajiao & Blanca Fernánadez

tel	+34 985 402525
fax	+34 985 402622
email	laposadadebabel@retemail.es
web	www.laposadadebabel.com

Map 4 Entry 41

Hotel El Habana

La Pereda s/n, 33509 Llanes, Asturias

Lush meadows, grazing cows, dry-stone walls – is this the Cotswolds? Such is the rural beauty of Asturia, where gently rolling farmland gives way to the Guera Mountains. The hotel is modern, a contemporary version of the traditional Asturian house, and all is charming within. Plants, rugs on warm terracotta floors, modern art, subtle lighting. Much of the furniture comes from owner Mariá Eugenia's home in New Delhi and an air of colonial elegance – touched with modern Deco – prevails. The friendly atmosphere goes up a notch in the dining room, the elegant hub of the hotel. Here, regulars and visitors congregate to sample Sirio's excellent Asturian dishes, served from 9pm. Bedrooms are big and light, the two with patios leading to the garden (300 species of trees, shrubs and ferns!) being our favourites. Spin off on one of their bikes, take a put on the golf course by the sea, join Claudio on a coastal pony trek, loll by the pool. Your multi-lingual hosts will advise – and if sporting pursuits do not appeal, head for nearby Llanes with its handsome galleried buildings. *A Rusticae hotel.*

rooms	10: 9 twins/doubles, 1 suite.
price	€78–€95. Singles €68–€82. Suite €120–€135.
meals	Breakfast €6.50. Dinner €21 à la carte.
closed	15 December–end February.
directions	From N-634, at km301 marker, Llanes exit, do a U-turn & cross over N-634 for La Pereda, following signs on right for Prau Riu Hotel. 1.5km further, hotel signed.

	Marián Rivero
tel	+34 985 402526
fax	+34 985 402075
email	hotel@elhabana.net
web	www.elhabana.net

Map 4 Entry 42

Hotel Torrecerredo

Barrio Vega s/n, 33554 Arenas de Cabrales, Asturias

The views are stunning, more so even than the photograph below suggests – "a double glory for hearts and eyes". The hotel itself is a rectangular, modern building on a hillside just outside the busy town of Arenas de Cabrales – a hub for walkers and sightseers visiting the Picos. Bedrooms are simple, spartan affairs with no great charm, the best those on the first floor at the front. What lifts this place into the 'special' league for us is its pine-clad dining/sitting room in which guests are treated to simple home cooking – brilliant after a day trekking the mountains. Walking is the main activity here; Jim is a mountain guide and when not leading group walks can take you out. Few know the area as intimately as he and Pilar; they are generous with time and advice on routes and can help plan entire excursions, including nights in mountain refuges: how about canoeing, riding, gliding, caving, climbing, mountain biking? So, a good value place to stay but absolutely without frills. And be prepared for the bumpy track! *Ask about special offers in the low season.*

rooms	19: 15 twins/doubles, 4 singles.
price	€30-€75. Singles €20-€45.
meals	Dinner €10 set menu.
closed	January-February.
directions	From Santander N-634 for Oviedo; left on N-612 for Potes. In Panes C-6312 (A-S114) to Arenas de C. Through town & right after Hotel Naranjo de Bulnes. Signed.

	Pilar Saíz Lobeto & Jim Thomson
tel	+34 985 846640
fax	+34 985 846640
email	torretours@fade.es
web	www.picosadventure.com

Map 4 Entry 43

Casa de Aldea La Valleja
Rieña, 33576 Ruenes, Asturias

If you fancy turning your hand to preserve-making, cheese-culturing or mountain honey-gathering, then head for La Valleja. Tending the livestock and pottering in the garden are also a must: Paula is passionate about rural tourism and loves guests to muck in. The house was built in 1927 and the original materials – bricks, tiles, stones and chestnut beams – maintain the rustic charm. Each bedroom, gaily coloured, has been named after wild berries; if yours feels sombre, throw open the shutters and drink in the views – sensational. La Valleja is a working homestead but there's comfort too, in orthopaedic mattresses, good heating and scrumptious food. After a rugged walk in the Peñamellera Alta – don't miss the spectacular Cares gorge – you'll be well fortified: meals are hearty and the food organic and lovingly prepared. So whether you want to sit and enjoy the views, join in the chestnut harvest or birdwatch with binoculars, this is the place. Be sure to buy some of the jams and preserves to take home and pack a citronella candle in summer!

rooms	5 twins/doubles.
price	€39-€48.
meals	Breakfast €4. Packed lunch €7. Dinner €12.
closed	Chrismas & January.
directions	N-634; at Unquera left for Panes. Here, right onto AS-114 for Cangas de Onís. 10km beyond, at Niserias, right to Ruenes. Through Alles & 800m after Pastorias right up a steep track to Rieña. Park at top.

	Paula Valero Sáez
tel	+34 985 415895
fax	+34 985 415895
email	valleycas@yahoo.es

Map 4 Entry 44

La Tahona de Besnes

33578 Alles, Asturias

In a valley of the Picos de Europa, surrounded by oak and hazelnut trees with a crystalline brook babbling by – the lushest of settings – is this 'núcleo de turismo rural'. It's a dedicated complex of old village houses, neatly converted into holiday apartments and rooms. One building was a bakehouse, another a corn mill, a third a stable; at the heart of it all is the bakery-cum-restaurant, decorated with dried flowers, gentian-blue tablecloths and old farm implements. Breakfast may be nothing special, with its packeted pastries and jams, but the set menu is good value. The terrace beside the trickling brook is a restful place for a cool glass of cider before dinner. Rooms and apartments are decorated to suit the rustic feel, simple with comfy beds and spotless bathrooms. La Tahona has plenty of literature on the area and friendly, helpful staff can arrange for you to ride, walk, canoe, fish or take trips out by jeep. A useful stop-off point for those on their way to the Santander ferry; when you leave, be sure to take a local cheese and a bottle of honey liqueur.

rooms	13 + 6: 5 doubles, 8 twins. 5 studios + 1 apartment.
price	€49–€56. Apt/studio €50–€71.
meals	Breakfast €6. Lunch/dinner €12 set menu; €27 à la carte.
closed	Christmas Eve; 10-30 January open only weekends.
directions	N-634; left to Panes at Unquera. There, right after bridge for Arenas de Cabrales. After 11km right at Niserias for Alles; follow signs for hotel.

	Sarah & Lorenzo Nilsson
tel	+34 985 415749
fax	+34 985 415749
email	tahona@infonegocio.com
web	www.latahonadebesnes.com

Map 4 Entry 45

Casona de Villanueva

33590 Villanueva de Colombres, Asturias

Thanks to careful restoration and imaginative decoration of the Villanueva – the oldest house in the vllage – Nuria has created an exceptional place to stay. Bedrooms, not grand, vary in size and have smallish bathrooms – but what a sense of history! Ancient walls and floors are scattered with rugs and cushions from Morocco, paintings and rare etchings, unusual colours and heaps of antiques. One of the suites – once her grandmother's room – is noble in its simplicity. Then there are the details: the homemade preserves and flowers at breakfast, the classical music at mealtimes. Food is good – wholesome soups, fish fresh from the slate – and the wine list will enchant connoisseurs. Nuria's passion is her organic walled garden, the most peaceful of retreats surrounded by cool green spaces, sitting areas and scented climbers. Nuria, a doctor who works on international development projects, speaks good English and delights in helping plan your sorties. Visit romanesque churches and sleepy fishing villages, or walk the rocky coastline and the Picos de Europa. Authentic and special.

rooms	8: 6 twins/doubles, 2 suites.
price	€55–€70. Singles €50–€60. Suites €80–€100.
meals	Breakfast €7. Dinner €22.
closed	January–February.
directions	From Santander N-634/E-70 for Oviedo. 3km after Unquera, at km283 marker, left for Colombres. Through village; 2km to Villanueva. At T-junc. hotel opp. on left.

	Nuria Juez Núñez
tel	+34 985 412590
fax	+34 985 412514
email	info@lacasonadevillanueva.com
web	www.lacasonadevillanueva.com

Map 4 Entry 46

Posada de Tollo

c/Mayor 13, 39575 Tollo (Vega de Liebana), Cantabria

Imagine having the full majesty of the Picos de Europa at the bottom of your garden: Nature at her boldest looms at the door of this old house. High gates open onto a somewhat ramshackle garden while the full-length front window gives a hint of a more contemporary, though simple, interior – and there is the most antiquated wooden balcony above. The living room is modern and light with its polished oak floor and lovely log fire; beyond is the towering heart of the house. Here you find a super great mural of an American bar scene on one wall and black and white photographs of flamenco singers in the dining area. Sparkling Pepa is chef, likes to use organic produce, and may join you for a glass of wine. The guest quarters are in the former granary and reached by a central stairwell. Rooms are light, airy and modern, with striped bedcovers and chunky rafters. North rooms have sensational views, top-floor rooms have fireplaces; from the suite's shower you gaze on distant peaks. It is laid-back and easy, and the view from the back garden carries the day.

rooms	8: 7 twins/doubles, 1 suite. Whole house available to rent
price	€42-€56. Singles €30-€40. Suite €70-€90. Whole house (min. 12 people) €440.
meals	Breakfast €5. Dinner €12.
closed	February.
directions	From Santander, A-67/N-634 for Oviedo. At Unquera N621 to Potes. Vega de L. road for 3.5km, left for Tomo for 3.5km; 2nd right for Tollo de Arriba. 200m from junc.

	Pepa Estevez Ortega
tel	+34 942 736284
fax	+34 942 736284
email	posadadetollo@hotmail.com

Map 4 Entry 47

Casa Gustavo Guesthouse

Cillorigo de Liébana, 39584 Aliezo, Cantabria

In the beautiful Liébana valley lies the hamlet of Aliezo and this very old farmhouse. Lisa, Mike and their children have taken on their adopted land, have learned its language, know its history and its footpaths. Within the thick stone walls of their house are low beams, steps up, sidewards and down, and good smells wafting out from the kitchen. For home it is: don't expect hotelly trimmings. Rather, the house is organic and shambolic; some rooms are small, some large, some have balconies. But walkers will be happy with the country cooking, hot showers and decent beds. Redstarts nest beneath the eaves, there are dogs and cats, a cosy lounge with woodburner, balcony, toys and books, and a shaded patio with awesome views; the main protagonist is Nature and her Picos mountains. Mike and Lisa offer free transport to the beginning of walks, will advise according to what the weather is doing and should be able to provide you with the best maps of the area. Great for ornithology and botany buffs – ski-mountaineering courses in winter – and spot on for families.

rooms	7: 5 twins/doubles, 1 single, 1 family.
price	€40-€60. Singles €20-€30.
meals	Packed lunch €5. Dinner €15. VAT included.
closed	Rarely.
directions	From Santander A-67/N-634 for Oviedo. Left at Unquera onto N-621 for Potes. Shortly before Potes, through Tama; after 200m, left to Aliezo. Follow bend to top of village.

	Lisa & Michael Stuart
tel	+34 942 732010
fax	+44 (0)1629 813 346
email	stuartsinpicos@terra.es

Map 4 Entry 48

Casona de Naveda

Plaza del Medio Lugar 37, Hermandad de Campóo de Suso, 39211 Naveda, Cantabria

Step out of the front door and follow the river to the village – or pick your way through pastures of cows and wild flowers. The area is studded with romanesque churches, and nearby Reisona, with its galleried houses and fine central square, is quite a find. The *casonas* of Cantabria are cousins of the *pazos* of Galicia, and if this one is anything to go by they are every bit as wonderful. It was built 300 years ago by one of those enterprising *indianos* who returned from Cuba and sought a dwelling grand enough to proclaim his newfound status. Floors, ceilings and fire surrounds of rich oak and walnut have the soft patina that only centuries of polishing can achieve; ancient stone pillars in the sitting room would look quite at home in one of Cantabria's churches. Rooms 6 and 7, with their wooden galleried sitting areas, have a *Romeo and Juliet* charm, but all are distinctive in their own ways. The menu is a celebration of simple food superbly cooked, with a line-up of the best of Spain's wines. *A Rusticae hotel.*

rooms	9: 7 twins/doubles, 1 suite, 1 single.
price	€78–€86. Singles €63–€69. Suite €85–€105.
meals	Breakfast €7. Dinner €19.
closed	Rarely.
directions	From Santander, N-611 to Reinosa. Then CA-183 to turn for hotel. Left to Naveda, signed.

	Paloma López Sarasa
tel	+34 942 779515
fax	+34 942 779681
email	info@casonadenaveda.com
web	www.casonadenaveda.com

Map 4 Entry 49

Posada La Casona de Cos

Pueblo de Cos 87, 39509 Mazcuerras, Cantabria

In a quiet village of Cantabria, just a short drive from Santillana, this could be a super place to stay before or after you take the ferry. It is small, family-run, unpretentious – a place where locals still far outnumber foreign visitors and Spanish to the core. Bright-eyed, ever-smiling Natalia has built up the reputation of this little hotel over the past 30-odd years and what is so refreshing is not only her pride in her 400-year-old home but also the relish with which she greets you as hostess. Enter by way of a busy bar (where would the Spanish be without them?); beyond is the dining room, the hub of the place. Low, beamy, with marble-topped tables and a fire in the hearth, it has the feel of a French bistro. The reader who discovered the Posada for us enthused about Natalia's home cooking and waxed equally lyrical about the delicious fruit juices at breakfast (a mix of apple, pear, grapefruit and lemon). Upstairs you'll find simple, spotless guest bedrooms. There's also a quiet lounge along the corridor from your room. A great little place.

rooms	12 twins/doubles.
price	€50. Singles €35.
meals	Breakfast €3. Lunch/dinner €25.
closed	Rarely.
directions	From Santander A-67 to Torrelavega; from here on A-8. Exits 244 & 249 to Cabezón de la Sal on N-634. On CA-180 for Reinosa; over bridge at Santa Lucía; left on CA-812 to Cos. Casona on right.

	Natalia San Martin
tel	+34 942 701550
fax	+34 942 702434
email	lacasonadecos@mixmail.com
web	www.lacasonadecos.com

Map 4 Entry 50

El Jardín de Carrejo
Carrejo, 39500 Cabezón de la Sal, Cantabria

Swings and sequoias in the grounds, the odd swaying palm and weeping willow, vast lawns and ancient trees… a garden made for children. Everyone will love this small hotel – particularly those with a penchant for clean lines and modern design. The huge 1901 stable and hayloft have been stylishly re-crafted into a comfortable haven between the Cabuerniga Valley and the golden beaches of Comillas. Expect a cool symphony of creams, taupes and warm hues, stone floors, polished parquet, contemporary Spanish photography, masses of light and not a frill or a curlicue in sight. Recline on suave leather sofas in the living room/library, or perch on a pretty fauteuil: the odd 18th-century touch comes as a delightful surprise. The chestnut and walnut furniture is the best of modern, and bedrooms are serene, two with balconies, all with garden views. Bathrooms are chic and nothing falls short. Hire a tandem from the hotel, practice your golf in the grounds, head off for a Parque Natural – there are two close by – or laze under a posh parasol. Bliss. *Uninspected at time of going to press. A Rusticae hotel.*

rooms	10: 8 twins/doubles, 2 suites.
price	€78-€112. Singles €70-€90. Suites €108-€160.
meals	Breakfast €8. Dinner €20.
closed	Rarely.
directions	A-8 exit 249 for Cabezón de la Sal & Reinosa-Valle de Cabuérniga. Carrejo 1km before Cabezón.

	Isabel Alvarez García
tel	+34 942 701516
fax	+34 942 701871
email	info@eljardindecarrejo.com
web	www.eljardindecarrejo.com

Map 4 Entry 51

Casona Torre de Quijas
Barrio Vinueva 76, 39590 Quijas, Cantabria

This is a grand yet intimate little hotel within striking distance of Santander and only minutes from the beach. Pilar and her husband bought it as a family home, then transformed it into a delightful hotel. It's splendidly furnished with fine antiques; fresh fruit and dried flowers set the welcoming mood; the modern art reflects your hosts' taste and flair. A log fire and deep, comfortable chairs upholstered in white cotton make for an attractive sitting room. Polished chestnut floors run throughout, and the bedrooms are mostly pale with a fresh cotton theme. Our favourite is the Lemon Room, big, light and airy, with French windows to a balcony and renovated in such a way that the original arches still stand. The cosiest bedrooms are in the upper part of the house where ceilings are beamed. Inviting, too, is the small bar, with its cane furniture and lace-covered lamps; outside is a peaceful covered patio packed with greenery. No dinner, but there is a smart restaurant over the road. Perfect for a first or last night in Spain — and the staff are charming.

rooms	19: 15 doubles, 2 singles, 2 suites.
price	€66-€90. Singles €48-€67. Suites €77-€111.
meals	Breakfast €6.
closed	15 December-15 January.
directions	From Santander A-67/E-70 for Oviedo. Exit at km238 for Quijas. In village hotel on left, next to tower.

	Pilar García Lozano
tel	+34 942 820645
fax	+34 942 838255
email	informacion@casonatorredequijas.com
web	www.casonatorredequijas.com

Map 4 Entry 52

Hostal Mexicana

c/Juan de Herrera 3, 39002 Santander, Cantabria

Enter another era. This modest little *hostal* first opened its doors in 1955 and has barely changed since. It's far from grand: bedrooms are basic, walls textured, curtains netted, lighting dim, floors clad in worn carpet or new laminate, furniture unmistakably Spanish. Bathrooms are spartan (bring your own plug), the newest an improvement on the old. But… the staircases are gorgeous, the hall has been updated, and the best bedrooms are big, airy and have a nostalgic charm. Make sure you ask for one of them! You are right in the town centre, so shops, cafés, restaurants and parking couldn't be closer – and noise is not an issue, thanks to double glazing. As for the (tiny) restaurant: it comes with cornices, dated 50s furniture and a seaside B&B feel. Breakfasts and suppers are simple. Santander has the charm of a slightly down-at-heel port: watch boats on the quay, admire the peaks of Cantabrian Cordillera on a clear day, tuck into fish of the day in authentic sailors' restaurants.

rooms	32 twins/doubles.
price	€32–€56. Singles €30–€38.
meals	Breakfast €3. Lunch/dinner €12.
closed	Rarely.
directions	In town centre, close to Plaza del Ayuntamiento, next to Banco Zaragoza. Underground parking in square offers reduction for Mexicana guests.

	María Eufemia Rodríguez & Caridad Gómez Rodríguez
tel	+34 942 222350/54
fax	+34 942 222350

Map 4 Entry 53

La Torre de Ruesga

La Barcena s/n, 39810 Valle de Ruesga, Cantabria

On the lush banks of the Asón, the 1610 stronghold matches elegance with sobriety, and is surrounded by pretty gardens. Through a glazed arch you enter the stone-finished hall with a charming bar to your right. The grander rooms have been embellished with frescos by the Catalan painter, Leon Criach, the finest in the pink-washed banqueting hall on the first floor. On either side are special rooms for videos, games or quiet reads – a nice touch – and there's a piano to play. The bedrooms in the *palacio* itself have a delightfully rustic feel, with their terracotta floors, chunky rafters and antique beds. In the ornate restaurant dinner is a mixture of Cantabrian and international, accompanied by fine wines from the well-stocked bodega. Take tea on the terrace or lounge on the lawns; the views of Torre de Ruesga are stunning. There's also a large outdoor pool with a gym and sauna, and five new 'corporate' garden suites with hydromassage baths. Every possible need has been anticipated, from babysitting to room service, and Carmen is vivacious and charming. *A Rusticae hotel.*

rooms	10+5: 6 twin/doubles, 4 suites. 5 apartments.
price	€83–€108. Singles €60–€70. Suite €102–€120. Apartment €120–€138.
meals	Lunch/dinner €21; €35–€40 à la carte.
closed	Last 3 weeks in January.
directions	From Santander, S-10 for Bilbao. Exit 173 for Colindres; N-629 for Burgos to Ramales de V. Right on C-261 to Arredondo & Valle; right at sign. On right just over bridge.

Carmen Caprile & Giorgio García de Leaniz

tel	+34 942 641060
fax	+34 942 641172
email	reservas@t-ruesga.com
web	www.t-ruesga.com

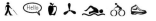

Map 4 Entry 54

Photo Jose Navarro

basque country,
navarra – la rioja

Hotel Arresi

c/Portugane 7, 48620 Armintza, Vizcaya

Driving off the ferry into a foreign land as night falls, fractious children in tow, can be a stressful start to a holiday. So, whether you're arriving at Bilbao or Santander, this hotel is a godsend: close at hand, civilised, friendly. From the outside, it may not look that special. Step in and you feel as though you have entered the home of a gracious friend. The approach is informal; the interior is anything but. An imposing staircase leads to an equally impressive landing and on to the bedrooms: all are smart, roomy and comfortable, with excellent bathrooms. In the morning, an amazing panorama – taking in the hotel's beautiful gardens and vineyard (do try their wine!), the cliffs and the hills, Armintza harbour and the sea. The children will by now have found the big Wendy house in the lush garden and the swimming pool (safely fenced off). You'll head for the shaded pergola by day, the cosy reading room by night. There's no restaurant as such, but they may well rustle up a meal for you if you ask in advance. An excellent little stopover. *A Rusticae hotel.*

rooms	10: 9 twins/doubles, 1 suite.
price	€96–€117. Singles €77–€93. Suite €150. VAT included.
meals	Restaurants 300m.
closed	24 December-8 January.
directions	From Bilbao for Mungia on N-631. At Mungia exit for Plentzia (BI-2120). On to Andraka on BI-3153. Here, right to Armintza. At entrance of town, hotel signed on left; at end of 200m uphill.

Arantza Aranbarri Uresandi

tel	+34 946 879208
fax	+34 946 879310
email	hotelarresi@hotelarresi.com
web	www.hotelarresi.com

Map 5 Entry 55

Atalaya Hotel

Itxaropen Kalea 1, 48360 Mundaka, Vizcaya

Atalaya is one of the most 'family' of Vizcaya's small hotels and owner María Carmen is a bundle of positive energy. You couldn't better the position: a clam's throw from the lively fish market, and a step from the beach and fishing boats of this deep inlet carved by the Cantabrian sea. The house was built in 1911, and is now protected by the Basque authorities as a building of national importance. An open galleried frontage lets in the ever-changing light, and allows you to contemplate sand, sea and the church tower of Santa María. The owners are kind, straightforward folk who proudly maintain their small hotel, and help you plan your visits. The best rooms have sea views but they're all worth a night: quiet, clean and comfortable with new oak furniture, king-size beds and every gadget in the book. A smart little bar serves sandwiches and snacks. This would be the perfect place to spend a last night before the ferry ride home, and your car and belongings should be safe in the car park. One of our favourites – and the fabulous Guggenheim at Bilbao so close by.

rooms	11 twins/doubles.
price	€85–€94. Singles €68–€75.
meals	Breakfast €8. Dinner approx. €20.
closed	Rarely.
directions	From Bilbao, A-8/E-70 exit 18 onto N-634. BI-635 via Gernika to Mundaka; left to village centre. Hotel near Santa María church. 50km from ferry.

María Carmen Alonso Elizaga

tel	+34 946 177000
fax	+34 946 876899
email	hotelatalaya@hotel-atalaya-mundaka.com
web	www.hotel-atalaya-mundaka.com

Map 5 Entry 56

Agroturismo Txopebenta

Barrio Basetxetas, 48314 Gautegiz-Arteaga, Vizcaya

Between Gernika and the rugged north coast, in an area of great natural beauty, the first *casa rural* to open in Spain. The house bears witness to the boundless energy and optimism of its owner Juan 'Txope' Bizkarra, who, in 1989, added an entire floor for guests. Old railway sleepers have been re-fashioned in every quirky and conceivable way: as lintels, stairs, roof supports, benches, tables, bedframes. The homely sitting/breakfast room (cosy with fire in winter) is a delightful spot for breakfasts served on Basque china and hand-embroidered linen: homemade pastries and cakes, toasted cheeses, freshly-squeezed juices. Bedrooms at the top (warm in summer) are small but charming; white walls are simply stencilled, beds crisply dressed. However, traffic noise is noticeable and the soundproofing is minimal. Don't miss the 'painted forest' in the Oma valley, or the biosphere reserve of Urdabai with its spectacular birdlife. Beaches are a walk away and the surfing at Mundara and Laga is magnificent.

rooms	6 twins/doubles.
price	€40-€47.
meals	Breakfast €5.
closed	Rarely.
directions	From Bilbao on A-8/N-634; exit 18 for Gernika & Amorebieta on BI-635. At Gernika BI-2238 for Lekeitio. After 6km left for Elantxobe. On right after 800m.

	Arantza Gantxegi & Juan Angel Bizkarra
tel	+34 946 254923
fax	+34 946 254923
email	txopebenta@terra.es

Map 5 Entry 57

Urresti

Barrio Zendokiz 12, 48314 Gautegiz de Arteaga, Vizcaya

A dream come true for Urresti's two friendly young owners – they have transformed the ruins of the farmhouse they found in green Vizcaya. From the outside it looks 17th century; inside is more contemporary in feel. Breakfast is excellent value, served in the large sitting/dining room: local cheeses, homemade jam, fruits from the farm, plenty of coffee. For other meals guests share an open-plan, fully-equipped kitchen/living area. Smart, impeccably clean little bedrooms have laminate floors and new, country-style furniture; the one under the eaves (hot in summer!) has a balcony; another is big enough for an extra sofabed. Ensuite bath and shower rooms are excellent. Outside: a small organic plot – you can buy the vegetables. The house stands in beautiful rolling countryside with stunning beaches not far away – bring buckets and spades. Gernika, too, is close. A brilliant place for families, with emus, sheep, goats, horses and hens to fuss over, and ancient forests of oak and chestnut to explore (borrow the bikes). The whole area is a Parque Natural and many come just for the birdlife.

rooms	6 + 2: 6 twins/doubles. 2 self-catering apartments: 1 for 2, 1 for 4.
price	€42–€49. Apartments €64–€70.
meals	Breakfast €5.50.
closed	Rarely.
directions	From Gernika for Lekeitio. At fork lower road for Lekeitio. After 6km, left for Elanchobe. On right, below road level, after 1.2km at sign 'Nekazal Turismoa agroturismo'.

	María Goitia & Jose María Ríos
tel	+34 946 251843
fax	+34 946 251843
email	urresti@wanadoo.es
web	www.toprural.com/urresti

Map 5 Entry 58

Ziortxa-Beitia

Goiherria 13, 48279 Bolibar, Vizcaya

Our inspector arrived with a bag of pears and green peppers and asked the owner – known as 'Paco' to all and sundry – if they could be incorporated into his evening meal. Without batting an eyelid, Paco whisked the ingredients off to the kitchen. The peppers later appeared with some freshly cooked pork and the pears poached in wine. This is not so much an example of Basque hospitality, rather an illustration of your gentle host's no-fuss-no-frills attitude. His old farmhouse sits in remote countryside below a Cistercian monastery on the famous pilgrim route to Santiago de Compostela; the drive here is stunning. The rooms are basic modern-rustic but comfortable and squeaky clean – perfect for pilgrims and walkers – and there's a laundry on the top floor. Food is of the home-cooked variety and although the bar can get quite lively in the evenings, the nights are blissfully quiet – just the hoot of the owl to lull you to sleep. Nearby Bolibar is the birthplace of Simon Bolivar, the liberator of South America, and the museum is well worth a visit – as is a stroll round the grounds of the monastery.

rooms	12: 6 twins/doubles, 6 rooms for 6.
price	€40-€45. Singles €30-€36. Bunkbed €14 p.p.
meals	Breakfast €4.50. Lunch/dinner €23.
closed	Christmas.
directions	From Bilbao A-8 for S. Sebastián; exit 17 to Durango; BI-633 for Markina. In Iruzubieta, right on BI-3334 to Bolibar. Here BI-4401 left for Colegiata. On right after 2.5km, below monastery; signed Taberna Aterpetxea.

	Francisco Rios Urbaneja
tel	+34 946 165259
email	ziortza-ostatua@terra.es
web	www.elatiko.com/ziortzabeitia

Map 5 Entry 59

Mendi Goikoa

Barrio San Juan 33, 48291 Axpe-Atxondo, Vizcaya

Donde el silencio se oye: a place of silence. Peaceful it is, and utterly beautiful. The hotel is made up of two handsome, 19th-century farm buildings surrounded by meadow, with mountain views from almost every room: extraordinary. The main restaurant, once the old barn, is vast and high-ceilinged and packed with fine country antiques; the emphasis is on traditional Basque cooking with a few of the chef's own delicious creations. There is a smaller breakfast room and a gem of a restaurant/bar in the stables, rustic with open-stone walls and rafters. It is a popular venue for the suit-and-tie brigade , but — thanks to a warm reception — you shouldn't feel uncomfortable if you are not one of them; it is, however, a wedding-feast place and gets lively at weekends. The bedrooms on the hayloft floor, not huge, are equally good-looking: original rafters and small windows, exposed stones, some lovely old pieces of furniture, carpeting and seductive views. Shower rooms are functional. There are great walks up to (or towards!) the surrounding peaks, so make sure you work up an appetite for dinner. Do book.

rooms	11 twins/doubles.
price	€90. Singles €60.
meals	Lunch/dinner €23.50 set menu; €50 à la carte. Restaurant closed Sunday evening & Monday all day.
closed	15 December–15 January.
directions	From A-8, exit 17 for Durango. N-636 for Elorrio. In Atxondo, right to Axpe. After 1km right following signs. Through village. House above village, on base of mountain.

	Agurtzane Telleria & Iñaki Ibarra
tel	+34 946 820833
fax	+34 946 821136
email	reservas@mendigoikoa.com
web	www.mendigoikoa.com

Map 5 Entry 60

Villa Soro

Avda. de Ategorrieta 61, 20013 San Sebastián, Guipúzcoa

Classy, different and in San Sebastián. Built in 1898 for a prominent Basque family, the conversion from house to hotel was completed in 2003. Only three of the original 20 chimneys remain – but this is a small price to pay for an exquisite transformation. The carpeted and carved oak staircase sets the tone of elegance and grace; drawings by the contemporary artist Orteiza adorn the walls; the radiators are not merely radiators, but beautiful examples of what can be done with cast iron... Parquet floors gleam, chandeliers glisten, staff glide. Retreat with tea or cocktail to one of two sitting rooms, light-filled in summer, fire-lit in winter. Big, serene bedrooms – some in the main house, others in the carriage house, equally good – have pure-wool carpets, classic furniture and exemplary beds. Marble bathrooms come with fine toiletries (for sale) and dressing gowns, while double glazing ensures peace from the nearby motorway to France. Michelin stars are a ride away, but don't motor in when the parking is tricky: spin off on one of the hotel's city-shoppers instead. *A Rusticae hotel.*

rooms	25: 23 twins/doubles, 2 singles.
price	€150–€225. Singles €125–€160.
meals	Breakfast €12. Room service available.
closed	Never.
directions	A-8 exit Donostia/Ondarreta. At Ondarreta up c/San Martín; over bridge & drive up c/Miracruz, which becomes Avda. de Ategorrieta. Hotel on left - on to next r'bout & turn around - very busy road.

	Pablo Carrington Londaiz
tel	+34 943 29 79 70
fax	+34 943 29 79 71
email	pcarrington@villasoro.com
web	www.villasoro.com

Map 5 Entry 61

Iketxe

Apartado 343, 20280 Hondarribia, Guipúzcoa

Another enchanting B&B in the rolling green Basque. Near the town of Hondarribia yet at the end of a maze of country lanes, Iketxe is a house that matches its owners: quiet and unpretentious. You can only wonder at the talent and energy of Patxi, who built the house virtually single-handed – and made much of the furniture too. You would hardly know the place was new, so chunky are the timbers, so authentic the building methods used. The pièce de resistance is the galleried sunlounge, the nicest imaginable spot from which to gaze on those glorious hilly views. Bedrooms are a delight, for their views and their decoration – kilims on rustic terracotta, white bedspreads on country beds, handsome bathrooms, no TV to break the spell. Top-floor rooms have balconies and are tucked under the rafters, but it would be hard to choose a favourite. Fátima will help you plan your day over breakfast, and knows all about the restaurants of attractive Hondarribia, a 20-minute walk (and its beach is superb). Hats off to these engaging hosts for realising their dream and sharing it with us.

rooms	6 twins/doubles.
price	€47-€55. Singles €37-€44.
meals	Breakfast €5.
closed	Rarely.
directions	From Irún for Hondarribia. 1km before airport, just after lights, Iketxe signed (yellow sign) to left. Follow signs from here. For last 2km single track, signed Arkoll at junc. from main road, leads to house. At end of narrow track.

	Patxi Arroyo & Fátima Iruretagoiena
tel	+34 943 644391
fax	+34 943 644391

Map 6 Entry 62

Gorbeia
c/Dominizubi 9, 01138 Murua, Álava

Gorbeia is a house of character, in the gentle, beautiful countryside of the Gorbeia National Park. And the old stable's stern façade, arched doorway and stone coat of arms conceal a wonderfully warm and cosy interior. The owners live next door, and the guesthouse is managed by their designer daughter Nagore. The restoration has been done to a high standard, with a strong, sometimes playfully rustic theme. Original beams and reclaimed wood are the order of the day, there are ochre and grey flagstones and, in the reception/bar, an open fire. One family room has striking yellow walls with fairy-tale patches of exposed stone, and the bunkbeds are delightful, with their quarry tile bases and chunky frames. Another family room, more sombre, has a mezzanine floor with coloured glass bricks that glow in the evening light. The double room is big and welcoming, with high beams and violet-washed walls. Bathrooms are rustically tiled. There's a suntrap garden behind, and two horses that experienced riders may borrow. Great value B&B – and the option to self-cater.

rooms	4: 1 double, 3 family.
price	€55. €15 per extra bed in family room. VAT included.
meals	Restaurants in Gopegui.
closed	Rarely.
directions	From Bilbao AP-68, exit 5 for Vitoria onto N-622. 3km after tunnel left for Gopegui. At entrance of Mona left for Gorbeia. After 300m, before 2nd speed bump, left. Over bridge; 200m up on left.

Nagore Camara Eguren
tel   +34 945 464201
email   casagorbeia@terra.es

Map 5 Entry 63

Antigua Bodega de Don Cosme Palacio
Ctra. Elciego s/n, 01300 Laguardia, Álava

Don Cosme Palacio is one of Rioja's most reputed bodegas: this is what you come for. Vines thrive in the gentle micro-climate of La Rioja, and the tempranillo grape has been working its magic here, in casks of French oak, for over a century. Visitors were calling in from all over the world to taste and buy so it seemed right and proper that they should be offered sustenance at the same time; thus was born the restaurant. It is large rather than homely, ever-changing artwork adorns its open-stone walls and it is popular for weddings. Before or after dinner head down to the cellars where there is a bar for tastings in the main wine stores, decorated with a series of frescos depicting all things oenological. Bedrooms upstairs, each named after a different grape variety, are newly decorated with a half-rustic, half-motel feel; some overlook the road, others the new warehouse. The car-free village is medieval and the walking very good, but the emphasis here is more 'esteemed *bodega*' than 'charming hotel'.

rooms	13: 12 twins/doubles, 1 suite.
price	€69-€76. Singles €61-€66. Suite €87-€97.
meals	Breakfast €6.95. Lunch/dinner €22-€30 menu.
closed	24 December-24 January.
directions	A-68, exit 10 for Cenicero. Through village, left to Elciego, on to Laguardia. Hotel on right on entering village.

	Begoña Viñegra Uzquiano
tel	+34 945 621195
fax	+34 945 600210
email	antiguabodega@cosmepalacio.com
web	www.habarcelo.es

Map 5 Entry 64

Etxatoa

31879 Oderitz, Navarra

The stunning forests are an open invitation to walkers, the old railway track is a gift for cyclists (horses, wheelchairs and pushchairs too), and the road up to the Santuario de San Miguel caves is spectacular. The house is a listed 17th-century building with a coat of arms and a three-sided roof; its plain stone exterior, awaiting renovation, conceals the charms of this young guesthouse. Inside, Maxux and Juanes have recycled as much as possible – the washstand made of reclaimed oak is charming – and Juanes has done a fine restoration job on the antique pieces he has so carefully collected. The large, frill-free living/dining/kitchen area has both comfort and style, and the simple double rooms, with their chunky rafters, open-stone walls, new wrought-iron beds and country antiques, have a fresh, rustic appeal. Note that the suite, impeccably restored and with a small bathroom, has a private terrace under the plum trees. Breakfasts are deliciously organic, breads, cakes, yogurts, even *cuajada* cheese homemade, juices freshly squeezed. Maxux, a former English teacher, is a warm and lively presence.

rooms	5: 4 twins/doubles, 1 suite.
price	€55–€65. Suite €118.
meals	Breakfast €7.50.
closed	October–June: weekdays except bank hols.
directions	From S. Sebastián A-15 for Pamplona exit 127. Through Lekunberri; at exit of town NA-7510 for Baraibar. 500m, left at junc. for Madotz on NA-7500. 6.5km to Oderitz. House opp. as you drive into village.

Maxux Ariznabarreta & Juanes Rekalde

tel +34 948 504449
email info@etxatoa.com
web www.etxatoa.com

Map 6 Entry 65

Donamariako Benta

Barrio Ventas 4, 31750 Donamaría, Navarra

A mouthwatering address! Donamaría is hidden away off to one side of a pass through the mountains between France and Spain, within striking distance of Pamplona; it was a farmers' rest until this family arrived. They are sophisticated and delightful people – and proud of their 'Q' rating, the Spanish seal of quality. These two old village houses (guest rooms in one, restaurant in the other) are packed full of old furniture, vintage toys, dried flowers and a few surprises to boot; the atmosphere is intimate, genuine, laid-back. This is a place to linger long over lunch or dinner; connoisseurs rave about the traditional Navarra cooking with a modern French touch. Menus change according to season; mushroom salad with foie gras is a speciality, all of it is memorable. Bedrooms are basic, clean and well looked after, bathrooms are pristine but small; one room has a superb little terrace overlooking the river. Mother, father and daughters welcome you most graciously into their home, set among old oak forests to make the heart soar. *Wine-tasting courses available; also salmon fishing.*

rooms	5 twins/doubles.
price	€60.
meals	Breakfast €5. Lunch/dinner €12; €25-€30 à la carte. No meals Sunday evenings or Mondays.
closed	Rarely.
directions	From San Sebastián, N-121-A for Pamplona. Right into Santesteban (Doneztebe); here just before bridge left for Saldías. On for 2km to junc. with Donamaría road; hotel opp. junc. on right hand side.

Elixabet Badiola & Imanol Luzuriaga

tel	+34 948 450708
fax	+34 948 450708
email	info@donamariako.com
web	www.donamariako.com

Map 6 Entry 66

Hotel Peruskenea

Beruete-Jauntsarats, 31866 Basaburua Mayor, Navarra

The journey up to Peruskenea is by way of Navarra's deep forests; you are headed for a place of great natural beauty. The old ruin has become one of the area's most attractive small hotels. The solar-panelled building stands alone, its whitewashed façade and bright wooden galleries facing a glorious valley. Breakfasts have this vista, guaranteed to inspire you to don boots and head off along one of the many pathways that criss-cross the countryside. The chunky raftered bedrooms on the first and attic floors have handsome parquet floors, textured walls and ceilings, large and comfortable beds, fat duvets, big framed prints. The mood is more hotel than B&B but the rooms are light, white and airy, bathrooms are modern and good, and the apartment/suite is delightful with an open fire (and a loo in the main room, behind a muslin drape!). You get two rustic lounges, one with a fireplace, and two dining rooms, one with views. The owner is charming, and you are surrounded by forest and vineyards – the tempranillo grape rules supreme. *A Rusticae hotel.*

rooms	10: 9 twins/doubles, 1 suite.
price	€80-€90. Singles €50-€60. Suite €150-€200. VAT included.
meals	Breakfast €10. Lunch/dinner €20. VAT included.
closed	Rarely.
directions	From Pamplona, A-15 for San Sebastián. Exit 117 onto NA-411 to Udabe. On to Jauntsarats; at end of village left for hotel (signposted). From here 900m to hotel.

	José María Astíz & María Cruz Barberena
tel	+34 948 503370
fax	+34 948 503284
email	peruskenea@ctv.es
web	www.peruskenea.com

Map 6 Entry 67

The Lake House in Navarra

Casa della Lago , 101010 Navarra

Singularly, originally and particularly unique – but, if the truth be told, the lake came afterwards when the valley was flooded by one of Franco's lunatic dam-building schemes. Some buildings are built unique and others have uniqueness thrust upon them. The architect was a stubborn fellow. He was warned about the dam but said to his builder: "Build and be dammed." That was a wise, intuitive move for the lake has given to an otherwise unremarkable folly a sheen of shimmering loveliness. The kings of Navarre used to hunt wild boar in this valley, now overrun by only the tamest of bores. But you may fish for trout; indeed, you are encouraged by the hotel to do so for the menu is otherwise limited. The house was built for a vastly rich tortilla tycoon, a setting for lavish but secret tortilla tastings away from the prying eyes of the over-zealous local hygiene inspector. The tycoon, however, was caught adulterating his tortillas and went bankrupt. The building has never recovered – that is why it is available for you as a very special albeit slightly run-down resting place.

rooms	5 doubles (submerged); 1 rooftop single (2-10 families, at a squeeze).
price	Cheap as tapwater.
meals	Freshwater fish served straight to your room.
closed	Never, but tends to drop out of sight during wetter months.
directions	N-101, North, then AS-909 towards Bel Aqua. Keep going until you reach the water, then a little further. When you feel a liquid slosh around your ankles, you've arrived.

	Señor Moje Manta
tel	+34 777 787878
fax	+34 777 787878
email	pumproom@navarra.es
web	www.feelthetrout.es

Map 0 Entry 68

Hospedería Señorío de Briñas
Travesía de la Calle Real 3, 26290 Briñas, La Rioja

Briñas is one of the prettiest villages of La Rioja. Its stately houses and ornate churches pay witness to its golden age, the 16th century, when the region reached its economic zenith and noble families set up house. The stern façade of this *casona* gives no hint of the character and classiness that lie within. Charming, gregarious Angela is a designer who embarked on this project when the building was little more than a ruin; impossible to believe now! A rustic elegance prevails – chunky terracotta floors, antique chairs, embroidered linen, chandeliers. Most intriguing of all are the trompe l'oeil frescos, the surreal creations of a Polish artist that will have you gazing out of an imaginary window or pulling back a lavish drape... Treasures and treats galore: a vast, individually decorated, blissfully quiet bedroom with an old and creaky pine floor, a mezzanine suite perfect for families, good breakfasts with freshly squeezed juices, and a cosy bar where you can get to grips with Rioja's most famous export, its oaky red wine. *A Rusticae hotel.*

rooms	14: 11 twins/doubles, 3 suites.
price	€115. Singles €75-€89. Suite €136-€170.
meals	Evening snacks available. Wide choice of restaurants in Haro.
closed	Rarely.
directions	From A-68, exit 8 for Zambrana. N-124 for Logroño. Through tunnel, up hill, after 8km, left for Briñas. After 300m right; 50m down dead-end road. Park in front, or in car park.

	Angela Gómez
tel	+34 941 304224
fax	+34 941 304345
email	brinas@hotelesconencanto.org
web	www.hotelesconencanto.org

Map 5 Entry 69

Hospedería Señorío de Casalarreina

Pza. Santo Domingo de Guzmán 6, 26230 Casalarreina, La Rioja

The Hospedería's windows look to the great portico of the monastery of St Dominic – a large, impressive edifice that dominates the village square, with bandstand and weekend market. The rest of the hotel as been transformed by Pedro, who won his hospitality spurs by creating a similar transformation in nearby Briñas. The Hospedería is grand, its furnishings idiosyncratic, even lavish, and its bathrooms a medieval extravaganza: all bricked hydromassage corner baths, heraldic scenes on walls and swagged drapes. Yet somehow the whole gorgeous place manages to avoid being impersonal, and local knowledge and expertise have been brought to bear at every stage. The frescos are by a local friend of Pedro, the curtains and covers are made by his sister, the floorboards (American oak) were riojan wine casks. A bar and lounge here and, just around the corner, the justly renowned restaurant, La Vieja Bodega, owned by another of Pedro's friends and said to offer some of the best food and wine in the region – and that's saying something. *A Rusticae hotel.*

rooms	15 twins/doubles.
price	€155–€140. Singles €105.
meals	Excellent restaurant 5-minute walk.
closed	Rarely.
directions	From Bilbao, A-68 for Logroño. Exit 9 for Haro; N-126 to Casalarreina. Hostal part of monastic building in main square.

	Pedro Ortega
tel	+34 941 324730
fax	+34 941 324731
email	infocasalarreina@hotelesconencanto.org
web	www.hotelesconencanto.org

Map 5 Entry 70

Photo Jose Navarro

aragon & catalonia

La Choca

Plaza Mayor 1, 22148 Lecina, Huesca

Lecina de Bárcabo is for lovers of vertiginous places; in a tiny (yet easily accessible) hamlet in a wild part of Huesca. Miguel and Ana restored this centuries-old fortified farmhouse, in a privileged positon on the village square, for themselves... but La Choca cried out to be shared so they opened to all. Fall asleep to the hooting of the owl, wake to the sound of the church bells: the peace is intoxicating. Inside, stone walls, ancient timbers, stone stairs and an attractive rusticity. The bedrooms are simple: without air conditioning (it gets hot in summer) but with captivating views... The lightest are the twins at the front, three are big enough for a family, and the top one has its own terrace. You'll eat well (perhaps to background classical music): homemade jams at breakfast, regional dishes with a French twist at main meals, and Ana's own recipes. There's a garden flanked by the church, and an ancient green oak for shade. Cave paintings nearby, bikes in the hamlet, walks from the door, and exceptionally kind hosts. Delightful self-catering apartments were added three years ago.

rooms	9 + 2: 9 twins/doubles. 2 self-catering apartments for 4-6.
price	€80 half-board; singles €50. Apt €40-€54 for 2 (min. 2 nights).
meals	Dinner half-board. Lunch available, weekends only, €25-€30 à la carte.
closed	December-March closed weekdays.
directions	From Barcelona AP-2/E-90 to Lleida (Lérida). Ring road exit N-240. On approach to Barbastro right into town after hospital. At r'bout to Alquezar; then Lecina.

	Ana Zamora & Miguel Angel Blasco
tel	+34 974 343070
fax	+34 974 318466
email	chocala@wanadoo.es
web	www.staragon.com/lachoca/

Map 7 Entry 71

Hostería Sierra de Guara
c/Oriente 2, 22144 Bierge, Huesca

There's inn-keeping in the family; Rosa's parents set up the well-established *hostería* across the road. This unassuming new building, still a little *al dente* when we visited, has lots of potential, thanks to its position in a Parque National – and to the unaffected charm of its owners. Rosa's husband works at the celebrated Vinos del Vero and can arrange a free guided tour of the *bodegas*. And you can go rafting, riding, climbing and ravine-spotting – or book onto a birdwatching tour and see eagles and vultures feeding. Birds are a bit of a theme here – note the painted wooden panels at reception. Bedrooms have the usual tiled floors, beds come with slender metal bedheads and flouncing muslin drapes, perhaps an armchair or two. Enjoy a sundowner on the terrace with its hilltop (floodlit) church views – wonderful. In the large dining room, make the most of dishes cooked on the open fire, and sample the 'olive oil menu': they produce their own. At the back of the house is an almond orchard, a cloud of white and pink in February when the blossom begins. *A Rusticae hotel.*

rooms	14: 11 twins/doubles, 3 suites.
price	€63–€69; half-board €90–€96. Singles €46–€51; half-board €62. Suites €88–€95; half-board €115–€122.
meals	Lunch/dinner €20.
closed	January.
directions	From Huesca, N-240 for Lleida. 5km after Angües, left to Abiego, then left to Bierge. Hostería on left at village entrance.

	Rosa Viñuales Ferrando
tel	+34 974 318107
fax	+34 974 318107
email	info@hosteriaguara.com
web	www.hosteriaguara.com

Map 7 Entry 72

Hospedería de Loarre
Plaza Miguel Moya 7, 22809 Loarre, Huesca

This modest 16th-century 'palace' graces the prettiest of main squares in the little village of Loarre; breakfasting on the terrace is a treat. The building was not so long ago restored, thanks to local government initiative, and no corners were cut in its complete facelift (full facilities for the disabled, for example). You'll probably mention the food first on the postcard home: Aragonese and French Basque cooking and the very best cuts of meat. Stay in autumn when wild mushrooms and game are on the menu – and do try one of the Somantano reds (be guided by your waiter): they are honest, robust wines and reasonably priced. The bedrooms are sober, comfortable and clean, with new beds, spotless tiles and the occasional antique; the best have balconies giving onto the square while those at the back gaze over the rooftops to the almond groves beyond. Do visit the medieval castle (see photo) and the fabulous rock formations of the nearby Mallos de Riglos range. Jorge and wife Anna are young and friendly and make a great team; this is a place at ease with itself.

rooms	12: 10 twins/doubles, 2 singles.
price	€52–€71. Singles €41–€57.
meals	Lunch/dinner €16 set menu; €30 à la carte.
closed	Approx. 30 days in November & December.
directions	From Huesca, A-132 to Ayerbe. Here, right onto HU-311 Loarre. Hotel in main square; garage for 3 cars.

	Jorge Valdés Santonja
tel	+34 974 382706
fax	+34 974 382713
email	info@hospederiadeloarre.com
web	www.hospederiadeloarre.com

Map 6 Entry 73

Posada Magoría
c/Milagro 32, 22728 Ansó, Huesca

This 1920s family home has a genuine mood and has been caringly restored by the much-travelled Enrique. It's a warm and well-insulated house, whose ancient radiators belt out heat. Louvred shutters let in the light, the pale interior is finely furnished, and the traditional bedrooms are uncluttered and soberly attired: good quality mattresses lie on 1920s beds and bathrooms have glass-brick walls to let the daylight in. But the real heart of the place is the communal dining area where a huge rock juts into the room beside the long table and the full-length wall tapestry lends the space weight. Here you will be served the most delicious, organic, vegetarian food – salads, soups, cheeses and homemade bread with lashings of cider. Breakfast is a purifying selection of muesli, cereals and mountain honey. Enrique, a pioneer of eco-tourism and a perfect host, has an intimate knowledge of the region and will deepen your understanding of this undiscovered peak. Walking, mushroom-picking, yoga… it's worth making a trip to this wonderfully remote place. The village, too, is special. *Vegetarian food only.*

rooms	7 twins/doubles.
price	€46-€51. Singles €31. VAT included.
meals	Breakfast €6. Dinner €12. VAT inc.
closed	Rarely.
directions	Pamplona-Jaca N-240. Left at Berdun on HU-202 to Ansó. Here, 2nd left into village past mill; left along narrow street to church; last house on right. Steep walk from car park: unload at house first.

	Enrique Ipas & Teresa Garayoa
tel	+34 974 370049
email	posadamagoría@telefónica.net

Map 6 Entry 74

El Privilegio de Tena

Plaza Mayor, 22663 Tramacastilla de Tena, Huesca

The name of this gorgeous place echoes the privileges granted long ago by the kingdom of Cataluna. Because of the valley's isolation, it suffered terrible hardship in the long winter months; there's still a remoteness and silence but you'll find the privations hard to credit now. Big, beautiful bedrooms and quirky, designer bathrooms have a generous, stylish comfort which is entirely 21st-century; the history of the place is still apparent in the ancient detail, rough golden stone and huge great beams. Juan inherited the two buildings – one a 15th-century abbey, the other a hotel – from his family; until 10 years ago they were used to shelter cows... If you really want to push the boat out, book the Suite Privilegio – it's quite something. There's even a brass telescope so you can make the most of the stunning views (the breathtakingly sheer rockface of Pena Telera down in the valley is a classic landmark). Juan and his wife are thoroughly nice people – she's from Zaragoza and used to teach Italian – and very proud of their collaboration with top Spanish chef Martín Berasategui.

rooms	28: 22 twins/doubles, 6 suites.
price	€114–€154. Singles €77–€100. Suite €140–€600.
meals	Lunch/dinner €18; à la carte €30.
closed	Rarely.
directions	From Huesca N-136 for Jaca. Follow road round to Biescas. 12km on, at junc. for Biescas, on towards France. 10km after junc. left & 1.5km to Tramacastilla. Through village; hotel behind Ayunatmiento.

	Anabel Costas & Juan Ignacio Pérez
tel	+34 974 487206
fax	+34 974 487270
email	info@elprivilegio.com
web	www.elprivilegio.com

Map 7 Entry 75

Casa de San Martín

22372 San Martín de la Solana, Huesca

It's quite an approach. Once you've left the main road, prepare to stay in second gear; a long, rough, two or three mile track leads to the hotel. Casa de San Martín rests on a little green summit surrounded by the foothills of the Pyrenees – what views! A dwelling is said to have stood here since 1200 but the present building is 18th century, and has a tall, galleried front. Pass the Spanish water dogs sunning themselves on the patio – and enter the hall, where pride of place is given to the Goya on the wall (a copy, not an original!); it's the portrait of an earlier owner who gave the artist shelter during the War of Independence. In the stone-walled sitting room – once a chapel – are smartly clad tartan sofas and country chairs, soft lighting and a big fire; the feel is rustic contemporary. Bedrooms, too, are decorated in stylish good taste. Some of dinner's ingredients come straight from the garden so couldn't be fresher; Mario describes his seasonal dishes as a mix of regional Spanish and Brazilian. The Somontano wines are delicious, too, and Mario and David are natural hosts. *A Rusticae hotel.*

rooms	10 twins/doubles.
price	€120-€180. Singles €90.
meals	Dinner €30 set menu.
closed	Rarely.
directions	From Barcelona, A-2/E-90 for Lleida. Junc. 6, N-240 for Huesca. Before Barbastro, right on N-123, then A-138 to Aínsa. Left to Boltana; N-260 for 10km to San Martín. 5km track to hotel.

	David Robinson & Mario Reis
tel	+34 974 503105
fax	+34 974 341456
email	info@casadesanmartin.com
web	www.casadesanmartin.com

Map 7 Entry 76

Hotel Los Arcos
Plaza Mayor 23, 22330 Aínsa, Huesca

At the heart of the enchanting village of Aínsa is a cobbled square overlooked by a fine church tower. Tucked away down its medieval alleys, many tempting restaurants and cafés – no wonder Aínsa is so popular. On one side of the square is a delightful terrace of old houses, built of warm stone, with shuttered windows and tiny iron balconies. Oscar, an engineer born in Aragon who decided to return to his roots, has turned one of these tall, slender houses into a charming little hotel. He is gentle and eager to ensure that his guests are comfortable. The communal areas are of necessity small, but the spaces have been cleverly used and on the walls are paintings by a Barcelona artist. Exposed stone, reclaimed beams and quarry tiles coexist with ultra modern steel and glass; soft, tawny colours and fabrics contrast with dazzling white linens. The bedrooms are generous and pleasing, some facing the square, others the Peña mountains. The 'special' room has a splendid four-poster. Ordesa National Park is close by: go there for great walking and, perhaps, a glimpse wild boar, vultures and deer.

rooms	7 twins/doubles.
price	€70–€150.
meals	Restaurants in village.
closed	Rarely.
directions	From Barcelona to Lleida (Lérida) on A-2; exit 458 onto N-123 for Huesca. Before Barbastro right for Aínsa. Left at main x-roads in Aínsa. After 250m right at sign 'casco historico'; 500m to car park. 5-min walk to hotel.

	Oscar Fantova & Carlota Dorado
tel	+34 974 500016
fax	+34 974 500136
email	info@hotellosarcosainsa.com
web	www.hotellosarcosainsa.com

Map 7 Entry 77

Posada La Pastora

c/Roncesvalles 1, 50678 Uncastillo, Zaragoza

Uncastillo, as the name implies, is an attractive castle-topped town – all too often passed by – in the Sierra de Santo Domingo. Just behind the beautiful, romanesque Iglésia Santa María is this grand, 18th-century house: the nicest place to stay in town. The traditional elements of old flagstones, wrought-iron grilles, terracotta tiles and wooden beams have been preserved and restored. Massively thick outer walls mean that even at the height of the Spanish summer it remains cool inside; in winter, a woodburner keeps the little lounge as warm as toast. Inma and Miguel are as charming and unassuming as the guesthouse they have created. Guest rooms have no delusions of grandeur but, with those heavy stone walls, checked bedspreads and antique washbasins they feel wonderfully snug. Another medieval town to visit is Sos del Rey Católico; its claim to fame is that the local-boy-made-good was Fernando II, whose marriage to Isabela would so radically change the course of Spanish history. *A Rusticae hotel.*

rooms	8 twins/doubles.
price	€66. Singles €47.
meals	Breakfast €5.
closed	Rarely.
directions	From Pamplona N-121 south, then N-240 Huesca; NA-127 to Sangüesa. There, A-127 to Uncastillo. Here, round church of S. María; park in small cobbled square. 20m to house.

Inma Navarro Labat & Miguel Pemán

tel	+34 976 679499
fax	+34 976 679499
email	lapastora@lapastora.net
web	www.lapastora.net

Map 6 Entry 78

Hotel Monasterio de Piedra

Afueras s/n, 50210 Nuévalos, Zaragoza

Enter a secret world of natural beauty. This 800-year-old monastery up in the hills is one of those gems of Spanish culture that ravish the senses and make exploring Iberia a joy. Impressive corridors still invite contemplation but there's not a horsehair mattress in sight: uncluttered bedrooms – each converted from a quartet of monks' cells – are antique-smart and delightfully cool in scorching summer. Best of all, they overlook an oasis of monastic garden. Vaulted sitting areas echo; food is mouthwatering; ancient cream stone walls and alabaster windows soothe the soul. So unwind, and take a guided tour of the cloisters, altars and tombs – and the first European kitchen where chocolate was made. In one of the former cellars, the Wine Museum gives another glimpse of life in days gone by, and there's the Life of the River Centre with its 3D audio-visual presentation of the life cycle of the trout. But the dense natural ecosystem of the park is the jewel in this particular Aragonese crown. A 174-foot waterfall, a mirror lake, a sunken grotto... go and lose yourself in the gardens and walkways.

rooms	61: 60 twins/doubles, 1 suite.
price	€121. Singles €68-€96. Suite €157.
meals	Breakfast €9. Lunch/dinner €23.
closed	Rarely.
directions	From Barcelona & Zaragoza exit 231 for Monasterio de P. In Nuévalos, signs for Monasterio de P. Hotel 2.5km outside village in grounds of monastery.

	Antonio Carmona Fernández
tel	+34 902 196052
fax	+34 976 849054
email	hotel@monasteriopiedra.com
web	www.monasteriopiedra.com

Map 13 Entry 79

Hostal Los Palacios
c/Palacios 21, 44100 Albarracín, Teruel

Albarracín is one of Teruel's most amazing walled towns, its medieval streets tumbling down the hillside to a beautiful square and blue-domed cathedral. Los Palacios is a tall, balconied building just outside the city walls whose earthy colours appear to fix it to the hillside on which it stands. The 50-year-old building was not long ago thoroughly revived and thus was born this small *hostal*. Bedrooms are furnished with workaday wooden furniture, floors are decked in modern tiles and the fabrics are a shade satiny, but forgive this little lapse – these are authentically Spanish rooms, impeccably clean and, from their small balconies, have views that are second to none. More breathtaking views from the breakfast room/bar. An unpretentious little place, amazingly cheap, and wholeheartedly recommended if you are happy in simple surroundings. Make time for the new animal farm nearby, Masia Monteagudo, with its horse riding and restaurant. *Lunch/dinner available July/August, Easter and bank holiday only.*

rooms	16: 15 twins/doubles, 1 single.
price	€33–€36. Singles €20–€23. VAT inc.
meals	Breakfast €2. Lunch/dinner €9. VAT included.
closed	Rarely.
directions	From Teruel N-234 north for Zaragoza. After 8km, left on TE-901 to Albarracín. Here through tunnel, right after 150m. Hostal 2nd house on right.

	Valeriano Saez & Maite Argente
tel	+34 978 700327
fax	+34 978 700358
email	hostallospalacios@montepalacios.com
web	www.montepalacios.com

Map 14 Entry 80

Hotel Esther

44431 Virgen de la Vega, Teruel

The high mountains and villages of the Maestrazgo are beginning to awaken the curiosity of those in search of new pastures to walk and ski. At its heart: the little Esther inn. This is a family affair run by father, mother and son, with the focus firmly on the restaurant. Expect a memorable meal in a modern but semi-rustic room, whose sloping timbered ceiling lends an intimate feel. Specialities are dishes from Aragón: roast lamb, pork and kid, stewed broad beans with chorizo, junket with honey for dessert – wholesome home cooking. There is a decent choice of wines and you can trust Miguel's recommendations. Decoration is the same upstairs and down – tiled floors, light pine; bedrooms have small bathrooms and printed drapes. The settlement of Virgen de la Vega is nothing to write home about, virtually deserted out of season, but there are some pretty villages nearby – head for Mora de Rubielos. Skiing is at Valdelinares, five miles away. Honest prices, and you may well be the only foreigner staying here.

rooms	24: 14 twins/doubles, 5 singles, 2 family, 3 suites.
price	€62–€83. Singles €44–€54. Suites €119.
meals	Breakfast €4.50. Lunch/dinner €15, €27 à la carte.
closed	8-25 September.
directions	From Valencia for Barcelona; at Sagunto, left on N-234 for Teruel. A-232 to Alcalá de la Selva. V de la Vega 2km before Alcalá. 200m before church, on right.

	Miguel Andrés Rajadel García
tel	+34 978 801040
fax	+34 978 808030
email	hotelesther@sierradegudar.com

Map 14 Entry 81

Masía del Aragonés
44586 Peñarroya de Tastavins, Teruel

Its 16th-century tower rising majestically above open pastures, at the end of a long, long track, this lovingly restored, Aragonese farm. It was once a weekend retreat for wealthy locals; today it is more simply furnished. Its airy, sitting/dining room has stone walls hung with old farm implements, contemporary tiles, pine furniture and a fine wood-burning stove. This is where you enjoy Pilar's cooking with nearly all ingredients home-grown or reared: she prepares wholesome soups and stews, simple puddings and gorgeous pastries accompanied by her liquers and home-brewed wine (and she doesn't mind a bit if you bring your own!). Bedrooms, some basic, are a good size and have iron bedsteads, homespun curtains, spotless bathrooms, exposed stone walls. With arched windows and an open layout (sharing an open bit of wall), we liked those on the top floor best, in spite of the steep stairs. The scenery is epic, the mountains home to ibex and eagles, there are crystalline rock pools above Beceite, and Valderrobres is worth a visit. The Andreu family go out of their way to make sure your stay is memorable.

rooms	6 twins/doubles.
price	€32–€45. VAT inc.
meals	Lunch/dinner €12–€16, by request. VAT included.
closed	Never.
directions	Barcelona A-7, exit junc. 38 for L'Hospitalet de L'Infant. On to Valderrobres. There, left to Fuentespalda, on for Monroyo, left for Peñarroyo de T. After 500m right to Herbes; following signs to Masía. After 2km right for 3km on track.

	Pilar Andreu & Manuel Lombarte
tel	+34 978 769048
web	www.masaragones.com

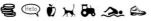

Map 15 Entry 82

La Torre del Visco

44587 Fuentespalda, Teruel

Bajo Aragón is the 'Tuscany' of Spain: beautiful, wild, unspoilt, and stacked with natural and man-made treasures. Set well back from the coast – a 90-minute drive – the hotel is surrounded by its own large farm… such tranquillity. Inside the superbly converted estate house, each piece of furniture, be it antique, rustic or modern, fits perfectly with the 15th-century tiles, brickwork and beams. And everywhere there are flowers. The food is another reason to come, and standards are high in the beautiful, split-level restaurant where the emphasis is on seasonal dishes: fresh fruit and vegetables from the farm, black truffles and wild mushrooms, local game (including wild boar), the freshest fish. Then there are the gardens, the summer breakfasts on the terrace, the large library, the medieval wine cellar (great wines) and the huge original kitchen where you can observe work in progress. Although this singular and exclusive hotel is owned and run by an English couple, Piers and Jemma, the majority of guests are Spanish. A treat never to be forgotten. *Ask about their cookery courses.*

rooms	15: 12 twins/doubles, 3 suites.
price	Half-board only, €220-€270. Suites €330.
meals	Dinner included. Lunch €38.
closed	Rarely.
directions	From Barcelona A-7 S for Valencia; junc. 38 for L'H.de L'Infant y Móra, then Gandesa. There for Alcañiz; left in Calaceite to Valderrobres. There, left for Fuentespalda; 6km; right. Follow track.

	Piers Dutton & Jemma Markham
tel	+34 978 769015
fax	+34 978 769016
email	torredelvisco@torredelvisco.com
web	www.torredelvisco.com

Map 15 Entry 83

Hotel El Convent

c/El convento 1, 44596 La Fresneda, Teruel

Its massive front door is set in a creamy stone archway, flanked by a pair of cypresses; one quarter of the door swings open to admit you. The site was acquired around 1900 by a forebear of today's owners; with the land came the ruins of a church built in 1613. By the time the said forebear arrived on the scene, little more remained than the church's outer walls – the shell for an elegant new dwelling. Now it's a delightful hotel run by a smiling family. Spaces are lofty and unexpected, and there's an arresting mix of ancient and modern: beamed, vaulted ceilings and glass floors, exposed stone walls and contemporary fittings, conventual austerity and secular comfort. The bedrooms have huge period appeal and old frescos; those on the top floor are more contemporary and have terrific views. Particularly striking are the central patio and restaurant in the old choir and nave, the former side chapels providing intimate dining areas. The food is mediterranean with an elegant, contemporary slant. Gardens are vast, sunny and tranquil, watery sounds abound and there's a modest pool.

rooms	13: 11 twins/doubles, 2 suites.
price	€83-€105. Suites €115-€125.
meals	Lunch €36. Dinner €30.
closed	7-20 January.
directions	From Alcañiz N-232. 1km after junc. with N-420 left onto A-231 for Valderrobres. 5km before Valderrobres right to La F. There, left fork to square. Park. Hotel 50m below square on right, at bottom of dead-end alley. Staff will show you how to get to hotel car park.

	Ana & Diana Romeo Villoro
tel	+34 978 854850
fax	+34 978 854851
email	hotel@hotelelconvent.com
web	www.hotelelconvent.com

Map 15 Entry 84

La Parada del Compte

Finca la Antigua Estación, 44597 Torre del Compte, Teruel

The 1940s railway station in the forested valley has been given a new lease of life. At the end of the road cutting down from the village a surprising, original and luxurious hotel awaits. Public spaces are large, cool and airy, colourful not cosy: high rafters, sweeping glass and metal, designer sofas and chairs. In contrast, bedrooms and bathrooms are intimate and enticing – among the best in this book. Each room is inspired by a different place – 'themed', but in the chic-est way. Istanbul has sloping rafters and a bright red wall; New York is purple and metropolitan; Sevilla is a symphony of rose, citrus and white; Valencia has sliding doors to the garden. It's hard to choose a favourite but we would go for França because it gets the sun first thing. Bathrooms are state of the art, lights sparkle, cushions tumble; this is Spanish contemporary design at its best. Head off along the old railway track, on foot or by bike, to discover the wilderness and wonders of this part of Spain; return to mediterranean food so good looking you hesitate to consume it. Amazing. *A Rusticae hotel*

rooms	11 + 5: 6 twins/doubles, 5 suites. 5 self-catering apartments for 2.
price	€100–€125. Suites €160–€200. Apts €80–€90.
meals	Breakfast €12. Lunch/dinner €30 set menu. On request only.
closed	10-31 January.
directions	Zaragoza-Alcañiz N-232. A-231 for Valderrobres. Turn left into T. del Compte. Exit village and follow road to left. Signposted.

José María Naranjo & Pilar Viles
tel	+34 978 769072
fax	+34 978 769074
web	www.hotelparadadelcompte.com

Map 15 Entry 85

Mas de Ibáñez

Apartado de Correos 33, 44580 Valderrobres, Teruel

As hideaways go, few are as hidden as this old farmhouse in Aragón. You'll need a 4x4 to negotiate its four-mile track – it's worth every jolt. This is the land that time forgot, deep in the pine-covered Pena valley; you are surrounded by the peaks of Picosa and La Caixa, while a creek babbles below. Peter and Laureen, who live here with their three dogs, have carried out a thoughtful restoration. Each apartment has a double and a twin bedroom, a well-equipped kitchen, a bathroom and an open-plan living-dining room. The furnishings are modern – and functional, with boisterous youngsters in mind – and the ground-floor apartment is next to a communal playroom-lounge, so the children can spread. Outside, an unobtrusive garden with lavender and a perfectly manicured lawn. They also farm organically, so fresh vegetables, olives, grapes, almonds and figs are yours for the asking. Awesome nature beyond, and, for history buffs, the ancient town of Valderrobes at the other end of the track. *Communication by email preferred.*

rooms	3 apartments for 4. Extra beds available.
price	€80–€120. Extra bed €10. Minimum stay 2 nights.
meals	Self-catering.
closed	Rarely.
directions	From Valderrobres towards Fuentespalda & Monroyo. After 1km right up track for 'Embalse de Pena', unpaved from here ; 1km beyond, after bridge, bear right following signs.

Peter Bromwich & Laureen Rundle Bromwich

tel	+34 687 315131
fax	+34 978 890854
email	mail@masdeibanez.com
web	www.masdeibanez.com

Map 15 Entry 86

Cal Mateu

c/Mayor 27, 43372 La Bisbal de Falset (Priorat), Tarragona

To stay at Cal Mateu is rather like rediscovering a lost relative; guests have been known to shed a tear when they take their leave! Carmen has created a warm and comfortable home in the little medieval town of La Bisbal – known for its olive oil and its mansion houses. Cal Mateu is of more recent construction but has the spirit of an older building. Its lounge, dining room and kitchen are low-beamed and interlinked, connected by stone arches; two more sitting rooms on the upper floors have splendid views of the Montsant, a region known for its canyons and dry-stone terraces. The six little bedrooms take their decorative cue from the rest of the house, with their rough plaster walls, simple iron or wooden beds and red or mint checked fabrics. Basic bathrooms have showers or sit-up-and-beg baths. The whole house breathes an air of unaffected charm, while meals are tasty and wholesome. The sleepy village produces prize-winning olive oil – pop into the Agrituebda and take some home. Extraordinarily good value, a peaceful setting, and the most *simpática* of hostesses. *Self-catering option for big group.*

rooms	6: 4 twins/doubles, 2 family.
price	€29-€47. Singles €21. VAT included.
meals	Breakfast €6. Lunch/dinner €11.
closed	Rarely.
directions	From Reus N-420 to Falset; there right on T-710 to Gratallops then La Vilella Baixa. On via Cabassers (Cabacès) to La Bisbal de Falset. House on right at dead end of main street, past church.

	Carmen Perelló Masip
tel	+34 977 819003
fax	+34 977 819285
email	casapagesmateu@terra.es

Map 7 Entry 87

Mas Passamaner

Camí de la Serra 52, 43470 La Selva del Camp, Tarragona

Slip through the gates, spot the helipad to your right, and you're in uber-luxury land. This stunning house, built in 1922 by the renowned Domenech i Montaner, has been restored and transformed into a modernist boutique hotel. It is fabulously and faithfully detailed. The 26 rooms, each named after a Catalan architect, are ultra-designed. Colours are silky creams, aubergines and charcoals, furniture smoothly functional, lighting understatedly modern; it's a design-junkie's dream. Decoration is bold and clean, perhaps a ceiling-high bedhead or a broad framed mirror. Bathrooms are razor sharp in chrome, slate and marble with plenty of pampering potions. Rooms in the old building have terraces while the two Royal Suites come with their own pools. Sprawl on the sitting room sofas, laze by the swimming pool, take a nightcap to the reading room. There's a shimmering, minimalist spa – candlelit, with every treatment imaginable – as well as gym and tennis. The restaurant is classy, intimate, modern, and the chef comes garlanded with two Michelin stars. *A Rusticae hotel.*

rooms	26: 19 twins/doubles, 7 suites.
price	€170–€215. Suites €240–€300.
meals	Breakfast €15. Half-board extra €60 p.p.; full-board extra €90 p.p.
closed	Rarely.
directions	From Barcelona on A-7; exit 34 to Reus & airport. On C-14 for Montblanc. Exit for La Selva del Camp & Constantí. Follow signs for Constantí; after 2.5 km right for hotel.

	Mireia Olivé
tel	+34 977 766333
fax	+34 977 766336
email	hotel@maspassamaner.com
web	www.maspassamaner.com

Map 8 Entry 88

Hotel Rural Les Vinyes

c/Vilardida 13, 43812 Vilardida-Montferri, Tarragona

Josep and Manja's backgrounds in property and interior design have transformed a former hostel for mill workers into a hotel of imagination and personality. A quirky candelabra key-holder is the first of many surprises, and each themed bedroom and suite is individual, colourwashed walls inspired by the name: reds and greens for La Vinya, warm yellows for El Sol, soft blues and whites for El Cielo… Manja has added handmade soft furnishings and lampshades, prettily painted antique furniture and many more touches, making each room special. Bathrooms are brilliant with marble basins and powerful showers; the high standards carry through to the elegantly comfortable dining and sitting rooms. You're in the heart of a small wine-making community and vineyards surround you. Make the most of Manja's Spanish and Dutch dishes – organic vegetables come fresh from the garden – and the local wines: such tiny vintages that each bottle is numbered. If you want to explore, borrow bikes – nothing is too much trouble for these enthusiastic and friendly hosts.

rooms	8: 4 twins/doubles, 4 suites.
price	€80–€140. VAT included.
meals	Dinner €20–€30 à la carte.
closed	Rarely.
directions	AP-2, exit 11 onto C-51 to Vendrell. After 2km, in hamlet on left.

	Josep Ruiz Camps & Manja Jonker
tel	+34 977 639193
fax	+34 977 639193
email	info@lesvinyes.com
web	www.lesvinyes.com

Map 8 Entry 89

Can Cuadros

c/Major 3, 25211 Palouet-Massoteres, Lleida

Arriving in the dreamy silence of siesta time, you'd never imagine the hamlet of Palouet could contain such a place as Can Cuadros. The labyrinthine, 900-year-old castle is more museum than hotel, each room a step back in time. Josep and Àngels are seeking to relive the traditions and culture of this corner of Catalonia. Not even the shower rooms escape the hand of history – each has beams and antique fittings – while bedrooms, darkish yet appealing, and mercifully cool in summer, are full of fine old beds and fascinating curios. There's a library of 4,000 books, and a dining room with an old wine press for a fireplace: it's like a magical fairy grotto at night. For summer suppers there's a walled patio with goldfish pond and plants. You dine on medieval recipes, painstakingly researched and expertly cooked by Àngels: Segarran pancakes, melon soup (memorable), medieval Jewish puddings... Wines (over 200 bins) are organic, laurel brandy homemade. Josep's vast knowledge of Catalan folklore, local artisanal activity and walks add to the whole wondrous experience.

rooms	7: 6 twins/doubles, 1 triple.
price	€50. Singles €35. Triple €70.
meals	Breakfast €5. Dinner €15.
closed	Rarely.
directions	From Barcelona N-II to Cervera. Here, right to Guissona; right to Massoteres; follow signs to Palouet.

	Josep Arasa & Àngels Miró
tel	973 294106
fax	mob: 0034 678 606906
email	cancuadros@telefonica.net
web	www.cancuadros.com

Map 8 Entry 90

Can Boix de Peramola

Can Boix s/n, 25790 Peramola, Lérida

Ten generations of the Pallarés family have lived and worked at Can Boix; three of them have turned this seductively located inn into something of an institution. And this is not a family to sit back on its laurels. Bedrooms are big, attractive and awash with modern comfort: air conditioning, minibar, TV and DVD, mirrored wardrobes, jacuzzi. Those in the main building have a small balcony or terrace, those in the annexe a larger terrace overlooking gardens or stunning valley – and direct access to the hotel sauna and solarium. The food is a celebration of what is locally grown or raised; the half-board option is excellent value. The presentation is superb, the wine list long, and, even if the dining room is big enough for a banquet, the accompanying views are as scrumptious as the meal and it still feels welcoming. The great ridge lowering above the hotel is a constant reminder of the sublime scenery of the Pyrenees. An immensely friendly hotel which caters for business people and travellers alike. *A Rusticae hotel*

rooms	41 twins/doubles.
price	€87–€121. Singles €70–€97. Half-board from €142; singles from €97.
meals	Breakfast €9. Lunch/dinner €19, €39–€49 à la carte.
closed	2 weeks November; 4 weeks January/February.
directions	Barcelona-Lleida (Lérida) on A-2. Exit Cervera & on through Cervera to Ponts; there, right on C-14 to Oliana. 3km after bridge, left to Peramola. 4km to hotel.

	Joan Pallares Oliva
tel	+34 973 470266
fax	+34 973 470281
email	hotel@canboix.com
web	www.canboix.com

Map 8 Entry 91

Casa Pete y Lou

Toló, San Salvador de Toló, 25638 Tremp, Lleida

Crystal clear air, heady views, snug farmhouse – Pete and Lou serve up an intoxicating mix at their traditional Catalan home perched high in the foothills of the Pyrenees. Every day a tough decision: trekking, rock climbing, whitewater rafting, hang-gliding, horse riding, swimming in cascade ponds... Pete will help you, with maps and routes, transport and his own good company. But there's nothing to stop you staying put here, gazing from the terrace on the alpine flowers, perhaps spotting a griffon vulture or short-toed eagle. The stone-built farmhouse, surrounded by colourful gardens, is warmly rustic inside. The three bedrooms have beamed ceilings, rugs on wooden floors and colourful wall-hangings, and you share a bathroom and sitting room. In the brightly cluttered kitchen it's all too easy to linger over one of Lou's suppers; dine in several nights a week on home-grown organic fruit and veg (and homemade bread and preserves breakfast). The site may be remote, but there are other eateries to discover. Warm, friendly, laid-back, the mood is one of 'mi casa, tu casa'.

rooms	3: 2 doubles, 1 twin.
price	€40.
meals	Dinner €12 set menu. Packed lunches available.
closed	Rarely.
directions	A-2 Barcelona-Lérida, to Tárrega; C-14 to Agramunt and on to Artesa de Segre; L-512 for Tremp; at Col de Comiols left for San Salvador; after 6km, just past bridge over river, left track for 1km. Signed.

	Peter Dale & Lou Beaumont
tel	+34 973 252309
fax	+34 973 252309
email	lou@casapeteylou.com
web	www.casapeteylou.com

Map 8 Entry 92

Casa Mauri

Santa Engracia, 25636 Tremp, Lleida

Few villages in Spain can match spectacular Santa Engracia for setting; from its rocky ledge you look across to hill, lake and mountain. The heady magic of the place worked its spell on Anne and Mike, who fell in love with this 200-year-old farmhouse and cottage and took them on. Both Casa Mauri and El Pajar lead off a shared, walled courtyard – with barbecue, seating and inflatable pool. You get character and modern comfort: exposed beams, open stonework, white-plastered walls... radiators, woodburners, videos, up-to-date kitchens and showers (not ensuite). Pretty rugs, beds and bamboo lights add a homely touch. One of Casa Mauri's bedrooms has a balcony, El Pajar's living room has a picture window that overlooks the courtyard and village church; both houses have terraces. Should you tire of that grandest of views you could follow dinosaur footprints from the door – or swim in the nearby lake, visit the market in Tremp, whitewater raft, ride, ski or choose between any number of fabulous walks: Anne and Mike have compiled a guide. They'll also carry your bags for you up the old 300m mule track from your car!

rooms	1 + 2: 1 double. 2 self-catering cottages for 6 and 4.
price	€66. Singles €33. Houses €225-€785 per week. VAT included.
meals	B'fast €7.50. Dinner €18. VAT inc.
closed	Rarely.
directions	From Tremp, north for La Pobla de Segur on C-13. After garage on right, pass left to Talarn; after bends, left for S. Engracia. Under r'way, on for 10km to village. Park & walk 300m up to house.

	Anne & Mike Harrison
tel	+34 973 252076
fax	+34 973 252076
email	casamauri@hotmail.com

Map 7 Entry 93

Casa Guilla

Santa Engracia, Apartado 83, 25620 Tremp, Lleida

A matchless position. As you soar higher and higher to the hamlet perched on a rocky crag you can only wonder at the tenacity of Santa Engracia's earliest inhabitants. Richard and Sandra Loder, who have a head for heights, restored the old buildings that make up Casa Guilla 20 years ago. A fortified Catalan farmhouse, parts of which go back 1,000 years, the labyrinthine dwelling twists and turns on many levels... all is deliciously organic. There's a large sitting room with an open hearth, and a library on the mezzanine floor. The bedrooms are plainly but comfortably furnished: terracotta tiles, heavy old beams, low ceilings, ensuite showers. In the dining room or on the terrace, tuck into big breakfasts with home-baked bread and generous dinners with lots of game – accompanied by that incomparable view. Geologists, lepidopterists, ornithologists and botanists will be in their element, but anyone seeking seclusion in a fascinating part of Catalonia will love it. Richard and Sandra are caring and informative hosts, and suppers at the big table are good value.

rooms	4: 2 twins/doubles, 2 family.
price	Half-board only, €110 for 2. Singles €55. VAT included.
meals	Packed lunch €6. Dinner included.
closed	1 November-29 February.
directions	After 1.5 km on C-13 from Tremp to Pobla de Segur, left on road signed 'Santa Engracia 10km'. House next to church, reached by own road; parking at house.

	Richard & Sandra Loder
tel	tel/fax +34 973 252080
fax	mob +34 620 911935
email	info@casaguilla.com
web	www.casaguilla.com

Map 7 Entry 94

Besiberri

c/Deth Fort 4, 25599 Arties-Valle de Aran, Lérida

If you're headed for the Val d'Aran (Valle de Aran), stay at the Besiberri; it is delightful, intimate and managed by the friendliest of families. The geranium-clad building looks to the Alps for its inspiration. Enter via the little sitting room with a dining area to one side – a cosy beamed space, made even cosier by its collection of pewter and Carmen's flowers. Wonderful to warm yourself after a day's hiking before the winter fire… Smallish bedrooms are cheerfully pine-clad, and have deeply comfortable beds. Each floor has a balcony gazing out across the river rushing by – but splurge out and take the suite at the top, with windows to both sides and a small sitting room. Bathrooms are excellent, while the recently converted village house opposite holds five new suites. No meals apart from breakfast here, but you are up the road from one of the finest restaurants in the Pyrenees. Carmen is a warm presence and the village is breathtakingly lovely – visit before it becomes too well-known!

rooms	22: 16 twins/doubles, 6 suites.
price	€67-€87. Singles €53-€69. Suites €120-€150.
meals	Restaurants in village.
closed	May-June; 15 October-November.
directions	From Lleida (Lérida) N-230 to Viella; C-142 to Arties. Signed to right on entering village.

	Carmen Lara Aguilar
tel	+34 973 640829
fax	+34 973 642696
email	info@hotelbesiberri.com
web	www.hotelbesiberri.com

Map 7 Entry 95

Fonda Bíayna

c/Sant Roc 11, 25720 Bellver de Cerdanya, Lérida

The meeting place and heart of the village for many generations, this *fonda* proudly upholds its tradition of hospitality. It is bang in the heart of huntin', shootin' and fishin' country; its busy proprietor, Jordi, can organise a pass for the trout fishing nearby – and point you in the direction of the Camino de Buenos Hombres, named in reference to those who passed along it while fleeing the Spanish Inquisitors. On your return, head for the restaurant where hearty regional food and impressive array of Spanish wines are enjoyed by a fast turnover of visitors and locals alike. Bedrooms have polished wooden floors and are soberly furnished with iron beds and looming wardrobes reminiscent of a great aunt's; some on the upper floor open onto a wooden balcony edged with geraniums. The bathrooms are unremarkable but have good-sized baths (on which you cannot always count in Spain!). A place for those who love the great outdoors – the Cerdanya mountains are there to be explored – and who are happy to return to the communal warmth of a village inn.

rooms	17 twins/doubles.
price	€55. Singles €49. VAT included.
meals	Breakfast €6. Lunch/dinner €16. VAT included.
closed	25 December.
directions	From Barcelona, C-1411. After Cadi tunnel, towards El Seu de Urgell & Bellver. In Bellver, park in Sant Roc square. c/Sant Roc leads to Fonda from square.

	Jordi Solé
tel	+34 973 510475
fax	+34 973 510853
email	fondabiayna@ctv.es
web	www.fondabiayna.com

Map 8 Entry 96

Can Borrell

c/Retorn 3, 17539 Meranges-La Cerdanya, Gerona

Can Borrell was once the shelter of mountain shepherds who brought their flocks up to the high slopes of La Cerdanya for the rich summer grazing. This rambling old Pyrenean farmhouse of granite and slate is in the tiniest of villages, with meadows to the front (so children can roam) and conifer-clad mountains behind. Wood is all about in beam, shutter and chair, while slate floors mirror the building's exterior. Its conversion from home to hotel has been sensitively accomplished; it is not over-prettified but has a delightful intimacy. And there are board games for families and paintings on the walls. Bedrooms are inviting with polished floors, fabulous views and excellent beds. They vary in size, following the idiosyncrasies of an old house, and are simple and characterful. Expect something special at your well-dressed table in the popular restaurant: the mouthwatering cooking is "Catalan with a special touch". Uniformed waiting staff add a surprising note for such an off-the-beaten-track place. There are waymarked walks to neighbouring hamlets and cycle trails aplenty.

rooms	9: 7 twins/doubles, 2 family.
price	€73–€145. Singles €61–€67.
meals	Lunch/dinner €24, €33 à la carte.
closed	November: Mon & Tues; December-April: Mon-Thurs. Open daily summer & Easter.
directions	From Barcelona, A-18 via Terrassa & Manresa; C-1411 to Berga. Through Tunel del Cadí, then towards Andorra. After 5km, right for Puigcerdá on N-260; left at Ger to Meranges. Signposted in village.

	Laura Forn Solé
tel	+34 972 880033
fax	+34 972 880144
email	info@canborrell.com
web	www.canborrell.com

Map 8 Entry 97

Cal Pastor

c/Palos 1, 17536 Fornells de la Muntanya-Toses, Gerona

Ramón and Josefina are gentle folk whose families have farmed this valley for generations. Two rooms next to their house were originally opened to guests; now four new guest rooms have been added. They are simple, not cosy but spotless, with tiled floors, modest Spanish fabrics and comfortable beds. Those in the attic have a warmer feel and bigger windows. The dining room is slightly soulless but don't be put off: there's eggs and bacon at breakfast – just ask – and Josefina's dinners are hearty and delicious; don't miss her *croquetas*. She's happy to cook vegetarian dinners, too, and there's a little restaurant you could also visit next door. The trans-Pyrenean, Mediterranean-to-Atlantic footpath runs right by the house and you may feel inspired to do part of it – or go trout fishing in the hills. This is a good place to come back to – unpretentious, authentic, peaceful – and the hamlet is delightful and friendly. Be sure to visit the Museo del Pastor – a testimony to the work of four generations of Ramón's farming family.

rooms	6: 3 twins/doubles, 3 triples.
price	€47–€58.
meals	Breakfast €7. Dinner €13.
closed	Rarely.
directions	From Barcelona, N-152 for Puigcerdà via Vic & Ripoll. Just past Ribes de Freser, left at km133.5 marker; 2km to village. House by restaurant.

	Josefina Soy Sala
tel	+34 972 736163
fax	+34 972 736008
email	apartrural@hotmail.com

Map 8 Entry 98

Hotel Grèvol

Ctra. Camprodón-Setcases s/n, Vall de Camprodón, 17869 Llanars, Gerona

Close to ski slopes, mountain trails and a swag of romanesque churches. Carved pine balconies and exposed stone – it's the Alps without the cuckoo clocks and the perfect backdrop for après-ski. The high-raftered sitting and dining rooms have the best of modern: central hearths and big windows to pull in the light. Pine-panelled, carpeted bedrooms, each named after an alpine flower, are four-star swish; those on the first floor open onto the balcony that wraps itself around the building; attic rooms have little ones you can stand up on. *Grèvol* means 'holly' in Catalan (a protected species here) and the décor uses the leaf for its leitmotif. The hotel has a warm, enveloping feel and the food is really special: a mix of regional, international and 'haute'. "It tastes good and looks good," says Antonio. There is also a vast choice of wines: a rare treat in this quiet corner of the Catalan Pyrenees. The hotel, bustling in season with skiers heading for the slopes in Vallter, has an indoor pool and bowling alley, and, new this year, a spa: a serious pull for skiers and walkers.

rooms	36: 30 doubles, 6 suites.
price	€128-€168. Suites €180-€210.
meals	Lunch/dinner €30.
closed	2 weeks in May; 2 weeks in November. Phone for dates.
directions	From Barcelona A7 for France; C-17 (former N-152) via Vic to Ripoll. There C-151 to Camprodón. Hotel 1.5km from Camprodón on road to Setcases.

	Antonio Solé Fajula
tel	+34 972 741013
fax	+34 972 741087
email	info@hotelgrevol.com
web	www.hotelgrevol.com

Map 8 Entry 99

Hotel Calitxó

Passatge el Serrat s/n, 17868 Molló, Gerona

Molló is a pretty mountain village, 3,000 feet up in the Pyrenees, on the edge of the French border. Hotel Calitxó has more than a hint of the Tyrolean chalet; strange to say, this building was once was a warehouse for the potatoes for which the village is famous. It's well set back from the road with an attractive balconied façade brightened by summer geraniums. You enter through a barn-like restaurant, where the menu is a mix of Catalan and traditional Spanish. Bedrooms, named after trees, are a good size, nothing remarkable but with all you need. You get new pine, matching floral curtains and bedcovers and amazing views – green in summer, white in winter. The suites verge on plush, and some rooms have balconies; breathe in the mountain breezes as you listen to the gentle tinkling of cowbells. Orchid-strewn fields in spring, skiing in winter, beautiful romanesque churches all year round. Come back to comfortable sofas in the sitting room and a wood-burning stove – and be won over by the young Fajula family's easy cheeriness.

rooms	26: 23 twins/doubles, 3 suites.
price	€76–€150; singles €40–€127; suite €97–€186. VAT inc.
meals	Breakfast €2.80. Lunch/dinner available.
closed	Rarely.
directions	From Ripoll C-151 to Camprodón, then C-38 to Molló. In village on left.

	Susana Sole Hernandez
tel	+34 972 740386
fax	+34 972 740746
email	info@hotelcalitxo.com
web	www.hotelcalitxo.com

Map 8 Entry 100

Mas el Guitart

Santa Margarida de Bianya, 17813 La Vall de Bianya, Gerona

Toni and Lali are young, friendly hosts; he left television and she design to launch themselves into the restoration of this old dairy farm. Thanks to their hard work and unpretentious good taste they have succeeded in creating one of Catalonia's very best *casas rurales*. We loved the rooms, each decorated in a different colour with Lali's stencilled beds to match; there are wooden floors and old rafters, window shutters and washstands, little rugs, decent bathrooms and good views. The sitting rooms are decorated in a similar vein. Although no meals are available there are two fully-equipped kitchens as well as a washing machine at your disposal: this would be a great choice for a longer stay. Gaze on the gorgeous green pastures from the hammock, drift off by the safely fenced pool, explore the surrounding mountains. Delightful Toni knows everything: restaurants, walks, history, reflexology – why not book in for a massage? Swings, slides and a mini football pitch in the garden, cows and cow bells, kittens, ducks and hens – it's heaven for families. *Minimum stay two nights.*

rooms	4 + 2: 4 twins/doubles. 2 apartments for 4.
price	€47. Apartments €95. VAT included.
meals	Self-catering.Various restaurants nearby.
closed	Rarely.
directions	From Gerona, C-66 to Besalú. On to Castellfollit de la Roca. Here follow signs for Camprodón on C-26. House signed in La Vall de Bianya.

	Lali Nogareda Burch & Antoni Herrero Pere
tel	+34 972 292140
email	maselguitart@garrotxarural.com
web	www.turismerural.com/guitart

Map 8 Entry 101

Mas Colom

17857 Sant Joan les Fonts, Gerona

Stay here and your conscience will be squeaky-clean. Soap is hand-made, food organic and furniture recycled. Pilar and Jodi, an enthusiastic and friendly young couple, care about the environment yet are never preachy. And their 14th-century mas, perched on the forested hills outside St Juan les Fonts, has an easy mood: a cat curled up in the sun, Greenpeace magazines scattered around, help-yourself biscuits and teas. Rooms are earth-coloured with exposed stonework, tiled floors and chunky furniture. The sitting room has an open wood fire, comfy sofas and hand-sewn cushions; the dining room, in the former stable, jolly tablecloths and colourful shutters. Paintings and sculptures by an artist friend dot the walls and add character. The bedrooms are similarly bright and rustic with appealing touches, perhaps a polished antique bedhead or rush-seated chair. Bathrooms, mostly ensuite, are small but well-designed. Walk, cycle, hunt for medicinal mushrooms, visit the botanical gardens of Olot, ask Pilar to point you towards secret rock pools for swimming. Return to peace, views and a wholesome tranquillity.

rooms	6 twins/doubles.
price	Half-board only, €43 p.p. VAT inc.
meals	Half-board dinner.
closed	Rarely.
directions	A-7 exit 6 for Gerona Nord-Olot. N-260 & Gl-522 to St Joan les F. Through & right for "Residencia Torreblanca". Turn left at "Residencia Torreblanca". On for about 500m; sign for Mas on left. Follow road for 300m; sign on left, Mas Colom just there.

	Pilar Quintana Laduz
tel	+34 972 290802
fax	Mob. +34 627 419679
email	mascolom@telefonica.net
web	www.mascolom.com

Map 8 Entry 102

Rectoria de la Miana

17854 Sant Jaume de Llierca, Gerona

Not for those looking for standardised luxury – but poets, romantics and history buffs will love it. In the middle of a vast stand of beech and oak, at the end of three miles of rough, winding track, a former rectory in a fabulous setting. History is ever present: in the eighth century there was a fortified manor; in the 1300s a monastery was built, complete with escape tunnel and chapel. It took courage and vision for Frans to embark on the restoration – and from the ruins has emerged a beautifully simple hostelry. Flagged floors and undressed walls have been left intact; old sepia photographs are touching in their directness (a group of locals marvelling at the first radio to arrive at La Miana.) Bedrooms vary in shape and size, one is ensuite, and all are furnished with a mix of rustic pieces and new pine, perhaps a bright kilim or an ancient tiled floor. In the vaulted dining room (circa 800AD!) with its century-old pews, you'll be treated to creative Catalan cooking, and vegetables from the garden. Watch the sunset from the sitting room balcony, revel in the history and the peace.

rooms	8: 6 twins/doubles, 3 family.
price	Half-board only, €76; children under 7 half-price.
meals	Breakfast & dinner included.
closed	Rarely.
directions	Figueres N-260 Besalú & Sant Jaume de Llierca. Left into village, 2nd left into c/Industria. 6km track to house following signs. Just past Can Jou farmhouse.

	Frans Engelhard & Janine Westerlaken
tel	+34 972 190190
email	rectoriadelamiana@yahoo.com

Map 9 Entry 103

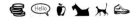

Can Jou

La Miana, 17854 Sant Jaume de Llierca, Gerona

You won't forget your arrival at Can Jou: as you drive up the three-mile track – best negotiated by 4x4 – you feel you are leaving the rest of the world behind. Round the final bend you catch sight of the farm, high on a hill, overlooking miles of forest of oak and beech – superb. No wonder Mick and Rosa were inspired to revive this old place in search of the good life: by working the land, by giving the house a family (they have four children), and by restoring the once-derelict barn. Bedrooms are basic with a mix of old and new and lively colour schemes; six come with balconies. It's a good place for a family holiday: a farm to explore, horses to ride (ideal for beginners, and with marked forest bridleways) and, close by, a beautiful spring-filled rock pool. Rosa does shiatsu and aromatherapy; Antonio has taken over the cooking reins and offers an inventive take on Catalan cuisine. Dinners are friendly affairs around one vast table. Riders and hikers, families and those looking for nature without luxury, head here.

rooms	15 twins/doubles.
price	€80. Half-board €110 p.p. Full-board €136 p.p. VAT included.
meals	Lunch and/or dinner included.
closed	Rarely.
directions	From Figueres, N-260 to Besalú & Sant Jaume de Llierca. Left into village, then 2nd left into c/Industria. On for 6km along track to house; signposted.

	Rosa Linares & Mick Peters
tel	+34 972 190263
fax	+34 972 190110
web	www.canjou.com

Map 9 Entry 104

Mas Salvanera
17850 Beuda, Gerona

In a blissfully quiet corner of the wooded Pyrenean foothills this solid, semi-fortified farmhouse has been transformed into a small luxury hotel. Your hosts still glow with enthusiasm for the project that changed their lives. The guest bedrooms, in an olive mill next to the main house, are named after signs of the zodiac and are large and elegant. Beneath old, darkening beams are colourful fabrics and antiques, many of which Ramón has restored himself, while Rocío's decorative flair is on show throughout. Bathrooms are generous and lovely. The main building has a pretty old well, vaulted ceilings, open hearths, exposed stone, an authentic country feel; the dining room is up one level, its centrepiece a fine 18-place dining table. Everyone eats together (but no meals in summer) and many of Rocío's recipes are Basque. Paella and rabbit are specialities, rioja is the wine of choice. Breakfasts are big and buffet, taken whenever you like. Outside, a peaceful walled garden and a big sculpted pool beneath the olive trees, great for families.

rooms	9 twins/doubles.
price	€120; half-board €174.
meals	Dinner €27. Restaurant 8km.
closed	1-10 January; 1-10 July; 11-19 September. No meals July-Sept.
directions	Barcelona A-7 Gerona. Exit 6 for Gerona Norte; C-150 to Banyoles & Besalú. Right on N-260 Figueres; left for Maià de Montcal. Follow signs to Beuda; 1.6km to hotel.

	Rocío Niño Ojeda & Ramón Ruscalleda
tel	+34 972 590975
fax	+34 972 590863
email	salvanera@salvanera.com
web	www.salvanera.com

Map 9 Entry 105

Mas Falgarona

17742 Avinyonet de Puigventós, Gerona

This easy, engaging couple spent years searching for Mas Falgorana and what a find it is; built from golden stone, the 11th-century farm is said to be the oldest in the region. The restoration is a deft blend of ancient and modern: light, modern colours lift the spirits as does their passion for old things. If the interior is a minimalist's dream, cypresses, olives and palms, an aquamarine pool and stunning views over the Pla d'Estany are the gilding on the lily. Dominated by beautiful arched ceilings, lounge and dining room have cool, neutral tones; good, plain fabrics blend with old flagstones and terracotta tiles. Bedrooms and bathrooms are exquisite, their walls dotted with photographs taken by a talented artist son. A small, chic and cosy room has been set aside for aperitifs; in summer you eat under the stars. Cooking, based on aromatic herbs and olive oil, is inventive and mediterranean, with vegetarians well looked after. Wines are local and delicious. After more than 30 years in the business Severino has achieved his dream, summarised by a favourite quote: "One eye sees, the other feels".

rooms	11: 8 twins/doubles, 3 suites.
price	€168-€195. Suites €240-€315. VAT included.
meals	Dinner €29-€58. Restaurant closed Monday & Tuesday.
closed	January.
directions	From Figueres N-260 for Besalú & Olot. After 5km right to Avinyonet; follow signs to Mas Falgarona.

Severino Jallas Gándara & Brigitta Schmidt
tel	+34 972 546628
fax	+34 972 547071
email	email@masfalgarona.com
web	www.masfalgarona.com

Map 9 Entry 106

Finca Paraíso Darnius

Cami del Club Nautic, 17722 Darnius, Gerona

You are an oar's throw from the water's edge – 200 metres to be exact – in an area of astonishing natural beauty. There is enough walking, riding, bathing, tennis and fishing to satisfy the most enthusiastic outdoor fanatic. Finca Paraíso is a modest place to stay, rustic and authentic, with six comfortable, reasonably priced rooms and two apartments. Beyond the cosy, whitewashed sitting room is a lovely terrace – very much a highlight – with a huge pine table and pretty lamps. And a large grassed garden, full of spring colour, with chairs and sunloungers dotted about in the shade of the cork trees. Christiane is French, and will give you a good continental breakfast in the garden or on the terrace. For other meals, you can nip across to the Club Nautic on the edge of the reservoir – or to attractive Darnius, with its bars, bakery and one good restaurant. The bedrooms are unremarkable but adequate, some with good bamboo and reed furniture. Not for Sybarites, then, but an excellent springboard for lovers of the great outdoors.

rooms	6 + 2: 6 twins/doubles. 2 self-catering apartments for 2.
price	€55. Singles €45. Apartments €450-€600 p.w. VAT included.
meals	Excellent restaurants nearby.
closed	10 December-15 January.
directions	From Figueres, N-II for La Jonquera. After 9km left to Darnius. At lights left to Club Nautic, signposted. Finca further on, on left.

	Christiane Vernet
tel	+34 972 535662
fax	+34 972 535662
email	fincaparaiso@hotmail.com
web	www.darnius.net

Map 9 Entry 107

Can Xiquet
Afores s/n, 17708 Cantallops, Gerona

Stylish modernity on ancient foundations. With the lovely white and blue fishing village of Cadaqués up the road – the favoured haunt of Salvador Dalí – one might expect nothing less. Indeed, this whole region is steeped in the art of the early 20th century. Matisse and the Fauves spent time up the coast at Collioure, and works by local artists hang here – the tradition lives on. This immaculately reconstructed building takes full advantage of its site, its huge windows keeping the sea and the hills permanently in view. In the entrance hall: gleaming tiles, chunky rafters, modern wicker. The living area has blue armchairs and logs for winter. Bedrooms are awash with natural light and neutral colours; some open onto private terraces, all are beautifully and soberly furnished. If you like space, splash out on a suite. Dine under the cork oaks by candlelight, laze by the pool on a perfect lounger, make the most of the gleaming new gym. Young and enthusiastic staff complete the picture – a super, stylish, multi lingual hotel.
A Rusticae hotel.

rooms	14 doubles & suites.
price	€160–€250.
meals	Breakfast €9. Dinner €30 à la carte.
closed	Rarely.
directions	From Figueres, N-II for La Jonquera. Before La Jonquera, right to Cantallops. Hotel signed on left after 5km. Follow track.

	Xenia Roura Roig
tel	+34 972 554455
fax	+34 972 554585
email	info@canxiquet.com
web	www.canxiquet.com

Map 9 Entry 108

El Molí

Mas Molí, 17469 Siurana d'Emporda, Gerona

Unusually for this guide, El Molí is modern – but more than earns a place in the 'special' category alongside its older Catalan neighbours. A relative B&B newcomer, it has already been awarded official recognition for excellence. The house is modelled on the traditional Gerona *mas*. Big bedrooms have rustically tiled floors, wafer-bricked and ochre-washed walls, crisp linen drapes and views across the garden to the fields and woods beyond. And there's a beautifully furnished terrace. Young María and Josep's welcome is warm, and their food exceptionally good value. Vegetables, chicken and beef come straight from the farm, accompanied by a good local red wine and an infusion of *hierbas* to finish. For breakfast there are delicious breads and homemade yogurt and jams. This would be a great place in which to break the journey travelling north or south, and María, who speaks excellent English, will help you plan your trips. Choose between the Roman ruins at Empuries, the pretty fishing village of Cadaqués, the Dalí Museum at Figueres or the beach at San Pere Pescador, a 10-minute drive.

rooms	6 + 1: 5 twins/doubles, 1 suite. 1 apartment for 2-3.
price	€60–€75. Suite €72. Apartment €60–70. VAT included.
meals	Dinner €12. VAT included.
closed	1 week in January.
directions	AP-7 exit 4 for Figueres on N-II. After 3km, right on C-31 Vilamalla; there follow signs for Siurana & then for hotel.

	Maria Sanchís Pages
tel	+34 972 525139
fax	+34 972 525139
email	casaelmoli@teleline.es
web	www.elmolidesiurana.com

Map 9 Entry 109

Can Navata

Baseia, 17469 Siurana d'Empordà, Gerona

Amparo has lived among this small farming community all her life, and has named her 19th-century farmhouse after her father's native village. Enter through a shady porch a warren of living areas, darkish but cool, arched and decorated in colourful regional style. Bedrooms are furnished with family heirlooms and kitschy touches, four with a seasonal theme; the 'summer' room is light and airy with an antique embroidered sheet for a curtain, a warm red and yellow colour scheme and French windows that open to the upstairs terrace. Bathrooms are functional. Winter suppers are served at a long table in the vaulted basement, and dishes are hearty. Families can truly unwind: there's a playroom on the ground floor, swings and boules in the garden, and farm animals to meet. Amparo has also provided those in need of peace, a quiet refuge with a room full of books. Ever obliging, she will send you details of places to visit, make bookings and prepare cycling and walking routes. Can Navata and its delightful owner are as Catalan as it's possible to be – full of *amistat* (Catalan for friendship).

rooms	6 + 1: 6 twins/doubles. 1 self-catering apartment for 6.
price	€60–€70. Apt €120–€130 (min. stay 3 nights).
meals	Dinner €13, with wine (winter only), on request.
closed	Rarely.
directions	From Figueres N-II then GI-31 (C-252) for L'Escala. After 4km right for Siurana. On left as you enter Baseia.

	Amparo Pagés
tel	+34 972 525174
fax	+34 972 525756
email	info@cannavata.com
web	www.cannavata.com

Map 9 Entry 110

Hostal Empuries

Platja Portitxol s/n, Apartado Correos 174, 17130 L'Escala, Gerona

You couldn't be closer to the beach. A hundred years ago, this was a snack bar;
then a vast Roman necropolis was discovered in L'Escala. Archaeologists flocked
and rooms were added to accommodate them. Later, in the 40s and 60s, the place
acquired the reputation of a love nest, and its slow decline began. No longer!
Since Cinta and Guillermo stepped in two years ago, its fortunes have been
transformed. Today Hostal Empuries is a fascinating, minimalist beachside hotel,
with a stylishness all of its own. Don't be disappointed by the approach; once
you're on that terrace overlooking the sands everything looks wonderful. The
atmosphere is friendly, relaxed and charmingly assured; the walls are pale and the
décor subtle, with dashing floor tiles and comfortable sofas and chairs dressed in
crisp white linen. There's a woodburning stove in the big sitting room overlooking
the sea, and, next door, an enticing reading room. Cinta and Guillermo, their two
young children and their delightful staff make you feel instantly at home. The food
is local, unpretentious and very good.

rooms	38: 27 twins/doubles, 10 family, 1 suite.
price	€84–€125. Singles €67–€100. Suite €97–€121.
meals	Breakfast €8. Half-board €22.
closed	Rarely.
directions	From Barcelona on A-7; exit 5 for L'Escala. At L'Escala follow signs for Ruinas de Empuries. Hostal on right on beach; car park.

Cinta Fernández Camps

tel	+34 972 770207
fax	+34 972 770207
email	info@hostalempuries.com
web	www.hostalempuries.com

Map 9 Entry 111

Can Fabrica

17845 Santa Llogaia del Terri, Gerona

On top of a gentle hill sits this 17th-century *masía* surrounded by fields, woods and Pyrenean views. Ramón is an engineer, Marta a designer, and their carefully restored farmhouse is now a characterful holiday home – the perfect place for a family reunion. Bedrooms are smallish, nicely furnished with old pieces and soft materials that set off the bare stone walls. The kitchen/dining room is beautifully equipped, the sitting room cosy with woodburning stove (there's central heating, too), and there's a swimming pool in the garden. Your hosts have environmentalist leanings, and by planting trees and farming their 17 acres of land have created a blissful corner of peace from which to explore the villages and romanesque churches of the region. They'll tell you all you need to know about the many walks and cycling routes in the area. A lovely place with an exceptionally kind, vivacious hostess; without question, one of our favourite places to stay in Spain. Be sure to try Marta's delicious sauces and jams. And if you are here in summer, do visit the Dalí museum – by night! *Minimum stay two nights.*

rooms	House for 8.
price	€206-€216; €1,030-€1,236 p.w.
meals	Self-catering.
closed	4 weeks-February.
directions	AP-7, exit 6; C-66 for Banyoles. After 8km bear right for Cornellà del Terri then at r'bout towards Medinya. After 2.5km left to Santa Llogaia; through village, 400m of track to house on left.

	Marta Casanovas Bohigas
tel	+34 972 594629
fax	+34 972 594629
email	info@canfabrica.com
web	www.canfabrica.com

Map 9 Entry 112

Mas Crisaran

c/Proccessó 2, Fonolleres, 17133 Parlavá, Gerona

Two bronze, Indian horsemen hint that this 15th-century country mansion, tucked among the villages inland from the coast, might be grand. But they do not prepare you for the lavish and exotic interiors. Indian, African and Panamanian art and antiques are set against a Spanish colonial background, reflecting Cristina's passion for Afro-Asian cultures. Batik hangings, handmade quilts and modern Spanish art flow over whitewashed walls; even the lift doors have frescos. The barrel-vaulted drawing room is striking with its red carpet, grand piano and deep leather sofas; the light-filled dining room overlooking the gardens feels colonial. Food is super-fresh and imaginatively prepared. Bedrooms have beamed ceilings, tiled floors and rich fabrics, are immodestly large and quixotically furnished. Book into Ajanta, whose arched bay windows lead to a private stone terrace. Or blow the budget and go for the glorious Portobelo suite. Arantxa and Cristina are friendly and characterful hosts; the place pure indulgence. Beaches, golf and riding beckon – but you may find it impossible to leave.

rooms	9: 8 twins/doubles, 1 suite.
price	€240-€270.
meals	Dinner €35.
closed	January-February.
directions	AP-7 to Gerona (Girona); exit 6 for Palamós & on C-66. At km18 marker left for Pals & Torroellei. Hotel 1km past Parlavá, on right.

	Arantxa García
tel	+34 972 769000
fax	+34 972 769219
email	agrolodge@ctv.es
web	www.mascrisaran.com

Map 9 Entry 113

Aigua Blava
Platja de Fornells, 17255 Begur, Gerona

It's something of an institution in Catalonia, this large hotel – and, thanks to exceptional management and clever design, manages to feel as intimate and as welcoming as the best B&B. The bedrooms are individually decorated and ranged on several terraced wings that look out across gardens to a delicious hidden cove; so rugged a coastline would be hard to spoil. Run by the same family, nourished by the same chef, tended by the same gardener for 40 years, the hotel has a long history of personal attention. Señor Gispert genuinely cares for – and remembers – every one of his guests; customer loyalty is strong. Breathe in deeply the sweet-smelling pinewoods, bask beside the pool, savour lobster straight from the cove; views from the immaculately dressed tables sail across the sparkling waters. So many places to relax: the pub-like bar, the comfortable lobby, the trellised terrace, the parasoled garden, the beach bar just below. The village is one of the prettiest on the Costa Brava, and you are close to the medieval towns of Pals and Palafrugell. This is Spain at its best – light-years from Benidorm.

rooms	85+ 10: 77 twins/doubles, 5 singles, 3 suites. 10 apartments for up to 6.
price	€133-€214. Singles €99-€130. Suites €174-€269. VAT included.
meals	Breakfast €13.90. Lunch/dinner €36 menu. VAT included.
closed	November-February.
directions	From Gerona C-255 to Palafrugell. From here, GE-650 to Begur. Signed on entry to village.

Josep María de Vehí Falgás
tel	+34 972 622058
fax	+34 972 622112
email	hotelaiguablava@aiguablava.com
web	www.aiguablava.com

Map 9 Entry 114

Hotel Sant Roc

Plaça Atlàntic 2, 17210 Calella de Palafrugell, Gerona

The Costa Brava remains a stunning stretch of coastline and this quiet little hotel could restore your faith in seaside holidays in Spain. It's a family affair – not only family-run but a place where guests are treated like old friends. Many return. The setting is marvellous: a perch at the edge of a cliff, surrounded by pine, olive and cypress, the sea ever present. Its colours change with every hour, and from the dining room and large canopied terrace are delightful views across the bay: bobbing boats, hillsides and and the village beyond. The best rooms have seaward terraces but we like them all, so light and pretty with their hand-painted headboards and watercolours painted by an artist friend. Bathrooms are new. With Franco-Catalan owners you can expect something special from the kitchen; fish is a speciality and the fairly-priced wines are good. A path from the hotel winds down to the beach and there are longer walks around the bay. Young Bertrand and Teresa are humorous and charming, even in high season: their generosity permeates this exceptional, family-friendly hotel.

rooms	47: 44 doubles, 3 suites.
price	Half-board only, €130–€240. Suites €232–€300.
meals	Breakfast €9.90. Lunch/dinner €20–€30.
closed	Early December–mid-March.
directions	From Barcelona A-7 north to exit 6 (Girona Norte); follow signs for La Bisbal via Palamos then on to Palafrugell; from here to Calella; hotel signposted.

	Teresa Boix & Bertrand Hallé
tel	+34 972 614250
fax	+34 972 614068
email	info@santroc.com
web	www.santroc.com

Map 9 Entry 115

Xalet La Coromina

Ctra. de Vic 4, 17406 Viladraú, Gerona

Viladraú is an elegant little town close to the stunning Natural Park. Woodlands are grandiose, water flows and falls, rare plants flourish and the walking is superb. This building dates from the 1900s when wealthy Catalans first started to build summer retreats away from sticky Barcelona. The building, which looks more French than Spanish, has kept its elegant exterior but has been thoroughly modernised inside. The old-modern mix is full of personality, the smartly sofa-ed sitting room has its original fireplace, and each bedroom combines English and French fabrics with turn-of-the-century antiques. Rooms vary in size (ask for a larger one), bathrooms are excellent, views are stupendous. And the car rally memorabilia? Gloria's husband, Antonio Zanini, was one of Spain's most successful drivers. The Coromina prides itself on its food too, winning a Michelin star in its very first year. Come for the very best of local, seasonal produce – such as delicious mushroom dishes made with local *setas* when they spring up after the rain. Outside are gentle gardens and a pretty pool. *A Rusticae hotel.*

rooms	8 twins/doubles.
price	€94–€120. Singles €76–€80. Weekends and bank holidays, half-board only.
meals	Breakfast €8. Lunch/dinner €18 menu, €25–€35 à la carte.
closed	26 January–20 February.
directions	From Girona C-25. Exit km202, then GI-543 to Viladraú. In village towards Vic: hotel on right after 50m.

	Gloria Rabat Blancafort
tel	+34 938 849264
fax	+34 938 848160
email	xaletcoromina@xaletcoromina.com
web	www.xaletcoromina.com

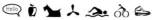

Map 8 Entry 116

Mas Vilarmau

Ctra. de Sant Marçal s/n, 17406 Viladraú, Gerona

Delightfully idiosyncratic. That just about sums up Pep and Pilar's approach to interior design. In just two years, they've added verve and fun to a secluded 12th-to-18th-century farmhouse that was already crammed with character. Each bedroom has a theme: *mimbré* means 'rushes' so, if this is your room, you'll find a rush canopy over the bed, a wicker-framed mirror and chair, a bouquet of rushes in the bathroom… you get the idea. The beds are blissful, but comfort and cosiness spread right through the house: on each floor is a sitting area with old wooden beams and planked floors, stone walls and an open fire. "Park your car and forget it for your whole stay", says Pep. He's right, so take his advice. You're on the edge of the mountainous Montseny nature reserve, a rambler's paradise, yours to discover – if you can drag yourself away from your hammock in the garden. Or the swimming pool, the chickens and the ducks, the game of ping-pong, the fresh seasonal dishes… or that great bottle of red that Pep has just brought up from the cellar. *Two nights minimum stay at weekends.*

rooms	8 twins/doubles/family.
price	Half-board €60 p.p.; full-board €70 p.p. VAT included.
meals	Half- or full-board only.
closed	Never.
directions	From Viladraú road to Cubells. Right after 5km & on for about 1km until wooden sign on left. Follow lane for 1.5km to hotel.

	Pep Bochaca & Pilar Masmuntal
tel	+34 659 446613
email	info@masvilarmau.com
web	www.masvilarmau.com

Map 8 Entry 117

El Jufré

08511 Tavertet-Osona, Barcelona

The hilltop villages of this part of Catalonia rival those of Provence. And the drive up to Tavertet, past craggy limestone outcrops and stands of forest, is an adventure in itself. El Jufré is perched over a craggy ledge and the views are superb: look out over the plain below and be captivated. Wonderful to stay with Josep and sweet Lourdes and their two children in this very old house; rebuilt in the 1600s, some parts date back as far as 1100, and Lourde's family have been in residence for over 800 years! Bedrooms are simple and attractive, marrying together ancient beams and exposed stones with new beds, baths and lighting. We liked best the big room with the iron bedstead and the mountain-drop view. Linger later on the terrace over an aperitif, distant cowbells signalling the end of the day. The food is another reason to come: good, simple dishes make full use of their own organic beef, pork and vegetables. At breakfast there's milk from the cows. El Jufré is for lovers of high places and tranquillity (full-time residents in the village number 40), and walkers will be in heaven.

rooms	8 twins/doubles.
price	Half-board only, €80. VAT included.
meals	Dinner included.
closed	22 December-7 January; 1-15 September.
directions	From Vic C-153 for Olot & Roda de Ter to L'Esquirol & Santa María Corco. Here, right to Tavertet. House on left on entering village.

	Josep Roquer & Lourdes Rovira
tel	+34 938 565167
fax	+34 938 565167

Map 8 Entry 118

Hotel Torre Marti

c/Ramón Llull 11, 08504 Sant Julia de Vilatorta, Barcelona

Wow! This boutique hotel, opened last year by father Pere and son Roger, is, quite simply, stunning. You may be forgiven for thinking you'd pulled up to a Tuscan villa – the solidity and the squareness, the porticoed first floor, the rich, red exterior. Enter a world of more reds – and ochres, pistachios and Moroccan blues. A classy, chic backdrop for flamboyant furnishings: gilt mirrors, twinkly chandeliers, Asian and modern art (including Pere originals), old theatre seats for dining on, a barber's chair on the landing – it's eclectic in the nicest possible way. Be soothed by soft classical music and incense as you float down for dinner – Pere's sublime cooking lures locals, always a good sign. Big windows allow views onto the terrace and lawn with its fountained pond. Bedrooms, some in the main house, some with balconies, the rest in the old guards' house next door, are surprising, original and come with sparkling bathrooms. And there's more: the vivid blue library with its traditional leather chairs, the open fires, the warm and charming staff… what a treat. *A Rusticae hotel.*

rooms	8: 5 twins/doubles, 2 singles, 1 suite.
price	€110-€135. Singles €88-€110. Suite €215.
meals	Lunch/dinner €30.
closed	Rarely.
directions	From N-II exit for Cervera on C-25. After Vic follow signs to Sant Julia de V. From Barcelona on C-17 towards Vic, follow signs to Sant Julia de V.

	Roger Morral Palacín
tel	+34 938 888372
fax	+34 93 8888374
email	hoteltorremarti@yahoo.es
web	www.hoteltorremarti.com

Map 8 Entry 119

La Morera

08553 El Brull, Barcelona

If you get the urge to head for the hills, head here. This is precisely what these relaxed young Catalan owners did some years ago, when they found a 17th-century *masía* in inspiring surroundings. The laid-back atmosphere is palpable the minute you step into the walled courtyard and meet the dogs dozing in the sun. (And there are donkeys and cows in the fields.) In the cosy, shambolic dining room is a magnificent Catalan fireplace and a communal dining table; this takes pride of place in winter when the aromas of home-reared meats mix with lively conversation, strains of Catalan rock and robust Priorat wines. The sitting room is furnished with a beguiling mix of old furniture, sofas and ancient chandeliers; restoration is ongoing, so some unvarnished floors and exposed plasterwork may be expected. Bedrooms are split-level with old, carved beds on the mezzanine (stairs are steepish) and antique mirrors. Shower rooms are small but fine. Breakfast are simple and delicious: charcuterie, cheese, homemade jam — try the apple, apricot and banana. Easy for families.

rooms	8 twins/doubles.
price	Half-board €76-€114. Full-board €90-€145. VAT included.
meals	Lunch and/or dinner included.
closed	Rarely.
directions	From French border, A7 to Girona; west on Eix Transversal. Exit Viladraú on to Seva, then signs for El Brull. Just past village at km30.5 marker, house signed on right (easily missed); 2km track.

Ramón Casamitjana, Sergi Peytibi & Juan Carlos Cano

tel	+34 93 8840477
email	lamorera@tiscali.es
web	www.lamorera.net

Map 8 Entry 120

Masía El Folló

Ctra. C-17 km36, 08593 Tagamanent, Barcelona

So unexpected, this mountain-top farmstead one hour from Barcelona. A Catalan *casa pairal* (father's house), it has been masterfully restored by Merce and Jaume. Rustic bedrooms have huge charm, their rough stone or pine-clad walls invigorated by bold colours and a fruit and flower motif throughout. Hues range from the vibrant red of the Strawberry Room to the gentler tones of Mallow. Lighting is subdued and complements the beamed ceilings, the muslin curtains, the natural fabrics, and there are bunkbeds for kids. Bathrooms have free-standing tubs and oodles of towels; two have astonishing views. Reminders of a rural past are never far away: one of the dining rooms, dominated by a long table, is in the old stable. A feeling of abundance and well-being abounds, and Mercè is proud of her cooking: robust, organic, vegetarian (and she cooks for meat-eaters too). Don't miss out on the amazing breads – granary, onion, courgette, rye – or the goat's cheese with quince jelly. Dogs, cats, chickens, views; it's a sociable place, great for children. *Pre-dinner cookery classes held twice-weekly.*

rooms	8 twins/doubles.
price	€60. Singles €80.
meals	Breakfast €10. Lunch/dinner €25.
closed	Rarely.
directions	From north A-7 for Barcelona, exit 14; C-17 for Vic. At km36 (opp. petrol station) right then ahead at r'bout. Follow signs for 2km to El Folló.

	Merce Brunés & Jaume Villanueva
tel	+34 938 429116
fax	+34 938 429116
web	www.elfollo.com

Map 8 Entry 121

Can Rosich

Apartado de Correos 275, 08398 Santa Susanna, Barcelona

Handy for Barcelona, close to the beach, yet deep in 20 hectares of bucolic loveliness. This *masía* is more than two centuries old but has been virtually rebuilt. Bedrooms, named after the birds and animals of the region, are a good size and large enough to take a third bed. Beds may be antique but mattresses are new, and you'll find a be-ribboned, neatly-ironed bundle of towels on your duvet – a typical touch from a gracious hostess. To one side of the large hallway is the white-walled dining room, its six tables decked in bright checks. Cooking is wholesome, delicious and great value when you consider that the price includes good local wine. Among Montserrat's specialities are rabbit, pork from the farm and *asado de payés*, a thick stew with three different meats, plums and pine nuts (order this one in advance!). Breakfast, too, is hearty: cheese and charcuterie, fruits, fresh juice. You are a five-minute walk to the station and trains that get you to Barcelona in an hour. A favourite with our readers. *Multi-lingual hosts.*

rooms	6 twins/doubles.
price	€50–€55.
meals	Breakfast €7. Dinner with wine €15.
closed	November.
directions	From AP-7, exit 9 Maçanet; N-II for Barcelona to Santa Susanna; here, right at 1st r'bout for 'nucleo urbano'; signs for 2km to Can Rosich.

	Montserrat Boter Fors
tel	+34 93 7678473
fax	+34 937 678473
email	canrosich@canrosich.com
web	www.canrosich.com

Map 9 Entry 122

Hotel Masferrer

08474 Gualba, Barcelona

It takes boldness and sensitivity to turn a grand Catalan masía into a boutique hotel without losing its charm. Montserrat and her husband spent two years restoring Masferrer, in the little town of Gualba on the edge of the Parque Natural, and have achieved a beguilingly simple blend of ancient and modern. Rustic oak beams and exposed stones have been invigorated with earthy and pastel coloured walls and designer lighting. Elegant antiques mix with modern sofas. Bedrooms are pared down but not chilly: a cream rug on polished tiles, muslin curtains at a stone window. Bathrooms are a stunning mixture of designer-sleek and rough-cast. Choose the split-level suite for huge windows onto a private terrace. The dining room is breezily elegant with white linen and simple vases of flowers. Montserrat has gained a reputation for her *cocina temporada*, using produce from the garden whenever possible. In several acres of woodland and garden – with a pool – it's hard to believe the coast is 15 minutes away and Barcelona half an hour. Country peace without the isolation. *A Rusticae hotel.*

rooms	11: 9 twins/doubles, 2 suites.
price	€105. Singles €90. Suites €132–€146.
meals	Breakfast €9. Lunch/dinner €25.
closed	Rarely.
directions	From Barcelona AP-7 to Gerona; exit 11 onto C-35 to Hostalric; left at r'bout to Gualba. Hotel signposted on right after 200m.

	Montserrat Guinovart
tel	+34 93 8487705
fax	+34 93 8487084
email	hm@hotelmasferrer.com
web	www.hotelmasferrer.com

Map 9 Entry 123

El Trapiche

Can Vidal, Els Casots, 08739 Subirats, Barcelona

Imagine waking from a deep sleep to see the crags of Montserrat against a blushing dawn – and vineyards all around. It's not hard to see what drew this couple to the charming, 400-year-old *masía*. Michael is front of house, and very good cook. Book in for dinner and you'll eat with the family; the focus here is wonderfully relaxed and your hosts are generous with the wine. Bedrooms vary from big to huge; two rooms have their own sitting areas and the Pink Room has a terrace overlooking the valley and the mountains. All have simple pine furniture, warm walls, darkened beams, wooden floors, and central heating for the colder months. If you are interested in wine, visit the Codorniu cellars – this is cava country and they're just down the road – or Bodegas Torres a few miles on, past Vilafranca, where there is also an interesting wine museum. There are a number of pleasant strolls nearby and the Johnstons' two dogs will be only too happy to accompany you. Dreamy countryside – yet a 40-minute train ride from Barcelona; friendly Michael and Marcela will even drive you to the station.

rooms	4 twins/doubles.
price	€95–€110.
meals	Dinner €35 set menu.
closed	Christmas & New Year.
directions	From AP-7 exit 27 Sant Sadurni. On leaving m'way towards Barcelona & Ordal on N-340. On for 3km to Els Casots; 600m beyond hamlet, 1st track on left.

	Marcela & Michael Johnston
tel	+34 93 7431469
fax	+34 93 7431469
email	michael.johnston@bmlisp.com

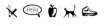

Map 8 Entry 124

Cal Mestre

c/Torre Romana 2-4, 08793 Les Gunyoles d'Avinyonet, Barcelona

Breakfast overlooking the rugged outline of Mount Montserrat, then toss up whether to spend the day on the beaches or lapping up Barcelona's riches: this very old village house is within easy reach of both. Marion and Martin (multi-lingual Dutch) lovingly restored the house, smoothly blending old with new to create sleek, understatedly stylish rooms. Polished wooden floors, timber beams and exposed stonework mix with oversize lampshades, abstract art and sea-blue or white bedcovers. Modern, clean-lined furniture stands next to handsome originals, perhaps a grandfather clock or an old school desk. Choose Penedès for its free-standing bath or Horse Stable for its shuttered doors to the village street – perfect for walkers with dogs. Spend the day exploring Roman Tarragona, hiking in Garraf Nature Park or wine-tasting in the Penedès vineyards. Or relax with a book from Marian and Martin's library in the terraced gardens around the house, Spanish guitar music drifting from inside. Suppers are served around the communal dining table, and your hosts are gentle, friendly and relaxing.

rooms	5 twins/doubles.
price	€80–€105.
meals	Lunch/dinner €14.
closed	November.
directions	From Barcelona N-340 to Vilafranca. At Avinyonet follow signs to Olessa-Gavá-Beguer. After 100m right; hotel is yellow house near church.

	Marian & Martin Badoux
tel	+34 938 970761
email	info@cal-mestre.com
web	www.cal-mestre.com

Map 8 Entry 125

Hotel Santa María

Passeig de la Ribera 52, 08870 Sitges, Barcelona

Sitges has been fashionable among wealthier Catalans for years. The crowd is international now, but the place has kept its intimate feel and life still centres on the promenade and beach. At the heart of it all: the Santa María. It is a pretty building, its white façade enhanced by apricot awnings, the largest one spanning the entire front terrace. It could be a smart British seaside hotel, only the food is better and cheaper; there's a glistening array of fresh seafood and a modern open kitchen. The sea almost laps to the table and everything ticks over beautifully – thanks to the indefatigable Señora Ute, who manages to switch between half a dozen languages at any given time. Some bedrooms have beautiful shuttered balconies and a view across the palm trees to the bay; all are light and well furnished, some with modern furniture, others with floor tiles and traditional pieces. There are prints on the walls and vases of fresh flowers. For Sitges it's well priced – but you must book ahead in season; if there's no room here, there may be space in the sister hotel, La Nina.

rooms	57: 54 twins/doubles, 3 family rooms.
price	€80-€108. Singles €68-€91. Family rooms €112-€130.
meals	Lunch/dinner €12, €25 à la carte.
closed	20 December-1 February.
directions	From Barcelona, A-16 through Tuneles de Garaf. 2nd exit for Sitges centre, follow signs to Hotel Calipolis. Hotel on sea front; car park.

Antonio Arcas Sánchez
tel   +34 938 940999
fax   +34 938 947871
email   info@lasantamaria.com
web   www.lasantamaria.com

Map 8 Entry 126

Photo Michael Busselle

castilla-leon, castilla-la manche, madrid

El Tiempo Recobrado

Avda. de Villanueva 33, 24550 Villamartín de la Abadía, León

What used to be two modest workers' houses is now an attractive and astonishingly good-value place to stay. The hotel, a gentle mix of rough stone, apricot plaster and gleaming slate roofs, has only been open for a year but is already proving a draw, as is its restaurant. What a delight! The food is superb, from the starter of leeks with Cantabrian anchovies to the delectable homemade puddings. The wine list, too, is worth going out of your way for: this region is famous for its fine Bierzo wines. The buildings have been well and stylishly renovated, the big, airy bedrooms are simple and natural – exposed stone, polished wooden floors, chestnut beams, wrought-iron bedheads – and everything is of the highest quality. It's quiet, too, the only sound that of the river pulsing past. This is a relatively unknown part of Spain yet there is so much to see and do. The village is full of interesting and ancient houses, and a good road network gives easy access to a whole host of places, including the Médulas, the church at Peñ Alba de Santiago and the thatched houses of Campo de Agua.

rooms	9: 5 twins/doubles, 4 suites.
price	€60-€65. Suites €70-€75. VAT included.
meals	Lunch/dinner €15.
closed	7-31 January.
directions	From León A-6 for Coruña. After Ponferrada exit at km399 for Villamartín. Hotel signposted at village entrance.

	Juan Jóse Alonso
tel	+34 987 562422
fax	+34 987 562422
email	eltiempo@eltiemporecobrado.com
web	www.eltiemporecobrado.com

Map 2 Entry 127

Guts Muths

c/Matanza s/n, Barrio de Abajo, 24732 Santiago Millas, León

This and other villages in the area drew their wealth from the transport of merchandise by horse and cart throughout Spain. The coming of the railways put an end to all that, but what remains are some grand old village houses of which Guts Muths is a fine example. Enter through the imposing arch to find yourself in a large gravelled courtyard, dotted with shrubs and a couple of palms. The interior is bohemian and bold, cosy and warm; these effusive hosts have created an easy feel. Expect exposed stone and heavy beams, dried and fresh flowers, potted plants and pictures, sofas round a rustic, well-used hearth. The dining room comes with a stocked bodega and an old bread oven – a proper backdrop for Mari Paz's delicious cooking and homemade liqueurs. Bedrooms could be better soundproofed, but new pine beds are comfortable and murals and modern art add an individual touch. Sjoerd is great fun, and interested in local history and folklore. He may even be persuaded to take you out to explore the gorges on foot or bike... or attached to the end of a rope. *A Rusticae hotel.*

rooms	8 twins/doubles.
price	€67.
meals	Breakfast €8. Dinner €17.
closed	Rarely.
directions	From Astorga, LE-133 for Destriana. 1km before S. Millas left at sign Barrio de Abajo. Into village past playground. Signposted to left past triangle in centre; 1st left. 2nd house, 2nd on left.

	Sjoerd Hers & Mari Paz Martínez
tel	+34 987 691123
fax	+34 987 691123
web	www.gutsmuths.com

Map 3 Entry 128

Posada del Marqués
Plaza Mayor 4, 24270 Carrizo de la Ribera, León

There are few places to stay in Spain as special as this old pilgrim's hospital, originally part of the monastery next door. Pass through the fine portal to a pebbled cloister and beautiful, mature gardens with a gurgling brook, a big old yew and walnut trees: with its high walls and rambling roses it may remind you of an English rectory garden. Sombre but charming bedrooms are set around a gallery on the first floor and are filled with family heirlooms: Portuguese canopied beds, oil paintings, old lamps and dressers. One has a terrace over the cloisters for summer, there are big old radiators for the winter months, and spotless marble bathrooms. The sitting and games rooms downstairs are similarly furnished – antique Castillian doors, carved chests, tapestries, comfy armchairs and an English sofa in front of the hearth. At dinner there's delicious regional food from a short menu (roast leg of pork, trout with red peppers) washed down with robust wines. Afterwards, a post-prandial game of snooker. Kind and erudite hosts in the most peaceful and beguiling of settings. *Balloon flights available.*

rooms	11 twins/doubles.
price	€69-€92. VAT included.
meals	Dinner €14. VAT included. Book ahead.
closed	10 January-end February.
directions	A-12 (León-Astorga) exit 23 to Hospital de Orbigo; cross old N-120 for La Madalena on LE-420; Carrizo de la Ribera on km16. In Carrizo, follow wall surrounding Monastery; left into Plaza Mayor; Posada though archway.

	Carlos Velázquez-Duro
tel	+34 987 357171
fax	+34 987 358101
email	info@posadadelmarques.com
web	www.posadadelmarques.com

Map 3 Entry 129

Posada Regia
c/Regidores 9-11, 24003 León

The stained-glass windows of the cathedral are reason enough to come to this historic and lively town. And the best place to stay, in our view, is the Posada Regia, plumb in the centre of the medieval quarter – a bright star in the firmament of newly-opened hotels in Spain. The building first saw the light in 1370 and the dining room incorporates part of an even older (Roman) wall. The warm ochre and beamed reception strikes a welcoming note as you arrive and the staff could not be nicer. A fine old staircase leads to the bedrooms which are among the cosiest and most delightful in this book. Be welcomed by soothing colours, bright kilims, shining planked floors, carved bedheads, brightly painted radiators, and snazzy bathrooms with all the extras, from bathrobes to embroidered towels. Avoid the attic rooms in summer, and expect some noise at night. The hotel's restaurant, La Bodega Regia, which was founded by Marcos's grandfather and predates the hotel by some 50 years, is one of Léon's most renowned. Make room for the chocolate and chestnut tart! *Pets by arrangement*.

rooms	37: 31 twins/doubles, 6 singles.
price	€90. Singles €55.
meals	Lunch €18 set menu; €36 à la carte. Dinner €36 à la carte. Restaurant closed 15-31 January & 1-15 December.
closed	Rarely.
directions	Hotel in town centre 150m from Cathedral. Park in Parking San Marcelo on Plaza de Santo Domingo, then 100m walk to hotel.

	Verónica Martínez Díez
tel	+34 987 213173
fax	+34 987 213031
email	marquitos@regialeon.com
web	www.regialeon.com

Map 3 Entry 130

Posada de la Casa del Abad de Ampudía

Pza. Francisco Martín Gromaz 12, 34160 Ampudía, Palencia

The impressive church of San Miguel summons you to Ampudía, a peaceful village whose wooden colonnaded streets date from the 1600s. In the abbot's house on the main square, old timbers and stones combine with modern comforts and colours to create this thoroughly hedonistic hideaway. Enter the stately porch to a vast, vaulted, orange-hued hallway, where beams are ancient and décor modern. Colour-washed pinks and blues mix with columns, arches, cornices and adobe-bricks to create an informal and hospitable mood. The central patio, a verdant spot, is a great place for a pre-dinner aperitif. And you'll eat well, in the rustically atmospheric dining room stuffed with red-clad tables. The menu is imaginative, the food delicious, the wines good Spanish. There's also an intimate little bar, with its own entrance and garden. Bedrooms are havens of luxury, each a surprise: earthy colours, sumptuous beds, stainless steel basins, the internet (the hotel attracts a business clientele). All this and a domed, solar-heated swimming pool, a sauna, a gym, a tennis court and delightful staff. *A Rusticae hotel.*

rooms	16: 9 twins/doubles, 7 suites.
price	€105–€124. Suites €144–€170.
meals	Breakfast €12. Lunch/dinner €30–€35 set menu.
closed	Rarely.
directions	Burgos A-62 Valladolid. 12km south of Palencia, right at km92 to Dueñas. Here, right for Ampudía; bear left at petrol station on P-943 & follow wooden columns to square with willow. Posada on left.

	Begoña Mínguez
tel	+34 979 768008
fax	+34 979 768300
email	hotel@casadelabad.com
web	www.casadelabad.com

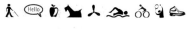

Map 4 Entry 131

Casa Zalama

c/La Fuente s/n, 09569 San Pelayo de Montija, Burgos

Not to be missed! In this little known area of northern Spain, the Casa Zalama is a place in which to linger. Maria and Graeme uprooted from Brighton in search of a guesthouse in Spain, and found this farming village purely by chance. Maria's attractive furnishings in the carefully converted house are matched by Graeme's green fingers – he is an ex-landscape gardener. Beamed bedrooms have comfortable double beds and lovely earthy colours; those with balconies get stunning views of the Merindad hills. Dinners, served in the chunky-raftered dining room, formerly the stables, are country Spanish and delicious: local sausage, home-grown veg, superb pear tart. And the garden… you and the hens may wander at your leisure, and into the countryside beyond. Next to the house is a studio where Graeme and Maria run workshops; join them if you're feeling creative, or use the workspace to do your own thing. Your hosts will give you plenty of advice about where to go and what to do, and the birdwatching is brilliant. A grand little place, and only an hour from Bilbao and Santander.

rooms	6: 5 twins/doubles, 1 suite.
price	€50. Suite €70. VAT included.
meals	Breakfast €5. Dinner €15 set menu. VAT included.
closed	Rarely.
directions	From E-70 for Bilbao, exit km173 for Colindres. N-629 up over Alto de los Tornos. At Aguera, left for San Pelayo. Past church, on left.

	Maria Cruz Totorika
tel	+34 947 565961
fax	+34 947 565961
email	info@casazalama.com
web	www.casazalama.com

Map 5 Entry 132

El Prado Mayor

Quintanilla del Rebollar 53, 09568 Merindad de Sotoscueva, Burgos

The impressive façade of the 16th-century Prado Mayor is concealed behind a solid arched gateway. Via a small garden with a columned terrace – perfect for summer breakfasts – you enter a warm family home. The cream-coloured stone gives the house a sheltered and peaceful air and the stylish, understated décor is in perfect harmony with the architecture. Wooden-floored bedrooms are rustic and inviting: expect period antiques, rocking chairs, colourful blankets, dried flowers, pretty country cabinets under basins, ornate framed mirrors. All have their own shower rooms. Breakfast is a must: your gentle hosts, who live on the upper floor, serve homemade cakes, biscuits, local bread baked in a wood oven, organic milk. Lunch and dinner are hearty affairs with home-grown vegetables and good local meats; the rabbit is excellent. The lush landscape is one of Spain's best-kept secrets, breathing culture and history – and the Ojo Guareña cave system, from where you can trace humanity's religious expression from Paleolithic times, is one of the biggest in the world. *Unsuitable for families with young children.*

rooms	8: 6 twins/doubles, 2 suites.
price	€48–€54. Singles €36–€42. Suite €65–€70.
meals	Breakfast €5. Dinner €15. Packed lunches available.
closed	Rarely.
directions	Burgos N-623 Santander. At Cilleruelo de Bezana C-6318 Bilbao. Village 7km before E. de los Monteros. Left at entrance of village; on for 500m to fountain. 50m to hotel, right at no. 52.

	Fernando Valenciano & Olga Fernández
tel	+34 947 138689
fax	+34 947 138689
email	info@pradomayor.com
web	www.pradomayor.com

Map 4 Entry 133

Casa La Engaña

Ctra. de la Estación 5, 09574 Pedrosa de Valdeporres, Burgos

While searching for Tiggy, Duncan and his Spanish partner, Mila, fell in love with this handsome village house – and bought it. (The cat turned up nine months later.) They then spent two and a half years restoring the early 20th-century manor, keeping the history and adding, subtly, 21st-century comforts. Oak beams and pillars, exposed stone, wooden floorboards and polished terracotta work their magic to create a warm, relaxing, sophisticated place to stay. Bedrooms could not be simpler – pale-washed walls, wrought-iron bedsteads, a bentwood chair, a row of hooks for your clothes. (The bigger rooms have wardrobes.) A colourful bedspread or abstract print adds a homely touch. Bathrooms are classic, white, sparkling. But the most alluring feature is the glass-and wood-veranda that spans the width of the house – a gorgeous sun trap. Hire a bike, discover birds, vultures, deer, wild boar – all can be spotted nearby – or learn Spanish; Duncan and Mila are foreign language teachers. Young, enthusiastic, caring, they are great hosts – and much of the food is organic.

rooms	6 twins/doubles.
price	€48–€54. Singles €38–€42.
meals	Breakfast €4.50. Dinner €13.
closed	Rarely.
directions	From Santander N-623; N-232; C-6318 to Santelices. After 400m left to Casa La Engaña; over level crossing 300m & follow road round for 50m; on left.

	Duncan Holt & Milagros García
tel	+34 947 138073
email	turismo@laengana.com
web	www.laengana.com

Map 4 Entry 134

Posada Molino del Canto

Molino del Canto s/n, Barrio La Cuesta, 09146 Valle de Zamanzas, Burgos

This jewel of a place is remote and heavenly in an Eden-like valley, lapped by the river Ebro. It is a 13th-century millworkers' home, restored by the young owner Javier, and the simplicity of the façade is reflected inside – authentic and exquisite. Through the dim little entrance hall – cool for summer, warm for winter – to a chunkily beamed, stone-walled sitting room scattered with country furniture, kilim, sofa and good log fire. Then to bedrooms upstairs, a splendid surprise: a cosy, delightful sitting room down, a sofabed for children, and sleeping quarters up (hot in summer). There are generous beds, large classic wardrobes, stylish white-and-terracotta bathrooms, big sky windows to gaze at the stars... drift off to the sound of the river. Breakfast is a great start to the day and the regional cooking is good. Javier will happily advise on birdwatching routes – and will show you how the watermill works. On a promontory down by the river it's a thousand years old and still contains the old flint wheels that spin into action when the sluice gate is opened. You'll fall in love with this place.

rooms	6: 3 twins, 3 doubles.
price	€82. Singles €68. VAT iincluded.
meals	Lunch €20. Dinner €23. VAT inc.
closed	Rarely.
directions	From Burgos N-623 for Santander. North of Quintanilla de Escalada, at km66, exit for Gallejones. On for Villanueva Rampally. There left for Arreba. Posada signed to right after 2.6km.

Javier Morala & Valvanera Rodriguez

tel	+34 947 571368
fax	+34 947 571176
email	info@molinodelcanto.com
web	www.molinodelcanto.com

Map 4 Entry 135

La Gándara
c/La Paloma s/n, 09572 Crespos, Burgos

The biggest noise around here is cicada hum and birdsong. The road stops at the village; remote, rustic, relaxed. The old farmhouse reflects this simplicity but there is a generous degree of comfort. Floors are oak, stairs creaky, windows shuttered, and walls are a pleasing mix of stone and plaster. The low-beamed bedrooms are furnished in elegant cottage style – brass or carved bedheads, embroidered covers, muslin curtains, perhaps a china basin or pine wash stand – even an old-fashioned typewriter. Bathrooms are elegant with their buttercup or sage walls. The top-floor suite is heaven: spot deer from the windows or gaze at the stars from the your tub. This is a place of simple pleasures – canoeing on the river, forest walking, exploring romanesque churches or visiting the spectacular gorge at Palancas. In the early evening, drink in hand, spot vultures from the balcony that overlooks the house's inner courtyard. Owners Javier and Isabel serve delicious meals with vegetables from their organic garden, and join their guests for supper. With no television, conversation lingers well into the night.

rooms	6: 5 twins/doubles, 1 suite.
price	€54–€58. Suite €80–€85.
meals	Breakfast €5. Dinner €15.
closed	6–31 January.
directions	From Santander N-623; left at km70 for Arreba & Manzanedo and on for 4km. Left & on for 1km to Crespos. House 1st on right.

	Javier Moyano & Isabel Villullas
tel	+34 947 573184
fax	+34 947 573042
email	lagandara@teleline.es
web	www.lagandaracasarural.com

Map 4 Entry 136

Mesón del Cid

Plaza Santa María 8, 09003 Burgos

Hard to say whether the star attraction is the views or the food. The position, opposite the gothic spires of Burgos cathedral, is matchless. And the restaurant's rich stews, succulent roasts and superb regional cheeses have been attracting diners for years. The 15th-century townhouse – named after a manuscript produced here when it housed a printing press – has an old-fashioned, understated elegance. Ceilings are beamed, tiled floors are patterned, gilt-framed mirrors and dark antiques line the corridors. Choose between bedrooms above the restaurant, with brass bedsteads, rugs on tiles, and exposed brickwork or stone, and the modern ones across the square, with gleaming parquet and pale wood. All are light-filled and have big beds, pretty bedspreads and lavish, marble bathrooms. (And from the rooms at the front you can almost touch the cathedral buttresses…) José Luis is on hand with a welcoming smile – and excellent advice on how to get the most out of your stay. In the heart of Burgos, amid cobbled steps and traffic-free plazas, Mesón del Cid is considered *the* place to stay.

rooms	55: 49 twins/doubles, 6 suites.
price	€125. Suites €147.
meals	Breakfast €10. Lunch/dinner €30.
closed	Never.
directions	In old town directly opposite main entrance to cathedral on Plaza de Santa María. Private car park next door.

	Lopez Alzaga family
tel	+34 947 208715
fax	+34 947 269460
email	mesondelcid@mesondelcid.es
web	www.mesondelcid.es

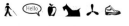

Map 4 Entry 137

Hotel Arlanza

c/Mayor 1, 09346 Covarrubias, Burgos

Mercedes and Juan José have created somewhere as charming and intimate as Covarrubias itself. The little town is well off the beaten track but is a must if you love places where tradition holds strong. The Arlanza sits right on the lovely, medieval, colonnaded central square. Inside, tiny polished terracotta floor tiles, heavy panelled doors, original lintels, wrought-iron chandeliers. Public rooms are on the dark side – beams are black and windows are small – but the restaurant is light and airy. Bedrooms are reached by an impressive staircase, and are a good size, those that overlook the square being the lightest. Expect good fabrics, panelled bedheads, pretty country furniture, perhaps an armchair or two. And the Castillian cuisine is excellent: this is the best place to eat in the village. (Note, medieval costumed banquets – fun but boisterous! – are held out-of-season on Saturday nights.) All the staff are friendly, but do find a moment to chat to the owners – anglophiles, they particularly enjoy meeting their British guests.

rooms	40: 38 twins/doubles, 2 suites.
price	€60. Suites €67. VAT included.
meals	Breakfast €4.20. Lunch/dinner €11.
closed	15 December-February.
directions	From Burgos A-1 for Madrid. In Lerma, left on C-110 for Salas de los Infantes. Hotel in Covarrubias on Plaza Mayor.

	Mercedes de Miguel Briones
tel	+34 947 406441
fax	+34 947 400502
email	hotel@hotelarlanza.com
web	www.hotelarlanza.com

Map 5 Entry 138

Hotel Santo Domingo de Silos II

c/Santo Domingo de Silos 14, 09610 Santo Domingo de Silos, Burgos

Catch vespers at 7am: the highlight of a stay is the Gregorian chant in the monastery chapel. For this reason alone it's worth stopping off at Santo Domingo on the journey north or south; the stunning church with its magnificent bells is one of the finest in Spain. Consider staying a night at this simple family hotel, recently doubled in size thanks to its extension. Its real raison d'être is its restaurant: delicious meats roasted by Eleuterio in a wood-fired oven pull in a family crowd at weekends. On weekdays you might feel a touch lonely in this vast space, but you can always ask for dinner to be served in a second, smaller dining area, or in the cosy bar next door. The cuts of lamb, kid and suckling pig are worthy of a medieval banquet, and the prices astonishingly low. The bedrooms in the new extension are the best: lavish and a good size, spotlessly clean and with hydromassage showers or tubs. This is a good, down-to-earth place to stay: hearty food, lovely people, great value for money – and exquisite Gregorian chant.

rooms	50 twins/doubles.
price	€50-€60. Singles €38-€45.
meals	Breakfast €3. Lunch/dinner from €10.
closed	Rarely.
directions	From Burgos, A-1 for Madrid; N-234 for Soria. Right in Hacinas on BU-903 to Santo Domingo. Hotel on right on passing through village.

	Eleuterio del Álamo Castillo
tel	+34 947 390053
fax	+34 947 390052
email	reservas@hotelsantodomingodesilos.com
web	www.hotelsantodomingodesilos.com

Map 5 Entry 139

Posada del Acebo

c/de la Iglesia 7, 40165 Prádena, Segovia

Prádena sits snug in the lee of the Guadarrama Sierra, the high chain of mountains that lie just north of Madrid. Its older houses are surprisingly grand, from an age when the villagers were granted royal privileges for the magnificence of their livestock's meat and wool, famous throughout the land. You enter the house through the small dining/sitting room, cosy and snug with its rustic bench seating, scent of seasoned timber, small open fire and proud photographs of shepherds and their flocks. Ramón will show you upstairs by way of a fine old bannistered staircase to the bedrooms, a truly charming mix of old (washstands, wrought-iron bedsteads, lamps, prints) and new (central heating, firm mattresses and double-glazing to keep the fearsome winters at bay). There are mountain walks from the door, the mighty Duratón river gorges to explore on foot or by canoe, a feast of romanesque churches; then back to dinner in that cosy dining room. Both rooms and food are excellent value; if you're missing eggs and bacon at breakfast, just ask!

rooms	8: 5 twins/doubles, 1 single, 2 family.
price	€54–€64. Singles €40.
meals	Dinner €12.
closed	Rarely.
directions	From Madrid, N-1 for Burgos. At km99 marker, exit S. Tomé del Puerto; N-110 for Segovia. After 12km, right into Prádena. House off main square.

	Ramón Martín Rozas
tel	+34 921 507260
fax	+34 921 507260
email	acebo@tursegovia.com
web	www.el-acebo.com

Map 12 Entry 140

La Tejera de Fausto

Ctra. La Salceda-Sepúlveda km7, 40173 Requijada, Segovia

The stone buildings of this rustic homestead stand in glorious isolation, a mile from the nearest village, close to the banks of the Cega river. Of course the roofs are terracotta: tiles (*tejas*) were made here, hence the name. Decoration is warm, simple and appealing: bedrooms, in an outbuilding, have a mix of old and new furniture – and no phone or TV to distract you from the views. Hostess and restaurant make this place special. In a series of snug, interconnecting rooms where fires blaze in colder months, guests tuck heartily into the best of regional cooking; specialities are roast lamb, suckling pig and boar. The gardens are lovely, too, with many trees for shade. Next door is a romanesque chapel whose foundation stones were pillaged from a Roman villa. This is a remote corner of Castille: a fertile valley in the lee of the Guadarrama mountains that cut a jagged scimitar between Madrid and the Meseta. Walk out along the old transhumance routes that criss-cross the region: Castillian to the core. Note that there are wedding parties on summer weekends, so treat yourselves to a midweek stay.

rooms	9: 7 twins/doubles, 2 suites.
price	€75. Suites €110–€150.
meals	Breakfast €6. Dinner €27 à la carte.
closed	Rarely.
directions	From Segovia, N-110 for Soria to La Salceda. Then left for Pedraza. Hotel on left, after Val de San Pedro, by signpost km7.

	Jaime Armero
tel	+34 921 127087
fax	+34 915 641520
email	reservas@latejeradefausto.com
web	www.latejeradefausto.com

Map 12 Entry 141

El Zaguán

Plaza de España 16, 40370 Turégano, Segovia

People flock to cobbled, walled Pedraza, and little Turégano gets forgotten. But it is every bit as lovely, with its porticoed main square and enormous castle dominating the skyline. On that very same square is El Zaguán – every inch the grand Castillian house. Casement windows, dressed stone, stables, grain store and *bodega*… a warm, quiet and cosy hostelry awaits you. Downstairs is a lively bar and dining room, with pine timbers, wafer-brick pillars and terracotta floors, well-dressed tables and soft lights, and a wood-fired oven where roasts are prepared – beef and lamb as well as the ubiquitous suckling pig. In the lovely upstairs sitting room you could almost be stepping into the pages of an interiors magazine – in the bedrooms too. The sitting room has smart sofas, a huge woodburner and a view of the castle; the bedrooms, no two the same, are undoubtedly handsome. And the under-terracotta-floor heating is a boon during the Castillian winter. A special hotel, with hardworking, cheerful, likeable Mario at the helm.

rooms	15: 12 twins/doubles, 3 suites.
price	€66. Singles €42. Suites €96.
meals	Breakfast €5. Lunch/dinner €18 set menu; €24-€30 à la carte.
closed	22 December-8 January.
directions	From Segovia, N-601 Valladolid. After 7km, right for Turégano & Cantalejo. Hotel in main village square.

	Mario García Heredero
tel	+34 921 501165
fax	+34 921 500776
email	zaguan@el-zaguan.com
web	www.el-zaguan.com

Map 12 Entry 142

La Abubilla

c/Escuelas 4 posterior, 40181 Carrascal de la Cuesta, Segovia

The delightful Oneto family have lavished love and decorative savoir-faire on this old farmhouse in a hamlet with a population of 12. La Abubilla (meaning 'hoopoe') is a typical Segovian farm, its house and outbuildings wrapped around a sheltered courtyard where two ash trees provide shade during the Meseta's sweltering summer. (Perfect for summer breakfasts.) Every detail of the guest bedrooms has been fussed over by Alfredo Oneto; even the light switches have been individually crafted. The bigger suites in the old hay barn are the prettiest imaginable: tiles are hand-painted, beds country four-poster, paints and fabrics sober, low-beamed bathrooms charming. The rustic, raftered, split-level sitting and dining room, where a log fire glows and classical music plays, is equally inviting. Indulge in a spot of hydrotherapy in the grounds, before settling down to a delicious meal; the kitchen is the hub of this house. Segovia is near, and you could easily visit Madrid, Ávila *and* Salamanca – should you choose to stay several nights. Peaceful, friendly, special. *A Rusticae hotel.*

rooms	5: 1 double, 4 suites.
price	€99-€128. VAT included.
meals	Dinner €17. VAT included.
closed	24-25 December.
directions	From Segovia N-110 towards Soria. In Sotosalbo left for Turégano to Carrascal de la Cuesta. House on right as you arrive in village.

	Hermanos Oneto
tel	+34 921 120236
fax	+34 916 617278
email	oneto@oneto.com
web	www.laabubilla.com

Map 12 Entry 143

Hotel Los Linajes

c/Dr. Velasco 9, 40003 Segovia

A stone's throw from Segovia's Plaza Mayor and wondrous cathedral, Los Linajes stands cheek-to-jowl with the old city wall; the land drops away steeply here so the building is 'stepped' to give most of the rooms a view across the valley. The amiable Miguel Borrequero officiates in reception; in charge at Los Linajes for years, he strives for perfection. The oldest section of the building is 17th century, and parts, it's true, feel a little dated; a thorough revamp is under way. The lovely old portal of dressed sandstone leads to a beamed reception area furnished with oil paintings and dark Castillian pieces. Bedrooms are pale, serene and comfortable, but what makes them special are those views across the green river valley. The best have small balconies and terraces, where you can breakfast if the weather is right. You're only really aware this is a 53-room hotel when you enter the huge dining room and bar; food is classic Castillian, but should you prefer a cosier venue for dinner, there are masses of restaurants close by. A brilliant site, and the underground car park is a big plus.

rooms	53: 39 twins/doubles, 5 singles, 9 suites.
price	€83–€99. Singles €62–€73. Suites €117–€129.
meals	Breakfast €9. Lunch/dinner €15, €25 à la carte.
closed	Rarely.
directions	As you arrive in Segovia from Madrid, follow signs 'Zona Oriental & Acueducto'. By Roman aqueduct, signs for El Alcázar, then for hotel.

	Miguel Borrequero Rubio
tel	+34 921 460476
fax	+34 921 460479
email	hotelloslinajes@terra.es
web	www.loslinajes.com

Map 12 Entry 144

Hostal de Buen Amor

c/Eras 7, 40170 Sotosalbos, Segovia

When Madrid folk tire of the capital they head for the green valleys of Segovia – and tradition demands that a roast meal completes the excursion. Dora and Victor's restaurant has long been popular, while their delightful small hotel, yards away, opened its heavy old doors more lately. Their niece, a designer, took on the job of nursing Sotosalbos's finest old house back to health; the result is a warm blend of authenticity and stylish comfort. The house is unbelievably peaceful: all you hear is the tick-tock of the grandfather clock and perhaps the church bells. Dora, a self-confessed antique shop addict, has waved a magic wand over the bedrooms, where you'll be delighted and surprised by antique writing tables, flamboyant fabrics and the best mattresses (far from antique!). She and Victor have lived in England and speak brilliant English. Underfloor heating keeps you warm when temperatures plummet, the blaze from the central suspended chimney warms all sides, and hearty breakfasts set you up for the day. Sotosalbos's romanesque church draws visitors from miles around – don't miss it.

rooms	12: 11 twins/doubles, 1 suite.
price	€77–€107. Singles €61. Suite €144.
meals	Dinner €15.
closed	Rarely.
directions	From Madrid N-VI for La Coruña. After tunnel, right for Segovia on N-603. Here, N-110 for Soria. After 18km left for Sotosalbos.

	Soraya Tapias
tel	+34 921 403020
fax	+34 921 403022
email	hosbamor@infonegocio.com
web	www.telefonica.net/web/hostaldebuenamor

Map 12 Entry 145

Saltus Alvus

c/Tejadillo 1, 40170 Sotosalbos, Segovia

Once a stopover for the Romans crossing the Sierra de Guadarrama, Sotosalbos was – still is – prime hunting territory. Begoña grew up here and, after years working in international business and the London theatre, has returned to settle. The house, newly built on land owned by the family, has a reassuringly solid, traditional feel, thanks to heavy beams and thick stone walls. Generous windows make the most of the mountain views and let in plenty of light to big, delightful rooms. To describe the décor as rustic-chic does not do the place justice. Every last detail has been finely considered and all is brought together with style and panache – and yet the effect is homely and rural. The bedrooms have glowing terracotta tiles and rich pine ceilings, firm beds and comfortable armchairs or a sofa. The finest craftsmanship is evident throughout. Begoña and Victor are a friendly and erudite couple with a young son. They have a great love for the area, and tremendous enthusiasm for this new venture. Saltus Alvus serves breakfast only, but there's a super restaurant nearby – ask Begoña to book you a table.

rooms	4: 1 double, 3 suites.
price	€76–€110.
meals	Restaurant in village.
closed	Rarely.
directions	From Segovia N-110 for Soria. After 18km Sotosalbos on left. At restaurant Las Casillas, sharp left up track. 2nd right ('residents only' sign); house opp. church on left.

	Begoña del Barrio Martín
tel	+34 921 403057
email	saltusalvus@terra.es

Map 12 Entry 146

Posada de Esquiladores

c/Esquiladores 1, 05412 San Esteban del Valle, Ávila

The granite exterior and rush blinds at the windows give little clue as to the treats within. A surprise to discover, then, a big inviting sitting room, huge hearth and special atmosphere. In the lovely mountain village of San Esteban, the *posada* was a village shop until 1989: some of the original goods are still on display. Today's interior is a harmonious and contemporary mix of stone, terracotta and carefully chosen fabrics; bedrooms are delightful, bathrooms spotless, the restoration exquisite. All this has been achieved by Almudena, a former journalist who worked for *TV Espana*. She also happens to be a brilliant cook and if you book dinner you'll experience some of the dishes that have made Castillian cuisine famous. Explore the wild villages of the region from here; there's a twice-yearly festival in honour of St Peter Baptist, the Franciscan missionary martyred at Nagasaki (whose skull rests in the church), and an annual horse race, El Vitor, in which riders race bareback from the square to the cemetery.

rooms	12 twins/doubles.
price	€100–€125. Singles €71. VAT inc.
meals	Lunch/dinner €18 set menu; €21 à la carte. VAT included.
closed	Rarely.
directions	From Madrid, N-V/E-90 for Talavera de la Reina. At km123, right on N-502 for Arenas de San Pedro, then right for Santa Cruz & on to San Esteban. Posada opp. Ayuntamiento.

	Almudena García Drake
tel	+34 920 383498
fax	+34 920 383456
email	posada@esquiladores.com
web	www.esquiladores.com

Map 11 Entry 147

El Canchal

c/de La Fuente 1, 05400 Arenas de San Pedro, Ávila

Not the Ritz, but perfect for walkers, who come for some of the most memorable routes in central Spain. Little Arenas de San Pedro, topped by a medieval castle and sculpted into the southern flank of the Sierra, is in the heart of the trails. This nobleman's residence – in the middle of town but not easy to find – dates from the Middle Ages and Isabel knows all the history. She is the perfect innkeeper: unflappable, flexible, friendly. The feel is of a walkers' retreat, the furniture is darkly Castillian and the ceilings are low. Each bedroom is named after a variety of mushroom – the area is popular with gatherers – and is grandmother-cosy, thanks to antique beds and dressers, lace-edged curtains, antique washstands and dark beams. The lounge and dining room feel similarly homely, with their books, sofas, old tiles and ancient hearth. Try Isabel's homemade cake at breakfast and eat in at least once: meals are simple and excellent, and the house red is good. Don't miss the labyrinthine cellars deep below; one of Isabel's many projects is to fill them with her own judicious selection.

rooms	6 twins/doubles.
price	€50–€64.
meals	Breakfast €3. Lunch/dinner €18.
closed	Rarely.
directions	Madrid N-V for Badajoz. Exit Casar de Talavera; N-502 A. de San Pedro. Here, over r'bout for 'Centro Urbano'. Before castle, left into c/Isabel La Católica. Round church; park in Plaza del Ayuntamiento. Walk up c/Cejudo, right; on left.

	Isabel Rodríguez
tel	+34 920 370958
fax	+34 920 370914
email	reservas@elcanchal.com
web	www.elcanchal.com

Map 11 Entry 148

Centro de Turismo Rural La Josa

Paraje La Tijera, Apdo. de Correos 48, 05480 Candeleda, Ávila

As you look out from the veranda across the glorious plain, you could be excused for expecting herds of wildebeest and zebra to come sweeping by. Ornithologists only have to sit and wait, in wicker-chaired comfort, before interesting birdlife comes their way. As the sun sets, the town lights glow like little ships anchored on far-off coastlines; as night falls, you hear the bark of the fox and the hoot of the owl. Exquisite views… from an exquisitely maintained little farm. Mature fig trees (one older than the house), broadleaf trees and palms surround the old farmhouse, and roses clamber its walls; there's a lushly verdant feel. Antonia and Ricardo are utterly charming, and know and love everything about the area and this special place. Sleeping is in purpose-built, rustically styled, mezzanine rooms; a good size, those on the upper floor with verandas, and all sparklingly clean. En suite shower rooms are pristine. Expect excellent fresh meat, vegetables and goat's cheese, wine and home-grown fruit, figs in particular, at well-priced dinners. You'll come for a night and stay a week – a gem.

rooms	6 twins/doubles.
price	€58–€64. VAT included.
meals	Dinner €13. VAT included.
closed	Rarely.
directions	From Madrid A-5 to Orpesa. Here north to Candeleda. Through village on C-501 for Arenas de San Pedro. 1.5km outside, left up concrete track for 1.5km. Signed on right.

	Antonia Velasco Serrano
tel	+34 666 866659
email	info@casarurallajosa.com
web	www.casarurallajosa.com

Map 11 Entry 149

El Milano Real

c/Toleo s/n, 05634 Hoyos del Espino, Ávila

If, you espy this unassuming hotel and pass by on the other side, you miss a rare treat. Surrounded by the Gredos mountains, it has the feel of a new Swiss chalet, with balconies to the front and behind. The beautiful ornamental garden at the front, however, owes more to the Italians. Inside, all is comfort and ease. Bedrooms are colour-coordinated and a good size, and there are eight plush themed suites. One is Japanese, stunning with futon and low furniture (not for the stiff-jointed!), another is New York penthouse, another English, with wall-to-wall carpeting and four-poster. There are two lounges, with matching sofas and fauteuils, one up under the eaves, a super library and an observatory so you can check out the stars. But the dining room is the real draw, the food winning a mention in all the guide books. Francisco ('Paco') has a huge selection of favourite wines and alongside each he lists year, bodega and his own personal score out of 10. Food and rooms are good value, worth a detour, and the Gredos are one of Spain's better-kept secrets. *A Rusticae hotel*

rooms	21: 13 twins/doubles, 8 suites.
price	€95–€127. Singles €84–€112. Suites €165.
meals	Breakfast €12. Lunch/dinner €32–€47 à la carte.
closed	Rarely.
directions	From Ávila N-110 for Béjar & Plasencia. After 6km, N-502 left for Arenas de San Pedro; after 40km, right on AV-941 to Hoyos del Espino. Hotel to right.

	Francisco Sánchez & Teresa Dorn
tel	+34 920 349108
fax	+34 920 349156
email	info@elmilanoreal.com
web	www.elmilanoreal.com

Map 11 Entry 150

La Casa Inglesa
37700 Béjar, Salamanca

Many guests are Spanish: they come for fine food, good company and to escape the capital. La Casa Inglesa is both home and retreat, tucked away in a forest of chestnut trees from which the nearby village of El Castañar takes its name. Decoration has a traditional *Inglesa* feel: antique drop-leaf tables, crystal decanters, books, candelabras and oriental vases. Bedrooms have knick-knacks and chintz, bathrooms are dated but fine. Anna likes the good things of life so expect candles at dinner, classical music at most times and very good food: she had three restaurants in London during the Sixties and fed everyone from Nureyev to the Rolling Stones. Anna is no typical ex-pat: since setting up home in Spain she has never been one to search out fellow compatriots, and her cooking looks both west and east, with a fine choice for vegetarians. Dinners have a Lebanese slant and she will happily prepare you a cooked breakfast. A charming hostess and home; stay a couple of nights and visit the exceptional village of Candelario 10 minutes away.

rooms	4: 3 twins/doubles, 1 triple.
price	€50–€60. VAT included.
meals	Lunch €25. Dinner €20.
closed	Rarely.
directions	From Salamanca for Cáceres & Béjar. In Béjar pass 2 petrol stations, left for El Castañar. Immed. opp. Hotel Los Duques, sharp left down cobbled track. At 3rd loop sharp left to black gate. Ring bell.

	Anna Antonios
tel	+34 923 404499 or 636 363476
email	lacasainglesa@telefonica.net

Map 11 Entry 151

Hotel Residencia Rector

Paseo Rector Esperabé 10, 37008 Salamanca

In a city of ineffable loveliness, one of western Spain's most perfect small hotels. Señor Ferrán like things to be 'just so' and examples of his meticulous care are found in every corner. There are two serene stained-glass windows in reception, and wood is used to fine effect: sparkling parquet floors in the public rooms, inlaid tables, writing desks and hand-crafted bedheads in the bedrooms. You may not need the phone in the bathroom, or the fax point in the bedroom, but you'll surely appreciate the double-glazing, the air conditioning and the deeply comfortable beds. Bathrooms, are quietly lavish: silver-grey marble, double basins, thick towels. Superb standards at breakfast too, and the staff are quiet, discreet and kind. Leave your car safe in the hotel car park – a big plus – and head out on foot to explore: the cathedral is two minutes away, the incomparable Plaza Mayor a step further, and next door is the Casa Lis, a fascinating museum dedicated to Spanish Art Nouveau and Art Deco. A charming, much-praised hotel.

rooms	13 twins/doubles.
price	€112–€146.
meals	Breakfast €10.
closed	Rarely.
directions	From Madrid on N-501, 1st right at signs 'Centro Ciudad'. At r'bout, left into P. Rector Esperabé. After 300m, hotel in front of 2 walls, by museum. Drop bags; reception will direct you to car park.

	Eduardo Ferrán Riba
tel	+34 923 218482
fax	+34 923 214008
email	hotelrector@telefonica.net
web	www.hotelrector.com

Map 11 Entry 152

Posada Real La Vadima

Ctra. Ledesma-Bermillo km7, 37100 Ledesma, Salamanca

If it is Old Spain you're seeking, come here. For generations this family have been living off the land, raising bulls, and live in a 300-year-old, character-steeped house. The old granite and timbers embrace you and there's history at every turn. And kindness, from special, well-travelled hosts who truly cherish their guests. Isabel's is a long established Castillian family, and her love for this place gives life to every ancient nook and cranny. The sitting room has checked sofas, hunting trophies and a roaring fire; idiosyncratic bathrooms, some more modern than others, have lashings of water; and each bedroom, named after a family member, is different. Isobel's grandparents' room comes with matching Deco furniture and astonishingly effective plumbing, while the room with the best view has an Austro-Hungarian wardrobe and a library of rare books. Doors are carved and heavy, curtains handmade, ceilings solid chestnut. And Eduardo's wines and Isobel's cooking – whatever she decides to produce that day – are as enjoyable as all the rest.

rooms	10: 7 twins/doubles, 1 single, 2 suites.
price	€80-€90. Singles €60-€65. Suites €100-€125.
meals	Breakfast €6. Lunch/dinner €15.
closed	10-31 January.
directions	From Salamanca cross Rio Tormes. Follow signs for Valladolid and N-620. Exit onto SA-300 for Ledesma. At bridge right on SA-311 for La Vadima. Posada on right after 7km.

	Eduardo Verastegui & Isabel Marin
tel	+34 923 570230
fax	+34 923 570329
email	info@lavadima.com
web	www.lavadima.com

Map 11 Entry 153

Posada Real del Pinar

Pinar de San Rafael, 47450 Pozal de Gallinas, Valladolid

This small hotel, secreted away in 300 acres of pine forest at the end of a long, dusty track, exudes quality and comfort. The low vaulted brickwork in the centre of the building is 17th century; the new brickwork is the colour of the earth in the fields. The sitting room, with its fire and plush seating, is an intimate and relaxed place to be; the dining room is elegantly vaulted and has a woodburning oven. Mouthwatering roasts are a speciality, there's a good little menu for children, and the local wines are delicious (and well priced). Behind the hotel is an old chapel, whose airy grandeur is perfectly suited to business receptions and weddings – if you prefer not to clash with a party, you much check when you book. Bedrooms, named after *mudéjar* towns, are smartly furnished, the largest in the old part of the building. Newer rooms are accessible by lift. The coloured mosaics in some of the bathrooms could be considered garish, but the overall impression remains classy. Historic Olmedo is worth a visit, there are plenty of natural marvels to see, and a thermal spa nearby. *A Rusticae hotel.*

rooms	19: 14 twins/doubles, 2 singles, 3 family.
price	€80–€125. Singles €70.
meals	Breakfast €6. Lunch/dinner €17.50.
closed	7-27 January.
directions	From Valladolid, A-6 for Tordesillas; A-6 for Madrid. Exit km157 for Olmedo. Follow CL-112 for 5km to Pozal de Gallinas. Posada signed to right as you pass through village; 3.2km down track.

	Marina Fernández
tel	+34 983 481004
fax	+34 915 646191
email	info@laposadadelpinar.com
web	www.laposadadelpinar.com

Map 11 Entry 154

Finca Corral de Ramas

Ctra. 3203 Elche de la Sierra-Liétor km76, 02410 Liétor, Albacete

Begoña and her brother Javier inherited the family farm 10 years ago, in this wild, beautiful and unknown part of Spain. With flair, vigour and dedication, they procceded to launch themselves into converting the old barn and stables – with pretty dovecote at one end – into a stylish restaurant-hotel. The hunting and country memorabilia that adorn the walls, the country chests, the vases of dried flowers, the family heirlooms – all reflect the finca's past. The raftered lounge, though lofty, is warm and inviting – particularly in winter, with its baronial log fire. Simple, twin-bedded rooms are decorated in good earthy colours and attractive prints, and have their own individually coloured showers. Sunlight dances through every window. The food is very special for such an out of the way place: José Antonio Cebrián Martínez's dishes are fresh, inventive, exquisite. (Just make sure you book ahead.) For those who value their independence, there's also an attractive duplex apartment with a great little kitchen, a mezzanine room for four and a courtyard.

rooms	9 + 1: 9 twins/doubles. 1 apartment for 4.
price	€60. Apartment €120.
meals	Breakfast €4.50. Dinner €25.
closed	October-May: closed weekdays.
directions	From Murcia A-30 for Albacete. At Hellin left on CM-412 to Elche de la Serra. Here right on CM-3203 for Ayna. After 6km right for Liétor. Finca signposted on left after 0.5km. 0.5km up track.

	Begoña Vidal
tel	+34 967 584004
fax	+34 967 236776
email	info@corralderamas.com
web	www.corralderamas.com

Map 20 Entry 155

Hotel Albamanjon

Laguna de San Pedro 16, 02611 Ossa de Montiel, Albacete

Like Tennyson's eagle, who clasps the crag with crooked hand, this hotel seems to cling to the very rock, or even grow out of it. The upper rooms are embedded in those fascinating rock formations that characterise the vast plains of Quixote's la Mancha, and their terraces have views down to a turquoise lake – an oasis in this rocky terrain. The hotel has a distinctive windmill frontage and was built in the 1970s in traditional style. The nine bedrooms, in which the rock sometimes appears unannounced, are comfortable and large, each with an open fire or woodburner that's lit every winter evening. You can sample Raúl's cooking from the lakeside dining room, or the large terrace in summer, which sparkles with lamps and fairy lights as dusk falls. The food is traditional Manchegan, with such diverse and pungent flavours as partridge with green beans, and *atascaburras*: puréed cod with nuts, potatoes and peppers. This is the Ruidera National Park, so expect some fine walking and birdwatching. You can also hire rowing boats, kayaks or mountain bikes from the hotel and explore, pioneer-style.

rooms	9 + 2: 5 twins/doubles, 4 suites. 2 studios for 3.
price	€85-€120. Singles €65. Suites €120. VAT included.
meals	Lunch/dinner €20-€35 à la carte. VAT included.
closed	Rarely.
directions	From N-IV, exit Manzanares & head east on N-430 for Albacete. At Ruidera follow signs to lakes. Hotel signposted from lakes.

	Raúl Arés Espílez
tel	+34 926 699048
fax	+34 926 699120
email	hotel@albamanjon.net
web	www.albamanjon.net

Map 19 Entry 156

Hotel Rural Antigua Casa de la Bodega

c/Clérigos Camarenas 58, 13200 Manzanares, Ciudad Real

From the dusty-hot streets of Manzanares, slip through handsome doors into a shuttered space of polished tiles, rich furniture and gleaming elegance. This 19th-century former bodega has all the slow, unhurried charm of a mature wine; one that demands you slip off your shoes, sink into a sofa and drink deeply. Isabel and Rafael spent three years lovingly restoring the house, giving it a swaggering exterior of white walls, wrought-iron balconies and gay awnings; the interior is classically traditional. Be soothed by plump upholstery, antiques, fine porcelain, bowls of fruit and acres of fabulously ornate floor tiles. The high-ceilinged bedrooms are all lace curtains, brass bedsteads, cool walls and dark wood. Elegant touches work their magic: monogrammed bed linen, a pretty glass chandelier, a petite writing desk, a cosy window seat. And always flowers. In one room, tiled steps lead up to a love nest. Bathrooms sparkle whitely. Beyond the shady, plant-filled breakfast terrace, a small pool is tucked into the high-walled garden, and the owners are as kind and refined as their house.

rooms	5 twins/doubles.
price	€70. VAT included.
meals	Restaurants nearby.
closed	Rarely.
directions	From Madrid N-IV south; 1st exit for Manzanares. At r'bout follow signs for 'Centro Ciudad'; through tunnel; hotel on left.

	Isabel Blanco & Rafael Bermejo
tel	+34 926 611707
fax	+34 926 612105
email	info@antiguacasadelabodega.com
web	www.antiguacasadelabodega.com

Map 19 Entry 157

La Casa del Rector

Pedro Oviedo 8, 13270 Almagro, Ciudad Real

One of the jewels in the crown of La Mancha, the town was once tipped to become home to the next Spanish university. It never happened, and the Casa del Rector and a couple of other grand 17th-century edifices passed into private hands. Five years ago, restaurateur Juan Garcia bought the old building and, with the help of local craftsmen, gave its ashen features a rosy, healthy glow. Behind the sandstone façade are these charmingly furnished rooms and suites, all opening onto a galleried central patio, where water cascades into carved stone troughs. Most of the bedrooms have their own sitting area, plus woodburning stoves and smart (even open-plan) bathrooms. Windows are small, so rooms are darkish, and there's an idiosyncratic touch to each: an Indian four-poster, a sauna/shower, a mosaic hot tub straight out of James Bond. The young, friendly staff serve excellent breakfast with Manchegan cheese and charcuterie; for supper look no further than the owners' restaurant, El Corregidor, close by. *A Rusticae hotel.*

rooms	15: 12 twins/doubles, 1 single, 2 suites.
price	€85–€132. Singles €75. Suites €180.
meals	Breakfast €7. Lunch/dinner €22–€30 at El Corregidor.
closed	Rarely.
directions	From Ciudad Real, CM-412 to Almagro. At 1st r'bout follow hotel signs; right, then 2nd on right.

	Luis R Horcajada Almansa
tel	+34 926 261259
fax	+34 926 261260
email	recepcion@lacasadelrector.com
web	www.lacasadelrector.com

Map 18 Entry 158

Los Baños de Villanarejo

13193 Navalpino, Ciudad Real

Time stands still in this 1939 lodge, whose pale cherry façade glows in the evening sun. You can imagine hunting parties gathering in winter, swapping exploits round the open fire. At the end of a two-mile track, discover a place of great beauty: 2,000 hectares of olive, cork and evergreen oak, teeming with foxes, boar, mongoose and deer. Guests are unlikely to meet the Marquis and Marchioness – unless they're suited and booted, of course – but the estate manager and his wife take good care of you, in best Spanish. There are rugs, oils, antiques, a tapestry, the odd trophy; Los Baños is more quaint than grand. Large bedrooms have ornate period tiles and Casablanca fans; bathrooms boast Seventies' colours. Breakfast is hearty (bacon and eggs, croissants, cakes, cold meats) in the dining room filled with mahogany tables; later you may dine on pumpkin soup and estate game. Wine is *à volonté*. There's a vast swimming pool in the grounds, and bikes to borrow; archery, clay pigeon shooting, riding and cycling beyond. *Address for correspondence: c/San Bernardo 97-99, 28015 Madrid.*

rooms	12: 9 twins/doubles, 3 suites.
price	€70. Singles €100. Suites €140. VAT included.
meals	Breakfast €6. Lunch/dinner with wine €21. VAT included.
closed	Rarely.
directions	From Madrid N-IV. Then N-430 to Cuidad Real. On to Piedrabuena; CR-721 via Arroba de los Montes & Navalpino for Horcajo de los Montes; at top of pass, left at green gate; track to house.

	Alvaro Colomina Velázquez-Duro
tel	+34 914 488910
fax	+34 915 933061
email	acolomina@fincarural.com
web	www.fincarural.com

Map 18 Entry 159

Casa Bermeja
Plaza del Piloncillo s/n, 45572 Valdeverdeja, Toledo

Angela González happened upon this old house in a peaceful village and realised a long-nurtured dream: to escape the noise of Madrid and retreat here with friends. Luckily for us, she later decided to stretch a point and share her home with paying guests too. Architect brother Luis took renovation in hand and Angela, a designer, took care of the rest. Beyond the exuberant terracotta and cream façade and the stately entrance is a bright and seductive interior, its warm tones inspired by the red earth of Castille. Antique mingles with modern, there are huge rafters and polished tiles, immaculate checked sofas and contemporary wrought iron, generously dressed dining tables and a scattering of magazines and books in many languages. Bedrooms are attractive, comfortable and blissfully quiet. This corner of the Meseta is an ornithological wonderland; children bored by birdwatching can look out for the one-eyed turtle said to live in the garden, where a blissful pool beckons. *A Rusticae hotel*

rooms	16: 7 twins/doubles, 9 suites.
price	€72–€95. Singles €76. Suites €110–€170.
meals	Lunch/dinner €20–€25.
closed	Rarely
directions	From Madrid, N-V/E-90 for Badajoz. Exit at km148 marker for Oropesa. From here, signs to Puente del Arzobispo; then right to Valdeverdeja. In main square, opp. Ayuntamiento, left to house.

	Angela González
tel	+34 925 454586
fax	+34 925 454595
email	info@casa-bermeja.com
web	www.casa-bermeja.com

Map 11 Entry 160

Casa Los Arcos

Finca El Egido de Oritranca, Ctra. de Extremadura km142, 45687 Alcañizo, Toledo

Conchita works on the best take-us-as-you-find-us principle of hospitality, and many will find the slightly shambolic charm of the place appealing. With its numerous outbuildings (some in use and some not), paddocks and stables, Los Arcos is strung together like a charm bracelet of agrarian elements. Inside, a sitting room peppered with Conchita's oil paintings, and mellow 200-year-old tiles on the floor. Bedrooms are comfortable, some with bright Mexican fabrics; the twin rooms with their alcoved sitting areas and windows onto the garden are particularly charming. Before you eat dinner – around a large table in the family dining room – you may be offered a drink on the open porch where tables and chairs jostle with assorted bits and pieces of a vaguely agricultural nature. Ask Conchita for a taste of the local chorizo as an accompaniment to your rioja. There are sunburnt fields all around, some geese, a friendly dog, and your hostess's horse in the paddock – you feel you are miles from the city, yet Toledo is a 45-minute drive.

rooms	3: 2 twins/doubles, 1 suite.
price	€62. Suite €74.
meals	Breakfast €5. Lunch/dinner €20.
closed	Rarely.
directions	From Madrid, N-V/E-90 to Talavera de la Reina. After Talavera, exit 142 for Alcañizo. Follow road to Finca El Egido; straight on, ignore 1st T-junc. on left. Entrance on left; 800m along track.

	Conchita Granda Lanzarot
tel	+34 625 609758
email	casalosarcos@terra.es
web	www.terra.es/personal9/casalosarcos

Map 11 Entry 161

Hotel Pintor El Greco

c/Alamillos del Tránsito 13, 45002 Toledo

At the heart of Toledo's old Jewish quarter, yards from El Greco's house and the synagogue museum, this onetime bakery, now a friendly small hotel. Its restoration has been a success, and both façade and patio have been restored to their former glory. Although the main building is 17th century, parts were standing when Toledo was the capital of the Moorish kingdom – there is still an escape tunnel, built when the Inquisition was at work. The interiors are cool, quiet and plush, much of the furniture is hand-crafted and new, there are paintings and ceramics by local artists, and the odd potted aspidistra. Guest rooms on three floors are wrapped around the inner patio, some with balconies – and vary in size. Colours are warm, beds have good mattresses and thick Zamora blankets, there are yet more paintings and sometimes space for an armchair or an extra bed for a child. Note that the lift only goes up to the second floor and is not the quietest, and that the rooms overlooking the patio are the smallest. Buffet breakfasts are enjoyable. *Residents-only parking opposite, €12 per day.*

rooms	40 twins/doubles.
price	€103–€135. Singles €82.
meals	Breakfast €6.
closed	Rarely.
directions	From Madrid N-401 to Toledo; follow signs to old town. At town walls right; on with wall on left until r'bout. Left; on to end of tree-lined avenue. Left through wall; along street to hotel.

	Mariano Sánchez Torregrosa
tel	+34 925 285191
fax	+34 925 215819
email	info@hotelpintorelgreco.com
web	www.hotelpintorelgreco.com

Map 12 Entry 162

Hostal Descalzos

c/de los Descalzos 30, 45002 Toledo

Hostal Descalzos sits high up by the old city wall, yards from El Greco's house. It is neither grand nor beautiful, but it is very good value, quiet, friendly, and with the only outdoor pool in Toledo. There are great views, too. The corridors leading to the rooms have not yet been refurbished but don't let that put you off: the bedrooms themselves are fine. Fittings are modern, floors white-tiled, fabrics coordinated and beds both comfortable and spotless. Each one has a little shower room. Ask for a room at the back, overlooking the pool and jacuzzi – these get the views, and the views are among the best in Toledo… unforgettable at night, when the old bridge across the Tagus is illuminated. The family who run the *hostal* are unassuming, friendly and enthusiastic about this modest little place. Breakfasts and cheap meals are served in the cafeteria, due to reopen in 2005. At the foot of the hostal is a walled garden with a fountain and flowers – a pretty place to sit out and watch the sun set over the Meseta after a day exploring this fabulous city. *Hotel garage €10 per day.*

rooms	12 twins/doubles.
price	€44-€60. VAT included.
meals	Breakfast €4. Meals available.
closed	Rarely.
directions	In Toledo, signs to old town. At town walls (Puerta de la Bisagra), right; on with wall on left until signs for hostal to left; hostal signed to right in front of Hotel Pintor El Greco.

	Julio Luis García
tel	+34 925 222888
fax	+34 925 222888
email	h-descalzos@jet.es
web	www.hostaldescalzos.com

Map 12 Entry 163

Hostal del Cardenal

Paseo de Recaredo 24, 45003 Toledo

Toledo is quintessentially, gloriously Spanish, having absorbed the richest elements of Moorish and Christian Spain. Tempting, then, to stay at the Cardenal, built 700 years ago as a mansion for the Cardenal Lorenzana on the edge of the city walls. All of Toledo's character and charm is reflected within its soft ochre walls, and the gardens are almost as lovely: fountains and ponds, geraniums and climbers. Go through the elegant main entrance to discover patios, screens, arches and columns... and rooms whose walls glow with fine old oils and *mudéjar* bricks. A peaceful mantle lies softly over it all, to the background tick-tock of the grandfather clock. Wide *estera*-matted corridors and a domed staircase lead to majestic, subtly lit bedrooms upstairs, with gleaming parquet floors and dark Castillian furniture. Bathrooms are small but opulent. Choose between several small dining areas, one under the trees, and feast on roast lamb, suckling pig, stewed partridge. No views, church bells at 5am – but a truly great place. The El Greco museum is the shortest of strolls.

rooms	27: 23 twins/doubles, 2 singles, 2 suites.
price	€83–€106. Singles €52–€66. Suites €114–€146.
meals	Breakfast €7.60. Lunch/dinner €25.
closed	Rarely.
directions	From Madrid N-401 to Toledo. On arriving at old town walls & Puerta de la Bisagra, right; hotel 50m on left beside ramparts.

	Luis González Gozalbo
tel	+34 925 224900
fax	+34 925 222991
email	cardenal@hostaldelcardenal.com
web	www.hostaldelcardenal.com

Map 12 Entry 164

La Almazara

Ctra. Toledo-Argés y Polan km3.4, Apartado 6, 45004 Toledo

One of Toledo's most illustrious cardinals built this delectable house as a summer palace in the 16th century. El Greco often visited for inspiration. High on a hillside overlooking Toledo, it catches the breezes that sweep in across the Meseta. Oil was milled here and there are still vats of the stuff deep below. You arrive by way of a grand old portal and long drive to be greeted by the charming owner, Paulino, or one of his friendly staff. Downstairs is a large sitting room with vast fireplace for winter; in summer, linger over breakfast in the white vaulted dining room that overlooks the orchards to Toledo. And take a closer look at those oil paintings, the work of Paulino's teenage daughter. Bedrooms are straightforward and comfortable; bathrooms have repro taps and lashings of hot water. Rooms 1-9 are our favourites, with double windows opening onto large terraces where you can gaze down at the old gardens below and the ochre-roofed city. The private car park is a big plus and the town is a 20-minute stroll downhill. Very reasonably priced so book well ahead.

rooms	28: 26 twins/doubles, 2 singles.
price	€41–€45. Singles €30.
meals	Breakfast €4.
closed	10 December-20 February.
directions	From Madrid, right in front of town wall for Navahermosa. Over bridge (Puente de San Martin), left; hotel on left after 2km ('Quinta de Mirabel' over entrance).

	Paulino Villamor
tel	+34 925 223866
fax	+34 925 250562
email	reservas@hotelalmazara.com
web	www.hotelalmazara.com

Map 12 Entry 165

Casa Palacio Conde de Garcinarro

c/Juan Carlos I, 19, 16500 Huete, Cuenca

The owner spent his childhood just along the street from this baroque mansion – and has given the building back its dignity. He was helped in this formidable task by his wife Encarna, an artist and antique restorer; every last corner shows an eye for detail and a feel for what's right. This is every inch a Castillian residence: a fine portal of dressed sandstone with coat of arms above, grilled windows, and an enormous studded door leading to a central, colonnaded patio-garden with wooden balustrade above. Sweep up the wide walnut staircase to the first floor; to one side, a vast lounge (formerly the chapel) decked in rich burgundy colours; to the other, a second, less imposing living room. Uncluttered bedrooms are vast, high-ceilinged, terracotta-tiled and painted in wonderful pastel colours. Old prints, window seats, cushions, easy chairs and hand-painted furniture: surprisingly sumptuous given this small hotel's prices. Breakfast in the old kitchen at bright checked tablecloths, then head off to discover the delights of this wild, relatively undiscovered corner of Castille. *A Rusticae hotel*

rooms	14: 10 twins/doubles, 3 suites, 1 quadruple.
price	€55–€85. Singles €50–€65. Suites €55–€65.
meals	Breakfast €6. Various restaurants nearby.
closed	Rarely.
directions	Madrid-Valencia on N-III. Exit for Tarancón, follow signs for Cuenca; CM-310 to Huete. In village centre next to Santo Domingo church.

	Antonio Reneses Sanz
tel	+34 969 372150
fax	+34 91 5327378
email	garcinar@teleline.es
web	www.casapalaciocondedegarcinarro.com

Map 13 Entry 166

Posada de San José
c/Julián Romero 4, 16001 Cuenca

Cuenca is a town that astonishes and engraves itself on the memory. Perched on the rim of its unforgettable gorge, this is an inn to match. A magnificently crumbling portal beckons you to enter; you would never guess what lies beyond. Inside, a multi-levelled and labyrinthine dwelling, where twisting staircases take you up, across and down... Your bedroom may be large or small, perhaps with a balcony or terrace or a canopied bed, probably its own bathroom. All have fresh white walls, uneven floors and are furnished with old country pieces and decorative flair; these owners value a vase of fresh flowers over trouser-presses and satellite TV. The best and quietest rooms are at the back and have views to make the spirit soar – but all of them are worth a night. Good smells waft from the welcoming little restaurant with its heart-stopping view; you'll be glad you cut across the Meseta to reach this out-of-time place. Cuenca is fascinating though parking is tricky; you may have to park at the bottom of the hill. And do make time for the wonderful museum of contemporary art. *A Rusticae hotel.*

rooms	27: 23 twins/doubles, 1 triple, 1 single, 2 family.
price	€31–€124. Singles €20–€48.
meals	Breakfast €7. Snacks (good tapas!) available in the evenings.
closed	Rarely.
directions	From Tarancón, N-400 to Cuenca. Follow signs to Casco Antiguo. Posada 50m from cathedral main entrance. Protected parking 150m down (avoid Plaza Mayor: cars often clamped).

	Jennifer Morter
tel	+34 969 211300
fax	+34 969 230365
email	info@posadasanjose.com
web	www.posadasanjose.com

Map 13 Entry 167

Las Nubes

Camino de Cabanillas, 19117 Albalate de Zorita, Guadalajara

'The Clouds' is well named – clinging to a hilltop with breathtaking views of the Marques valley... Carlos has taken the lofty position and added a dash of Hollywood: from the glass-fronted sitting room you may follow the sun from its rising to its setting. Space and light and subtle neutral colours are the hallmarks of this contemporary hotel. Enter friendly reception, then down to a huge open-plan sitting area with a suspended canopy over the central open fire. In the dining room, Bruno the chef serves lovingly prepared regional dishes using vegetables from the garden. Lavender-scented bedrooms have sliding windows that open to a communal balcony – what a view to start the day! The whole feel is lavish-modern, with good lighting and wooden headboards that incorporate huge black and white photographs; the suite has a stunning four-poster stylishly draped in cream silk. Hire a horse or a boat, try clay pigeon shooting or hunt wild boar. Then back to splendid isolation at the end of a long track, a bird's eye view of the world and incomparable peace. *New luxury cabins opening in 2005. A Rusticae hotel.*

rooms	6: 5 twins/doubles, 1 suite.
price	€125. Suite €150.
meals	Lunch/dinner €20.
closed	Rarely.
directions	Madrid A-2 Guadalajara; exit 23 Alcalá de H. M-300; M-204 through Villabilla to Yebra. Left for Pastrana, right for Almonacid de Z. to Albalate de Z. Here for Ermita & Ruinas Históricas; house signed.

	Carlos Sánchez
tel	+34 949 101009
fax	+34 949 826897
email	lasnubes@csh.e.telefonica.net
web	www.casarurallasnubes.com

Map 13 Entry 168

El Nido de Valverde

c/Escuelas 1, 19224 Valverde de los Arroyos, Guadalajara

Escape to one of Guadalajara's furthest-flung corners. At the end of an immensely long and winding road, a delightful village – at its prettiest under a coating of snow. This house is a superb example of Guadalajara's *arquitectura negra*, its dark slate rooftops glinting like fish scales after the rain. A lover of good food and conversation, your hostess cares beautifully for her guests, just as she cared for the children she once taught. She is also a passionate defender of the fragile ecosystem, and nearly all of the food is organic. The house wraps you in its embrace the moment you enter and catch that first delicious waft of linseed oil or baking bread. The colourful kitchen is the hub (join in!), there is the cosiest of dining rooms and above, two split-level suites whose tiled floors are heated and whose mattresses are the best. (And you can incline your bedhead.) A waste to stay one night only: it may be 50km to the nearest petrol station but you are surrounded by sierra and birdsong – and Concha, the loveliest hostess. *A Rusticae hotel.*

rooms	2 suites.
price	€170.
meals	Breakfast €14. Dinner €36.
closed	Rarely.
directions	From Madrid on A-2 to Zaragoza. Exit 51 for Cabanillas; follow signs for train station to Fontanar. CM-101 to Tamajon. After 1km right for Valverde. House on main square.

	Concha Sanz Hipólito
tel	+34 949 854221/949 307448
fax	+34 949 854221/949 307448
email	informacion@nidodevalverde.com
web	www.nidodevalverde.com

Map 13 Entry 169

Hospedería Rural Salinas de Imón

c/Real 49, Imón, 19269 Sigüenza, Guadalajara

Prize-winning salt is still produced at Imón: you see the crystallising beds as you arrive. Just beyond is a tiny square and the Hospedería. This elegant house began life as a convent, then became a lowly salt warehouse. The heavy studded door now opens onto a second conversion: an unusual and exquisite mosaic of different styles. A sitting room hums with bright sofas, antiques and ornaments, old dolls and books, framed prints and huge repro paintings by Luis Gamo Alcalde, whose art enhances the whole house. Up the colourful stairway to bedrooms individually, historically themed. One has musical scores and signed photographs of musicians, another a Louis XVI-style cradle; Carlos III is graced by Empire beds and family photos; bathrooms are beamed and subtly lit. Right at the top, a cosy log-fired library leads to a patio and a stunning garden where the two towers of the original building rise… a secluded swimming pool blends in. There's a fine new spa close by – and furniture restoration and painting courses in three languages. Highly likeable, deeply cultural, and run with a personal touch.

rooms	12: 10 twins/doubles, 2 suites.
price	€57–€72. Suites €99.
meals	Breakfast €9. Dinner €25.
closed	Rarely.
directions	From Madrid A-2/E-90 for Zaragoza. Left to Sigüenza; here C-110 for Atienza to Imón. Hotel on main square of village.

Jaime Mesalles de Zunzunegui

tel	+34 949 397311
fax	+34 949 397311
email	sadeimon@teleline.es
web	www.salinasdeimon.com

Map 13 Entry 170

Hotel Valdeoma

19266 Carabias, Guadalajara

Friendly Gregorio left a busy life to restore a ruined house in the hamlet of Carabias. And his charming small hotel is unmistakeably modern – big windows, a dash of stainless steel, a minimalist décor. All blends beautifully with the ancient wood and granite. Enter via a metal stair to a low reception desk and parquet floor, laid by Gregorio himself: harmonious and restful. Lovely big bedrooms – five on the raised entrance level, the rest at ground level – have been finished in warm colours with pale marble bathrooms and walk-in showers. Both dining room and sitting room glow with a mix of modern and Victorian pieces; there are woodburners in winter and sliding glass doors to the terrace in summer. And the Guadalajara mountain views… whether you're having breakfast, dinner or just mooching around, they are a constant, splendid presence. Only nine inhabitants in the village, and that includes Gregorio! It's blissfully quiet in this very private valley. And don't miss the medieval magic of Sigüenza, a short drive. *A Rusticae hotel. Swimming pool planned.*

rooms	10 twins/doubles.
price	€90.
meals	Lunch/dinner €21.
closed	Rarely.
directions	From Madrid A-2/E-90 for Zaragoza; left for Sigüenza; there CM-110 for Atienza. After 7km left for Carabias. There, left past church, up hill; hotel at end of narrow street on right.

	Gregorio Marañón
tel	+34 600 464309
fax	+34 600 466921
email	valdeoma@vodafone.es
web	www.valdeoma.com

Map 13 Entry 171

Molino de Alcuneza

Carretera de Alboreca km0.5, 19264 Alcuneza, Guadalajara

Rural charm and fine taste: El Molino is proof of what can be achieved when love and energy are present in great measure. Little remained of the 400-year-old mill buildings when Juan and Toñi fell for this swathe of delicious greenery whose rushing millrace promised respite from the baking summers of the Meseta. It was to be a weekend bolthole for the family but then the idea of a hotel was mooted and Juan was hooked. Every last detail of the interior decoration has been carefully considered: pine floors, dark beams, wicker sofas, framed pressed flowers, fine table linen, beautifully tiled baths... and a glass floor under which flows a rivulet of crayfish and trout. Our favourite rooms are nos. 3 and 4 but all are special. Guests are given separate tables at dinner, a feast of locally grown produce: partridge with chickpeas, trout baked in Albariño wine, *cèpe*. Breakfasts are hearty and picnic hampers can be arranged. Sigüenza and Atienza, two great medieval villages, are a must-see. Arrive as a guest, leave as a friend – the Morenos are a delightful family. *A Rusticae hotel*

rooms	11 twins/doubles.
price	€108–€180. Singles €72.
meals	Breakfast €7. Dinner €27. Restaurant closed Sundays.
closed	Rarely.
directions	From Sigüenza towards Medinacelli. Molino well signposted before you reach Alboreca, on right.

	Juan & Toñi Moreno
tel	+34 949 391501
fax	+34 949 347004
email	molinoal@teleline.es
web	www.molinodealcuneza.com

Map 13 Entry 172

Best Western Premier Santo Domingo
Plaza Santo Domingo 13, 28013 Madrid

In spite of its size, the Santo Domingo feels intimate and friendly. And it's slap bang in the middle of old Madrid, close to the Opera, the Plaza Mayor, the shopping on the Gran Vía, and the metro. Step in to find reception and lounge smartly and flamboyantly decorated, with a sparkling marble floor and striped sofas to sink into. Masses of art is on display and each one of the 120 bedrooms is different. All are well decorated, beautifully clean, and contain every conceivable extra: mini-bars and TVs, bathrobes and toiletries, safety boxes, writing sets, and quiet air conditioning. Standard rooms are compact, so pay for a superior one with a patio and a jacuzzi – you'll be glad you did. The desire to be as customer-friendly as possible in the bedrooms holds true in the restaurant, too. Surprisingly, for such a big posh place, there's "good home cooking" on the menu, to quote Ana Hernández, the hotel's ever-friendly manageress. Part of the Best Western chain, Santo Domingo won its laurels long ago, still aspires to be first past the post, and, thanks to kind staff and huge comfort, succeeds.

rooms	120: 60 twins/doubles, 60 singles.
price	€159.50–€215. Singles €94.50–€162; free at weekends.
meals	Breakfast €11.50; Lunch/dinner €29 set menu; €40 à la carte.
closed	Rarely.
directions	Along Gran Vía away from Cibeles; pass Plaza de Callao, left into c/San Bernardo to Plaza Santo D. On right. Porter will park car.

	Antonio Núñez Tirado
tel	+34 91 5479800
fax	+34 91 5475995
email	reserva@hotelsantodomingo.com
web	www.hotelsantodomingo.net

Map 12 Entry 173

La Casa del Puente Colgante

Ctra. Uceda km3, 28189 Torremocha de Jarama, Madrid

A beautiful wooded spot on the banks of the Jarama river – hard to believe Madrid is a bus ride away. The modern ex-banker's home is named 'the house of the suspension bridge'. Currently the bridge, swathed in greenery, is under repair, but when it reopens you may pop across to a waterfall, a river pool (take a splash) and a grassy knoll – perfect for watching bird life. (You may well see a kingfisher and a heron or two.) The peace and beauty of the setting are reflected in the tranquillity of the house: no TV, just music and the lull of the river, and the nightingale's song in spring. There's a pleasant sitting room for guests to share, while pastel-painted bedrooms vary in size and are simple, clean and cosy, with white fitted wardrobes and comfy beds. Silvia loves this place dearly, knows its every shrub and tree, and encourages guests to completely unwind. She is also full of ideas for exploring the area. She prepares dinners using organic fruit and veg, local cheeses and cuts of meat, and her apple tart, served on special occasions, is delicious.

rooms	5 twins/doubles.
price	€60. VAT included.
meals	Dinner €20. VAT included.
closed	23-26 December.
directions	From Madrid A-1 Burgos; exit km50 marker for Torrelaguna & Patones de Arriba. Right to Torremocha. Through & follow signs 'farmacia & turismo rural'; 3.3km, 'casa rural' sign on left by white columns.

	Silvia Leal
tel	+34 91 8430595
fax	+34 91 8430595
email	info@casadelpuentecolgante.com
web	www.casadelpuentecolgante.com

Map 12 Entry 174

Sara de Ur

Corcho 26, 28751 La Cabrera, Madrid

Where else will you find such an assortment of finds? Such is the irrepressible enthusiasm of Alejandro for the antiques trade that the hotel is an Aladdin's cave of Nepalese rugs, French furniture, Art Deco and African sculpture. There is nothing cave-like about the building however, which is sprucely modern. Though a purist might raise an eyebrow at the sudden jumps from old to new, as a guest you will revel in it all. Colourwashed bedrooms are a good size, bathrooms are luxurious (a stainless steel basin, an antique mirror) and split-level suites come with kitchenettes. Gardens are maturing well, and complimentary tennis and swimming are round the corner, thanks to an agreement with the campsite 200m away. This is a fun place, with a hugely likeable host, at the foot of the dramatic craggy outline of Honey mountain. Make time for Patones while you're here, a 17th-century village untouched by modern times. And, in case you are wondering, Sarah of Ur was Abraham's wife, from that oldest of inhabited towns in Mesopotamia. *A Rusticae hotel.*

rooms	14: 7 twins/doubles, 5 duplex, 2 suites.
price	€85–€115. Singles €70–€75. Suites €110–€130. VAT included.
meals	Lunch/dinner €15–€18 set menu; €30 à la carte.
closed	24–25 December.
directions	From Madrid, N-I for Aranda de Duero. Exit 57 to La Cabrera. Left by petrol station for Valdemanco. Right to hotel after approx. 20m.

Alejandro & Cecilia Burgos

tel   +34 91 8689509
fax   +34 91 8689514
email   info@saradeur.com
web   www.saradeur.com

Map 12 Entry 175

Photo Michael Busselle

levante

Hospedería La Mariposa

Casa del Estanco 67, Gebas, 30840 Alhama de Murcia, Murcia

In the old days you climbed the winding road to stock up on vegetables, flour, eggs and baccy. Now the old farmstead – a ruin when Roberto and Yvonne discovered it – has become a welcoming country hotel. And what a site, here in the heart of hiking country. There's excellent rock climbing and mountain biking too, and strolls through the Barrancos de Gerbas nature reserve for the less energetic. But if nature and the vineyards won't tempt you out, stay here and loll by the pool. (There's a playpool to keep little ones happy.) Or browse the library, practice your scales on the piano, dream from the patio on the Barrancos views. Bedrooms are beautfully uncluttered and a very good size, enlivened by Yvonne's colourful paintings. Roberto is equally creative: opt for lunch or dinner and you're in for a treat. A professional chef, he concocts delicious variations of classic mediterranean dishes, served at a big table. He and Yvonne are an energetic pair, as keen to look after their guests as they are the environment. Water is recycled and solar power used, and much of the fruit is organically home-grown.

rooms	6 + 2: 5 twins/doubles, 1 family. 2 self-catering apartments for 2-4.
price	€44-€79.50. Apts €51.50-€69 for 2. VAT included.
meals	Breakfast €4. Lunch/dinner €14.
closed	2 weeks in September; 1 week in January.
directions	From Alhama follow signs for Mula & Gebas. Hotel on right on entering Gebas.

	Roberto van Eijk
tel	+34 968 631008
fax	+34 968 632549
email	info@hospederialamariposa.com
web	www.hospederialamariposa.com

Map 20 Entry 176

Molino del Río Argos

Camino Viejo de Archivel s/n, 30400 Caravaca de la Cruz, Murcia

Remote and beautiful, the fruit and walnut farm is secreted away beside a 135 million-year-old canyon cut by the Argos – paleontologist heaven. Its abundant waters explain why grain was milled here for centuries… now Carmen and Swedish Jan have restored the 16th-century mill and outbuildings and created an award-winning place to stay. The building's peachy colourwash makes the least possible impact on the setting, natural dyes have been used for doors and beams, floor tiles handmade according to an ancient technique, and organic orchards planted on the terraces. In earlier times the mill was a barter-inn – peasants came to exchange goods for flour. Now people travel for a perfect night's sleep (lulled by the sound of fountains and streams) in a rustically simple apartment or room. The food is simple mediterranean, occasionally Scandinavian, with wild meat a speciality. There are patios and pergolas in the garden, children will love the river walks and the outdoor pool, and the birdwatching's wonderful. Make time for Caravaca – the fifth holy city – and the Ethnologic Music Museum 4km away.

rooms	1 + 6: 1 double. 6 apartments for 2-6.
price	€46. Apartment €55-€96.
meals	Breakfast €4. Lunch/dinner €22.
closed	Rarely.
directions	From Alicante A-7 for Murcia, and after, Andalucia/Granada. Exit at C-415 for Caravaca de la Cruz. Then signs to Andalucia. After 7km, hotel on right.

	Carmen Alvárez
tel	+34 968 433381
fax	+34 968 433444
email	elmolino@molinodelrio.com
web	www.molinodelrio.com

Map 20 Entry 177

Casa del Maco
Pou Roig 15, 03720 Benissa, Alicante

It's described as a rustic farmhouse but it's grander than that. An imposing paved terrace, statuesque trees and Lloyd Loom loungers around the pool give the Casa a gracious air. The 18th-century rooms, their beamed ceilings and deeply recessed windows betraying finca origins, are similarly special, the décor revealing flair and restraint. The restaurant, too, is sophisticated rather than rustic – food and wines are delicious, indisputably 'haute' (lobster is the house special) and served by impeccable staff. Bedrooms are romantic, bathrooms luxurious. The remote valley setting is stunning, and the gardens overlook vineyards, olive groves and almond orchards; behind, a bare shoulder of rock juts through the pine-covered hills. Excellent walks lead from the door; from Calpe, you can hike up to the flat top of the Peñón de Ifach (experienced crag rats like to tackle the rock climbs on its south face). Either way, you'll get great views of the saltpans, the mountains and the precipitous coastline to Cape La Nao. If you long for the sea and can face the crowds, the Costa is a short ride. A heavenly place.

rooms	6 twins/doubles.
price	€66–€99. VAT included.
meals	Breakfast €9. Lunch €19. Dinner €35 à la carte. VAT included. Restaurant closed Tuesdays.
closed	January.
directions	From Alicante, A-7 for Valencia. Exit for Calpe & Altea; N-332 for Benissa. 900m after sign for Calpe, by BP petrol station, left for Casa del Maco, signed; turning easy to miss.

	Bert de Vooght
tel	+34 965 732842
fax	+34 965 730103
email	macomarcus@hotmail.com
web	www.casadelmaco.com

Map 21 Entry 178

El Sequer

c/Traviesa 17, Partida Frontó, 03769 Benimelí, Alicante

Impossible to imagine it raining here, yet the lush fertility of the valley suggests that it must do sometimes. This beautifully restored *riu-rau* (a farm building used for drying grapes) is full of light and colour. Orange trees beside a dazzlingly blue pool, corn-yellow walls and blue shutters... there's a sunlit mood. You are nicely tucked away, too, at the tail end of the village and with stunning views to the tiny villages ringed in a horseshoe around the valley. The garden is a delight, with its orange grove, fig tree and vegetable patch, and lovely tile-clad tables and chairs for leisurely meals. Your living space is open-plan and airy, thoughtfully furnished and with a well-equipped kitchen. The double has a great antique bed; the bathroom a whirlpool bath. The bamboo-slotted ceilings, intersected with stout blue beams, are a hallmark of this type of cottage. You have everything you need, from CD player to mountain bikes, while hospitable Jennifer greets you warmly, and provides a little welcome pack of tea, coffee, milk, juice, fresh fruit, bread... just what you'd hope for after a long drive.

rooms	1 cottage for 4.
price	Week €650–€840; weekend €300–€340. Minimum 2 nights; July/August 1 week.
meals	Self-catering.
closed	Rarely.
directions	A-7 from Alicante. Exit 62 for Ondara (N-332). Then CV-731 & CV-732 to Beniarbeig. At bridge, left to Benimelí. 1st road up to right, signed.

	Jennifer Pilliner
tel	+34 966 424056
fax	+34 966 424056
email	jpilliner@telefonica.net
web	www.mediterraneorural.com

Map 21 Entry 179

Casa Pilar

c/San José 2, 03793 Castell de Castells, Alicante

A proudly kept and genuinely friendly hotel of charm, full of family furniture, books and paintings. From here you can explore the mountains of the Sierra de Aitana and return each evening to a 13-course dinner, a favourite with hikers. The house has been in the Vaquer family for generations – both Pilar and her mother were born here – and is one of the largest in this quiet village; it was built originally for the priest. The dining room was once the stables, and still has its stone walls and hay manger – now filled with jams and marmalades. This is where Pilar dishes out her gargantuan meals, eaten around the great communal table. Bedrooms are light and bright and – best of all – deliciously cool in summer. Pilar is a warm presence, ready to help with maps, picnics or tips on places to visit. Those who prefer a more sedentary existence can choose a book from the shelves in the sitting room upstairs and retreat to an armchair with one of Pilar's newly picked herbal infusions. Don't miss the cave paintings of Pla de Petracos nearby.

rooms	6 + 1: 6 twins/doubles. 1 apartment for 4.
price	€60–€75. Singles €35. VAT included.
meals	Packed lunch €6. Dinner €18. VAT inc.
closed	Rarely.
directions	From Valencia A-7 exit 62 Ondara. Right at junc. to Parcent. Left at 1st junc., right at 2nd junc. opp. Pizzeria to C. de Castells. There, left at junc. for centre. At end of main road, left opp. bar.

	Pilar Vaquer Tomás
tel	+34 965 518157
fax	+34 965 518334
email	casapilar@grupobbva.net
web	www.casapilar.com

Map 21 Entry 180

Almàssera Vella

Carrer de la Mare de Deu del Miracle 56, 03578 Relleu, Alicante

The village's old olive press still stands – in the dining room. Derelict when Christopher and Marisa arrived, the house, in this beautiful mountain village, is both a stylish and inviting home *and* a cultural centre. Spanish Marisa is an expert seamstress and interior designer, and cooks like a dream; Christopher is a prize-winning poet. Courses, run mostly during the winter, include writing, painting, photography, tapestry and hiking. The bright, airy living room is stuffed with books (3,000 at the last count), the dining room is homely. Also in the main house are four cosy, cottagey bedrooms, with original artwork and photographs on the walls; two look over the terrace garden with pool and giant chess, and the valley with Moorish hilltop castle beyond. Opposite, a smaller house for self-catering – and an independent studio upstairs, an inspiring retreat for artists and writers. Not every room has its own but there are plenty of bathrooms in both houses. A place for grown-ups not children – there's far too much thinking and creating going on! *Min. two people in cottage & studio high season.*

rooms	4 + 2: 4 twins/doubles. 1 cottage for 6, 1 studio for 3.
price	€55–€70. Cottage & studio €40 p.p. (high season); cottage & studio from €225 p.p. p.w. (low season). VAT inc.
meals	Dinner €17.50.
closed	Rarely.
directions	From J-66 on A-7 (Villajoyosa); right (inland). After Orcheta left to Relleu. Street opp. church. Last property on right.

	Christopher & Marisa North
tel	+34 966 856003
fax	+34 966 856337
email	oldolivepress@tiscali.es
web	www.oldolivepress.com

Map 21 Entry 181

El Almendral de Relleu

Partida Rural El Terme, Ctra. CV-775 km18, 03578 Relleu, Alicante

It's remote, the track is bumpy, there's little to do. It's just you, 2,800 almond trees and uninterrupted views of the jagged peaks. This is switch-off and chill-out country. Bernard, a well-travelled French journalist, has renovated and extended his hilltop, 18th-century country house (20km, but a world away, from Benidorm) to provide quirky but sinfully commodious surroundings. Step inside and rooms spill off in all directions. Furnishings are stylish, spoiling and reflect Bernard's travels and his refreshingly irreverent attitude. The bedrooms, named after (most of) the deadly sins – Greed is yellow, Pride is purple – are furnished with elegance and comfort: huge American beds, gleaming French antiques, rich Catalan fabrics. The salon has Art Deco sofas and a cinema-size TV while the restaurant, with its cherry-red and white walls, oil paintings and thick napery, is classy and romantic. The Spanish/French menu is the big draw for returning guests. Cool off in the pool, doze on the shady terrace, wander among the palms, orange and lemon trees, gaze at the views… bliss.

rooms	6 twins/doubles.
price	€85-120.
meals	Lunch/dinner €15; €25 à la carte.
closed	Rarely.
directions	From Alicante on motorway; exit for Campello-San Juan. On CV-775 for Agues. At km18 marker 1st left for El Almendral.

	Bernard Vassas
tel	+34 659 165085
fax	+34 966 308875
email	info@almendral.com
web	www.almendral.com

Map 21 Entry 182

El Otero

c/Atalaya 60, 03569 Aigües, Alicante

Life is lived outdoors at this large hacienda tucked above Aigües village. Four bedrooms, big enough to be family rooms, spread across the ground floor, each opening onto a wide, shady terrace. Linger over breakfast, then amble down to the curved swimming pool with its many spots for sunbathing or sun-shading. Nearby is a well-equipped children's playground. Two Belgian families – a brother and sister team, their spouses and young children – live on the upper floors and run this simple, homely B&B with enthusiastic efficiency. They're keen to arrange activities, from quad-biking and trekking to sailing and picnic expeditions. Bedrooms (one with a kitchenette) are cool and modest with bright bedcovers, large windows and amusing trompe l'oeils – perhaps a fake bookshelf or a fantasy view. No meals as such, but there are restaurants in the village and sister and sister-in-law Marie and Evelyne are happy to rustle up something tasty and wholesome if you ask. Barbecues are a regular summer event. Not luxury living but a warm, lively, family place to stay, and the beaches a very short drive.

rooms	4 twins/doubles.
price	€65–€85. VAT included.
meals	Summer barbecue, €13. Good restaurants nearby.
closed	Rarely.
directions	From Alicante airport on E-15/A7 for Valencia; exit on N-332 for San Juan-El Campello; right immed. after exit for El Campello. After 3.6km exit Aigues-Playas. In village, hotel up steep hill.

Evelyne & Marie Kraft
tel   +34 965 690116
email   elotero2001@yahoo.es
web   www.fincaelotero.com

Map 21 Entry 183

Poco-a-Poco Orange Farm

Apdo. 517, 03330 Crevillente, Alicante

Whence the name? 'Poco a poco' was the neighbours' regular comment as they watched the Brettles building this house among the orange and pomegranate. groves. 'Modern', 'roomy' and 'comfortable' best sum up the result. There are no stairs so it's ideal for little ones and the less nimble, and the bedrooms are large, one with its own luxy bathroom. Outside: an enormous gravelled garden with a large pool and great views, and a boules court. A sauna and steam room are being built in the garden; *poco a poco*, naturally. Pauline and Chris couldn't be more accommodating: rent the whole house and cook for yourselves, or book a room with breakfast; ask for an evening meal, eat out in Crevillente or, if you pick up the ingredients for a barbecue supper, the Brettles will cook it for you – over orange wood! Golfers will love it here, with seven courses within driving distance – the motorway is very close, though out of noise nuisance range. There's the Vega Baja to explore, the beaches and the dramatic Sierra Crevillente… your hire company will thank you if you let the Bettles take you up there in their 4x4.

rooms	3 twins/doubles.
price	€44. €230–€280 p.w. Whole house: €715–€1,155 p.w.
meals	Dinner from €8, by request.
closed	Christmas.
directions	From Alicante A-7 for Murcia; exit 77 for 'Torrevieja'. Straight over at 1st r'bout; next roundabout right. Under m'way. Immed. right on tarmac road; left at fork & left again onto dirt track.

	Pauline Brettle
tel	+34 676 169649
web	www.poco-a-poco-orangefarm.co.uk

Map 21 Entry 184

Mas Fontanelles

Ctra. Biar-Bañeres km4, 03410 Biar, Alicante

Light-flooded rooms, burnished wood floors, high raftered ceilings – it is rustic, contemporary, beautiful. The huge, peaceful, 200-year-old farmhouse overlooks the pine, olive and almond trees of Benijama valley, and has been lovingly restored by Isabel and her Italian husband, Roberto. Colours are ochre and blue, fabrics are creamy, furniture is restored-antique or sleekly modern – chic but not pretentious. Bedrooms, named after trees, have a light designer touch making perfect use of natural colours and materials: creamy cotton bedspreads, rush-seated chairs, antique chests of drawers. Some rooms have balconies, one a terrace and two have loft-style additions, brilliant for children. There's a cosy sitting room with board games and a high-raftered, second-floor living room with comfortably elegant white sofas and books to browse. And, everywhere, stunning views. Isabel and Roberto will help you plan your days; walk, ride, quad-bike, paint, visit an Arab castle or two. Then back to a freshly prepared supper, and a terrace from which to gaze, wine in hand, on a perfect southern sunset.

rooms	8 twins/doubles.
price	€54–€60. Singles €48–€54. VAT included.
meals	Dinner €17.
closed	Rarely.
directions	From Alicante N-330 to Villena. Here follow signs for Biar. Hotel 4km outside Biar towards Bañeres.

	Isabel Aracil & Roberto Medoro
tel	+34 686 426126
fax	+34 965 979007
email	info@masfontanelles.com
web	www.masfontanelles.com

Map 21 Entry 185

Casa el Pinet

Masía el Pinet s/n, 03459 Alfafara, Alicante

Deep in the dramatic Sierra Mariola, this 200-year-old castellated beauty. The former summer residence of Dona Maria Luisa Gil-Dotz del Castellar y Catalina, grandmother of the present owner, it is a home that has been cared for by generations of Ortegas. Sergio and mother Dolores offer you El Pinet for delightful B&B: homemade pastries on a canopied terrace for breakfast and an exquisite pool, replete with changing rooms and chairs. Above, in the coachman's quarters, a cosy holiday home for six. Beams, terracotta floors and original features abound, ensuite shower rooms sparkle, the small kitchen is well-equipped, and furniture is a mix of rustic antique and new. Rugs, quilts, rocking chairs and log fire ensure a relaxed feel. There's a terrace too, with a barbecue. Birdsong, cicadas and perhaps the distant hum of a tractor are all you hear in these 60 hectares of pines, fields and hills. The area is known for its aromatic plants and herbs, you can visit nearby caves and ice-wells and the hiking and riding are magnificent. *B&B minimum two nights. El Pinet also available for self-catering.*

rooms	4 + 1: 3 doubles, 1 triple. 1 apartment for 6.
price	€70. Apartment €162 per day.
meals	B&B or self-catering. Restaurant 1km.
closed	Rarely.
directions	From N-330, exit at Villena & head east for Ontinyet. After Bocairent, right to Alfafara. House signed on left, 1.5km before village.

	Sergio Castelló
tel	+34 965 529039
fax	+34 965 510141
email	info@elpinet.com
web	www.elpinet.com

Map 21 Entry 186

Hotel Els Frares

Avda. del País Valencià 20, 03811 Quatretondeta, Alicante

Brian and Pat left the UK to head for the Spanish hills. Herculean efforts have borne fruit at their village inn – a 100-year-old ruin when they first set eyes on it. Now its attractive frontage and constant flow of visitors are adding life and colour to the tiny hamlet, and your immensely likeable hosts have made many Spanish friends. Behind, jagged peaks rise to almost 5,000 feet – the hotel takes its name from them – and the patio (bliss for summery meals) looks out across surrounding almond groves to the lofty crags. Good mattresses ensure deep sleep, fabrics are bright, there are framed photos of the Sierra Serella, and four bedrooms have terraces with vines and views. The cosy, spotless dining and sitting rooms are just the sort of rooms you'd want to return to after a hike in the hills – perhaps with Brian as your guide (though not in the height of summer). At supper choose from a menu that celebrates local dishes and tapas yet finds a place for imaginative vegetarian alternatives; the olive oil, fruit, vegetables and herbs are home-grown, the wines local and delicious. Walkers' heaven.

rooms	9 + 1: 9 twins/doubles. 1 cottage for 4.
price	€65–€70. Cottage €200 for 2, €300 for 4 (2 nights).
meals	Breakfast €7. Lunch €18. Dinner €20 set menu; €24 à la carte.
closed	Rarely.
directions	From Alicante A-7, junc. 70, onto A-36 Alcoi; CV-70 Benilloba, left to Gorga; sharp right through village. 5km to hamlet of Quatretondeta.

	Patricia & Brian Fagg
tel	+34 965 511234
fax	+34 965 511200
email	elsfrares@terra.es
web	www.inn-spain.com

Map 21 Entry 187

El Chato Chico

Plaza de la Iglesia 6, 03788 Beniaya - Vall d'Alcalá, Alicante

Don't expect much action in Biniaya: at the last count there were 13 inhabitants! Yet in the Middle Ages it was important enough for the Imam of the Moorish King Al-Azraq (the 'Blue-eyed one' – Jakki will tell you more) to have built himself a fine house next to the mosque. It is this very building that your hosts have nursed back to life; you'll see one of the original arches in the sitting room. The house has a snug, enveloping feel; bedrooms, library and bar are smallish and beamed but your well-being is guaranteed – thanks to good beds, Paul's paintings on the walls, central heating for winter, and very good country peace. Don't expect an all-Spanish dinner but do expect the food to be delicious value. Breakfast, on the terrace with stunning views, can be fresh fruit, yogurt and homemade cake – or cooked English if you order in advance. If you prefer holidays with a purpose, note that your friendly hosts arrange courses in cookery, Spanish conversation and painting. Easy to see why they gave up jobs in Benidorm to open this pretty guesthouse full of history. The walking is superb.

rooms	5 twins/doubles.
price	€48-€66. Singles €31-€40. VAT included.
meals	Dinner with wine €20. VAT included.
closed	Rarely.
directions	From Alicante A-70 for San Vicente; A-7 & N-340 to Alcoy. 3km before Alcoy, right to Benilloba & Gorga. At Gorga junc., take Facheca road. Left to Tollos, sign to Beniaya (4km).

	Paul Walmsley & Jakki Spencer
tel	+34 965 514451
fax	+34 96 551 4161
email	elchatochico@wanadoo.es
web	www.elchatochico.com

Map 21 Entry 188

Casa Rural Serrella

c/San Jose 1, 03812 Balones, Alicante

The steep, winding road passes almond and olive terraces while the air grows clear and pure. By the time you reach the mountain village of Balones (population 190) it's intoxicating – no wonder ex-pats Mike and Demelza brought up their family here. Their large, peach-coloured village house is a true family home. Guests are greeted by an exuberant dog and everyone chats around the kitchen table. The guest rooms and the apartment (with terrace) have a comfy, lived-in feel, with much of the rustic-style furniture made by Mike. Colourful bedcovers, pastel coloured walls, terracotta floors and beamed ceilings create a simple but cared-for atmosphere. Summer meals are taken to the flower-filled terrace. Demelza, helped by daughter Melissa, cooks wholesome, unfussy, seasonally based dishes. After a day visiting historic Alcoy, or a long hike, return for a dip in the village pool – and time your visit, if you can, for one of the colourful village fiestas. The Whittocks are easy, relaxed people who are happiest treating guests as part of the family.

rooms	4 + 1: 4 twins/doubles. 1 apt for 2.
price	€20. Apartment €25 per person.
meals	Breakfast €3. Dinner €15. Packed lunches on request.
closed	Rarely.
directions	On A-77 for Alcoy. Right to Benilloba. 1km past Benilloba left to Gorga. There, right for Facheca. 2nd entrance to Balones, park under pine trees on right. Walk into village; 1st left & 1st left again; just after phone box on left.

	Demelza & Mike Whittock
tel	+34 965 511222
fax	+34 965 511222
email	casaserrella@terra.es
web	www.quietspain.com

Map 21 Entry 189

Masía la Safranera

Partida Serratella 13, 46650 Alcoy, Valencia

You may have heard of Alcoy because of its annual Fiesta de Moros y Cristianos when the whole town engages in mock battle. You are less likely to have heard of La Safranera, a century-old farm and bodega, five miles from the mock-medieval madness. You are in the centre of a Parque Natural and a birdwatchers' paradise – forested hills stretch as far as the eye can see. The ever-courteous Rafael Llace Vila and his extended family have vested love and labour in nursing these old buildings back to good health. Simple guest rooms strike a balance between traditional and functional, with old beams, modern tiles and decent beds and bathrooms. More striking is the dining room with its enormous old wine barrels and other oenological instruments on display, and mounted boar's head above the inglenook; utterly Spanish. The plastic chairs feel less rustic but food is regional, the bottled cider excellent and they're packed for Sunday lunch. Families will enjoy the peace, the space and the pool up the hill above the house. And be sure to walk the route from here up to the old Sanctuary of Font Roja.

rooms	14 twins/doubles.
price	€28. Half-board €40; full-board €50.
meals	Breakfast €6. Lunch/dinner €16.
closed	Rarely.
directions	From Alcoy CV-795 towards Bañeres. 200m beyond signpost 'Bañeres 12km' left following signs to 'Alojamiento Turístico La Safranera'. Hotel 3km from junction.

	Rafael Llace Vila
tel	+34 609 617280
fax	+34 962 245383
email	lasafranera@teleline.es
web	www.lasafranera.com

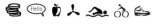

Map 21 Entry 190

Hotel L'Estacio

Parc de l'Estacio s/n, 46880 Bocairent, Valencia

The old railway station is today a light, bright hotel, run by friendly Dutch cousins Sebastian and Pascal. Reception is the station foyer, where an 'installation' of antique suitcases acts as a witty reminder of its history. Ultra-modern bedrooms, bathed in light from huge windows, have big comfy beds, elegant white blinds and a luxurious feel. The bathrooms match – generous and gorgeous. The large paintings you see everywhere are the work of Sebastian's talented mother. A vast building with vaulted ceilings – once the carriage shed – now houses a glass-roofed café/bar and a white-walled dining room, where you feast on regional dishes that make best use of local produce and herbs from the garden. A pool is planned for 2005, but there's also a good public one a walk away. Stroll round the lovely medieval town of Bocairent, see the Sierra Mariola from a hot-air balloon, pop down to the coast – or simply unwind in the glass-canopied lounge or palm-lined, shady gardens. A stylish bolthole, a treat for all ages.

rooms	15: 14 twins/doubles, 1 single.
price	€66–€94.
meals	Breakfast €9. Lunch/dinner €10 set menu; €25 à la carte (not weekends).
closed	Rarely.
directions	From Alicante airport N-332. At Campello N-340 for Alcoi. There, take smaller road for Bocairent. Hotel to side of r'bout before town.

	Sebastian Lodder
tel	+34 962 350000
fax	+34 962 350030
email	reservas@hotelestacio.com
web	www.hotelestacio.com

Map 21 Entry 191

La Casa Vieja

Carrer del Forn 4, 46842 Rugat, Valencia

This most peaceful of village houses combines 450 years of old stones with a contemporary feel for volumes and shapes. There are nobleman's arches and columns, ancient floor tiles, twisty beams, an indoor well and… a small, square, swimming pool in the verdant, Arabic courtyard. A double-height sitting area faces an immense inglenook where deep leather sofas envelop you as you sip a welcome sherry before dining. Many of the antiques have been in Maris's family for as long as she can remember – oil paintings and Persian rugs, a 16th-century grandfather clock, a carved mahogany table. Bedrooms, too, are stylish and homely, beds big and firm; there are terraces for some, books and baskets of fruit and no TV. Views stretch to the orange-clad hillsides, and summer meals are accompanied by jasmine and candles. People travel some way for the food, which follows the seasons; fish, fruit and vegetables are fresh from the market and there are interesting vegetarian alternatives. We enjoyed the grilled goat's cheese with fig and orange confit, and the excellent Spanish wines.

rooms	6: 5 twins/doubles, 1 suite.
price	€70-€85. Singles €60. Suite €120.
meals	Dinner €24.
closed	Christmas & New Year.
directions	Valencia A-7 for Alicante, exit 60. N-332 for Alicante. After tunnels fork right onto CV-60 for Albaida. After 19km right onto CV-691 for Rugat. Through Montichelvo, Rugat 2nd. village on left. Signed in village; behind church.

	Maris & Maisie Andrés Watson
tel	+34 962 814013
fax	+34 962 814013
email	info@lacasavieja.com
web	www.lacasavieja.com

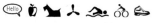

Map 21 Entry 192

Hostería Mont Sant

Ctra. del Castillo s/n, 46800 Xátiva (Játiva), Valencia

The Arab castle towers above; the views sweep dramatically over the red-roofed city and countryside below. Terraced gardens glisten with orange trees and 1,000 young palms soften the habitat of fascinating archaeology... Iberian and Roman shards, Moorish fortifications, Cistercian walls. A Moorish irrigation system has guaranteed water in all seasons since the 12th century and the mountain streams are channelled, refreshing the air as they go, into a vast cistern under the garden. Javier Andrés Cifre is proud of his old family house, including the relics he has uncovered during excavations. The natural gardens are full of idyllic nooks and corners; terraces are charming with canvas parasols. Cool, beamed living areas have intimate alcoves; bedrooms above have antiques and great views; large and sophisticated cabin rooms (air conditioning, TV, DVD) are dotted among the pines and the suite has its own pool. Bathrooms are luxurious. Tuck into elaborate Valencian dishes from state-of-the-art kitchens, and, should you over-indulge, recover in the sauna, small pool or jacuzzi. *A Rusticae hotel*

rooms	17: 16 twins/doubles, 1 suite.
price	€93–€130. Suite €149–€261.
meals	Breakfast €9. Half-board €41.
closed	7-20 January.
directions	From Valencia N-340 for Albacete. Xátiva (Játiva) exit; follow signs for 'Castillo'. Signed. From Alicante on N-340 north via Alcoy to Xátiva.

	Javier Andrés Cifre
tel	+34 962 275081
fax	+34 962 281905
email	mont-sant@mont-sant.com
web	www.mont-sant.com

Map 21 Entry 193

Casa del Pinar

Ctra. Los Isidros-Venta del Moro, 46310 Venta del Moro, Valencia

Ping-pong among the fragrant pines – what more could you wish for on a summer's evening? There is plenty here to delight all the senses. Ana María and Phillipe took over the old finca many years ago. Ana used to write about tapas for the BBC; Phillipe, whose culinary awards line the dining room, knows a thing or two about food: you'll eat well. Phillipe, who occasionally runs cookery courses, uses the best of local produce (such as the handmade Requena sausage, to which an entire festival is devoted in February). Choose between an attractively furnished room in the hotel, with its pretty, white-walled dining room and elegant, galleried sitting room, or one of the self-catering houses (one sleeping seven, the other eight), beautifully furnished in traditional style. The whitewashed buildings open onto a central courtyard and enjoy an unusually close relationship with the outdoors. Flowers are everywhere, rambling across the courtyard or amassed in great urns in the garden; beyond, almond orchards and olive groves. And a pool – shared by all – of Olympic proportions with a fine view.

rooms	6 + 2: 6 doubles. 2 self-catering houses for 7-8.
price	€75. Singles €65. Houses €650-€840 p.w.
meals	Breakfast €6. Lunch/dinner €24 set menu.
closed	December-January.
directions	N-322 for Albacete. After Los Isidros, right to Los Cojos. Pass turn for village. 1km further, on left.

	Ana María Castillo Serna
tel	+34 962 139121
email	diment@wanadoo.es
web	www.hotelcasadelpinar.com

Map 14 Entry 194

Hotel Mas de Canicatti

Ctra. Pedralba km2.9, 46191 Vilamarxant, Valencia

A late addition to this guide – and a rather splendid one. Private pools for the suites, a large pool overlooking a huge garden with the Camp de Turia beyond, tennis courts, a helipad and an all-singing, all-dancing spa (Turkish bath, massage, beauty treatments, sauna, jet pool)… this is a place for some serious pampering. This new, attractive, whitewashed hotel 20km west of lovely Valencia is built around a central patio with a fountain, and its bedrooms are both large and idiosyncratically luxurious. Cooling, calm walls, light parquet floors, traditional Spanish pieces, explosive colours and assertively modern accessories – all is impeccable. You'll eat well, too: the kitchens are supervised by the owner of the Michelin double-starred Girasol in Moraira. This extensive single-floor building – no stairs! – is surrounded by a large garden for children to roam: lawn, flowers, pines, palms, olive and carob trees with, beyond, more than 100 acres of orange groves – plenty of room for solitude. *Uninspected at time of going to press. A Rusticae hotel.*

rooms	27: 14 doubles, 13 suites.
price	€185-€221. Singles €155-€185. Suite €300-€420.
meals	Breakfast €18. Half-board €60 p.p. extra; full-board €90.
closed	Never.
directions	From Valencia A-3 for Madrid exit Ribarroja del Turia.

	Angeles Fuertes Llopis
tel	+34 961 650534
fax	+34 961 650535
email	direccion@masdecanicatti.com
web	www.masdecanicatti.com

Map 14 Entry 195

El Jardin Vertical

Carrer Nou 15, 12192 Vilafames, Castellón

Vilafames is a gorgeous hilltop village of red tiled roofs, turrets and towers, worn steps and an unmissable contemporary art museum. And El Jardin Vertical is *the* place to stay, with its stylish décor and views that sweep across cherry and almond groves (a feast in early spring) to the mountains beyond. This is a 400-year-old house exquisitely styled, a sophisticated yet rustic hideaway. Floors are solid terracotta or 1920s cement-tiled, walls are open-stone or colourwashed plaster. Original artwork and pottery, wicker chairs and Moroccan mosaics add personality to the cool, serene reception and the sitting room cosy with open fire. Gloria's gift for interior design extends to the quirky patio and the big, harmonious bedrooms; the one in the attic – hot in summer – has sensational views. Pale tiled floors reflect the muted but warm colours, the bed linen is the best, the paintings are by Gloria's daughter. Double-glazing and shutters mute village traffic noise. Food is home-cooked and mediterranean – so good that plans are afoot to open the restaurant to non-residents. *A Rusticae hotel.*

rooms	7: 6 twins/doubles, 1 suite.
price	€85-€90. Suite €95-€100.
meals	Breakfast €12. Lunch/dinner €20 set menu.
closed	Rarely.
directions	From Barcelona A-7 exit 'Castellón Sur'. After toll to Benicassim; exit for Borriol onto CV-15; on for San Mateo. Exit 38 onto CV-160 to Vilafames. At village entrance right to hotel. Up to Ayuntamiento & park. At far right of square.

	Gloria Diaz-Varela Parada
tel	+34 964 32 99 38
fax	+34 964 32 99 39
email	casarural@eljardinvertical.jazztel.es
web	www.eljardinvertical.jazztel.es

Map 15 Entry 196

Hotel Cardenal Ram

Cuesta Suñer 1, 12300 Morella, Castellón

Walled, hilltop Morella is a national heritage site: you'll realise why the moment you catch first sight of it. It's even better close to: traffic-free, cobbled and 14th-century. In one of its grandest mansions is a hotel as medieval as the town. Sited to one side of the colonnaded main street, its 15th-century arched windows give it a Venetian air – reflecting the onetime cultural exchange between Genoa and eastern Spain. Enter through the arched doorway beneath the Ram family coat of arms and you may be greeted by the genial Jaime Peñarroya. A vaulted stairwell sweeps up to the bedrooms – big, cavernous even, with white walls and original chestnut beams up high. Rooms have recently been renovated and come with hydromassage baths. They are also wonderfully peaceful. You should eat well; truffles and sweet tarts are specialities. Book for several nights and discover the wild beauty of the Maestrazgo: there's a superb long-distance GR pathway that links these remote hilltop villages. But Morella will stay longest in the memory. *Tricky parking outside city walls.*

rooms	19: 16 twins/doubles, 1 single, 2 suites.
price	€70. Singles €40–€50. Suites €80.
meals	Breakfast €6. Half-board €19 p.p.; full-board €33 p.p.
closed	Rarely.
directions	N-232 to Morella. Into old town through P. de San Miguel; follow road round town until hotel signs. 200m from cathedral. Unload & park by P. de los Estudios, outside city walls.

	Jaime Peñarroya Carbó
tel	+34 964 173085
fax	+34 964 173218
email	hotelcardenalram@ctv.es
web	www.cardenalram.com

Map 15 Entry 197

Photo Jose Navarro

extremadura

Monasterio Rocamador

Ctra Nacional Badajoz-Huelva km41, 06171 Almendral, Badajoz

Not easy to find, but worth it. The Franciscan monastery of Rocamador, long forgotten amid the wide spaces of Extremadura, has had new life breathed into old stones by remarkable owners, Carlos and Lucía. It is home and hostelry and so much more, for its food has earned a Michelin star. Inner patios are filled with lush greenery and fountains, labyrinthine buildings fan out from cloister and chapel... music and candlelight accompany dinners into the early hours. (You may even recognise some of the guests: it's that kind of place.) Bedrooms may not be the most brightly lit but are among the most extraordinary we've seen; most are vast. So are the bathrooms, some with shower heads 10 inches wide, others with a chaise-longue next to the tub so you can recline like Madame Récamier. There are hand-painted tiles, enormous beds, three-piece suites, rich fabrics, wafer-bricking, vaulted ceilings, open hearths, incredible views. Never mind the hum from the main road as you linger by the pool... the Rocamador stands in a class of its own: sumptuous, daring, escapist, unique. *A Rusticae hotel*

rooms	30: 25 twins/doubles, 5 suites.
price	€120-€200. Singles €130. Suites €265.
meals	Breakfast €13-€19. Lunch/dinner €55 set menu; €65 à la carte. Restaurant closed on Monday.
closed	Rarely.
directions	From Madrid N-V; exit La Albuera (km382 marker). Into village, then towards Jerez de los Caballeros. At km41, right, over bridge, follow drive to Rocamador.

	Carlos Dominguez Tristancho
tel	+34 924 489000
fax	+34 924 489001
email	mail@rocamador.com
web	www.rocamador.com

Map 16 Entry 198

Hospedería Convento de La Parra

c/Santa María 16, 06176 La Parra, Badajoz

Once you've stayed, you will become a devotee. This beautiful and tranquil place, formerly home to the nuns of the Order of St Clare, has been transformed into a hotel of understated elegance and serenity: cool white walls, muted colours, mellow tiled floors. Rooms open off a central cloister, with orange trees and fountain, on two levels; in winter, twin woodburning stoves add a glow to the raftered sitting room. Bedrooms have the simplicity of their former cell status but none of the austerity: the furniture is handmade, the tiling is impeccable. Some of the bathrooms have partly sunken baths and basins of beautiful earthenware or galvanised tin; others have double-arched ceilings; old and new have been brought together to provide comfort while preserving harmony. Set off on a donkey and take a picnic – it will be delicious; go paragliding, visit a castle. From the stork's nest on the bell tower to the exquisite turquoise pool to the sweet staff, this is a special place. And no televisions or children to disturb the peace. *Spanish cookery courses.*

rooms	21: 15 twins/doubles, 4 singles, 2 suites.
price	€105–€126. Singles €48. Suites €162. VAT included.
meals	Lunch/dinner €35 à la carte.
closed	Christmas.
directions	From Seville, N-630 for Mérida. N-432 for Badajoz. Left for Feria & on to La Parra. Pass petrol station, left & up into village. Hospedería signed.

	Javier Muñoz & María Ulecia
tel	+34 924 682692
fax	+34 924 682619
email	convento@laparra.net
web	www.laparra.net

Map 17 Entry 199

Hotel Huerta Honda

Avda. López Asme 30, 06300 Zafra, Badajoz

Do visit Zafra. There is a castle, a beautiful arcaded main square, any number of churches to visit, and Huerta Honda is the best place to stay. It's larger than life and unmistakably southern: geraniums, bougainvillea, fountains in abundance and, in places, décor positively kitsch. In the guest sitting room are log fires in winter and a miscellany of decorative styles – fat modern sofas, rustic kilims, a deer's head on the wall. The dining rooms feel snug with their ochre walls, heavy beams and beautifully laid tables, but other parts of the hotel feel less intimate; wedding parties and business folk come here and the richly timbered bar is ever busy. The food is excellent, the cook is Basque and you may be tempted to splurge. Bedrooms have been recently redecorated, most with balconies overlooking the plant-filled patio; three much grander, theatrical suites have been added that take Moorish, Christian and Jewish Spain as their touchstone. On one of the large roof terraces is a tiny, decked pool – another reason to stay at this friendly hotel.

rooms	42: 39 twins/doubles, 3 suites.
price	€74–€96. Suites €150.
meals	Breakfast €8. Lunch/dinner €11 set menu; €25 à la carte. Closed Sunday evenings.
closed	Rarely.
directions	From Mérida south to Zafra. Hotel in city centre, near Palacio de los Duques de Feria.

	Darío Martínez Doblas
tel	+34 924 554100
fax	+34 924 552504
email	reservas@hotelhuertahonda.com
web	www.hotelhuertahonda.com

Map 17 Entry 200

Finca Santa Marta

Pago de San Clemente, 10200 Trujillo, Cáceres

The farmer lived on the top floor and the olive oil was pressed below. Now the old farm has been transformed by designer Marta Rodríguez-Gimeno and husband Henri into a delightful country retreat. Some of Santa Marta's bedrooms are tiny but each has a character of its own: antiques in some, hand-painted Portuguese furniture in others. Those in the next-door *finca*, the Santa Teresa, are more rustic in character, and the effect is equally pleasing (the bathrooms are charming). In the vaulted olive-pressing area is an enormous, cool and elegant sitting room with *estera* matting, neo-*mudéjar* ceiling, antique furniture and subtle lighting. And innumerable South American bits and pieces; Henri was Dutch ambassador to Peru and it was the Latin readiness to share that inspired him to open his home to guests. He and Marta are not always here, but when away, a charming housekeeper steps in. There is outstanding birdlife in this part of Spain – and some excellent cabernet sauvignon wines, too. *A Rusticae hotel.*

rooms	14 twins/doubles.
price	€85. VAT included.
meals	Dinner €28 set menu. VAT included.
closed	Rarely.
directions	From Trujillo, EX-208 for Guadalupe. After 14km, Finca on right where you see eucalyptus trees with storks' nests (km89 marker).

	Marta Rodríguez-Gimeno & Henri Elink
tel	+34 927 319203
fax	+34 927 334115
email	henri@facilnet.es
web	www.fincasantamarta.com

Map 17 Entry 201

Hotel Rural Viña Las Torres

Ctra. Ex-208 km 87.6, 10200 Trujillo, Cáceres

The setting is spectacular, the area a birdwatcher's heaven. Perched on the side of a hill, this unusual building – a private house that was built for a Belgian entrepreneur – has views of epic proportions, particularly if you are lucky enough to get one of the tower suites with a 180° panorama. These suites have lots to offer in way of comfort – a vast sofa to lounge on and a chair or two (essential for those who wish to keep to their tower like Rapunzel). Bedrooms are on the whole straightforwardly furnished with modern furniture; bathrooms have a Seventies' air. But the kindness of the young owners more than makes up for any stylistic shortcomings, and the main living room is inviting in winter, with its velveteen sofas and big log fire. In summer you can sit outside in the shade of the long colonnaded patio, or wander around the grassy gardens to the pool, floodlit at night for midnight swims. There's a tennis court, too, and a sauna.

rooms	8: 5 twins/doubles, 3 suites.
price	€68–€117. Singles €56–€60. Suites €93–€99.
meals	Restaurants nearby.
closed	Rarely.
directions	From Trujillo, EX-208 for Guadalupe. After 10km, take track on right (Camino de Buenavista), signed to hotel, for 900m.

	Juan Pedro Gonzalez Montes
tel	+34 927 319350
fax	+34 927 319355
email	info@vinalastorres.com
web	www.vinalastorres.com

Map 17 Entry 202

Finca El Jiniebro

Casrío Aceña de la Borrega, 10515 Valencia de Alcántara, Cáceres

For two centuries, this was a working farm. Then the land was planted with pines and the stone buildings converted into self-catering cottages. All went swimmingly – until a fierce fire swept up the valley in 2003, leaving it almost treeless. Most people would have given up, but vivacious Inocencia and husband Luis – a carpenter by trade – are made of sterner stuff! Though the valley has not yet recovered, there are plans afoot to replant it with chestnut trees – and El Jiniebro stands proud and the garden blooms again. Luis's excellent handiwork can be seen in all the cottages. The old and new pine furniture is simple, and Inocencia makes sure you have everything you need, from kitchen equipment to logs for winter fires. In summer, the pool and the terraces, each with a barbecue, come into their own. Walking is still a pleasure in this peaceful valley; there are megalithic stones and numerous birds. For restaurants, head for Valencia de Alcántara – or the border. You could be settling down to lunch in Portugal within minutes of shutting the door. *Please call/email to give arrival time.*

rooms	1 studio for 2; 2 houses for 3-4; 1 house for 9.
price	Studio €50. Houses €60-€170. VAT included.
meals	Self-catering.
closed	Rarely.
directions	N-521 Cáceres-Lisboa; exit for Valencia de Alcántara. Turn off for Alcorneo & Aceña. On for 10km to Aceña de Borrega; right at signs for Jiniebro.

	Inocencia Rey
tel	+34 927 584062
fax	+34 927 584062
email	jiniebro@hotmail.com
web	www.eljiniebro.com

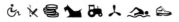

Map 16 Entry 204

Casa Salto de Caballo

La Fontañera s/n, 10516 Valencia de Alcántara, Cáceres

An intriguing place, this onetime shop and contraband centre, whose front entrance is in Spain and whose back terrace is in Portugal. Follow a narrow road across glorious, rolling hills to this, the furthest reach of the province of Cáceres – and, indeed, of Spain. This is where the smugglers plied their trade, saddlebags brimming with bread, coffee and garlic. These days you walk, or ride, straight out into Portugal's São Mamede Natural Park along those same secret pathways with not a thought for border patrols. Eva was so taken with it all she left Germany to restore this village house. The old floor tiles are still there, and the chestnut shutters and beams, along with a wholesome simplicity and a lack of modern luxury. Eva prepares innovative vegetarian meals if you would like them (she is a nutritionist and dietician) and three-course suppers. Sadly, the gardens and landscape have been scarred from a recent fire, but life is returning and Eva's spirit is upbeat. Generous hostess, generous prices and as far from the madding crowd as you could wish to get. *Walking and fasting weeks can be arranged.*

rooms	5 + 1: 5 twins/doubles. 1 apartment for 4.
price	€45. Apartment €90. VAT included.
meals	Lunch/dinner €12, on request only.
closed	Occasionally in winter.
directions	From Cáceres N-521 for Portugal; through Valencia de Alcántara, then right for San Pedro. After 2km, right for La Fontañera; last house on left in village, signed.

	Eva Schuster
tel	+34 927 580865
fax	+34 927 580865
email	saltocaballo@gmx.net

Map 16 Entry 205

Pomar Velho

Galegos, 7330-072 Marvão, PORTUGAL,

A rural paradise on the Spanish frontier... the tinkling of bells as the shepherd drives his flock home, the rumble of the mule cart further down the valley. A sense of timelessness pervades the 18th-century farmhouse in its five terraced acres of fruit, olive and cork oak trees, and the ancient mulberry shading the slate terrace, perfect for an aperitif. From the pool, gaze at the spectacular Sao Marmede range; if the weather's not too warm, head for the hills – the walking is great. There's a chestnut-beamed lounge with blue sofas and board games, and a spiral wrought-iron stair down to a dining room whose bread oven makes a fine open fireplace. And the granite grape press is as old as the house. Bedrooms are fresh with a French feel: blue limed furniture, big square pillows, crisp white beds; bathrooms are spotless. Marvão Castle dominates this mountain village where many festivals take place; come in November for the Chestnut Festival when the council subsidises the wine! Carole and Ken have been here for years, have an interesting wine cellar and love to cook. Breakfasts are feasts.

rooms	4 twins/doubles.
price	€60-€80.
meals	Dinner €35, with wine.
closed	22 December-2 January.
directions	From main road to Spain, left at Galegos. Through village then, as road starts to descend, 1st track on right for 200m. Park at end of track & ring bell at gate.

	Ken & Carole Parr-Young
tel	+351 245 964465
email	parryoung@pomarv.jazznet.pt
web	www.pomarv.jazznet.pt

Map 16 Entry 206

El Vaqueril

Ctra. Extremadura EX-207, 10930 Navas del Madroño, Cáceres

The big skies and cork-oaked hillsides make the area one of Spain's grandest visual feasts. Reached by an immensely long track, and in the middle of 320 hectares of cattle ranch, this old farmhouse stands amid carob, olive and palm. Its ochre and white frontage gives it a southern face and the house is classic cortijo: things gravitate towards a large central patio, the South's most effective technique for ensuring shade at any time of the day. No two bedrooms are the same: big, decorated with bright fabrics and family antiques, there are pretty tiles in the bathrooms, framed etchings and prints, open hearths. There is a vaulted lounge with a riotous ceramic hearth and a cavernous, candlelit dining room; pork comes from the farm, of course. This is a hotel that specializes in catering for large numbers at local events — weddings, bullfighting spectacles etc — so it may be lively and staff feel rushed. Laze by the big pool with views, rent a bike, stride off into the estate or jump into the car: Cáceres and Mérida are an easy drive.

rooms	14: 13 twins/doubles, 1 suite.
price	€66. Singles €47. Suite €84.
meals	Breakast à la carte. Dinner €24, €30 à la carte. VAT included.
closed	Rarely.
directions	From Cáceres, N-521 for Valencia de Alcántara. Then EX-207 for Navas del Madroño. Just before village, left at sign for house; follow long track (have faith!).

	Beatriz Vernhes de Ruanu
tel	+34 927 375257
fax	+34 927 191001
email	elvaqueril@elvaqueril.com
web	www.elvaqueril.com

Map 16 Entry 207

Finca El Cabezo

Ctra. Hoyos - Valverde del Fresno km22.8, 10892 San Martín de Trevejo, Cáceres

It is an awe-inspiring journey across the western reaches of Cáceres to the farm: rolling hills, cork oak forests, eagles above, the road to yourself. You are headed for a working farm (9,000 olive trees, 300 head of cattle) but don't expect a scruffy old ranch. Pass through the gates of this ivy-festooned building and you enter a magical inner courtyard of rambling virginia creeper and massed potted plants. The bedrooms are in the eastern wing and their size and elegance come as the greatest surprise: antiques on parquet or ancient terracotta, warm colours and modern art, chunky rafters and carved shutters. Bathrooms are fabulous. The sitting room, too, would have design mags purring: slate floors, open-granite walls, warm fabrics and good paintings. Feast on organic eggs fried in olive oil, goat's cheese and homemade cakes at breakfast; at dinner, choose between cheerful restaurants in San Martín or a Michelin-listed treasure down the road. This may be in one of Spain's furthest flung corners but it is worth a long detour and you couldn't hope to meet more special hosts. Sawday *Grand Cru!*

rooms	6: 5 twins/doubles, 1 suite.
price	€80. Suites €94.
meals	Restaurants nearby.
closed	Rarely.
directions	From Salamanca for Ciudad Rodrigo. Here, towards Cáceres; once over pass of 'Puerto de los Perales', right for V. del Fresno on EX-205. House on left at km22.8 marker. Signed.

Miguel Muriel García & María Moreno

tel	+34 927 193106
fax	+34 927 193106
email	correo@elcabezo.com
web	www.elcabezo.com

Map 10 Entry 208

Casa Manadero

c/Manadero 2, 10867 Robledillo de Gata, Cáceres

What's so thrilling about Spain are these vast, untamed parts of its interior. All-but-unknown Robledillo lies at the heart of the Sierra de Gata, yet is still within easy reach of Salamanca and Portugal. This village – one of the region's prettiest – makes much use of the local slate; it may be christened *arquitectura negra* by the locals but it is far from gloomy. Here is an inn where you can self-cater in a warm and rustic style. The tiny restaurant has heavy old beams, subtle lighting and excellent regional food. "One hundred per cent natural products," says Caridad, who has pillaged the family recipe books for your benefit; there's plenty for vegetarians to get excited about, too, and no less a man than Cervantes was fond of the local wines. The apartments vary in size and layout following the dictates of the original building, but all have a cheerful décor, good kitchens, central heating and views. The latest edition is a little cabin for two. You are surrounded by forests of oaks, olive groves and vineyards, wonderful for horse riding or bikes. And there's a natural swimming pool close by.

rooms	7 self-catering apartments: 5 for 4, 2 for 6.
price	Apt for 2, €39–€52. Apt for 4, €70–€75.
meals	Breakfast €5. Lunch/dinner €10.50 set menu; €15 à la carte. VAT inc. Set menu weekdays only.
closed	Rarely.
directions	From Madrid on N-V to Navalmoral; EX-108 to Plasencia; EX-370 to Pozuelo. Exit for Robledillo.

	Caridad Hernández
tel	+34 927 671118
fax	+34 927 671173
email	info@casamanadero.com
web	www.casamanadero.com

Map 10 Entry 209

La Sierra de Monfragüe

Ctra. EX-208 km14, 10590 Estación de Monfragüe, Cáceres

The track to the deer farm is dusty and long, the setting remote. On the edge of Monfragüe National Park, the open pastures, scattered with cork and holm oak, stretch for miles and miles. This is no Galicia! Yet the wild life is rich: wild boar, wildcat, otter, beech marten, pole cat, little bustard, black vulture and rare Spanish lynx and Imperial eagle. Emilio, friendly and helpful, will show you to your rooms. In a long purpose-built block attached to the main building, these are plain but comfortable, and you'll be glad of the air conditioning when temperatures soar. There's also central heating for winter. Bedrooms come with small sitting rooms and extra sofabed, bathrooms are bang up to date. Breakfasts and simple weekend dinners are served in a smart little dining room, each table jauntily topped with a red pepper plant. Once you have exhausted Monfragüe – the best-known raptor site in Spain – head off for something different: the spectacular Tuesday market in Plasencia. This is a new venture, the gardens will mature, and a swimming pool is planned for 2005.

rooms	6 twins/doubles.
price	€70. VAT included.
meals	Breakfast €7. Dinner €15, weekends only. VAT included.
closed	Rarely.
directions	From Plasencia S on EX-208 for Trujillo. After 10km campsite on left. After 4km left at sign La Sierra/Venta Quemada. Follow track for 5km.

	Jose Ignacio Solís Zúñiga
tel	+34 676 450 921
email	sierramonfrague@terra.es
web	www.lasierrademonfrague.com

Map 11 Entry 210

La Casa de Pasarón

La Magdalena 18, 10411 Pasarón de la Vera, Cáceres

Susana is young and friendly, proud of the 1890s village house in which her grandparents once lived. An elegant portal of carefully dressed sandstone in the unusual, burgundy façade leads into the entrance hall with its vaulted ceiling. The lounge mixes old and new furnishings piecemeal: cushioned sofas, a brass chandelier, photographic portraits and Impressionist prints. But the vaulted dining room has a really nice feel to it with just five attractively laid tables and the original marble-topped dressers; start your day here with a breakfast of oven-warm bread, local cheeses and fruit compotes made by the family. Dinner is excellent value, and homemade; perhaps soup followed by meatballs or kid stew. Bedrooms are reached via a heavy granite staircase: most are on the first floor and four are in the attic, with skylight windows. They are simple, spotless and quiet. At the back, a garden full of walnut and lemon trees (and new apartments and parking planned). Do visit the nearby monastery of Yuste where Charles V spent his final months, in this very lovely corner of Spain.

rooms	12 twins/doubles.
price	€60–€75. VAT included.
meals	Lunch €18. Dinner €10 set menu. VAT included.
closed	10 January–10 February; 2nd fortnight in June.
directions	From Plasencia towards Jaraiz to Tejeda del Tietar. Here, left to Pasarón. Enter village, 1st left. Signed.

	Susana Ayala
tel	+34 927 469407
email	pasaron@pasaron.com
web	www.pasaron.com

Map 11 Entry 211

Antigua Casa del Heno

Finca Valdepimienta, 10460 Losar de la Vera, Cáceres

The old farm stands superbly isolated on the southern side of the Gredos mountains, at the end of a long riverside track. You pass vineyards and olives, granite boulders and ferns to reach this enchanting spot. A crystalline stream – its banks studded with late spring flowers – meanders by, beyond are the mountains, criss-crossed with ancient footpaths. Inside, a sympathetic restoration, with granite, timber and cork the decorative leitmotif. Guest bedrooms get the balance just right: good beds, no television and views across the farm. The whole of the valley is at its most magical in spring when thousands of cherry trees come into blossom; book ahead if you want a room during this annual spectacle. Ornithologists come from all over Europe to focus their binoculars on azure-winged magpies, kites, vultures and great bustards. Javier and Graciela, quiet and caring, offer their guests time-tried home cooking in Heno's slightly oversized dining room, and use the very best cuts of meat. A reading room has recently been added – and there's a wonderful natural pool just a 20-minute walk.

rooms	7 twins/doubles.
price	€52–€60.
meals	Dinner €14.
closed	7 January–7 February; 10 days in June.
directions	From Madrid, N-V to Navalmoral de la Mata. Right onto ex-119 for Jarandilla to L. de la Vera. Pass Ayuntamiento; right at sign 'Hotel Tipico Rural Casa del Heno'. Follow signs past pool to hotel.

	Graciela Rosso & Javier Tejero Vivo
tel	+34 927 198077
fax	+34 927 198077
web	www.antiguacasadelheno.com

Map 11 Entry 212

Photo Guy Hunter-Watts

andalucia

Hotel Posada de Valdezufre

c/Santa Marina 1, Valdezufre, 21209 Aracena, Huelva

Alfonso XII may have secretly visited this house to meet his illegitimate daughter... a romantic notion that adds to the charm of the 19th-century farmhouse. Surrounded by olive, cork and oak groves and on the edge of Picos de Aroche Park Natural, its roadside setting (don't worry, bedrooms are double-glazed) makes it perfect for exploring this quiet corner of Andalucía. The white and brick-red exterior, with pretty grilled windows and cobbled inner courtyard, is typically Andulaz. Inside, a breezy, country feel with bold check armchairs, toile du Jouy curtains, polished surfaces and elegant mirrors. And, everywhere, fresh flowers. Bedrooms are large, light and uncluttered with pastel colours, beamed ceilings and handsome rattan bedheads. Well-equipped bathrooms are fresh in creamy white marble. Breakfast on the terrace overlooking the pool and walled garden before a day of cycling, walking, birdwatching – or popping into Portugal. Suppers in the rustic dining room reflect the area's prime ingredients: pork, wild mushrooms, sweet chestnuts. A relaxing, homely place to stay. *A Rusticae hotel.*

rooms	18: 11 twins/doubles, 2 singles, 5 suites.	
price	€95. Singles €70–€75. Suites €130.	
meals	Breakfast €6. Lunch/dinner €21, by request.	
closed	Rarely.	
directions	From Seville A-66/N-630 for Mérida; N-433 towards Portugal. Before Aracena 2nd entrance into Valdezufre. House on right.	

	Jose María Fernández
tel	+34 959 463322
fax	+34 959 463310
email	administracion@valdezufre.com
web	www.valdezufre.com

Map 17 Entry 213

Finca Buen Vino

Ctra. CN-433 km95, 21208 Los Marines, Huelva

After years in the Scottish Highlands, Sam and Jeannie knew that to settle happily in Spain they would need to find another place of wild natural beauty; this divinely isolated spot hides among the thick oak and chestnut woods of the Aracena mountains. Buen Vino was built in the 1970s but many of the materials used were ancient, shipped in from far corners of Spain; the panelled dining room, the arched doors and the wooden staircase have a seductive, timeworn patina. The house's decoration is unaffected yet elegant, and the bedrooms Scottish-cosy, with our favourites in the attic. You get easy chairs and cushions, cheery oil paintings and family memorabilia, books and magazines, comfortable beds and good linen, perhaps a bathtub with a view (two rooms have their own). There are also three independent cottages to rent, hidden away on the edges of the estate, each with its own pool. The feel is house party, particularly over star-lit dinner (farm meat, eggs, veg cooked by Jeannie) or barbecue by the pool: friends, friends' children, guests, farm manager… all are free to join in the fun.

rooms	4 + 3: 4 twins/doubles. 3 self-catering cottages; contact for details.
price	€100–€150.
meals	Lunch €15, on request; summer only. Dinner €35.
closed	Christmas & New Year.
directions	From Seville A-66 N 37km; CN-433 for Aracena. Los M 6km w of Aracena; 1.5km w of Los Marines; right at km95 marker.

	Sam & Jeannie Chesterton
tel	+34 959 124034
fax	+34 959 501029
email	buenvino@facilnet.es
web	www.fincabuenvino.com

Map 17 Entry 214

Molino Rio Alájar

Finca Cabezo del Molino s/n, 21340 Alájar, Huelva

Rustling leaves and birdsong. Come for the peace, or for the famously delicious ham or, in November, for the mushrooms. This gentle complex of self-catering stone cottages seems as much part of the natural scenery of this secret valley as the cork trees that surround it. Each has its own terrace, and each is finished to a high standard by the Dutch owners, Peter and Monica. Peter, who once walked from Amsterdam to Santiago de Campostella, has written a guide to local walks – you will not be left to wander aimlessly. The larger houses have underfloor heating, rafters and log fires, and steep stairs to the upper sleeping area; the smaller house is open-plan and has no kitchen (but you can cook in the reception building). Each dwelling is beautifully modern: tiles from Seville, woven rugs, painted ironwork beds, warm colours, There is a beautiful pool, and plenty of eateries in cobbled Alájar, up the lane. Portugal is over the border – but you may not wish to venture very far. You drift off to sleep with a mantle of stars above, and wake to birdsong – why leave? *Four-week Spanish courses November & March.*

rooms	5 houses for up to 6.
price	€460-€770 per week.
meals	Self-catering.
closed	Rarely.
directions	From Seville, N-630 for Mérida; N-433 to Aracena. Left on A-470 to Alájar. After Alájar, at km13/14, left & follow signs.

	Peter Jan Mulder
tel	+34 959 501282
fax	+34 959 125766
email	rioalajar@wanadoo.es
web	www.molinorioalajar.com

Map 17 Entry 215

La Posada de Alájar

c/Médico Emilio González 2, 21340 Alájar, Huelva

Just as well that the Sierra de Aracena is famed for its walking: you'll need the exercise to justify your over-indulgence at this mouthwatering *posada*. Lucy and Angel's cooking, making full use of excellent local produce, is irresistible: *Ajo Blanco* (almond soup), pork loin in sweet chestnut, layered apple pie... The vivacious young couple from Seville spent years searching for the right place but fell instantly for this 18th-century inn in Alájar village. It feels welcoming and warm the moment you step into the beamed, slate-floored and log-fired living room. As if by magic, you are drawn to the tiny bar beyond, then into the cosy, buttercup yellow dining room with its country tablecloths and Angel's collection of olive oils. The low-beamed bedrooms make the most of their limited spaces and are decorated in breezy colours with simple furnishings. Front rooms have French windows and balconies overlooking the street while those at the back are the quietest, but all assure a good night's sleep. Genuine warmth, a friendly welcome, five-star cooking and a great mountain position.

rooms	8 twins/doubles.
price	€55. VAT included.
meals	Dinner €18. VAT included.
closed	Rarely.
directions	From Seville, A-66 towards Mérida; N-433 towards Portugal & Aracena. At Aracena on towards Alájar; 2nd entrance to village. Hotel just before main square, on left.

	Lucy Arkwright & Angel Millán Simó
tel	+34 959 125712
email	laposadadealajar@telefonica.net
web	www.laposadadealajar.com

Map 17 Entry 216

Las Navezuelas

Ctra. A-432 km43.5, Apdo. 14, 41370 Cazalla de la Sierra, Sevilla

A place of birds and natural beauty, a 16th-century olive mill set in 136 hectares of green meadows, oak forest and olive groves… exceptional. Water streams down from the Sierra, often along Moorish-built channels, swallows and storks nest, boar and deer roam, and pretty Cazalla is two miles away. The house and converted outbuildings are pure Andalucía with beams and tiles; the garden is a southern feast of palms and orange trees, wisteria, vines, jasmine… and lazy pool. Bedrooms vary in shape and size, the most characterful in the rambling main house; all are fresh and light with old bits of furniture and a homespun feel. Apartments are lovely though minimally supplied. There are two sitting rooms and two dining rooms, the oldest aromatic with log fires in winter, and the menu includes delicious local dishes and produce from the farm. And there's homemade jam for breakfast. These friendly, energetic, eco-aware owners go out of their way to help and give advice on expeditions on foot, horse or bike and where best to watch birds: the whole area is an ornithologist's dream.

rooms	6 + 6: 4 twins/doubles, 2 suites. 4 self-catering studios for 2; 2 apartments for 4-6.
price	€53-€57. Singles €34.50-€41. Studios, €80-€85. Apt €95-€100.
meals	Lunch/dinner €17. VAT included. Lunch in summer only.
closed	7 January-25 February.
directions	From Seville A-431 to Cantillana. Here, A-432 for Cazalla. Pass km43 marker; after 500m, right at sign.

	Luca Cicorella & Miriló Tena Martín
tel	+34 954 884764
fax	+34 954 884594
email	navezuela@arrakis.es
web	www.lasnavezuelas.com

Map 17 Entry 217

Palacio de San Benito

San Benito s/n, 41370 Cazalla de la Sierra, Sevilla

Four-star treatment and an informal feel… the sandy brick façade, nuzzling up to the 15th-century church with quirky triangular tower, gives no clue as to what lies within. The raised swimming pool with its spouting fountain, the sumptuous 19th-century library with its up-to-date CDs and DVDs, the curved, ornately-tiled stair: a splendid theatricality pervades this *palacio*. The owner, whose noble lineage is attested to in the stately interiors, was a set designer for the opera and inherited the palace from his grandmother. By a curious feat of stage management he had the building moved, brick by brick, then let his design flare run riot inside, using bold juxtapositions of colour and style. The Room of the Infanta is one of the least dramatic, with its rose-strewn sofas and fine potraits on aqua walls, while bedrooms on the ground floor have terraces and tinkling fountains. Bathrooms are sumptuous and the central sunny terrace with glazed cloisters is a gem. With a top-class chef and a memorable dining room, this place promises as much glamour as a night at the opera.

rooms	9 twins/doubles.
price	€120–€210. Singles €120.
meals	Lunch/dinner €30 set menu; €36 à la carte.
closed	Rarely.
directions	From Seville, N-630 for Mérida, right on A-431 to Cantillana; A-432 to El Pedroso & onto Cazalla. Palacio on right, up hill, at village entrance.

	Manuel de Mata & Manuel Sánchez
tel	+34 954 883336
fax	+34 954 883162
email	info@palaciodesanbenito.com
web	www.palaciodesanbenito.com

Map 17 Entry 218

La Cartuja de Cazalla

Ctra. A455 Cazalla - Constantina km2.5, 41370 Cazalla de la Sierra, Sevilla

The 15th-century Carthusian monastery, one of the most remarkable buildings in Andalucía, lay empty for 150 years until Carmen Ladrón, visiting in the 1970s, nursed it back to life. Passionate about history and art, she has introduced a series of extraordinary paintings by Peruvian artist Espinoza to the five restored chapels and created a ceramics workshop in her 'centre for contemporary culture.' (Painters, sculptors and musicians have been known to exchange art for their stay.) The guest bedrooms, which finance the centre, are divided between a contemporary block and the original, well-restored, monks' cells, where light streams through a huge skylight. They have modern furniture and bathrooms, and, in keeping with the spirit of the place, no telephones or TV; heating is hit or miss in winter. Country cooking – fixed menu, no frills – is extremely good. Unwind in the healing centre, ride horses from the Cartuja stables, roam the surrounding 100 acres, slip into the spring-water pool. We have magical memories of wandering from chapel to chapel in the early morning light. *A Rusticae hotel.*

rooms	12 + 1: 6 twins/doubles, 2 singles, 4 suites. 1 apartment for 6.
price	€80-€90. Singles €50-€55. Suites €100-€120. Apt €120.
meals	Lunch €15. Dinner with wine, €25.
closed	24-25 December.
directions	From Seville C-431 to Cantillana; A-432 to El Pedroso & Cazalla. There, right onto A-455 for Constantina. La Cartuja at km2.5 marker.

	Carmen Ladrón de Guevara Bracho
tel	+34 954 884516
fax	+34 954 884707
email	cartujsv@teleline.es
web	www.skill.es/cartuja

Map 17 Entry 219

Cortijo Aguila Real

Ctra. Guillena-Burguillos km4, 41210 Guillena, Sevilla

Aguila Real is every inch the classic, whitewashed cortijo. You are surrounded by fields of cotton, sunflowers and wheat, yet are no distance at all from the charms of Sevilla (catch a glimpse of the Giralda's tower from the gardens). Passing under the main gate you enter a vast inner courtyard where bougainvillea romps; an old dovecote and water trough are reminders that this was a working farm. The public rooms, the best with beautiful barrel-vaulted ceilings, are decorated in ochres and terracottas with a smart mix of modern sofas and heavy antiques and the odd painting and hunting trophy on the wall. In the new, purpose-built dining room and on the elegant summer terrace dinner comes with silver cutlery and classical music; the food is upmarket Andalucían and the wine list is long. Bedrooms, set around the inner courtyard, are swish affairs, with huge beds, patterned and coordinated fabrics and lots of space; bathrooms have double sinks, some bedrooms get a terrace and the tower room has views. The palm-filled garden where white doves coo is subtly illuminated at night – and there's a pretty pool.

rooms	13: 8 twins/doubles, 5 suites.
price	€80–€120. Suites €120–€190.
meals	Breakfast €10. Dinner €24.04 à la carte.
closed	Rarely.
directions	Seville ring road SE-30 to Merida A-66. Exit No. 798 towards Guillena (A-460). In Guillena turn right at the second traffic light. Hotel on Guillena-Burguillos (A-461) road; signed.

	Isabel Martínez
tel	+34 955 785006
fax	+34 955 784330
email	hotel@aguilareal.com
web	www.aguilareal.com

Map 23 Entry 220

Casa el Marqués

c/En medio 40-42, 41950 Castilleja de la Cuesta, Sevilla

The Dukes of Sevilla came to this area to escape the oppressive heat of the city. You might be tempted to do likewise; you'll still be a five-minute bus ride from the historic city centre. There is a strong sense of being hidden away here, tucked behind the high wall of the Casa de Cultura, in the grounds of a former olive mill. Your modest holiday home belongs to Juan and Macarena, whose knowledge of the history and culture of the city will set you on the right track. Via a small courtyard (your hosts live opposite) you enter a simply furnished house, cool with white walls and tiled floors and stairs. Furniture is traditional-plain. The two bedrooms, one with a balcony that overlooks the courtyard, are clean and uncluttered. Downstairs are the bathroom and living room – and chairs on the patio should you wish to spill into the sun. There are flashes of colour from the pots outside. Those who like to escape the noise and dust of the city will be very happy here – and relish the prospect of a dip in Juan and Macarena's pool.

rooms	Houses for 2 and 4.
price	€70–€130 for 2; €100–€180 for 4.
meals	Self-catering. Good restaurants close by.
closed	Rarely.
directions	Seville-Huelva A-49. At km3, exit for Castilleja. Over 1st r'bout, then left. Next r'bout, left onto main street. Right at 'Telepizza' for Casa de Cultura. Next to Casa de C., behind high wall.

	Macarena Fernandez-Palacio & Juan Castro
tel	+34 629 791188
fax	+34 954 165379
email	informacion@casaelmarques.com
web	www.casaelmarques.com

Map 23 Entry 221

La Casa del Maestro
c/Almudena 5, 41003 Sevilla

You may be compelled to dance a flamenco inside this classic Sevillian townhouse.
It was once the home of the maestro guitarist, Nino Ricardo, and photographs of
his handsome face and passionate playing cover its walls – evoking the heady days
of the 1900s. The house has kept that era's gracious style while carefully
introducing 21st-century comforts. The focal point is the central covered
courtyard with its mosaic floor, elegant chairs and tables, and double tier of
wrought-iron balustraded galleries. The upper galleries lead to the bedrooms.
These are stylishly classic with creamy stucco walls, rugs on tiled floors, elegant
bedheads and embroidered bed linen. Antiques, fresh flowers and glossy
magazines add a warm, homely feel. Well-designed bathrooms are neat and bright
in white and blue. Take breakfast in your room or in the courtyard before stepping
out into the maze of streets of the Santa Cruz district. After a busy day's
sightseeing, cool off in the courtyard or watch the sunset from the plant-filled,
rooftop terrace. This place captures the true intimacy of Seville. *A Rusticae hotel.*

rooms	11 twins/doubles.
price	€99–€218. Singles €88–€176.
meals	Restaurants nearby.
closed	Some dates in August.
directions	In Seville S-30 for Córdoba, exit S. Justa. At S. Justa station 1st right; 1st left. Right for P. de Osario. Right on c/Escuelas Pías, past church, 1st left. Straight to Plaza S. Leandro; turn into c/Francisco Carrión Mejías. 1st left.

	Patricia Zapardiel
tel	+34 954 500007
fax	+34 954 500006
email	reservas@lacasadelmaestro.com
web	www.lacasadelmaestro.com

Map 23 Entry 222

Hotel Simón
c/García de Vinuesa 19, 41001 Sevilla

Two steps from the Giralda cathedral is the Simón – a friendly little place, well-worn but not shabby, and ideal for those on a budget. Gentle-mannered Francisco ('Frank') enjoys receiving guests and practising his excellent English. The hotel is utterly Sevillian; pass through the main portal, then a second wrought-iron door, then into a cool, columned, inner patio. Here tables and chairs are dotted among an abundance of aspidistras and ferns: a pleasant retreat from the throbbing heat. The dining room has grand old mirrors and Moroccan-tiled walls, period tables and chandeliers, and bedrooms, a touch dated but reasonable for those on a budget, are set around the patio and reached via a marble staircase – another reminder that this was a nobleman's residence. Rooms are simply decorated and air conditioned, the best at the front; those at the back can be gloomy. Breakfast is table service although it appears to be buffet. There are innumerable restaurants and tapas bars outside the door; ask the helpful staff to advise. Light sleepers note that local bars can stay open late.

rooms	29: 19 twins/doubles, 5 singles, 5 suites.
price	€70–€92. Singles €46–€55. Suites €100–€140.
meals	Breakfast €4.25.
closed	Rarely.
directions	From Plaza Nueva in centre take Avda. de la Constitución (if closed, tell police you are going to hotel); right onto c/Garcia de Vinuesa. On left, half-way down.

	Francisco Aguayo García
tel	+34 954 226660
fax	+34 954 562241
email	info@hotelsimonsevilla.com
web	www.hotelsimonsevilla.com

Map 23 Entry 223

Casa Numero 7

c/Virgenes 7, 41004 Sevilla, Sevilla

The owner, an aristocrat from Jerez, has a great fondness for Britain and the British; the result – a touch of Chelsea in the heart of Seville. Perhaps it was memories of England's country houses that inspired his conversion of fine Moorish townhouse into exceptional small hotel. A mood of privileged intimacy prevails, with six bedrooms – very quiet for the centre of town – grouped around a central courtyard. And there's a roof terrace from which you can gaze on the Giralda. Bedrooms are regal affairs, every one different, from the smallest to the largest, the Yellow Room with its 'Juliet' balcony. All is immaculate, fabrics, furniture, lighting; beds are sumptuous and large. Yet there's a delightfully homely feel, thanks to books (*Who's Who!*), magazines and photos of the owner's famous forebears. The cool and elegant drawing room is a distinguished spot for a glass of sherry – from the family's Jerez bodega, of course – and breakfasts are perfectly English, served by two butlers in white gloves. María is a sparkling manageress, and Seville lies outside the door.

rooms	6 twins/doubles.
price	€177–€275.
meals	Restaurants nearby.
closed	Rarely.
directions	Park in Aparcamento 'Cano y Cueto' at junc. of C/Cano y Cueto & Menendez Pelayo (next to Jardines de Murillo). Tell attendant staying at Casa No. 7. From here 5 minutes' walk to hotel.

	Gonzalo del Río y González-Gordon
tel	+34 954 221581
fax	+34 954 214527
email	info@casanumero7.com
web	www.casanumero7.com

Map 23 Entry 224

El Triguero

Ctra.Carmona-El Viso del Alcor km29, 41410 Carmona, Seville

El Triguero is cradled by low hills looking out across the rich farmlands of Seville's hinterland: fields of wheat and sunflower are interspersed with pastureland where beef cattle and fighting bulls are reared. Although you are very close to the treasures of Seville and Carmona, you are a mile from the nearest road and the setting could not be more bucolic. As you enter the grand reception hall and are shown up to your room by the friendly housekeeper, a veil of silence wraps itself around you. The best views are from the tower room; warmly and traditionally furnished, with a tiny shower room. Other bedrooms are larger, full of family antiques, old writing desks and dressers, religious figurines, gilt-framed portraits on the walls, perhaps fresh flowers or a brightly painted rush-seated chair; white bathrooms shine. Ask for a room with a terrace and watch the sun rise or set across the vast plain – beautiful. This feels like a grand family home – not studied, but with a simple, warm elegance. Though breakfast is no feast, meals and rooms are excellent value.

rooms	9 twins/doubles.
price	€48-€58.
meals	Lunch/dinner €15 with wine, on request.
closed	Rarely.
directions	From Seville towards Córdoba on NIV then right to Carmona. Here, N-392 for El Viso del Alcor. Entrance on left at km29 post, then 1km dirt track. Signposted.

	Carmen Vega
tel	+34 955 953626
fax	+34 955 953626
web	www.galeon.com/eltriguero

Map 23 Entry 225

Casa de Carmona
Plaza de Lasso 1, 41410 Carmona, Sevilla

The glossy brochure urges you to enjoy the lifestyle of a Spanish aristocrat... wander the indoor and outdoor spaces of this Renaissance palace and do just that. The style is on a decidedly grand scale and the 'state' rooms are especially splendid – though not without those occasional spots of peeling paint which mark many a nobleman's residence. However, the addition of some essentially modern luxuries – sauna, hairdresser, elegant elongated pool – nudges us into the 21st-century. The warm apricot walls of the interior patios, their mass of dark green foliage marshalled into serried ranks of terracotta pots, set the tone, and bedrooms are swish, even sumptuous, with smart repro furniture and varying décors. But it is the beauty of the building and its setting within the walls of the ancient town of Carmona that puts the Casa into the 'special' catergory; the amazing sandstone façade is first sighted from the square where you park. Dinner is decidedly posh, breakfast is a spread; for tea, expect silver platters of Mars Bars for the children and delicious pastries for you. Extraordinary.

rooms	33: 25 doubles, 8 suites.
price	€120-€300. Singles €115-€215. Suites €700-€1,000. VAT included.
meals	Lunch/dinner €45 à la carte.
closed	Rarely.
directions	From Seville, N-IV for Airport & Córdoba. After 25km, exit for Carmona. Head for city centre, following signs to Centro Histórico & hotel.

	Ana Julia Alvarez Brea
tel	+34 954 191000
fax	+34 954 190189
email	reserve@casadecarmona.com
web	www.casadecarmona.com

Map 23 Entry 226

Palacio de los Granados

c/Emilio Castelar 42, 41400 Écija, Sevilla

Push the boat out and come here – this 18th-century baroque palace makes every guest feel like a prince or princess. Rooms sparkle with chandeliers, comfort oozes from every corner... heavy tasselled fabrics, deep sofas, thick rugs. Moorish arches, lanterns and brassware, reflecting the city's Arabic past, add an exotic touch – and the inner courtyards are magical. In one there are pillared archways, soothing fountains and glossy ferns; the other, with an elegant pool and 120-year-old palm, is scented with orange and pomegranate trees. Sheer delight to breakfast in! The high-ceilinged bedrooms are grand in every detail: queen-size beds, jewel-bright fabrics, exotically coloured walls, mosaic-tiled bathrooms. Some have chandeliers, others Moorish alcoves; yet others get draped beds straight from *The Arabian Nights*. Dinner menus change daily – a mix of Andalucían and South American. Explore Écija with its Roman remains and baroque churches, then return for a nightcap around the pool. Pablo and his staff are as gracious as you would expect: prepare to be hopelessly spoiled.

rooms	13: 10 twins/doubles, 2 suites.
price	€120-€150. Suites €160-€190.
meals	Lunch/dinner €35-€40.
closed	Rarely.
directions	From Seville on A-4; exit for Écija & Osuna on A-351. At r'bout follow signs for 'Centro urbano, Ayuntamiento, Palacio de Granados'. Hotel at end of c/Emilio Castelar, on right.

	Pablo Ojeda O'Neill
tel	+34 955 905344
fax	+34 955 901412
email	info@palaciogranados.com
web	www.palaciogranados.com

Map 23 Entry 227

Palacio Marqués de la Gomera
c/San Pedro 20, 41640 Osuna, Sevilla

Calle San Pedro was *the* address in Osuna in the 18th century. Many of the local aristos had their townhouses here, and could afford to do themselves proud. (The Duke of Osuna owned so much land that he could ride from Sevilla to Málaga without leaving his estate.) The result is a remarkably pretty street in a lovely town dating back to Roman times. Even in this competitive setting, the Marqués de la Gomera is stunning. Above its long, white frontage, the gilded edge of the roof flows in crested waves. The baroque entrance, topped by a marble balcony and coat of arms, is flanked by ornate columns. Exquisite, too, is the galleried central patio inside, with a 17th-century chapel leading off it. Cavernous, luxurious rooms are furnished with 18th-century pieces, as well as more modern, and comfortable, sofas. The most spectacular of the bedrooms is the tower suite, built on two levels: step onto its balcony for a 360° view of Osuna and the countryside. The softly lit restaurant is another treat: in spite of its star rating, it is relaxed and unstuffy, serving succulent food and excellent wines.

rooms	20: 18 twins/doubles, 2 suites.
price	€88–€94. Singles €68–€75. Suites €156–€180.
meals	Breakfast €10. Lunch/dinner €30, €36 à la carte.
closed	Rarely.
directions	Seville-Malaga A-92. Exit km82 Osuna. Over level crossing to r'bout, 1st right for 'Centro Urbano' on c/Sevilla. Left at church into c/Cristo, 2nd right into c/San Pedro. Halfway up on left.

	Francisco José Mulero Molino
tel	+34 954 812223
fax	+34 954 810200
email	info@hotelpalaciodelmarques.com
web	www.hotelpalaciodelmarques.com

Map 23 Entry 228

La Casa Olivada

Via Antiguo Desperdicios, 999999 Sevilla

The tiles tumble towards the street, tossed and turned by time. Yes, the whole house is a cliché. But unashamdely so for it has seen most of the main events of Sevillan history, including the lavish celebrations by King Peter for Muhammed V in 1360. So wildly did the citizens celebrate that a wooden column holding the overhang collapsed and was quickly replaced by a hastily cut-down tree. It is as crude now as the day it began life as a column. The timbers within are original, rotten and weak – but have stood the test of all this time, so you should not fear for your safety. The house is a 'survivor', just like its indomitable owner, Dona 'La Vieja' Miseria. She is a woman of vast and uncertain age, sustained throughout her life by an impassioned hatred of foreigners. As she never ventures out you are bound to encounter her. Be brave, for the battle for acceptance is worth winning. Once she is persuaded that you really are Spanish, vast will be her embrace. The hotel has few comforts, but we include it in a spirit of frivolity. Anyway – it is a historic gem.

rooms	3: we think. Difficult to tell what's rubble and what's a wall.
price	No charge, but trowels, cement and spare lintels not provided. Guests are recommended to take out life insurance prior to arrival.
meals	Dusty.
closed	If only.
directions	Ask in the tourist office. Expect pitying looks and some laughter.

	Dona 'La Vieja' Miseria
tel	+34 999 666666
fax	+34 999 666666
email	miseria@antigua.com
web	www.crumblingrubbish.com

Olla de la Margarita

41660 Villanueva de San Juan, Sevilla

Leave the low-slung sports car behind – the track is rough and steep. Liz moved from Africa to this remote corner to raise her family, and stayed. She is gentle and kind, makes delicious chutney and has great stories to tell. Goats, pigs, hens, ducks and geese roam the small organic farm, and olives and Seville oranges grow; make the most of Liz's marmalades and olive oil. The old farmstead is as ramshackle as you like, deeply authentic and with sensational views. It – and your little whitewashed cottage with its ochre highlights – are perched high, surrounded by eucalyptus, alder and ancient olive. Inside the one-storey home: a dear little kitchen/sitting room with square windows and a woodburner in the hearth, a two-hob Baby Belling, yellow gingham curtains, an old-fashioned kettle. It could be cramped – but most of the year you spill outside, onto a makeshift terrace with views. For evenings in, there's Spanish furniture, an old sofa and an alcove stuffed with books. Bedrooms have twin beds, and are modest and clean. Kick off your shoes (but leave the kitten mules at home!). This is real Spain.

rooms	Cottage for 2-4.
price	€35 for 2; €45 for 4; prices per night.
meals	Self-catering. Restaurants 8km.
closed	August.
directions	A92 Malaga airport-Antequera. After 50km, Campillos turn off; 7km past Almargen Right to Algarnitas. In Algarnitas, right; after 2km, left for Villanueva. Track on left; 800m to last house. Signed.

	Liz Hart
tel	+34 955 958 049

Map 23 Entry 230

Cortijo Alguaciles Bajos
Ctra. SE-445 km22.6, 41710 Utrera, Sevilla

Bed and breakfast in the rolling wheatlands of the Sevillian hinterland, where the only passing traffic is the tractor from the next village. Arrival is up a lovely palm-lined drive, then into a cobbled courtyard where beautiful whitewashed walls are offset by ferns, gcraniums and jasmine. The housekeeper greets you and shows you the sprucely furnished bedrooms in the old grain stores, whose furniture and paintings form part of the collective memory of the Mencos family (who live in Madrid for most of the year). Our favourite is the massive Naranjo room whose swish bathroom is the size of a studio in London or Paris – but all are roomy, comfortable and full of original and interesting features. (And water is solar-heated.) No meals in the Corijo, apart from a rudimentary breakfast, but for dinner there is a wonderfully authentic *venta* (roadside restaurant) a short drive away. The silence at night envelops you; after a day or two here you will feel closer to understanding the elusive Andalucían character. This is great value, and an enchanting anthisesis to chain hotels.

rooms	8 twins/doubles.
price	€48. Singles €36.
meals	Two restaurants nearby.
closed	Rarely.
directions	From Seville N-IV for Cádiz to Cabezas de San Juan. There, at x-roads left on A-371 for Villamartín; after 6.5km left again on SE-445 for Montellano. Farm on left after km22.6 marker.

	Maribel Gómez
tel	+34 630 561529
fax	+34 91 5641071
email	alguaciles@alguaciles.com
web	www.alguaciles.com

Map 23 Entry 231

Hacienda de San Rafael

Apartado 28, Ctra. N-IV (km594), 41730 Las Cabezas de San Juan, Sevilla

As southern Spanish as can be, the hacienda lies handsomely amid the undulating farmlands of Sevilla's hinterland. Half a mile or so of olive-lined drive leads to its sunny white and ochre façade. Andalucía! Olives were once milled here; Kuky recalls it all from her earliest days. She could scarcely have imagined that she and her English husband would be at the helm — and they are delightfully enthusiastic hosts. Bedrooms — split-level, immaculate, with their own verandas and attractive wicker furniture — give onto the exquisitely cobbled central patio, the inner sanctuary of any true cortijo. Geranium, jasmine and bougainvillea romp. In the gardens are three thatched *casitas*, beautifully furnished in the country style, with a piece of terrace each and sharing an infinity pool. There are two supremely elegant drawing rooms where oriental furnishings and prints collected on trips to the East blend with local pieces, and a thatched dining area in the garden for summer meals. The views are vast, golden with sunflowers in summer. *Children 12 and over welcome.*

rooms	11 + 3: 11 doubles. 3 self-catering cottages for 2.
price	€210. Cottages €480.
meals	Lunch €25 à la carte. Dinner, 3 courses with wine, €55.
closed	1 November–17 March.
directions	From Seville south on N-IV, San Rafael is 1st turn on right-hand side after km594 marker, before Repsol petrol station.

	Kuky & Tim Reid
tel	+34 955 872193
fax	+34 955 872201
email	info@haciendadesanrafael.com
web	www.haciendadesanrafael.com

Map 23 Entry 232

Posada de Palacio

c/Caballeros 9-11, 11540 Sanlúcar de Barrameda, Cádiz

Wonderful Sanlúcar… this sleepy place, at the mouth of the Guadalquivir estuary, gets surprisingly few visitors yet it is one of Andalucía's most appealing towns, famous for its manzanilla wine, a fino-type sherry, and its fish restaurants. A sleepy town whose streets are there to be wandered with no destination in mind – happening upon tapas bars and shops reminiscent of another age. La Posada is an inn to match the town – a place plucked from another era; indeed, the Palacio was once used for the filming of a 19th-century period drama. Two large and elegant mansion houses have been joined to create this hotel, and the latest owner has restored and renovated what was already a delectable place. Some of the rooms are tiny, but beds and linen are top of the range, the whole place has been repainted from top to toe, and antiques have been brought in from all over Spain. There's a new restaurant in the old bodega and dinner should be good, if breakfast is anything to go by. Be sure to pay a visit to the covered market just below, and immerse yourself in the brouhaha of Andaluz life.

rooms	15: 9 twins/doubles, 6 suites.
price	€75–€90. Singles €65–€80. Suites €95–€120.
meals	Breakfast €6. Dinner €18 set menu.
closed	10 January-15 February.
directions	From Seville A-4/N-4 & A-471. From Jerez on A-480. At entrance of town, right after r'bout into Camino de la Vía; 2nd on left (Avda. Dr. Fleming), pass Castle & Palacio Ducal. Posada opp. Town Hall.

	Federico Galera
tel	+34 956 364840
fax	+34 956 365060
email	posadadepalacio@terra.es
web	www.posadadepalacio.com

Map 22 Entry 233

CasaCinco

c/Sancho IV el Bravo 5, 11150 Vejer de la Frontera, Cádiz

Fascinating Vejer de la Frontera is perched on a hilltop, its winding, cobbled streets brimful of shops, restaurants and cafés. CasaCinco is in its middle, a townhouse wrapped around a small patio, with a beautiful arch of wafer brick. The tiled floors and beamed ceilings add to the traditional feel, but what makes this place special is your hosts' exquisite feel for contemporary design. Peaceful bedrooms fuse Andalucían pieces with English antiques, the functional with the eclectic, and every room is unique... grey-blue ceiling beams here, a metal deco bed there, an orange glass bowl in a rose-red alcove. Delightful bath and shower rooms, tiled, light and clean, are en suite and open plan (no doors). Colette and Glen are a friendly pair who serve great breakfasts – accompanied by flamenco music, if you so desire – and like to get everything right. The living room is small, but its books, magazines, woodburner and leather sofas make it intimate. A tiny door leads to a roof terrace with views that sail over the rooftops to the beach at Zahara and the mountains of Morocco. Superb.

rooms	4 doubles.
price	€80-€105.
meals	Dinner €30, twice a week.
closed	January.
directions	From Algecíras N-340 for Cádiz; 2nd left at km36 for Vejer. On uphill; follow signs for 'Ayuntamiento' to Plaza de España. Park, through arch, right & CasaCinco on left.

	Colette & Glen Murphy
tel	+34 956 455029
fax	+34 956 451125
email	info@hotelcasacinco.com
web	www.hotelcasacinco.com

Map 23 Entry 234

Escondrijo

Callejón Oscuro 3, 11150 Vejer de la Frontera, Cádiz

Even here – down a backstreet of whitewashed houses – you can smell the sea.
Vejer is one of Andalucía's most alluring little towns and Escondrijo a most
beguiling place to stay. It's in the old quarter – the fashionable part of town in the
1800s – and was built on the site of a church destroyed in the 1776 earthquake.
Bits of that old church, cleverly incorporated, make attractive features and infuse
the patio bar with history: an arch here, a stained-glass window there, a little
niche… Nigel and Netty spent 18 months restoring it all before opening in 2004,
and it's been delightfully done – a vivid, unusual blend of traditional and top-spec
contemporary. A maximum of eight guests ensures a friendly atmosphere and
there's no sense of overcrowding. Nigel and Netty are young, easy, sophisticated
hosts who gladly share their collection of 400 CDs, and there's broadband
internet and TV. Three of the generous bedrooms have their own kitchen areas,
two have private terraces with stunning views over the rooftops to the mountains,
all have excellent bathrooms. Ravishing beaches are close by.

rooms	4 doubles.
price	€70-€115.
meals	Lunch/dinner €12, on request. VAT included. Good restaurants close by.
closed	January.
directions	From Algecíras N-340 for Cádiz; 2nd left at km36 for Vejer. On uphill; follow signs for 'Ayuntamiento' to Plaza de España. Park, through arch, left at Vera Cruz restaurant; 1st left.

	Tenette Ludlow & Nigel Anderson
tel	+34 956 447438
fax	Mob. 34 669 950305
email	info@escondrijo.com
web	www.escondrijo.com

Map 23 Entry 235

Casas Karen

La Fuente del Madroño 6, Los Caños de Meca, 11159 Vejer de la Frontera, Cádiz

Recline among the broom and mimosa in your Mexican hammock on one of the last wild coastlines of southern Spain. Karen worked in the music business before recognising, in this group of old farm buildings, an outlet for her creativity. Her guest accommodation, between pinewoods and beach, has grown organically over the years. *Casa Karen 1* and *Casa Karen 2* are the most independent; other rooms and apartments are better if you want to be sociable. Decoration takes its inspiration from the local surroundings and local here means Andalucían and Moroccan – the high mountains of the Magreb are visible on clear days. The place attracts people with a creative impulse and the atmosphere is totally laid back – like Caños itself, so popular with young travellers. There's walking, riding, biking in the Parque Natural – and personal advice on where to eat. If self-catering seems daunting, a friend of Karen's can come and cook for you (veggie, local) and a massage with aromatic oils is always available as well as reiki, tai chi and yoga. There's even a life coaching session for you, on the house.

rooms	1 + 8: 4 houses & studios for 2-4; 2 houses for 4-6; 2 thatched houses for 2-3; 1 double.
price	Houses €42-€125. Studio €36-€92. Room €30-€70.
meals	Self-catering.
closed	Rarely.
directions	Cádiz-Tarifa N-340. At km35, right for Vejer; at 1st r'bout right for Los C; 10km to next r'bout; left. 500m after F. T'gar exit, left at 'Artesanía Levante'; for 'Apts. y B.lows T'gar'. 500m, right; 50m, right.

	Karen Abrahams
tel	+34 956 437067
fax	+34 956 437233
email	casas@casaskaren.com
web	www.casaskaren.com

Map 23 Entry 236

Hotel La Breña

Avda. de Trafalgar 4, 11159 Caños de Meca, Cádiz

What immediately strikes you about this place is the friendly, light-hearted mood. The staff are happy and helpful and genuinely enjoy what they do. It's a modern, beach-side hotel which only opened recently, although it has been a successful restaurant for five years. And the food is fresh and very good – try the seafood carpaccio and the luscious homemade puddings. Local wines as well. If you eat out on the wide, bamboo-covered terrace, you'll have the additional pleasure of an uninterrupted view across the sea to Morocco – the hotel is on the very edge of the Atlantic. Inside is an enormous dining/reception area with acres of honey-coloured marble and lots of interesting modern art. The bedrooms are all big, too, and pleasingly decorated in earthy colours. Some have their own private terraces and all have excellent bathrooms. The beaches are good – if you're into skinny dipping, you'll appreciate the nudist beach to the left of the hotel – and a Parque Natural runs all the way from here to Barbate, so there's no difficulty in finding somewhere attractive to walk. A great place to unwind.

rooms	7 twins/doubles.
price	€55-€100. VAT included.
meals	Breakfast €2.50. Half-board €20 extra p.p. VAT included.
closed	15 November-January.
directions	From Cádiz N-340 for Tarifa. At km35 right for Vejer; at r'bout right for Caños. Here, through village parallel to sea; signposted at far end of Caños.

	Carlos Cortes & José Manuel Morillo
tel	+34 956 437368
fax	+34 956 437368
email	info@labrena.com
web	www.labrena.com

Map 23 Entry 237

Hotel Restaurante Antonio

Bahía de la Plata, Atlanterra km1, 11393 Zahara de los Atunes, Cádiz

A short drive from the workaday little fishing village of Zahara de los Atunes, with gardens that lead straight onto one of the best sand beaches on the Atlantic coast, Antonio Mota's two hotels share a special site. We prefer his first, smaller, family-run affair, popular with the Spanish. The newer venture is huge and four-star. Both are southern in spirit, with repro prints on the walls – romantic swans, grisly bullfights – but rooms and restaurants are light, cheerful and clean. Choose dinner in the 'old' restaurant: fish fresh from the tank and excellent white local wine. Breakfasts are feasts of eggs, fruit, cheeses and hams. Bedrooms in the new hotel are of a very good size and come with balconies or terraces and every mod con, but the older ones have more character, particularly those with terraces overlooking the palm-filled gardens to the sea. There's a lovely pool, a beach bar, too, and horses for hire; stay long enough for a ride along the beach to Bolonia, where there are Roman ruins and restaurants. No wonder the faithful return.

rooms	Old hotel: 22 doubles, 3 singles, 5 suites. New hotel: 17 doubles, 16 family, 4 suites, 1 wheelchair room.
price	€58–€122. Singles €34.50–€60. Suite €71–€101.
meals	Lunch/dinner €19, €30 à la carte.
closed	November-December.
directions	Algecíras E-5/N-340 to Cádiz. 25km after Tarifa left to Barbate; Zahara on left after 10km. Signed.

	Antonio Mota Pacheco
tel	+34 956 439141
fax	+34 956 439135
email	info@antoniohoteles.com
web	www.antoniohoteles.com

Map 23 Entry 238

100% Fun

Ctra. Cádiz-Málaga km76, 11380 Tarifa, Cádiz

With a name like this you expect something out of the ordinary – and this young, funky hotel should catch your imagination. The busy N-340 lies right between it and that oh-so-desirable surf but, in the exuberant greenery of the garden with thatched roofs overhead, we felt we were in the deepest Amazon. You pick up your key and make your way to your bungalow and terrace – perfect for drying out all the gear. Inside, expect a simple combination of terracotta tiles, sponged walls, fans to beat the sizzling summers, and big comfortable beds. You are surrounded by gurgling fountains, a gorgeous swimming pool and an airy, Polynesian-thatched restaurant serving spicy Tex-Mex and vegetarian alternatives. Here, too, are the best-equipped surf shop on the Tarifa coast, selling hand-crafted windsurfing boards, and a new 'chill out' area for high summer. You are five miles west of surf city, and a sprint from the finest surfing stretch in Spain. Not for wallflowers: this is a young fun paradise for sporting dudes. It's even better value out of season.

rooms	22: 16 twins/doubles, 6 quadruples.
price	€53–€102. Quadruples €87–€140. VAT included.
meals	Lunch/dinner €18 à la carte.
closed	November-February.
directions	From Cádiz, N-340 Algecíras. At beginning of Tarifa Beach, hotel flagged on left, next to La Enseñada, close to km76 marker.

	Ursula Walter & Barry Pussell
tel	+34 956 680330
fax	+34 956 680013
email	100x100@tnet.es
web	www.tarifa.net/100fun

Map 23 Entry 239

Dar Cilla Guesthouse

c/Cilla, 11380 Tarifa, Cádiz

As you laze on the roof terrace you gaze on Morocco: Zoe's spiritual home. With energy and flair this English woman has created a corner of Maroc in Tarifa. Handsome, 100-year-old Dar Cilla was built smack into the 12th-century town wall and wraps itself round not one but two patios. These studios and apartments are truly lovely: wafer bricks, sienna-washed plaster, polished stucco, illuminated nooks and crannies, kilims on terracotta, and double glazing to keep out traffic hum; the finishes are superb and all been perfectly orchestrated. You get bedrooms and dining/sitting areas, shower rooms and kitchenettes in the fashionable Arab-Anduluz style, dotted with decorative features and fabrics that Zoe has picked up on her trips to Tangier. No lounge – bar that amazing terrace, with shower! – but a new breakfast/brunch spot, Café Gusto, managed by Zoe's daughter-in-law. Surf the golden beaches of the wind- and kite-surfing capital of Europe, gallop in the hills, dip into the many bars of the old, labyrinthine town – or do that ferry hop to Morocco. *Multi-lingual house.*

rooms	7 studios/apartments for 1-5.
price	Single studio €30-€65. Apt for 2 €70-€130. Apt for 4-5 €100-€195. VAT included. Min. stay three nights. Reduced rates Oct-March.
meals	Breakfast €3-€5. Restaurants 5-10 minutes.
closed	Rarely.
directions	N-340 Algecíras-Cádiz; then first exit for Tarifa. Dar Cilla 1km further, on left.

	Zoe Ouwehand-Reid
tel	+34 653 467025
fax	+34 956 627011
email	info@vivatarifa.com
web	www.darcilla.com

Map 23 Entry 240

Huerta Las Terrazas

c/Sierra de Lucena, Pelayo, 11390 Algecíras, Cádiz

Climb up through honeysuckle, mimosa, oleander, cypresses and shady corners, and reach the cool, blue pool. Turn and gaze southwards to the exotic outlines of the Moroccan mountains. The three-acre terraced gardens, dizzy with scent and colour, are the draw of this white casa, teetering below the foothills of the Sierra de Ojen, on the edge of the Alcornocales Park. In the bedrooms – choose La Casita for a self-contained hideaway – the eager young English owners have blended cool modern design with traditional furnishings. Seagrass matting, white walls and soft bed linen mixes with dark wooden furniture, rich cushions and hints of Morocco. The sitting and dining rooms are emboldened with warmer colours, lamps and candles. Breakfasts are from their organic fruit and veg garden while their own spring feeds the pool as well as the taps. But don't forget this is the countryside: neighbouring farm dogs are not always quiet. Swim, surf or ride on the beaches, explore cosmopolitan Tarifa, enjoy one of Amy's expert massages or birdwatch; the house is under the African migration route.

rooms	4 + 1: 2 doubles, 1 twin/double. 1 cottage for 2.
price	€85–€100. House €600 per week (minimum 2 nights).
meals	Light lunch €12, on request.
closed	Rarely.
directions	From Algecíras on N-340 for Cádiz. Pass km97, under foot bridge; next right past restaurant Las Piedras. On uphill; 2nd left at fork. Follow road up to green gate.

	Alistair & Amy Farrington
tel	+34 956 679 041
email	alandamy@huertalasterrazas.com
web	www.huertalasterrazas.com

Map 23 Entry 241

Cortijo La Hoya

Ctra. N–340 Tarifa–Algecíras, km96, 11280 Tarifa, Cádiz

Two miles of cork tree-fringed track lead to the farm and Fabiola's *casitas*, tucked away among the eucalyptus and cork oaks in an exquisite corner of the Alcornocales Park. These three lovely self-catering apartments have been created in buildings whose chicken-shed origins are hard to credit. Fabiola has great decorative nous, her colour schemes inspired by the earthy washes of the Mahgreb, her patterned fabrics gorgeous. Kitchenettes are well-equipped and there's central heating for winter. The wonderful garden leads to an 'infinity' pool where the water of the pool merges with that of the Straits of Gibralta – sensational – above which rises the Moroccan Rif, its colours changing as subtly as the iridescent coastal light. Fabiola is mindful of guests' privacy, but, should you ask, will tell you all you need to know. Do note her recommendations about where to eat in Tarifa; the ancient town pulsates on a Friday and Saturday night – and its white sand beaches are superb. And then there are the dogs… at least half a dozen of all shapes and sizes, ever ready with a wag.

rooms	3 apartments for 2.
price	€90–€110. Minimum stays peak season.
meals	Self-catering. Hamper on request. Restaurants in Pelayo, 3km.
closed	Rarely.
directions	From Algecíras, N-340 for Cádiz. Through Pelayo; by Youth Hostel U-turn & head back. 100m past km96 marker, sharp right. Follow signs for 3km.

	Fabiola Dominguez Larios
tel	+34 956 236070
fax	+34 956 236070
email	cortijohoya@hotmail.com
web	www.cortijolahoya.com

Map 23 Entry 242

Monte de la Torre

Apartado de Correos 66, 11370 Los Barrios, Cádiz

Quentin Agnew's family has farmed this estate for generations. Puzzling to come across this utterly Edwardian building in the very south of Spain – it was built by the British when they were pushing the railway through the mountains to Ronda. This commingling of northern architecture and southern vegetation and climate is as seductive as it is unexpected. The house stands alone on a hill, surrounded by resplendent gardens; bask in the shade of the trees, gaze onto the Bay of Gibraltar, dip into the pool. The drawing room is panelled, the dining room elegant, there are masses of books, family portraits, a grandfather clock and dogs... this is a home, not a hotel, and the living is easy. The bedrooms (reached by a grand staircase) are high-ceilinged, decorated with family heirlooms and have period bathrooms – a festival of tubs and taps. Each is different, all lovely in an old-fashioned way. The apartments are in the former servants' quarters – unrecognisable now! Sue and Quentin are charming hosts; only breakfast is on offer but there are many good restaurants within easy reach.

rooms	3 + 2: 3 twins/doubles. 2 self-catering apartments for 5.
price	€110-€130. Apts €550-€850. VAT inc.
meals	Restaurants & tapas bars nearby.
closed	15 Dec-15 Jan; July/Aug.
directions	Málaga N-340 for Algecíras. 8km after S. Roque, A-381 to Los Barrios. At r'bout with fountains, left onto CA-231 Algecíras; at km2.8 right opp. black/white post, up track.

Sue & Quentin Agnew Larios

tel	+34 956 660000
fax	+34 956 634863
email	mdlt@mercuryin.es
web	www.andalucia.com/montedelatorre

Map 23 Entry 243

Hostal El Anón

c/Consuelo 34-40, 11330 Jimena de la Frontera, Cádiz

Five wonderful old townhouses have been amassed into a catacomb of beamed and low-ceilinged rooms on a myriad of levels and intimate terraces: such a delicious little piece of authentic Spain. Suzanna has lived here for years, knows the people and country like her own, and always has time for tea and a chat. She will delight in disentangling the rich web of local history for you, and can organise riding, painting, birdwatching, walking and flora-spotting expeditions. The countryside has treasures galore: see it from the little rooftop swimming pool with views over the tile-topped village all the way to Gibraltar. Enjoy the cool peace of the arched main courtyard and the exotic banana and custard-fruit trees, rejoice in the furnishings collected over the years (wall-hangings, paintings, sculptural bits and pieces), then dine on delicious spare ribs or tapas on the verdant terrace or in the bustling restaurant/bar. Rooms – and plumbing! – are basic; come for quantities of Spanishness in an unusually laid-back place.

rooms	13: 11 twins/doubles, 1 single, 1 suite.
price	€58. Singles €35. Suite €68. VAT inc.
meals	Lunch/dinner €25 à la carte. VAT inc.
closed	2 weeks June; 2 weeks Nov.
directions	From Málaga, N–340 Algecíras; at r'bout in Pueblo Nuevo de Guadiaro right for Jimena. In village centre left by taxi rank; 2nd right. Parking tricky.

	Gabriel Delgado & Suzanna Odell
tel	+34 956 640113
fax	+34 956 641110
email	reservas@elanon.net.
web	www.andalucia.com/jimena/hostalanon

Map 23 Entry 244

Casa La Loba

c/La Loba 21, 11170 Medina Sidonia, Cádiz

Relax in the wicker armchairs of the flower-filled courtyard before climbing, rioja
in hand, to the roof terrace and the sunset flaming over Cádiz. A classic
Andalucían townhouse, in a classic Andalucían hill town, the house seamlessly
mixes traditional with modern to create a relaxing, sophisticated home. Its
energetic owner used to run guest houses in France. High-beamed ceilings,
whitewash and terracotta are the background for red leather sofas, low wooden
beds and soft white bed linen. Decoration is simple but well-chosen: a carved
antique chair, a gilt table lamp or a splash of red vases. Help yourself to a drink
from the bar, a book from the library and move between courtyard and terrace to
escape or seek the sun. (For cooler weather: a log-burning stove in the living
room.) Refreshed, head for Cádiz, Seville or Jerez, the nearby beaches or the
marvellous walking of the Sierra de Cádiz. James – Leith's cookery school trained
– will cook supper or point you towards bars and restaurants where you will find
it hard to resist the charm, warmth and spirit of this unspoilt Andalucían town.

rooms	3 twins/doubles.
price	€95–€105. VAT included.
meals	Lunch/dinner €20.
closed	Rarely.
directions	From Jerez airport for Jerez; exit for Cádiz. Follow road round north of Jerez, join A-4; exit for Los Barrios. Left to M. Sidonia on A-381. Signs for 'Centro Urbano'; at Plazuela Santiago left into c/La Loba. On right.

	James Barr
tel	+34 956 412051
email	james@casalaloba.com
web	www.casalaloba.com

Map 23 Entry 245

Casa Viña de Alcántara
Ctra. Jerez–Arcos km8.6, 11400 Jerez de la Frontera, Cádiz

Senor Gonzalo del Rio y Gonzalez-Gordón is linked to the Gordon-Byass sherry dynasty – which means you'll be served an excellent glass of fino before dinner. A fervent anglophile, Gonzalo (who divides his time between the family estate and his hotel in Seville) is a charming man with a gift for gracious living. The 1890 hunting lodge, built by great-grandfather, has an instant allure, and is equally inviting within. First it was gutted, then subtly and exquisitely restored: polished limestone downstairs, oak parquet up. Bedrooms have refined elegance *and* warmth, thanks to fine family furniture and Gonzalo's mother's paintings. All is perfection, from taps to towels, and the bathrooms are some of the best in this book. Breakfast – English, with southern touches – is served by a white-gloved butler, as is dinner, simple and delicious. The Casa is fringed by a small forest of palms and pines, and surrounded by the vine-braided hills that nurture the palomino grape. Jerez, an architectural gem, is two minutes by car, thanks to the motorway (just a gentle hum). The beaches are not much further.

rooms	9 twins/doubles.
price	€150.
meals	Dinner €40, on request.
closed	Rarely.
directions	From Seville A-4 to Jerez. 1st exit for Jerez, follow signs Arcos & Circuito de Velocidad. Pass 'Meson La Cueva'. On right after 500m surrounded by trees.

	Gonzalo del Río y Gonzalez Gordón
tel	+34 956 393010
fax	+34 956 393011
email	info@vinadealcantara.com
web	www.vinadealcantara.com

Map 23 Entry 246

La Casa Grande
c/Maldonado 10, 11630 Arcos de la Frontera, Cádiz

La Casa Grande nudges right up to the very edge of whitewashed Arcos – a spectacular site. At night, from its terrace-of-terraces, you gaze onto two floodlit churches and mile after mile of surrounding plain. The house is almost 300 years old and many of the original features have survived to tell the tale. In true Andaluz style, a central, colonnaded, plant-filled patio is the axis around which the house turns; vaulted rooms lead off to all sides, nooks and crannies appear at every turn. A cosy lounge doubles up as a library with thousands of books – some of them written by delightful, multi-talented Elena. The decoration of the house reflects her and her husband's eclectic, bohemian taste: tiles from Morocco, blankets from Grazacema, David Hockney prints, a deco writing table topped by a designer lamp, a wickerwork chair. Stylish yet homely – and everywhere, the smell of woodsmoke and coffee. Guest bedrooms (two in the basement) are full of antiquey bits and pieces, with double glazing to protect you from night-time hum. Then wake to breakfast on that unforgettable terrace! *A Rusticae hotel.*

rooms	8: 6 twins/doubles, 2 suites for 4.
price	€65-€85. Singles €55 (low season only). Suites €77-€148.
meals	Breakfast €7.50.
closed	7 January-7 February.
directions	In Arcos follow signs to Parador. Park in square in front of Parador & walk to end of c/Escribano (just to left of Parador). Right, past Hotel El Convento, then left. House on right.

	Elena Posa Farrás
tel	+34 956 703930
fax	+34 956 717095
email	info@lacasagrande.net
web	www.lacasagrande.net

Map 23 Entry 247

Hotel Los Olivos del Convento

Paseo de Boliches 30, 11630 Arcos de la Frontera, Cádiz

Off a street leading to the old quarter of Arcos, Los Olivos is an Andalucían townhouse with breathtaking views. A huge oak door leads you into the hall and cool, wicker-furnished lounge; beyond is an arched inner courtyard with shade-bestowing canopy, aspidistra and palms, somewhat colonial in feel. The bedrooms give onto this light, airy courtyard and some have views across gentle hills and olive groves, down towards the Atlantic. If you're a light sleeper choose a quiet room at the back. All the bedrooms have high ceilings, freshly painted walls, modern fabrics, music systems and minibars. You can breakfast on the patio until the hotter summer days chase you indoors to the air-conditioned lounge. The old town with its *arcos* (arches) and narrow winding streets is just a 10-minute walk from Los Olivos and so too is the restaurant El Convento which is also managed by the hotel's owners: the food is excellent and has won many prizes. Great views, friendly staff, and the luxury of private parking; traffic wardens abound.

rooms	19: 17 twins/doubles, 2 singles.
price	€60–€70. Singles €40–€45. VAT included.
meals	Breakfast €6. Lunch/dinner €24 set menu; €30 à la carte.
closed	Rarely.
directions	In Arcos, signs for 'Conjunto Monumenta' & Parador. Follow one-way system into town; on left of road parallel to main street; own car park.

	María Moreno & José Antonio Roldán
tel	+34 956 700811
fax	+34 956 702018
email	losolivosdelc@terra.es
web	lasolivos.profesionales.on

Map 23 Entry 248

El Convento

c/Maldonado 2, 11630 Arcos de la Frontera, Cádiz

Arcos is spread like icing along the top of a craggy limestone outcrop; it was a great stronghold when Moors and Christians fought over the ever-shifting *frontera*. El Convento, a former cloister, is perched right at the edge of the cliff in the old town's heart. Behind the plain white façade lies a deliciously labyrinthine hotel and the wowiest, cliff-hanging balconies in Andalucía. Choose a room with one and enjoy stunning sunsets and views. José Antonio Roldán is proud of his home town and he and his wife have filled their hotel with works by local artists. Decoration is unfussy in the old part; furnishings are smarter in the annexe just across the rooftop terrace. Beds are very comfortable. Breakfast is served in an attractive beamed dining room with bar and there's a large terrace above, perfect for a sundowner as you watch the aerobatics of the kestrels nesting in the cliffs below. José Antonio and María own a restaurant in the covered colonnaded patio of a 16th-century palace just up the road; come to sample some of the best food in the Province of Cádiz.

rooms	11: 10 twins/doubles, 1 single.
price	€50-€80. Singles €35-€55.
meals	Breakfast €6. Lunch/dinner €24, €30 à la carte.
closed	10-24 January.
directions	In Arcos, signs to Parador & Plaza del Cabildo. Park in front of Santa María church, walk along c/Escribanos; at end, right into c/Maldonado.

	María Moreno & José Antonio Roldán
tel	+34 956 702333
fax	+34 956 704128
email	hotelelconvento@terra.es
web	www.webdearcos.com/elconvento

Map 23 Entry 249

Hacienda El Santiscal

Avda. El Santiscal 129, (Lago de Arcos), 11630 Arcos de la Frontera, Cádiz

This grand old cortijo overlooking the lake is a short drive from Arcos in a peaceful place where pigeons coo. Converted from a forgotten family home into an elegant but simple hotel, the building is Andalucían to the core: an austere whitewashed façade, a grand portal and the blissful peace and cool of that inner sanctum, the courtyard (pleasantly furnished with wicker chairs). The bedrooms lead off the patio, and almost all have magnificent long views across the estate. All are dark, classic Andaluz, with traditional beds and modern soft furnishings added. Bathrooms are good, with marble or tiles, and woodwork in Andaluz green. The suites are really special, and worth splashing out on. Children will enjoy the circular pool in the lawn. Mouthwatering aromas waft from the kitchen; dine in on classical Andalucían dishes (grilled meats, quail soufflé), or – when weddings are in the offing – head up to wonderful old Arcos where there are loads of interesting tapas bars and a few good restaurants. *A Rusticae hotel*

rooms	12: 10 twins/doubles, 2 suites.
price	€65–€99. Suites €84–€137.
meals	Breakfast €9. Lunch/dinner €25.
closed	Rarely.
directions	From Arcos A-372 for El Bosque; 1km after crossing bridge, left into Urbanización Dominio El Santiscal; follow signs (carefully) to El Santiscal.

	Francisca 'Paqui' Gallardo
tel	+34 956 708313
fax	+34 956 708268
email	reservas@santiscal.com
web	www.santiscal.com

Map 23 Entry 250

Cortijo Barranco

Ctra. Arcos-El Bosque (A-372) km5.7, 11630 Arcos de la Frontera, Cádiz

Grand Barranco stands alone, high on a hillside, across from the 'white' town of Arcos de la Frontera. Getting here is quite an adventure, at the end of a dusty one-mile track. This is every inch the classic olive-mill-cortijo, the private quarters and former stables wrapped around a central courtyard; they still make their own olive oil. The guest rooms and apartments are refreshingly sober with their terracotta floors, wrought-iron bedsteads, heavy linen curtains and hand-crocheted bedspreads; the most private of the apartments is charmingly authentic, with a big open-plan kitchen/living area. The sitting room is enormous with space for a billiard table, the dining room is lofty, with long tables and an open hearth at one end, and the huge, vine-clambered patio is a cool haven on hot days. A beautiful pool overlooking the Sierra de Grazalema completes the picture. Stroll out after dinner and abandon yourself to the beauty of the sun dipping behind the hills... later, let the owls hoot you to sleep. *The above address is for correspondence and is not that of the farm.*

rooms	14 + 5: 14 twins/doubles. 5 self-catering apartments for 4.
price	€70–€75. Singles €55. Apartments €90–€140.
meals	Lunch/dinner €21–€25, on request.
closed	Rarely.
directions	From Arcos de la Frontera, A-372 El Bosque. After 5.7km marker, at end of long straight section, left at sign onto track; 2km to farm.

	Maria José & Genaro Gil Amián
tel	+34 956 231402
fax	+34 956 231209
email	reservas@cortijobarranco.com
web	www.cortijobarranco.com

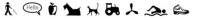

Map 23 Entry 251

Casa Margarita

Lista de Correos, 11630 Arcos de la Frontera, Cádiz

The house on the hill, reached via a bumpy track, lies in the last reaches of the rolling Jérez country, its landscape gentler than the jagged limestone of the Grazalema Park beyond. Bliss to rest by the pool surrounded by southern lushery, splashes of bourganvillea and dramatic views, the only sound that of the rooster crowing and the inevitable distant barking dog. The main terrace has Arcos views: spectacular at night when the churches are lit up. Guest bedrooms, set among the pine and citrus trees, have patios, simple shower rooms, breakfast in the fridge, orchard fruits on the table and a rustic, Spanish-Moroccan décor. The well-equipped apartment, in an independent part of the main house, has air-conditioning for summer and a woodburner for winter. Life at La Casa del Curandero is lived by Anne, her daughter Rebecca, horse Baltasar and two friendly dogs in a relaxingly cheerful manner: come to unwind. Anne also has lots of info on walks. The house takes its name from the healer who once lived here – these alternative doctors are still a part of life in the sierras of the south.

rooms	2 + 1: 2 twins/doubles. 1 self-catering apartment for 2-4.
price	€50. Singles €40. Apt €60. VAT inc.
meals	Good restaurants nearby.
closed	21 December-6 January.
directions	A-382 Arcos-Antequera; A-372 km5.5 El Bosque; pass lake & petrol station; right for Girasol onto old road; 300m 2nd Girasol sign; right; 5th on left.

	Anne Lacy
tel	+34 956 231204
fax	+34 956 231204
email	annelacyarcos@hotmail.com

Map 23 Entry 252

Hacienda Buena Suerte

Apartado 60, 11650 Villamartín, Cádiz

A grand arrival! Pass under the great portal and sweep up the drive to this beautifully renovated estate surrounded by Judas trees, bougainvillea and palms. Beyond: the rolling olive groves and wheat fields of the Grazalema foothills. But the main star here is the horse. Enchanting Magda and Raphael are rarely out of the saddle, either teaching in the riding school or trekking in the hills with their guests. And non-riders are every bit as welcome. Yoga, relaxation, horse-whispering classes, the walks are wonderful, and there are sauna and outdoor pool too. Bedrooms, most of them in the converted granary (a few air conditioned) are large and simply furnished, decorated with stylish prints of horses and animal skins on beautiful old floors. You may find sweets on the pillow or a candle in the corner. The restaurant/bar is the hub of the place and meals, taken round the huge dining table, are delicious – everything from goulash to bouillabaisse to couscous – mostly organic and home-reared or -grown. A classic cortijo with alternative touches and a wonderfully laid-back feel.

rooms	12 twins/doubles. 2 4-rooms. 1 Bungalow.
price	€60-€88. VAT included.
meals	Lunch/dinner with wine, €15.
closed	Rarely.
directions	From Ronda, C-339 Seville. At junc. with N-342, left for Jerez A-382. 7km before Villamartín, left at sign for El Bosque & Ubrique. Buena Suerte 1.5km on left.

	Family Dysli
tel	+34 956 231286
fax	+34 956 231275
email	magda-dysli@gmx.de
web	www.dysli.com

Map 23 Entry 253

La Mejorana
c/Santa Clara 6, 11610 Grazalema, Cádiz

Push aside the carved wooden door and step into an apparently ancient, mountain village house – gleaming with polished tiles, dark rustic furniture and white walls. A shock, then, to discover La Mejorana, tucked into a quiet corner of Grazalema, is 20 years old. Its other trick is that its one-storey appearance opens up into three floors that tumble down the hillside to a jasmine-scented garden and swimming pool below. The guest rooms, and their neat, colourfully tiled bathrooms, are furnished, as is the rest of the house, in Andalucían rustic style – with the cheerful addition of the modern art of Ana, one of the young and friendly owners. Beamed ceilings, tiled floors, shuttered windows, lacey bedcovers – there's a wholesome, uncluttered feel, while potted plants, decorative plates and checked cushions help create an individual atmosphere. Hope for a room with rooftop and mountain views! Breakfasts are taken in the glass-fronted gallery with more stunning vistas. An unpretentious but fetching place, close to Ronda and the wonderful walks of the Grazalema Natural Park.

rooms	5 twins/doubles.
price	€50.
meals	Restaurants in village.
closed	Rarely.
directions	In main square right up c/de las Piedras; at fountain, right, then right again. Park; signed.

Andrés Sánchez & Ana Vázquez
tel	+34 956 132327
email	info@lamejorana.net
web	www.lamejorana.net

Map 23 Entry 254

Cortijo El Papudo

11340 San Martín del Tesorillo, Málaga

An authentic old farmstead in the fertile valley of the Guadiaro river; there's a special feel here. And fruit trees flourish, thanks to the exceptional climate: everything from citrus to custard fruit, pomegranates to avocados. More recently a number of plant nurseries have sprung up and the Harveys have set up one of their own – an obligatory shop-over for the coastal ex-pat community. They are, of course, highly knowledgeable about all things botanical. Their own garden is an exotic, multi-coloured ode to southern flora, and laps up to the high, solid old cortijo whose rooms are simple and pleasing. The original wooden ceilings give character to the bedrooms, which have Casablanca-style ceiling fans for the summer, and central heating for the colder months. All have views of the garden and across the farm to the surrounding orange groves; one has a balcony overlooking the flower-fringed pool. The rustic breakfast room has a handsome flagged floor and a woodburner, and there's an honesty bar here. The beach is a 15-minute drive.

rooms	11 twins/doubles.
price	€64-€70. Singles €42-€46. VAT included.
meals	Good restaurants nearby, 1 mile.
closed	Rarely.
directions	N-340 Málaga-Cádiz. After 3km right for Algecíras. At km133 right on CA-514 for San Martín. At km10 bear left over river; before bridge right at sign for 2km, up hill & sharp left.

	Michael & Vivien Harvey
tel	+34 952 854018
fax	+34 952 854018
email	papudo@mercuryin.es
web	www.andalucia.com/gardens/papudo

Map 23 Entry 255

Hotel Casablanca

c/Teodoro de Molina 12, 29480 Gaucín, Málaga

Gaucín is one of Andalucía's most spectacular mountain villages. Its labyrinthine, car-challenged streets huddle against a hillside beneath a Moorish castle; eagles wheel overhead, the views stretch for ever. The Casablanca's restoration is majestic; pass through enormous wooden doors, beneath lofty inlaid ceilings, to emerge in the bar. Beyond is a glory of a garden, giving you both sanctuary and breathtaking views. Palms, magnolia and jacaranda lend colour and shade, a fountain murmurs beside the pool, sun-dappled terraces on varying levels look out across rooftops to the castle and the mountains of Morocco, and the sunsets are sensational. The Van Gogh and Goya bedrooms in the old house are perhaps the finest, but every room is special: polished parquet or terracotta floors, warm colours, huge beds, heavenly bathrooms (three with shower only). All bar two have private terraces – and those are studios a step from the pool. Dine in at least once; the new chef is working wonders in the kitchen, and his food follows the seasons. The owners live in Britain but regularly drop by to check all is perfect.

rooms	8 twins/doubles.
price	€110-140. VAT inc.
meals	Lunch/dinner €25 à la carte. VAT included.
closed	November-February.
directions	From Málaga N-340 for Algecíras. After Estepona right on MA-539 via Manilva to Gaucín (not Casares). Into centre to street of San Sebastián church; one-way system right for Ronda; on left, signed.

	Steve & Di Lloyd
tel	+34 952 151019
fax	+34 95 2151019
email	reservations@casablanca-gaucin.com
web	www.casablanca-gaucin.com

Map 23 Entry 256

El Nobo

Camino de Gibraltar, 29480 Gaucín, Málaga

Gaucín has long been popular among the more adventurous of the ex-pat community and the Von Meisters live in one of the area's most gorgeous homes. At the end of a dusty old track... a Moorish courtyard, fountains and a pool; impossible to believe that 12 years ago a lowly farm building stood here. The position is amazing: from the pretty, shaded terrace you can see Gibraltar, the Strait and the mountains of Africa. The gardens are awash with colour and the house feels as if it has always been anchored to its rocky hillside. The drawing room is the most memorable space and pays full homage to that view-of-views thanks to enormous French windows: an enchanting spot at both breakfast and dinner. Gregarious Sally loves good food and describes her culinary thing as "very mediterranean". She uses lots of fish, whatever veg are in season – delicious – and Tuffy knows his wines. The bedrooms at El Nobo are comfortably flamboyant, there's also a charming self-catering cottage with two large balconies and a plunge pool, andnyou may use the main pool too.

rooms	3 + 1: 2 twins/doubles, 1 suite. 1 self-catering cottage for 2.
price	€125. Suite €140. Cottage €750 per week. VAT included.
meals	Dinner €35 on request.
closed	July, August, Christmas, New Year.
directions	AP7 to exit 142; on to Gaucín. Right into village at T-junc; sharp right onto road marked 'Camino de Gibraltar'; 1 km downhill on left.

	Sally & Christopher Von Meister
tel	+34 952 151303
fax	+34 952 151083
email	elnobo@mercuryin.es
web	www.elnobo.co.uk

Map 23 Entry 257

La Herradura

Camino Romano, 29480 Gaucín, Málaga

Unforgivable not to make the most of a panorama like this. And the designers of the little pink-washed house have done just that: house, terrace and pool are perfectly positioned for maximum effect. Behind and to either side is wild, green mountainside; ahead, breathtaking views to Africa. La Herradura, owned by Christopher and Sally next door, has been newly built in an unobtrusive, rustic style, while flair and imagination have created an effect of rural simplicity tempered with sophistication inside. Pastel colours – pinks, blues and golds – glow gently against pale cream walls. In the airy, open-plan living room, a big woven rug contrasts with the austere white fireplace; a squashy sofa and armchairs are grouped companionably around. The ceiling is chestnut-beamed and slopes down towards two sets of double doors that open onto the terrace. There's a fireplace in the attractive kitchen/dining area, too – but you'll want to eat outside whenever you can. Below: a gorgeous pool, poised on the very edge of hillside; beyond: those unbelievable views.

rooms	1 villa for 4.
price	€1,650 per week.
meals	Self-catering.
closed	Never.
directions	AP7 to exit 142; on to Gaucin. Right into village at T-junc; sharp right onto road marked 'Camino de Gibraltar'; 1 km downhill on left.

	Sally & Christopher von Meister
tel	+34 952 151303
fax	+34 952 151083
email	elnobo@mercuryin.es
web	www.elnobo.co.uk

Map 23 Entry 258

Molino del Carmen
Barrio Alto 67, 29480 Gaucín, Málaga

The long white façade combines balconies, arches, delicate pillars and tumbling creepers to dazzling effect. Until 1967 this lovely, rambling place was still being run as a mill. Now Darryl and Marjukka live at the centre (where part of the old mill-workings can still be seen) and have turned the rest of the building into five unusual apartments. Moroccan drapes and mirrors add colour and drama to plain whitewashed walls, heavy old doors and gleaming floor tiles; the odd flight of steps gives a sense of the unexpected. The furniture is Moorish or rural Spanish and there are woodburning stoves to keep you warm in winter. Cooking and eating here will be a real pleasure. Though the kitchens have marble worktops and all mod cons, their intriguing stone shelves and recesses and pretty tiles give an impression of rural simplicity at its most engaging. Outside is a pleasant patio garden, a terrace with a pool and impressive views down to the Med and Gibraltar. Darryl and Marjukka, both enthusiastic motorcyclists, make delightful hosts, and Gaucín is the most attractive of the white villages.

rooms	5 self-catering apartments for 4.
price	€495–€925 per week. VAT included.
meals	Self-catering.
closed	Rarely.
directions	From Málaga airport N-340 for Cádiz. After 20km A-7 toll road to exit 142 for Gaucín. At junc. at entrance of Gaucín right & on downhill. Left at next junc. & next left onto Barrio Alto.

	Darryl & Marjukka Laurin
tel	+34 952 151277
fax	+34 952 151277
email	info@molinodelcarmen.com
web	www.molinodelcarmen.com

Map 23 Entry 259

El Gecko
Cañada Real del Tesoro, 29391 Estación de Cortes de la Frontera, Málaga

El Gecko (no, not that Spanish artist from Toledo) is a great name for a great place – next to the river in a sleepy hamlet, with a railway line that gets you to the gates of the Alhambra. (Though the Mediterranean beaches are an awful lot closer!). Large, lofty bedrooms have an elegant simplicity and are decorated with care and flair by Rachel: gentle colours, Indian bedspreads, good mirrors and prints. Two have bathrooms, the rest showers. There are cane-covered sun terraces so you can gaze on the river as you dine, a dear little bar, and a restaurant, stylishly simple, a crowd-puller with a reputation for good, fresh, seasonal food: chicken with couscous, orange and fresh mint; tuna with puy lentil salsa. Rachel used to work in the wine trade and knows her stuff, so if you stay long enough you can explore her exclusively Spanish selection. The place was once an old station inn, serving those who paused on their journey; now the British come here – and return. And there's a long, cool, turquoise pool.

rooms	5 twins/doubles.
price	€78–€103. Singles €55. VAT included.
meals	Lunch €15 à la carte. Dinner €25 à la carte.
closed	December–end February.
directions	From Málaga E-15/A-7 for Algecíras. Exit 142 for Gaucín. There, left, then right on Ronda road 1-396. Left to Cortes de la F., signed. Cross river; 1st left into village. Hotel 200m, on left.

	Rachel Dring
tel	+34 952 153315
fax	+34 952 153266
email	elgecko@mercuryin.es
web	www.hotelelgecko.com

Map 23 Entry 260

Banú Rabbah

Sierra Bermeja s/n, 29490 Benarrabá, Málaga

A good little place in a very grand setting. You're pretty much left to your own devices but all you need is here – restaurant, terraces, pool, and nightlife. (Local legend has it that the Moors built a secret tunnel between here and Gaucín.) The hotel, named after the first Berber tribesman who settled here, was built as a local council initiative, and is now run by a friendly group of six from the village. The lofty setting is what makes Banú Rabbah special: 2,000m up a mountain, with a magnificent sweep of rocky range, white village and densely wooded hillsides. The hotel has a rather cumbersome design but bedrooms are cosy, light and clean and come with generous terraces. The restaurant – open to the public, along with the pool, in summer – features local produce: try the *saltavallao* (a hot gazpacho) and the almond cakes. After dinner take a stroll through this very Spanish village: you are unlikely to meet many foreigners here (unlike in neighbouring Gaucín). There's a trek down to the sparkling waters of the Genal for the energetic – route maps provided – and mule rides and 4x4 trips for the idle.

rooms	12 twins/doubles.
price	€48–€60. Singles €39–€49, extra bed €10.
meals	Breakfast €3 Half-board €13.50; full-board €21.
closed	February.
directions	From Málaga N-340 for Cádiz. A-377 via Manilva to Gaucín. Here towards Ronda on A-369; after 4.5km, right to Benarrabá. Signed.

	Jesús García
tel	+34 952 150288
fax	+34 952 150005
email	hotel@hbenarraba.es
web	www.hbenarraba.es

Map 23 Entry 261

La Casa del Arriero

c/Cantón 8, 29380 Cortes de la Frontera, Málaga

No fewer than three of Andalucía's most beautiful natural parks are on your doorstep. The Guadiaro valley is criss-crossed with ancient drovers' paths and these young owners know its loveliest corners. They organise walking and riding holidays and have route maps of all their rambles. They've given new life and a twist of style to this traditional village house – all yours – with a roof terrace that looks to the church tower and across the rolling pastures of the valley. Things within work beautifully: an open-plan kitchen and diner, a small plant-filled patio for summery meals, a cosy lounge with a woodburning stove. There are two bedrooms, one vast with its own sun terrace, the second much smaller but fine for kids. The house takes its name from the muleteer who once lived here and the equine tradition continues: Mel, a rider all her life, organises full or half day rides from Cortes. Even if you're idle, this is just the place to recharge your batteries. Buy veggies fresh from the market, rub shoulders with the locals in any number of bars, get a taste of that fabled 'real' Spain.

rooms	House for 2-4.
price	€375-€450 per week.
meals	Self-catering.
closed	Rarely.
directions	From Málaga E-15 for Algecíras; exit for Gaucín. Here right to Ronda, left to Cortes de la F. Here, right opp. bullring then left up c/Alta. Park at top. Down pedestrian street; 1st left; last house.

	Melanie Dickins & Tiger Templer
tel	+34 952 153330
fax	+34 952 153330
email	enquiries@casaarriero.com
web	www.casaarriero.com

Map 23 Entry 262

Molino del Santo

Bda. Estación s/n, 29370 Benaoján, Málaga

Pauline and Andy moved south in search of the good life, and restored a century-old mill surrounded by national park. The setting is exquisite: water tumbles past flowered terraces, under fig trees and willows and into the solar-heated pool. (When it comes to things environmental, these owners are exceptionally green.) Pretty rooms and restaurant wear warm local garb – terracotta tiles, beams, carved beds, rush-seated chairs. Fresh flowers are everywhere and the Molino's reputation for good Spanish food is established – as organic and free-range as possible. Most hotel guests are British but the locals flock in at weekends to enjoy local hams and sausages, rabbit, fish and imaginative vegetarian. Staff and owners are generous with advice on walks from the hotel. From the sleepy little station you can take a train to Ronda or, in the other direction, pass some of the loveliest 'white' villages of Andalucía. The Molino, one of the Sierra's most enjoyable small hotels, has achieved the perfect balance between warmth and professionalism. Pay extra for a superior room with a terrace – and book in advance!

rooms	18: 15 twins/doubles, 3 suites.
price	€80–€112. Suites €134–€178. VAT included. High season half-board extra €24 p.p.
meals	Lunch/dinner €30–€40.
closed	Mid-November–mid-February.
directions	From Ronda, A376 Seville; after km118 marker, left for Benaoján. After 10km, having crossed railway & river bridges, left to station & follow signs.

	Pauline Elkin & Andy Chapell
tel	+34 952 167151
fax	+34 952 167327
email	molino@logiccontrol.es
web	www.molinodelsanto.com

Map 23 Entry 263

El Tejar

c/Nacimiento 38, 29430 Montecorto, Málaga

You look out from a hillside near to Ronda to a panorama of oak forest, almond groves and distant peaks. The house is the highest in the village and is made up of a labyrinthine series of spaces built on more than a dozen different levels. The decoration is ethnic, intimate and southern: an open hearth, ochre washes and terracotta impart an Andaluz flavour while textiles and rugs collected in Asia, Africa and South America add spice and colour. There are masses of books and magazines, two friendly dogs and a well-stocked honesty bar. Bedrooms have a Moroccan feel with kilims, brightly woven blankets and photos of travels in distant lands; the views of the jagged outline of the Grazalema Sierra are sublime. Dinners, prepared by housekeeper Paqui, are Andalucían, wholesome and delicious and served at a candlelit table; wine and conversation flow. Guy has written books on walking and can steer you towards the most enchanted, hidden corners of the Grazalema Park, with maps and route notes provided. *Special summer rental: rates on request. English, French, German, Spanish spoken.*

rooms	4: 3 twins/doubles, 1 suite. Whole house available June-mid-Sept.
price	€65. Suite €70. House €950 weekly (June-mid-Sept).
meals	Breakfast €5. Dinner with wine €22.50; not Saturday or Sunday.
closed	May-September when house rented.
directions	From Ronda A-376 for Seville for 20km. Right into Montecorto. Cobbled track opp. church & at end, right. Pass left of no. 54 & at very last house right up track to El Tejar.

	Guy Hunter-Watts
tel	+34 952 184053
fax	+34 952 184053
email	eltejar@mercuryin.es
web	www.rusticblue.com/zc111.htm

Map 23 Entry 264

Cortijo Las Piletas
Apdo. 559, 29400 Ronda, Málaga

Play the country squire: there are 100 hectares of wheat and sunflower fields, oak woodland and cattle grazing at your disposal. This sprawling cortijo, with its brilliant white walls and tomato-red shutters, is a fine example of an Andalucían country estate, owned by Pablo's family for 200 years. Staying here is like staying as a guest of the family. Light-filled bedrooms are elegant with polished furniture, pretty coloured or carved bedheads and soft white curtains. Flowers or plants add a fresh, country touch. The old farmhouse hall has been turned into a comfortable drawing room enriched with antiques, tapestries and oil paintings; a fire in winter and an honesty bar add to the relaxed feel. The beamed dining room – with terrace for summer eating – is small and cosy, its tables set with pretty china. This is terrific walking country with three natural parks, including Grazalema, on the doorstep. Return to a dip in the pool, a snooze on your private terrace; there are binoculars and books to borrow. From the gardens, watch the sun set over Grazalema, glass of wine in hand. Pablo keeps an excellent cellar.

rooms	7 twins/doubles.
price	€60-€75.
meals	Dinner €21.
closed	Rarely.
directions	From Ronda A-376f or Seville. After km108 left for Montejaque MA-505. Las Piletas has red windows: 1st farm on left.

Elisenda Vidal & Pablo Serratosa

tel	+34 605 080295
email	cortijolaspiletas@hotmail.com
web	www.andalucia.com/laspiletas

Map 23 Entry 265

Cortijo El Horcajo

Ctra. Ronda-Zahara de la Sierra km95.5, Apdo. 149, 29400 Ronda, Málaga

A remote and special setting. The old farmstead of El Horcajo lies on the northern boundary of the Grazalema Natural Park, at the end of a long, long track snaking down to the bottom of a deep valley. This is every inch the classic Andalucían cortijo, where outbuildings are wrapped around a sheltered inner courtyard, a welcome insurance against the summer's heat. There's unpretentious rusticity at every turn, in cobble, beam and tile. The large sitting, dining and reception areas are in the converted cattle byre, where the original vaulting has been preserved and new windows opened to pull in the light. Bedrooms are comfortable, if a little plain, the best expanding into private terraces. We prefer the rooms round the courtyard to those at the back, which feel somewhat removed from the heart of the place. Early sleepers should avoid those above the restaurant. Bathrooms are basic but clean. There are good walks close by, pretty Grazalema is 20 minutes by car and the birdwatching's a treat. Food is country traditional and Luis a gentle and accommodating host.

rooms	26: 15 twins/doubles, 1 single, 10 suites.
price	€61–€99. Singles €51–€63. Suites €69–€136.
meals	Lunch/dinner €15.30.
closed	Rarely.
directions	From Ronda, A-376 for Seville. After 15km, left for Grazalema on A-372. Don't take next left turn for Grazalema, continue towards Zahara & at km95.5 marker, left down track to farm.

	Luis González García
tel	+34 952 184080
fax	+34 952 184171
email	info@elhorcajo.com
web	www.elhorcajo.com

Map 23 Entry 266

La Fuente de la Higuera

Partido de los Frontones, 29400 Ronda, Málaga

Tina and Pom have travel in the blood; he chartered yachts, she worked for one of the big airlines. Then the Ronda mountains wrapped them in its spell and they realised their dream: a luxurious retreat to ease away urban cares. Tina is the 'spark', a charming and vivacious woman who has decorated the hotel with an understated panache. Pom is born to the role of host: a raconteur by nature and a connoisseur of wine. The conversion of their old mill has been accomplished with local expertise, smooth plastering and planked floors adding to the immaculate furnishings and the stylish feel; a refreshing change from the more rustic beam and terracotta. Each lovely suite has an open fire for cosy winter stays; Indonesian beds, muslin drapes, lamps, chairs and tables add an exotic feel. Bathrooms are generous. An honesty bar in the library, a laid-back feel… La Fuente is more home than hotel. The focus is poolwards; beyond, groves of olives and the changing colours of the mountains – a blissful backdrop to your sundowner. At dinner, feast on local food impeccably presented, and excellent wines.

rooms	11: 3 twins/doubles, 8 suites.
price	€135–€250. Singles €120. Suites €166–€260.
meals	Dinner €35.
closed	7 January–15 February.
directions	Bypass Ronda on A-376 towards Seville. Pass turning to Benaoján; right at sign for hotel. Under bridge, left at 1st fork; over bridge; left after 200m.

	Pom & Christina Piek
tel	+34 952 114355
fax	+34 952 114356
email	info@hotellafuente.com
web	www.hotellafuente.com

Map 23 Entry 267

Finca La Morera
Ronda, Málaga

The narrowest of country lanes passes sleepy bars, errant chickens and groves of medlar, quince and olives before eventually looping round, then ending, at La Morera. *The* classical vision of Arcadia: a solid whitewashed farmhouse, swaying palm fronds, jasmine-clad terraces, orchards stretching down to a river. Inside, a meticulous division of space and design from a team of friends from England. Their aim? To create one of the plushest, most exciting rent-a-homes in Andalucía. Enter a lofty hall-dining room with a huge fireplace and a table for 14, then a twin sweep of stairs that arcs one way to the master suite (with a claw-footed tub in the bedroom itself), the other to a gorgeous chestnut-floored drawing room with enticing valley views. Bedrooms, all ensuite, are fabulous; each has a balcony or private terrace, mattresses from England, cotton sheets from Egypt, perhaps a four-poster from Indonesia. Add to this a games room and cinema, two state-of-the-art kitchens, underfloor heating in the main house, a choice of two pools and a chef available at 24-hours notice. Exceptional.

rooms	House for 12.
price	£2,000–£4,000. Short low season lets available.
meals	Self-catering. Restaurant/bar 1.5km.
closed	Never.
directions	Owners will send directions on booking.

Richard Johnston, Richard Becher & Nicholas Smallwood
tel   +44 (0)1749 814 811
email info@fincalamorera.com
web   www.fincalamorera.com

Map 23 Entry 268

Finca La Guzmana

Apdo. de Correos 408, 29400 Ronda, Málaga

You'll want to stay here for at least a week – such a happy, relaxed place to be and Claire and Peter so welcoming and open. The house, a 150-year-old, single-storey Andalucían cortijo, is surrounded by five acres of olive trees and vines. Apart from the occasional train, or the put-put of the tractor as Peter works his fields, it's very peaceful. At the heart of the place is a tiled courtyard, wrapped around by the three whitewashed wings of the house. A dappled terracotta roof juts forward to provide cloister-like shade; vivid geraniums spill from supporting pillars. Breakfast out here by the lion fountain is a delicious way to start the day. The bedrooms – and the open-plan kitchen that guests are free to use – open off the courtyard; they are pleasant, inviting rooms, with square, deep-set windows and plenty of light and space. Outside is a superb, 20m salinated pool where you can swim and gaze up at the mountains. There's masses to do in the area if you can drag yourself away, and Claire is happy to provide packed lunches. For dinner, good food can be found at the *venta* at the end of the track.

rooms	7 twins/doubles.
price	€65–€85. VAT included. Weekly rates available.
meals	Packed lunch €6. Restaurant 300m.
closed	Rarely.
directions	Ronda-El Burgo road to km4. Take track ('Camino Privado') opp. La Venta; 300m.

	Peter McLeod & Claire Casson
tel	+34 610 826279
email	info@laguzmana.com
web	www.laguzmana.com

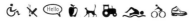

Map 23 Entry 269

Hotel San Gabriel ●
c/Marqués de Moctezuma 19, 29400 Ronda, Málaga

From the dusty cobbled street, slip beneath the tall cypress to discover a cool courtyard shrouded in foliage and set with curvy, wrought-iron tables. This 18th-century Andalucían house in the historic centre retains its gracious, family atmosphere. Care has been taken to preserve original features while traditional furnishings blend seamlessly with modern comforts, and chandeliers, columned archways and choice antiques make you forget you're in a hotel. Curl up in the sitting room with its plump sofas, play billiards or sink into red velour seats in the private cinema. Bedrooms are luxurious but not ostentatious: gleaming tiled floors, carved Castillian bedheads, rich brocades. Individual touches – perhaps a marble topped writing table or wooden screen – add to the home-like atmosphere. All have space for a little salon while the tiled and marbled bathrooms are top-notch. Only breakfast and evening tapas are served but the delightfully enthusiastic Arnal Pérez family will recommend local restaurants. This feels like staying with rather grand, but exceptionally welcoming, old friends.

rooms	16: 13 twins/doubles, 3 suites.
price	€73–€95. Suites €95–€105.
meals	Breakfast €6.
closed	21-31 July; 21 December-7 January.
directions	From north (Seville-Campillo) head for the main road, by Plaza de Toros. Cross new bridge; 2nd right. From south (San Pedro-Algecíras) up road next to ramparts; 2nd left.

	Arnal Pérez Family
tel	+34 952 190392
fax	+34 952 190117
email	info@hotelsangabriel.com
web	www.hotelsangabriel.com

Map 23 Entry 270

La Goyesca

c/Infantes 39, 29400 Ronda, Málaga

Don't be put off by the shabby entrance from the street to La Goyesca. You emerge into a verdant inner courtyard full of plumbago, medlar, Virginia creeper, ferns, jasmine and other plantery. Owners Javier Herrera Pérez and his wife, teachers by profession, always wanted to run a small guesthouse in Andalucía, and the 100-year-old building has a chequered history: it once housed a convent's garden, then became a small factory producing quince jam, later it was a grain store... now this delightfully quiet and friendly place to stay. Bedrooms are wrapped around the patio, the hub of the place, and have been recently redecorated with an uncluttered Moroccan feel; they are simple but cosy, and some come with sofas. Best of all – a bonus in this town – they are quiet; all you hear is the chirruping of the caged canaries. No restaurant, but the Pérez recommend the new Taverna Curro next door. Hilltop Ronda is lovely and you are bang in the town's heart – the famous and magnificent bull ring, the oldest in Spain, is around the corner. Come out of season if you can.

rooms	6: 4 twins/doubles, 2 family.
price	€72-€90. Singles €51-€36. VAT included.
meals	Available nearby at Taverna Curro.
closed	15 December-15 February.
directions	From Málaga, N-340 for Cádiz; A-376 to Ronda. 1st right for Ronda; follow road through old town, cross bridge, pass bullring, then 1st right. Pass Hotel Polo; hotel in 4th block on left.

	Javier Herrera Pérez
tel	+34 952 190049
fax	+34 952 190657
email	hotelgoyesca@ronda.net
web	www.ronda.net/usuar/hotelgoyesca/

Map 23 Entry 271

Alavera de los Baños ●

c/San Miguel s/n, 29400 Ronda, Málaga

A very fetching small hotel on the edge of the old Tanners Quarter – sheep-grazed pastures to one side, cobbled (steep!) ascents to Ronda on the other. *A-la-vera de* means 'by the side of' – your hotel is next to the first hammam of the Moorish citadel. Christian and Inma brim with enthusiasm for both hotel and restaurant, and staff are friendly. The new building is in keeping with the Hispano-Moorish elements of its surroundings: thus terracotta tiles, wafer bricks, keyhole arches without and, in the cosy little bedrooms, a softly oriental feel: kilims, mosquito nets, colour washes of ochres, blue and yellow. Shower rooms are compact but charming. Book one of the terrace rooms if you can; they lead to a lush little garden and delicious pool (crowded in high summer) with views. The dining room is lily-filled and candlelit, cut across by an arched central walkway leading to the rooms at either end. Breakfasts are freshly different each day; dinners have a Moorish slant: lamb is the speciality and there is tasty veggie food too, much organically grown. Come out of season for the Alavera as its best.

rooms	10: 9 twins/doubles, 1 single.
price	€75–€85. Singles €50. VAT included.
meals	Dinner €22–€25.
closed	December–January.
directions	In Ronda, directly opp. Parador hotel, take c/Rosario. Right at end & down hill to Fuente de los Ocho Caños. Here left, then 1st right to Arab Baths; hotel next door. Park here.

	Christian Reichardt
tel	+34 952 879143
fax	+34 952 879143
email	alavera@telefonica.net
web	www.andalucia.com/alavera

Map 23 Entry 272

La Cazalla

Tajo del Abanico, Apdo de Correos 160, 29400 Ronda, Málaga

If you want 'off the beaten track', make for this valley; spectacularly positioned at its head and built partly into the rock is La Cazalla. A Roman road once ran beside it – you can almost imagine the legionaries trudging by. A place of astonishing greenness and peace, and the house, part Roman, part Arab, exquisitely restored by María. On the big terrace, with views to the Tajo del Abanico, shade is provided by vines and willows. Keep cool in the spring water 'pool'. Everywhere there are fruit trees and the soothing sound of water – even in the delightfully unusual sitting room, where natural rock walls and white paint contrast with rich kelims and piles of books. Bedrooms upstairs are airy and elegant. Each bathroom has an intriguing domed shower, each bedroom a pair of binoculars for watching birds and deer. María lives here with her son Rodrigo, who does the cooking – the three-course dinners are "always a surprise" and you are encouraged to say if there is anything you don't eat. There's also a small but good wine list. Worth a long detour. *Minimum stay two-five nights. A Rusticae hotel.*

rooms	6: 5 twins/doubles, 1 suite.
price	€130. Suite €110-170.
meals	Dinner €30.
closed	Rarely.
directions	From Ronda, C-369 for Algecíras. Pass 1st r'bout; at next r'bout, to right of road, avoid track for 'ermita' & take next right. Follow blue-painted marks on stones for 2.8km.

	Maria Ruiz González
tel	+34 952 114175
fax	+34 952 114092
email	reservas@hotellacazalla.com
web	www.hotellacazalla.com

Map 23 Entry 273

Los Castaños

c/Iglesia 40, 29452 Cartajima, Málaga

You will be charmed the moment you step through the huge studded door. The Moorish influence seduces at once: water trickles in a little tiled fountain, arches beckon, geraniums splash the dazzling walls with colour. There's a fireplace, too, for the nippier months. Climb to the next floor and you'll find six cool, airy bedrooms – four with balconies – and windows framing the loveliest of mountain views. Handmade beds, old Spanish rocking chairs, low tables, Moroccan lights and super bathrooms add to the sense of well-being. Go up again and you emerge onto an entrancing roof terrace, benignly presided over by the white tower of next door's church. Set among pillars and pierced terracotta screens is a small, round, brilliant blue plunge pool: irresistible. A pampering, grown-up place, where Di and her daughter Lu, smiling and generous, know how to soothe and spoil. The food is delicious, the village is charming and there are good walks to the other villages glimpsed through the trees. As if that wasn't enough, there are fascinating Roman and Phoenician ruins to explore.

rooms	6: 5 twins/doubles, 1 single.
price	€110. Singles €50.
meals	Dinner €35. Not Sunday.
closed	Rarely.
directions	From San Pedro to Ronda on A-376/A-397. 10km before Ronda left after petrol station to Cartajima. There, bear right, pass recycling bins, then 1st hard right; park by phone box. On right.

	Di & Lu Beach
tel	+34 952 180778
fax	+34 952 180901
email	reservations@loscastanos.com
web	www.loscastanos.com

Map 23 Entry 274

Albero Lodge

Urbanización Finca la Cancelada, c/Támesis 16, 29689 Estepona, Málaga

A private villa reborn as a sophisticated small hotel. Young trees stand sentinel in front of the modern, ochred exterior (*albero* describes the sandy colour of the bull ring) lending it a ceremonious air. The interconnecting dining room, sitting room and bar are similarly formal. The bedrooms, by contrast, are triumphantly, stylishly individual, each inspired by a different city: Florence, Deauville, Berlin, Dover, Ronda, Madras, Djerba, Fez and New York. Those with an eastern theme are especially gorgeous. Walls are colourwashed, linen and fittings impossible to fault, every room gets its own patio, and bathrooms ooze rustic chic. The gardens are similarly groomed – lush with palm trees, jasmine, hibiscus, plumbago. There's a terrace dotted with colonial-style rattan furniture, and a delicious pool. Albero Lodge is part of a smart development of villas fairly close to the N-340; from outside there's a distant hum, but indoors the insulation is good. It's a five-minute walk to the beach, Gibraltar is a short drive to the west, and Morocco is not much further. Special.

rooms	4 twins/doubles, 5 suites.
price	€85–€155.
meals	Breakfast €7. Many restaurants with various types of food near the hotel.
closed	10 January–10 February.
directions	From Málaga, N-340 for Estepona. Exit after km164.5, signed Cambio de Sentido. Under bridge, left twice, right twice, past Park Beach. Hotel on right.

	Myriam Pérez-Torres
tel	+34 952 880700
fax	+34 952 885238
email	info@alberolodge.com
web	www.alberolodge.com

Map 23 Entry 275

Breakers Lodge Hostal

Avda. Las Mimosas 189, Linda Vista Baja, 29678 San Pedro de Alcántara, Málaga

Sharon, exhuberant ex-Londoner, ushers you in and offers you tea – properly chilled in summer. Her six-bedroom hotel is a quiet and welcoming refuge yet a short hop from the action, if action is what you're after: Golf Valley, the Golden Mile, the marina at Puerto Banus. Otherwise, stay put: the big modern white villa sits in a residential street that leads straight to the beach and the bars... five minutes and you're under a parasol. Sharon could not be more friendly and the mood is laid back; pour yourself a beer from the honesty bar, head for the terrace and tone that tan. This is not a family hotel so you are guaranteed peace around the pool – just the odd ripple as a toe is dipped idly into the water. Breakfast is served out here in the summer; in winter, you'll have to make do with a gilt-mirrored dining room and a gorgeous log fire. For dinner, it's got to be San Pedro's promenade and plaza, where you're spoiled for choice. Return to a good bed in a room attractively and comfortably furnished; those downstairs have sliding doors to private patios. Beyond, a mature and palm-lush garden.

rooms	6 twins/doubles.
price	€80.
meals	Restaurants nearby.
closed	Rarely.
directions	From Málaga N-340 for Algecíras. Through San Pedro, past garage & right after 100m. Straight over for 700m to Spar shop. Right & follow road for 200m; hotel on left.

	Sharon Knight
tel	+34 952 784780
fax	+34 952 784780
email	breakers@mercuryin.es

Map 23 Entry 276

Amanhavis

c/El Pilar 3, Benahavis, 29679 Marbella, Málaga

There's a real warmth to this place, thanks to Burkhard, Leslie and staff, and you sense it the moment you enter. The oasis-like Benahavis has long been known to Costa residents for its string of restaurants, and the most renowned is this one. Make the most of Burkhard's "creative mediterranean cuisine" in this intimate restaurant-hotel: fresh tiger prawns, fillets of monkfish, raspberry cream cake, mountain cheeses... no wonder they're popular with the Marbella set. Bedrooms, radiating off the gorgeous inner courtyard with plunge pool, are lavish and regal – nine flights of fantasy with themes harking back to Spain's Golden Age: the Astonomer's Observatory, the Spice Trader's Caravan, the Philospher's Study. Satellite TV, air conditioning and the internet speak of a more modern era. Bathrooms have a Moroccan feel and there's comfort and attention to detail throughout, from the snugs in the suites to the aromatic oils. In summer you dine by the pool, indoors is a convivial bar. This excellent place is five kilometres from the sea and all those golden beaches – and golf clubs abound.

rooms	9 twins/doubles.
price	€119-€179.
meals	Breakfast €11. Dinner €37.50. Restaurant closed Monday in low season & Sunday all year.
closed	7 January-12 February.
directions	From Málaga for Cádiz. Just past San Pedro, right for Benahavis. Hotel on far side of village, signed.

	Leslie & Burkhard Weber
tel	+34 952 856026
fax	+34 952 856151
email	info@amanhavis.com
web	www.amanhavis.com

Map 23 Entry 277

The Town House

c/Alderete 7, Plaza Tetuán, 29600 Marbella, Málaga

Kjell is eager for people to discover the simple elegance that is the real Marbella and there couldn't be a better launch pad than this. Plaza Tetuán is a lovely square in the very heart of the old town. It's not on any through route, so is surprisingly quiet (except during the Feria in the second week of June). The house is a rare and striking place to stay, with a peachy marble entrance placed at the corner of the building and bisected by a single white pillar. Originally an old family house — seven brothers lived here — it has been closed for the last eight years and gradually restored. Inside, Moorish and Modern have been married to arresting effect the whole place has an air of supremely tasteful decadence! The luxurious bedrooms are decorated in neutral colours or lustrous pastel shades and furnished with restraint: sumptuous beds, fine mirrors, the occasional superb antique… Each room is different; all are marble floored and subtly lit, with exuberant plants and suitably sybaritic bathrooms. You'll have to eat out but that should be a pleasure, with the fine array of good restaurants close by.

rooms	9 twins/doubles.
price	€95–€120. VAT included.
meals	Restaurants nearby.
closed	Rarely.
directions	From Málaga airport for Cádiz; exit for Marbella 'Centro Urbano'. On for 2km; right at junc.; follow signs for Hotel Lima. Last exit at r'bout into Av. Nabeul. On c/Najera to Plaza Tetuán. On corner.

	Kjell Sporrong
tel	+34 952 901791
fax	+34 952 901791
email	info@townhouse.nu
web	www.townhouse.nu

Map 23 Entry 278

El Oceano Hotel & Beach Club

Ctra. N-340 km 199, Urbanización Torrenueva, 29649 Mijas, Málaga

El Oceano may not be particularly Spanish, but is as spoiling as can be. Mooch around all day in your bathrobe in the new spa, get your nails polished and your hair done… then slip into something fabulous for dinner. Double bedrooms look onto the mountains, suites face the ocean; several have terraces, a few have outdoor jacuzzis. Floors are modern tiled, beds king-size, furnishings coordinated; life here is decidedly ritzy. There's a hint of Florida in the lounge/bar and a touch of the Far East in the outdoor pool, lush with palm trees and thatched bar – glide up for a generous measure of pink gin. The cuisine is international and immaculately presented, be it lobster, Thai fish cakes or sirloin steak, and is accompanied by fine wines and classical piano. In warm weather you dine on the wooden broadwalk overlooking the sea. Beyond the pool: a long sweep of ocean; the blue water shimmers, waves lap onto the rocks and the beach feels as though it's yours. Considering you are a short drive from Marbella, this patch of the Costa del Sol is blissfully crowd-free.

rooms	38: 14 twins/doubles, 24 suites.
price	€140–€240.
meals	Breakfast €10–€12.50. Lunch/dinner €40 à la carte.
closed	Rarely.
directions	From Málaga, N-340 for Marbella. Exit Riviera del Sol. At r'bout, left under m'way, back onto N-340 for Fuengirola. After footbridge, 1st exit. Hotel on right.

	John Palmer
tel	+34 952 587550
fax	+34 952 587637
email	info@oceanohotel.com
web	www.oceanohotel.com

Map 24 Entry 279

The Beach House

Urbanización El Chaparral, CN-340 km.203, 29648 Mijas Costa, Málaga

The Mediterranean could not be closer: it splashes and sparkles just below the balustrade at the end of the pool. An arresting spot: you may be sandwiched between the devil (the coastal N-340) and the deep blue sea, but it's easy to forget the devil. In a previous life, the house was the ritzy villa of a wealthy Arab; now Swedish Kjell – charming, friendly and immaculately well turned out – has turned it into a temple of design. This remarkable small hotel has a Japanese-minimalist feel and is wonderfully restful. Every detail counts – from the perfect flower floating in a bowl by your bed to the choice of music on the hotel's compilation CD (available for sale). It is a unique, meticulous creation, the sort of place that gets written up in the design magazines, yet manages to feels warm and inviting at the same time. Kjell and his staff are excellent hosts, and breakfast is a big buffet, served on the decked terrace in summer. This is like staying in a friend's beautiful villa, and is as close to the Med as you can get. The pool is heated all year, the lovely beaches of Fuengirola are a shake away.

rooms	9 twins/doubles.
price	€125–€175. Singles €110. VAT included.
meals	Good restaurants nearby.
closed	Rarely.
directions	From Málaga N-340 Cádiz. Keep on N-340; past km202, exit Cala de Mijas. Follow signs Fuengirola & Málaga back onto N-340. Keep hard right; past 1st footbridge, slip road to right. On right after 250m.

	Irene Westerberg
tel	+34 952 494540
fax	+34 952 494540
email	info@beachhouse.nu
web	www.beachhouse.nu

Map 24 Entry 280

Posada del Torcal

Partido de Jeva, 29230 Villanueva de la Concepción, Málaga

The fruit of the owners' conversion from bustling Costa to harshly beautiful Sierra is this award-winning small hotel. Inside and out feels thoroughly Andaluz, and the setting – not far from the Dalí-esque limestone formations of the Torcal Park – is sublime. Bedrooms are dedicated to Spanish artists and are lavish. The oils are local copies of originals, while many of the trimmings come from further afield; the beds, some brass, some gothic, some four-poster, were shipped out from England. The balcony rooms have the most outstanding views. Underfloor heating warms in winter, air conditioning cools... the only sound is that of the gardener clipping the meadow in summer. Food is elaborate: prawns in filo pastry with coconut milk, lamb wrapped in a spinach mousse, the range of vegetarian dishes wide and the wine list long. Terraced gardens run down to the pool, heated all year round, and there's tennis, sauna, mountain bikes and gym. Professional staff will point you in the right direction if walking or riding is your thing. Even helicopter trips can be arranged – not bad for a 10-bed hotel!

rooms	10 twins/doubles.
price	€155–€180. Singles €125. Suite €260.
meals	Lunch/dinner €35 à la carte. VAT included.
closed	January.
directions	Málaga N–331 for Antequera, exit 148 for Casabermeja. There, right for Almogía; next left to V. de la Concepción. At top of village, left at junc.; after 1.5km right for La Higuera. Hotel 3km on left.

Michael Soffe & Karen Ducker

tel	+34 952 031177
fax	+34 952 031006
email	hotel@eltorcal.com
web	www.eltorcal.com/PosadaTorcal

Map 24 Entry 281

La Fonda Hotel & Apartments

c/Santo Domingo 7, 29639 Benalmádena Pueblo, Málaga

There are some places on the Costa that have held onto their identity through the years of unbridled development, and one of them is Benalmádena Pueblo. Near the airport, even closer to the beach, yet in a quiet street off a pretty square, the Fonda was the creation of architect Cesar Manrique, known for his lifelong quest to bring together the best of old and new. The hotel – and its apartments in the streets nearby – is a hymn to the south: cool patios shaded by palms, geometric tiles and fountains and, from many rooms, tantalizing glimpses of the glittering sea. Bedrooms are large, light, airy and marble-floored; downstairs are white wicker armchairs to relax in, a shaded terrace and a central pool; reception is at the top (no lift). La Fonda's plant-filled restaurant doubles as a cookery school (the school closes during summer, when the hotel heaves) so treat yourself to an excellent southern lunch at half the cost of elsewhere. Or wander along to the square and watch the world go by, with a plate of olives and a chilled glass of sherry. *Apartments have laundry service.*.

rooms	26 + 26: 4 doubles, 18 twins, 4 singles. 26 s/c apartments.
price	€65-€115. Singles €47-€70. Apartments €30-€110. VAT inc.
meals	Lunch/dinner €20. Lunch Thursday-Sunday only.
closed	Rarely.
directions	A-7 Cádiz; exit 222 for Benalmádena Pueblo; 2nd exit at 1st r'bout, 2nd exit next r'bout, 1st exit 3rd r'bout. Park in village; lift up to hotel.

	José Antonio García García
tel	+34 952 568273
fax	+34 952 568273
email	lafonda@fondahotel.com
web	www.fondahotel.com

Map 24 Entry 282

Santa Fe Hotel-Restaurante

Carretera de Monda km3, Apartado 147, 29100 Coín, Málaga

Two young, enthusiastic and multi-lingual Dutch brothers have made a quite a name for themselves since taking over the Santa Fe. The old farmhouse sits among the citrus groves of the Guadalhorce valley, to one side of the road from Marbella up to Coín (traffic is audible, but never intrusive). The transformation from farm to guesthouse has been faithful to local tradition; simple bedrooms have rustic furniture, terracotta floors (tiles fired with the dog-paw print bring good luck!) and stencilled walls. Those with small windows are darkish in winter, two share a bathroom. No sitting room, but a great garden and pool, and a terrific little restaurant, popular with the locals – Spanish or Costa-cosmopolitan. Two new young chefs rustle up the likes of spicy king prawns, fillet steak with chanterelle sauce, pecan pie. There's a good selection of veggie dishes too, and wines. The dining room has a log fire in winter and the conservatory and bar are cosy – but most of the year you dine beneath the huge and ancient olive tree or the pool-side pergola. A friendly, relaxed atmosphere – and late breakfasts – reign.

rooms	3 twins, 2 doubles.
price	€66. Singles €58. VAT included.
meals	Lunch/dinner €20-€30 à la carte; not Tuesday.
closed	2 weeks in November; 2 weeks in February.
directions	From Málaga, N-340 for Cádiz. 1km after airport, A-366/C-344 to Coín. In Coín for Monda onto A355. Santa Fe just outside Coín, on left.

	Warden & Arjan van de Vrande
tel	+34 95 2452916
fax	+34 95 2453843
email	info@santafe-hotel.com
web	www.santafe-hotel.com

Map 24 Entry 283

El Castillo de Monda

29110 Monda, Málaga

What a position, high up above the village, reached by a series of switchbacks: the views from the Castillo are magical, taking in the sweep of the Sierra Nevada and the Ronda mountains. The first fortifications were built on Monda's hilltop by the Moors in the 11th century, and this new building owes much to that tradition: there are fountains, wafer-bricked arches, ceramic tiles and much use of *muqarna*, the delicate stucco bas-relief which is the delight of the Alhambra Palace in Granada. But there are English touches as well: a collection of watercolours of the English countryside suggest a certain nostalgia for Blighty. The main dining room evokes a medieval banqueting hall with its arches and flags, and the classical Andalucían mix spills over to bedrooms, too: four-posters and swish fabrics, Moorish arches, marbled and heated bathroom floors. Best of all is the terrace festooned with flora – retire with a post-dinner drink and watch the lights of the village twinkling below. Luxurious and fun, and with a tempting pool. *Week-long relaxation skills courses available.*

rooms	26: 14 twins/doubles, 11 suites.
price	€113. Singles €95. Suites €194–€224. VAT included.
meals	Breakfast €4.50–€11.50. Lunch/dinner €30 à la carte. VAT included.
closed	Rarely.
directions	From Málaga N-340 for Cádiz. Shortly before Marbella (don't turn off N-340), right for Coín. After 16km right into Monda; follow signs.

	John Norris & Bruce Freestone
tel	+34 952 457142
fax	+34 952 457336
email	mondas@spa.es
web	www.costadelsol.spa.es/hotel/monda

Map 23 Entry 284

Hotel Cerro de Híjar

Cerro de Híjar s/n, 29109 Tolox, Málaga

On a clear day you can see — well, if not forever, at least to the sea and the Sierra Nevada. It has a wonderful remote position, this hotel, on a bluff 2,000 feet above sea level, and an unrivalled view. (The walking is magnificent, for you are on the eastern edge of the Sierra de las Nieves Parque Natural.) From the ancient spa village of Tolox, follow the winding road up and up... The young hotel looks like a traditional hunting lodge and inside there is a terrific sense of light and space: creamy stucco walls, bright rugs and attractive furniture, a winter fire (it has been known to get a bit smoky in the dining room!) and modern Andalucían paintings and prints on every wall. The bedrooms are large, comfortable, beautifully finished, dazzlingly clean. You'll eat and drink brilliantly here for Martín's cooking is inspired — traditional Andalucían with a modern touch. No surprise to learn that he once worked in the area's only Michelin-starred restaurant... He, Guillermo and Eugenio run the place in an eco-friendly manner, all three have excellent English and are most welcoming. Memorable.

rooms	18: 14 twins/doubles, 4 suites.
price	€66–€92. Singles €59–€71. Suites €92–€104.
meals	Breakfast €7.20. Lunch/dinner €27 set menu.
closed	Rarely.
directions	From Málaga, on Cártama. Filter right to Coín, then onto A-366 for Ronda. Left to Tolox, through village to Balneario (spa); right up hill for 2.5km to hotel.

	Guillermo Gonzalez
tel	+34 952 112111
fax	+34 952 119745
email	cerro@cerrodehijar.com
web	www.cerrodehijar.com

Map 23 Entry 285

Molino Santisteban

Ctra. A-366 km50-51, 29108 Guaro, Málaga

Frits and Gisèle left Holland dreaming of warmer, more southern climes. Easy to see how this great old mill fitted that dream: it lies to one side of the lush valley, half an hour from the coast, enfolded by willow, eucalyptus, citrus, rose and every other verdant climber. Olives were once milled here and the mill race adds life to the pretty garden; a gaily painted little bar awaits by the pool. The main building has the feel of a small hacienda; bedrooms give onto the inner patio where a fountain gurgles, while a wooden balcony wraps itself around the upper floor. Andulaz bedrooms have big antique beds and a period feel; some have French windows that overlook the river. The original mill across the way is the breakfast/dining room, where you eat at a long rustic table on chairs that once graced a monastery. Your well-travelled hosts love to share their knowledge of hiking routes; the area is a birdwatchers' dream, and they are preparing their own routes. A simple restaurant is a step down the road, with more sophisticated eateries in Coín. *Note steep access to front door.*

rooms	6 twins/doubles.
price	€60-€75. Singles €49-€64.
meals	Dinner €17-€20, on request.
closed	1st November-1st March.
directions	From Málaga airport, N-340 for Torremolinos & Cádiz. After 200m right for Coín, then Ronda on A-366 & C-344. Hotel between km50 & km51 markers on right, just before Venta Gallardo.

	Frits Blomsma & Gisèle Gerhardus
tel	+34 952 453748
email	info@hotelmolino.com
web	www.hotelmolino.com

Map 23 Entry 286

Hotel la Era

Partido Martina, Los Cerrillos, parcela 85, 29566 Casarabonela, Málaga

Not for smokers – or for nervous drivers! The ascent is steep but the setting stupendous. Francisco and Isabel, originally Cuban but raised in Miami, fell for the view and built their dream home. It is named after the original *era* (threshing floor), still intact and surrounded by tiered gardens, walkways and pool. The spot is so lofty it overlooks the last village in Andalucía to fall to Isabel and Ferdinand... The interiors of this purpose-built eyrie may not be the last word in hotel chic, but the Era has a neat, tidy and cared-for feel. And the food is delicious. Locals brave the twisting road for Isabel's regional dishes: cream of courgette soup, grilled swordfish and amaretto pudding; vegans and veggies are equally well served. Nine comfortable, air-conditioned bedrooms are named after the municipalities that make up the Sierra de las Nieves; furniture is in traditional style, there are real paintings and prints on the walls, and balconies or terraces with gasp-worthy views. Come to get away from it all; hike, paraglide or pony-trek to your heart's content.

rooms	9 twins/doubles.
price	€105–€135.
meals	Dinner €25, on request.
closed	22 December-February.
directions	From Málaga for Motril. From ringroad, A-357 to Cártama-Universidad; left on MA-403 to Casarabonela. Before village right following signs to hotel; 2km on.

	Isabel Manrara Díaz
tel	+34 952 112525
fax	+34 952 112009
email	info@hotellaera.com
web	www.hotellaera.com

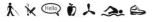

Map 23 Entry 287

La Posada del Canónigo
c/Mesones 24, 29420 El Burgo, Málaga

You won't forget your first sight of the mountain village of El Burgo: a splash of brilliant white amid the ochres and greys of the limestone massif. Little visited, it will give you as real a taste of Andalucían mountain life as can be found anywhere. The multi-levelled village house, all aged beams and lustrous tiles, is another reason for coming. No fewer than 13 brothers and sisters helped in the original restoration and decoration: a family affair! Bedrooms are simple and characterful, their prints, paintings and dried flowers lovingly arranged, your hosts proud of every corner. There is a small dining room leading to a little patio where you breakfast deliciously in the morning sun, and a snug basement bodega where simple dishes are served. Both sitting rooms have open hearths and exposed stonework and the whole place is uncannily quiet. Stay two nights and discover the land by foot – or let the owners take you riding in the virtually unknown National Park of the Sierra de las Nieves above Ronda. The scenery is spectacular.

rooms	12 twins/doubles.
price	€45–€65. Singles €32–€37. VAT included.
meals	Lunch/dinner €11 set menu. VAT included.
closed	24 December.
directions	From Torremolinos to Cártama then to Calea, Alozaina, Yunquera & El Burgo. Turn right into village; hotel next to San Agustín church. Parking tricky.

	Álvaro Pérez
tel	+34 952 160185
fax	+34 952 160185
email	reservascanonigo@telefonica.net
web	www.laposadadelcanonigo.com

Map 23 Entry 288

Molino de las Pilas

Ctra. Vieja de Ronda km1, 29327 Teba, Málaga

Could there be a link between this wild part of Andalucía and Scotland? Historically, yes. Above the old mill-farmhouse looms Teba Castle, scene of a fierce battle in 1331. Sir James Douglas, en route to the Holy Land with Robert the Bruce's heart in a casket, got caught up in a conflict with the Moors – and, to encourage his men, flung casket and himself into the fray. Molino de las Pilas is less ancient. Built in 1882, it was in ruins when Pablo chanced upon it; the restoration took three years. Simply but comfortably furnished in an elegantly rustic style, it has excellent beds and fine bathrooms; three rooms have coal-effect fires, and the sitting room is cosily beamed. But what makes this stylish inn unforgettable is the remarkable restaurant in the mill. All the old workings are in place: great grindstones for mashing the olives, massive beamed press, huge *tintajas* set in the floor to store the oil. Equally remarkable is Esmeraldas's cooking: superb fish, fabulous marinaded partridge, salads a delight – all at amazingly reasonable prices. Special.

rooms	6 twins/doubles.
price	€60-€70. VAT included.
meals	Lunch/dinner €21 à la carte.
closed	3 weeks in January.
directions	From Málaga, A-357 for Campillos. After Ardales, cross bridge at lake, left at km11 to Teba, on A-341. After 6km, right at petrol station, up hill. Signed to left after 1km.

	Pablo Moreno Aragón
tel	+34 952 748622
fax	+34 952 748647
email	info@molinodelaspilas.com
web	www.molinodelaspilas.com

Map 23 Entry 289

La Casa de la Fuente

c/Málaga 18, 29310 Villanueva de Algaidas, Málaga

Comfortable, spick and span B&B in an untouristy Spanish village, run with charm. Linda and John chanced upon the big old Aldalucían house after five years of searching. He worked on the restoration, she the décor. Lovely old floor tiles have been restored, the furniture is in traditional country style, and each bedroom is named after a favourite artist – Van Gogh, Picasso, Monet, Constable, Cézanne – with prints of their works on the walls. Bathrooms are hugely luxurious, big enough to tango in and graced with John's tiling. Painted frescos decorate the oriental-tiled staircase that leads to the nicest rooms on the second floor. The building centres on a courtyard with a heated plunge pool and ceramic-topped tables, a fountain, potted plants and welcome shade. Book dinner here – they do a simple *menú del día* – or drop in on the wonderful Bar la Tasca nearby. Great value – and excellently sited for day trips to Granada, Córdoba, Ronda and the old town of Málaga. Lovely old Antquera is even closer.

rooms	5: 4 twins/doubles, 1 family.
price	€65–€75.
meals	Dinner €15 set menu.
closed	Rarely.
directions	From Antequera N-331 N for Córdoba; right for Villanueva de A. on MA-206. In village left at junc. Down hill, left for Cuevas Bajas; after 75m left into c/Málaga. House on left.

	John & Linda Collie
tel	+34 952 745030
fax	+34 952 745030
email	lacasadelafuente@yahoo.com
web	www.lacasadelafuente.com

Map 24 Entry 290

Cortijo Valverde

Ctra. Alora-Antequera km 35.5, 29500 Álora, Málaga

You are in a landscape of hills and rocky outcrops – rural Spain at its best. The 40 acres around Valverde are still farmed (sunflowers, olives, citrus) and the farmhouse has a beautifully rustic feel. In one direction, you look up to the Torcal; in the other, to the Moorish castle and city walls of Álora. Dinner here after a day exploring the treasures of Granada or Seville is something to come home for: four evenings a week you are treated to Rod's cooking and the freshest produce brought in daily from the market. After aperitifs on the terrace, try the grilled goat's cheese or flambéd prawns and relax in the house-party atmosphere on the terrace. Rod and Moyra are the warmest of hosts. Bedrooms are in their own very private *casitas*, each with a walk-in shower and pretty terrace; fabrics and décor have a stylish simplicity, and the rooms are hugely comfortable, with air conditioning for summer. Scented gardens, southern views, a blissful pool – and the possibility of intensive Spanish courses should the pampering begin to pall.

rooms	7: 7 twins/doubles.
price	€96.
meals	Snack lunch €5. Dinner €25.
closed	12 January-7 February.
directions	From Málaga, A-357 for Campillos; A-343 to Álora. Don't go into village. Cross river; at T-junc. by Bar Los Caballos, left for V. de Abdaljis. Pass km35.5; sign to right; 300m; sharp left up to hotel.

	Moyra & Rod Cridland
tel	+34 952 112979
fax	+34 952 112979
email	cortijovalverde@mercuryin.es
web	www.cortijovalverde.com

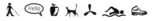

Map 24 Entry 291

Cortijo Jacaranda

Apdo. de Correos 279, 29500 Álora, Málaga

The problem with holidaying with young children is that so few places answer your needs and theirs. This is different: Ruth and Jeremy, ex-Londoners who mastermind the Cortijo, are as family-friendly as can be; they'll even run you to and from the airport. Their 16-acre farm in the hills, once the property of an enthusiastic planter of rare trees, has two purpose-built and simply styled *casitas* and an apartment – plus three small terraces with barbecue and a shared pool (replete with circular shallow area at one end and inflatable toys)… a boon during the blistering summer. You also get a big sun-trap terrace, purpose-built play areas, a gym, videos to rent, mountain bikes to borrow and loads more – a rare set-up for a remote mountain setting. Your hosts are also happy to provide a babysitting service on Tuesdays, ferrying you to and from your chosen restaurant. They put on a barbecue once a week and, in the cooler months, an Andalucían meal. Golf and riding can be arranged, and skiing is possible (a two-hour drive) between January and April. Quite a place! *Laundry €10 per load.*

rooms	2 houses for 4-6; 1 apartment for 2-4.
price	House €110–€120. Apartment €75–€85. VAT included.
meals	Self-catering.
closed	Rarely.
directions	From Málaga A-357 for Campillos. After 25km exit for Álora; 6km right at T-junc. Left into track after 0.7km, opp. bus shelter. 1.5km right fork. 2.8km on, at x-roads.

	Jeremy Henshaw
tel	+34 650 838410
email	bookings@cortijojacaranda.com
web	www.cortijojacaranda.com

Map 24 Entry 292

Casa Rural Domingo
Arroyo Cansino 4, 29500 Álora, Málaga

Domin, Cynthia and their young family left Belgium, headed south and opened their home to guests. Meet them and you'll realise why they were bound to succeed: their enthusiasm is infectious and they love their guests. They were inspired when they chose this site: high above Álora, with stunning views of the eastern ranges of the Ronda Sierra. Guests can choose between B&B rooms or well-equipped self-catering studio-bungalows with terraces. It's a super place, rich in creature comforts, with good new beds and bright rugs on terracotta floors. Modernist paintings add an artistic touch. Mature gardens offset the stylish house, and life in the warmer months centres on the poolside terrace with open kitchen and barbecue; guests mingle easily, perhaps over a game of boules or tennis. Domin and Cynthia don't do lunch or dinner but tapas are available, breakfasts are hearty, and Álora's restaurants are a few minutes by car. You won't be short of ideas for excursions, cultural or sportif. Children are positively liked, and families encouraged to cycle, hike or ride – by donkey if not by horse.

rooms	2 + 3: 2 twins/doubles. 1 apartment, 2 studios.
price	€60-€95. Apt €600-€700 per week. Studio €425-€500. VAT included.
meals	Restaurant/bar 1km.
closed	Rarely.
directions	Málaga A-357 for Campillos; A343 Alora; before village, corss river; cont. to T-junc, then signed.

	Domin & Cynthia Doms
tel	+34 952 119744
fax	+34 952 119744
email	casadomingo@vodafone.es
web	www.casaruraldomingo.com

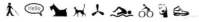

Map 24 Entry 293

Los Limoneros

Apdo de Correos 314, 29560 Pizarra, Málaga

Drift off to sleep in Morocco, China or Japan.. The bedrooms in this Andalucían farmhouse – half an hour inland, but a world from the Costa del Sol – are globally themed. Japan is neat with white walls, simple black furniture and pretty fans; Africa has rich red walls, exotic prints and mosquito netting. Enfolded by citrus groves and with views to the Arab town of Álora and the mountains and valleys of Guadalhorce, this hotel is guaranteed to help you unwind. Furnishings in the beamed and tiled public rooms are rustic and simple, enhanced with second-hand finds. While Anne-Marie looks after the cooking – menus are varied and flavoursome – Yvette, a complementary therapist, offers reflexology, massage and crystal healing. She and Anne-Marie are easy, laid-back people who have created a happy, wholesome place to stay. Lazing by the pool, in the shade of the bamboo-clad terrace, may be all you wish to do – the garden, with its lemon, fig and orange trees, is a soporific spot – but Granada, Seville and Ronda are too close to ignore, and the walking and riding are magnificent.

rooms	7 twins/doubles.
price	€90. Singles €60.
meals	Light lunch €5. Dinner €20.
closed	Rarely.
directions	From airport towards Málaga, then Motril. Exit on A-357 for Cártama. From A-357 exit on A-343 to Pizarra. Here, left, & at km49 right at sign 'Ermita de N.S. de la Fuensanta'. House 2nd on left.

	Anne-Marie Walker & Yvette Winfield
tel	+34 952 484072
fax	+34 952 484072
email	loslimoneros@hotmail.com
web	www.andalucia.com/loslimoneros

Map 24 Entry 294

Hacienda San José
Buzón 59, Entrerrios, 29650 Mijas, Málaga

This hilltop hacienda is a cool, calm sanctuary from the concrete and heat of the Valle del Golf, and looks down on seven golf courses with views to Mijas and the sea. Delightful Nikki opened one of the first small country hotels in Spain years ago; now she and Pepe have created another classy and comfortable Andaluz retreat. The building is not ancient but the smell of woodsmoke and beeswax, the terracotta floors, the high wooden ceilings and the many antiques give the place a traditional feel. Huge bedrooms have underfloor heated tiles, colourwashed walls, new beds and generous drapes; bathrooms come with double sinks and fancy handmade tiles. The high-raftered, ochre-walled sitting room has warmth and charm, and you breakfast on a cobbled patio – homemade patisserie and fruits from the orchard. Your hosts are mindful of your privacy yet there when you need them. Riding and golf in summer, sightseeing (Granada, Ronda) in winter – and one of the mildest climates in Europe. A genuine cortijo feel, a great garden (palms, tennis, pool) and bags of class.

rooms	7: 2 twins/doubles, 5 suites.
price	€105-110. Suites €140-150.
meals	Dinner €25.
closed	20 June-31 August.
directions	From Fuengirola for Marbella on N-340 (A7). In Cala de Mijas turn for La Cala Golf. At 1st r'bout right; at next fork right again for Entrerrios. 1.8km from here to hotel; signed.

	Nikki & José García
tel	+34 952 119494
fax	+34 952 119404
email	haciendasanjose@yahoo.co.uk
web	www.hotelruralhaciendasanjose.com

Map 24 Entry 295

Arcadia Artist Retreat

Antigua Venta de Santa María, 29150 Almogía, Málaga

A quiet mountain approach, a red-coloured building by the side of the road and inside, an unusual holiday complex. The main house is 300 years old and was run as a roadside restaurant; then Martina and Giorgio arrived, swapping pressurized London lives for peace, sunshine and aromatherapy in Andalucía. The largest self-catering unit is the Honeymoon Inn, sleeping 10 plus two babies. These old stables have become a cool and cosy living space, and the yard where the donkeys once brayed, an attractive patio with plants and cascades. There's a pool and a shared outdoor jacuzzi, bedrooms have gorgeous colonial antiques, walls are vibrant and gardens are on different levels. More bold paintwork in The Granary for six, more tropical terraces and a curvaceous saltwater pool. The Garden Cottage is simpler, its three bedrooms on one level, and there's a small pool in its untamed gardens. You can B&B here, too. In short, a colourful and stress-free spot less than a half-hour's drive from the coast, with fine views. *Painting, riding, massage, babysitting available. Shared barbecue & indoor pool.*

rooms	4 + 3: 2 twins/doubles, 2 suites. 3 self-catering houses for 10, 6 & 5.
price	€53–€64. Suites €96–€107. Houses €550–€1,500 p.w. VAT inc.
meals	Restaurants nearby.
closed	Rarely.
directions	From Málaga, follow signs for Hospital & Avda. Carlos Haya. Through Puerto de la Torre, to Almogía. On left, 1km after village.

	Giorgio Melis
tel	+34 952 430598
fax	+34 952 430547
email	stay@arcadiaretreat.com
web	www.arcadiaretreat.com

Map 24 Entry 296

Hotel Humaina

Parque Natural Montes de Málaga, Ctra. de Colmenar s/n , 29013 Málaga

Hotel Humaina is hidden deep in a forest of oak and pine, at the end of a mile and a half of steep, unbeaten track. It was a hunting lodge before being reborn as a small hotel; the area was popular with the shooting brigade, but its new status as a Parque Natural means that the local rabbits, foxes and hares are more likely to be of this world than the next. What strikes you when you arrive is the tranquillity of the place and it seems fitting that Juan María should greet you in such a gentle manner. The dining room and bedrooms are plainly furnished and nothing special; bedrooms at the front have the best wooded views. The hotel's cosiest room is the small lounge with chimney piece, furnished with books on the walking, flora and fauna of the area; set time aside to hike along the waymarked trail. This is an eco-aware hotel: water is heated by solar energy, food comes from the kitchen garden. Try the *plato de los montes* if you like fry-ups, followed by a glass of *vino de pasas*, the local raisin wine. A simple forest getaway.

rooms	14: 10 twins/doubles, 2 family, 2 suites.
price	€71-€92. Singles €52-€56. Suites €106-€118.
meals	Breakfast €7. Lunch/dinner €25. Half-board €22-€29p.p.; full-board €37-€39 p.p.
closed	24 December.
directions	From Málaga for m'way for Motril; exit 244 for Limonar. On for Camino Colmenar. After 15km on C-345, at F de la Reina, track on left for 3.8km.

	Juan María Luna
tel	+34 952 641025
fax	+34 952 640115
email	info@hotelhumaina.es
web	www.hotelhumaina.es

Map 24 Entry 297

Molino de Santillán

Ctra. de Macharaviaya km3, Apdo. de Correos 101, 29730 Rincón de la Victoria, Málaga

Carlo Marchini, tired of the cut and thrust of business in Madrid, moved to the softer climes of Andalucía, bought an old farmhouse and, after years of restoration, is harvesting the fruits of his efforts. The building is inspired by the hacienda-style architecture of the New World, its arched patio opening at the southern end to catch the light and a distant view of the sea. One wing is given over to the restaurant, an ochre rag-walled room where you may be treated to home-grown aubergines stuffed with hake, or loin of pork in a honey and apple sauce; the paella is excellent, too. Bedrooms feel properly Andalucían; stencilling and warm colours add zest, Casablanca fans keep the temperatures down, wrought-iron beds are prettified with mosquito netting. A new extension has been created for further rooms; they may lack the personality of the old ones but have French windows to private terraces and a well-finished feel. Outside: a pool and a verdant courtyard garden. Carlo, his daughter Adriana and their staff have created a comfortably laid-back restaurant-hotel. *A Rusticae hotel.*

rooms	22: 20 twins/doubles, 2 suites.
price	€90-€138. Singles €68-€89. Suites €142-€258.
meals	Breakfast €9. Lunch/dinner €20.
closed	Rarely.
directions	From Málaga for Motril on N-340. Exit for Macharaviaya; right at signs before reaching village. 1km of track to hotel.

	Carlo Marchini
tel	+34 902 120240
fax	+34 952 400950
email	reservas@molinodesantillan.es
web	www.molinodesantillan.es

Map 24 Entry 298

Hotel Paraíso del Mar

Prolongación de Carabeo 22, 29780 Nerja, Málaga

Nerja is one of the busiest resort of the Costa del Sol – hardly an auspicious beginning. But the Paraíso is a friendly little place, and pleasantly quiet, away from the main drag of restaurants and bars, and on the edge of a cliff looking out to sea. The main house was built in the Sixties by an English doctor, the annexe is newer, and all has all been thoroughly revamped thanks to charming young Enrique and his wife Alicia. Most remarkable perhaps are the hotel's terraced gardens that drop down towards the beach: a tumble of jasmine, palms, bougainvillea, bananas, morning glory and a washingtonia... an exotic, southern air prevails. Bedrooms are pleasant – marble floors, soft colours, modern furniture, big florals – and roomy; the suites have jacuzzis; all have fluffy bathrobes and good towels. From some, a spiral stair leads you up to your own patch of roof terrace – perfect for sunset-watching, or topping up your tan as you gaze over the sparkling bay. Beneath the hotel are a sauna and a hot tub dug out of solid rock – and you breakfast on the terrace overlooking the Med.

rooms	17: 9 twins/doubles, 8 suites.
price	€62–€120. Singles €52–€130. Suites €105–€146.
meals	Breakfast available. Restaurants nearby.
closed	Mid-November–mid-December.
directions	From Málaga N-340 for Motril. Arriving in Nerja follow signs to Parador; Paraíso del Mar is next door.

	Enrique Caro Bernal
tel	+34 952 521621
fax	+34 952 522309
email	info@hispanica-colint.es
web	www.hotelparaisodelmar.com

Map 24 Entry 299

Hotel Rural Almazara

Los Tablazos 197, Ctra. Nerja-Frigiliana, 29788 Nerja, Málaga

There's a surprisingly rural feel to this hotel in the vibrant resort of Nerja. Despite the old *almazara* (oil press) outside the front door, the building is new: it opened in 2002. After braving the beach or the shops, return to the sitting room with its cool tiles, sofas and armchairs – a comfortable place to relax. And there's plenty of opportunity to splash: a pool on the terrace, and a plunge pool in the blue and terracotta 'cave' in the basement. And a jacuzzi and sauna. In the dining room, opening to a long terrace in summer, you can watch the chef at work in the kitchen. The cooking here is truly creative – vegetable soup from local produce, angler fish served Arabic style, oxtail stew, duck. Wines are regional and very good. A good night's sleep is guaranteed in spotless, well-equipped bedrooms, air-conditioned and beautifully quiet. José Antonio is a genial host and his staff are friendly and helpful. Take a copy of this guide with you and they will give you a 10% discount.

rooms	22: 21 twins/doubles, 1 single.
price	€79–€118. Singles €60–€80.
meals	Breakfast €7. Lunch/dinner €21 set menu.
closed	Rarely.
directions	From Málaga, N-340 for Motril. At Nerja (exit 292), MA-105 to Frigiliana. Hotel on right after 100m.

	José Antonio Gómez Armijo
tel	+34 952 534200
fax	+34 952 534212
email	info@hotelruralalmazara.com
web	www.hotelruralalmazara.com

Map 24 Entry 300

La Posada Morisca

Loma de la Cruz s/n, Ctra. Montaña Frigiliana-Torrox, 29788 Frigiliana, Málaga

Simple comfort, stunning views. Sit on the terrace outside your room, lounge under a thatched parasol by the pool, gaze down to the distant sea… and unwind. The building gleams white and terracotta on the hillside, well away from the bustling village. This inn is new but traditional in style, with plenty of wood and wicker. Sara, who runs it, is from Frigiliana and her warmth and charm add greatly to the atmosphere. There is a sense of gaiety and simplicity about the whole establishment… brightly coloured tiles, latticed wardrobes, woodburning stoves (each bedroom has one). The rooms have a country cottage feel, and are nicely private. You eat at well-dressed tables in the cosy, cream-walled dining room, or on the terrace, and the cooking is mediterranean. There's a choice of traditional and 'creative' menus, and the wine lisst is small but select. When your batteries are thoroughly recharged, head for nearby Nerja, where there's lots going on. Come in May or June and you will see the folk dancing and the Pomeria of San Antonio. *A Rusticae hotel.*

rooms	12 twins/doubles.
price	€85-€100. Singles €50. VAT inc.
meals	Dinner €25 à la carte. VAT included.
closed	10-31 January.
directions	From Málaga m'way to Almería. Exit 292 for Nerja. There, MA-105 to Frigiliana. Round bottom of village, left at Taller los Cobos for Torrox. Signed on left after 1.5km. Down steep track & bear left.

	Sara Navas Sánchez
tel	+34 952 534151
fax	+34 952 534339
email	info@laposadamorisca.com
web	www.laposadamorisca.com

Map 24 Entry 301

Casa La Piedra
Plazoleta 14, 29754 Cómpeta, Málaga

Casa La Piedra is an old house in a little square in lively Cómpeta. The spectacular village is cradled by the Sierra de Tejeda and looks out across vine-clad hillsides to the Med; the muscatel grape is used to make the sweet wine for which the village is famous. This 400-year-old 'holiday home' has a higgledy-piggledy layout, simple Andaluz décor and a huge roof terrace from which, on clear days, you can see all the way to the mountains of north Africa. Be enchanted by an inner courtyard that brims over with jasmine and exotic plants, and many delightful architectural features: beamed ceilings and patterned terracotta floors, blue-painted shutters and millions of steps. There's a gorgeous, rustic, open-plan kitchen/dining room filled with colour and books. Sweet bedrooms have a Moorish feel. Sandra, a reflexologist and aromatherapist, lives in the lower section of the house and leaves you to your own devices, but is happy to pass on advice about walks, rides, picnic spots and bars and restaurants – you are spoiled for choice! *Linen, gas & electricity included. Call for weekly rates.*

rooms	House for 4.
price	€70 for 2; €100 for 4. VAT included. Minimum 2 nights.
meals	Self-catering.
closed	Rarely.
directions	From Málaga airport for Málaga; almost immed. to Motril & Almería on N-340. Exit for Algarrobo. At r'bout, left for Cómpeta. On arrival, phone Sandra.

Sandra Irene Costello
tel	+34 952 516329
fax	+34 952 516329
email	casa@2sandra.com
web	www.2sandra.com

Map 24 Entry 302

Hotel La Tartana

Urbanización San Nicolás, 18697 La Herradura, Granada

This has always been a focal point for the people of La Herradura and never more so than now; Penny, Barry, and Jo spent years on cruise ships catering for the rich and famous before coming here to roost. La Tartana, surrounded by trees, its arched entrance swathed in bougainvillea, is right by the road – noisy first thing in the morning – but there's an almost uninterrupted view of the sea, and a big terrace from which to enjoy it. The hotel is built Andalucían style, around a patio, with a fountain at the centre and rooms leading off; there's a mellow, established feel. The doors and beams come from a 16th-century convent and some of the furniture in the simple, comfortable bedrooms is antique. Downstairs is a vaulted bar – a great place to get to know your relaxed hosts over a drink and a salsa dip before settling down to enjoy Jo's inspired cooking. Both food and dining room are colourful. Dishes are American with an international 'fusion' (ribs, Irish beef, Thai curries, salads) and there is a good and unusual selection of Navarra wines. Save room for some fine desserts.

rooms	6 twins/doubles.
price	€55–€79.
meals	Dinner €15.
closed	Last 2 weeks in January
directions	From Málaga, N-340 for Motril. Urbanización San Nicolás on left-hand side of road, just before entrance to La Herradura. Hotel 1st house on left on entering Urbanización.

	Penny Jarret & Barry Branham
tel	+34 958 640535
fax	+34 958 640535
email	reservations@hotellatartana.com
web	www.hotellatartana.com

Map 24 Entry 303

La Casa de los Bates

Ctra. Nacional 340 km329.5, Apartado de Correos 55, 18600 Motril, Granada

It was built in 1898: a bad year for Spain with the loss of its last American colony. But not a hint of depression in this flamboyant Italianate villa. It stands far enough back from the coastal highway for noise not to be intrusive, and is surrounded by one of the most exquisite gardens in the south: huge and exuberant palms, catalpas, magnolias and Atlas cedars to make a plant-lover's heart quiver. Many of the trees and fishponds pre-date even the villa. When the Martín-Feriche family acquired the house it had long lain empty but thanks to careful restoration and the skill of an accomplished interior designer it is once again an elegant, beautifully furnished home. Marble-floored lounges are full of deco lamps, Japanese lacquered tables, screens and oils, a Bechstein piano, family photos, gilt mirrors, mounted pistols, a harp; bedrooms have a classic 1950s period feel, bathrooms are attractive modern. The mahogany table in the dining room sits up to 20 (great for small weddings); give your blue-blooded hosts enough warning and a candlelit dinner can be prepared. *A Rusticae hotel.*

rooms	4: 3 twins/doubles, 1 suite.
price	€135. Suite €180.
meals	Dinner €25-€45 à la carte. VAT included. On request only.
closed	Rarely.
directions	From Málaga N-340 east. Pass Salobreña; after 2km large warehouses on right of 'Frutas de Cara'. Exit, then N-340 back for Salobreña; after 200m, right for house.

Borja Rodríguez Martín-Feriche

tel	+34 958 349495
fax	+34 958 349122
email	borjar@jet.es
web	www.casadelosbates.com

Map 24 Entry 304

Palacete de Cazulas

Caserío de Cazulas s/n, 18698 Otívar, Granada

The oldest deeds of Cazulas date back to 1492 – and are in Arabic! The main building came later but its debt to Alhambra style is manifest. Wafer-brick, terracotta, fountain and palm combine exquisitely in this utterly southern summer palace. Five miles from the nearest village (three restaurants, two bars) at the end of a subtropical valley, you are blissfully secluded, the goatherd with his flock the only traffic. Come with a family party and take over the whole place for a week, or more: daily maid service is included in the price, and there are cooks, shoppers and babysitters should you desire them. Rooms are elegant, fabrics luscious, furniture antique; there are sparkling new bathrooms, a couple of four-posters, delightful curios and sweeping views. The vaulted lounge has an honesty bar and books, the kitchen is large and rustically modern. Outside: walled grounds full of hidden corners, a private chapel, a long, lovely pool flanked by high clipped cypress, tennis… and a heavenly walk along the valley floor to a towering gorge and crystalline rock pools. Monumental Granada is a short drive.

rooms	11: 5 doubles, 6 twins.
price	€100. Whole house (16): €9,000 p.w. Extra guests: €500 p.p. p.w. Cottage (2-4): €500 p.p. p.w.
meals	Restaurants in village.
closed	May-August. House for rent all year.
directions	From Almuñecar old road to Granada to Otívar. On for 5km; left at sign 'central Cazulas'. On for 1.5km.

	Brenda & Richard Russell-Cowan
tel	+34 958 644036
fax	+34 958 644048
email	info@cazulas.com
web	www.cazulas.com

Map 24 Entry 305

Cortijo del Pino
c/Fernán Núñez 2, La Loma, 18659 Albuñuelas, Granada

Little-known Albuñuelas – is only a short drive from the Costa and 30 minutes from Granada. It's a fetching little place surrounded by citrus groves, with wonderful walks along the rocky canyon that cuts south from the village. El Cortijo del Pino sits high on a bluff above, taking its name from the gargantuan Aleppo pine that stands sentinel over house and valley. The sober lines of the building have an Italian feel and the sandy tones that soften the façade change with each passing hour. Perhaps it was the endlessly shifting light that attracted artist James Connel. His painterly eye and his wife Antonia's flair for decoration have created a warm, enveloping place to stay, an open house for guests and friends. Bedrooms are big, beamed and beautiful, with comfortable beds and very good bathrooms. Outside, birdsong and church bells, roses, wisteria and a terrace with sweeping views, a dreamy pool… if you are inspired, grab a canvas and an easel and retire to James's studio. Art-lovers be warned: his paintings are on every wall and you may be tempted to part with your money! *House available for rent in summer.*

rooms	5: 4 twins/doubles, 1 suite.
price	€78-€90. Singles €50. Whole house: €1,650 p.w. VAT included.
meals	Restaurants nearby.
closed	Rarely.
directions	From Málaga towards Granada. Before Granada m'way to Motril, exit 153 for Albuñuelas. Opp. bus stop, right & follow steep road to house.

	James Connel & Antonia Ruano
tel	+34 958 776257
fax	+34 958 776350
email	cortijodelpino@eresmas.com
web	www.elcortijodelpino.official.ws

Map 24 Entry 306

Alojamiento Rural Cortijo del Pino

18194 Churriana de la Vega, Granada

Farmhouse B&B 15 minutes from the city, and a delightful family. Kind, artistic Concha and her mother make this place, and their grand old farmhouse, topped with tower and pigeon loft, is hard to resist. The approach is marvellous, the beautiful surrounding trees creating a warm, out-of-time atmosphere. The apartments in their converted cattle stalls are supremely comfortable – one a nest for two, another sleeping six, two sleeping four. Come for underfloor heating, woodburning stoves and characterful and well-equipped kitchens. Furnishings are antique, the beds a delight; ceilings are high, walls thick, tiles handmade. A gorgeous wisteria covers some of the outside patio, and each of the houses has its own terraced area. The swimming pool and laundry are shared. For the green-fingered and green-minded, there are workshops on recycling and nature, while summer guests are offered products from the holding's own *huerta ecologica*. And when you've had enough of home cuisine, there's an excellent *venta* nearby. Who would not love this place?

rooms	4 apartments for 2-6.
price	€64-€107; €385-€749 per week. VAT inc. Min stay 2 nights low season, 1 week high season.
meals	Self-catering.
closed	Rarely.
directions	From Ronda de Granada, exit 129. At r'bout to Clínica de la Immaculada. Cross river to C. de la Vega. At r'bout to C. de la Vega. 1.2km; right for Camino Viejo de Cullar. Follow signs.

	Concha Lopez
tel	+34 958 250741
email	info@cortijodelpino.com
web	www.cortijodelpino.com

Map 24 Entry 307

Molino del Puente

Puente de Durcal s/n, 18650 Durcal, Granada

The water that gushes from the high Sierras is the raison d'être for this old mill – and explains the prolific greenery and birdlife. Dori and Francisco started off making organic biscuits and jams; now they have a successful restaurant-hotel. The dining room has already made quite a name for itself with the locals, and rightly so: the food is Andaluz, the meats char-grilled, the desserts wood-fired, the fruits, vegetables and liqueurs home-grown. Note that they get very busy with wedding and christening parties at weekends. Bedrooms are modest affairs but full of creature comforts, there are cosy rafters and Impressionists on rag-rolled walls, and shower rooms full of towels. The sound of rushing water is never far away (competing with the cars crossing the bridges to either side) so a first-floor room might be a wise choice during winter. The newest bedrooms are in a separate wing, but our favourite is room 102 – a waterfall plunges down outside its window! Come for the food, the people and the lush setting; children will enjoy the new outdoor pool.

rooms	15 twins/doubles.
price	€70–€85. Singles €50. VAT included.
meals	Lunch/dinner €20–€30 à la carte.
closed	Rarely.
directions	From Motril, m'way north for Granada. Exit for Durcal & Cozvijar. Follow signs for Durcal. Just after crossing bridge, sharp right down hill.

	Miguel Angel Arcos
tel	+34 958 780731
fax	+34 958 781798
email	biodurc@teleline.es
web	www.elmolinodelpuente.com

Map 24 Entry 308

Hotel Reina Cristina ●
c/Tablas 4, 18002 Granada

A big 19th-century townhouse, two steps from the cathedral and the Bib Rambla square. The hotel comfortably strides past and present, able to please the most demanding of modern travellers. Carpeted corridors lead to marble-floored bedrooms with a pot-pourri of printed bedspreads and drapes and comfortable beds. Ask for one of the larger rooms set around the furnished, fountained courtyard (neo-*mudéjar* ceiling, pretty Andalucían tiles, marble columns: blissfully cool): they should be quieter than most. In one corner is a reproduction of the painting depicting the rendition of Granada; the dining room has the original Art Deco fittings and a collection of photos from the time of Spain's most revered poet, Garcia Lorca, whose friend, Luis Rosales, lived here. Make sure you eat in at least once: the Rincón de Lorca restaurant has won awards, the chef conjuring up a mix of traditional regional dishes and in-house specialities. The wine list is judicious and long. Excellent tapas in the café, too, and homemade cakes. Maria and her staff are relaxed and friendly – and the position is perfect.

rooms	43 twins/doubles.
price	€75-€111. Singles €50-€63.
meals	Breakfast €7.50. Lunch/dinner €23; à la carte €35.
closed	Rarely.
directions	From A-92 exit 128 onto Mendez Nuñez which becomes Avda. Fuentenueva. Before Hotel Granada Center, right into Melchor Almagro which becomes Carril del Picón. Left at end into c/Tablas. Hotel on left.

	María Gómez & Federico Jiménez
tel	+34 958 253211
fax	+34 958 255728
email	clientes@hotelreinacristina.com
web	www.hotelreinacristina.com

Map 24 Entry 309

Hostal Suecia

C/Molinos 8(Huerta de los Angeles), 18009 Granada

Hostal Suecia is hidden away at the end of a quiet little street at the very foot of the Alhambra hill – hard to imagine a better site. Come for the setting: you are surrounded by greenery, close to the café-spilled plaza – El Campo del Príncipe – and five minutes from one of the world's finest architectural wonders. And there's a huge roof terrace where you can catch the breezes and the palace views: no better place to read *Tales from the Alhambra*! The Suecia is every inch a southern house with its terracotta roofs and arched windows; to the front is an ancient Sharon fruit, at the back, some pretty trees in the garden – kaqui, nispero, lemon. There's a sitting room downstairs, a good little breakfast room above and bedrooms that are adequate rather than memorable. Varying considerably in comfort and size, most of them have their own small bath or shower rooms. More hostel than hotel, this would be a suitable resting place for budget travellers – and with the convenience of parking in the cul-de-sac right outside.

rooms	11 twins/doubles.
price	€40–€50. VAT included.
meals	Breakfast €4.50.
closed	Rarely.
directions	From Granada to Alhambra via 'Ronda Sur'. Through tunnel; at r'bout up hill to Alhambra; right at sign 'Calle Molinos'. Down hill, straight over at lights; round Campo del Príncipe; left, under arch.

	Mari-Carmen Cerdán Mejías
tel	+34 958 225044
fax	+34 958 225044

Map 24 Entry 310

Hotel Carmen de Santa Inés

Placeta Porras 7, 18010 Granada

An intimate hotel – it almost has the feel of a B&B – in the heart of one of Granada's most beautiful quarters. Behind the modest façade and heavy studded door lies a small flagged inner courtyard whose marble columns support ancient beams... a tinkling fountain, a potted aspidistra, squishy sofas. Off to one end, beyond another fine carved door, is a small formal garden filled with roses, vines, lemon trees and goldfish pond. With its view up to the Alhambra, it is blissful at any time of the day – and a most romantic spot for breakfast. Up the marble stair, past the tiny chapel are the bedrooms. Each one is different, and even the smallest is a delight. Expect fine rugs on polished tiles, a potpourri of old and modern art, lovely fabrics classic and plain, a vase of flowers. If you like space, opt for the suite: El Mirador is delectable and has its own terrace. Breakfast is served on cooler days in the little honeycomb-tiled dining room. Then wander the Albaicín's fascinating labyrinth of streets, bars, restaurants and tea houses, at their most magical at dusk. One of our favourite small hotels.

rooms	9: 8 twins/doubles, 1 suite.
price	€125–€200.
meals	Breakfast €10. Various restaurants closeby.
closed	Rarely.
directions	Park in Parking San Agustín & take a taxi.

Adriana Garrido Pérez

tel	+34 958 226380
fax	+34 958 224404
email	sinescar@teleline.es
web	www.carmensantaines.com

Map 24 Entry 311

Casa Morisca

Cuesta de la Victoria 9, Bajo Albaycín, 18010 Granada

Imagine yourself outside a tall, balconied, 15th-century house on the south-facing slopes of the Albaycín. The street drops steeply away and opposite towers the Alhambra. You are in the old Moorish quarter of Granada and Casa Morisca is an exquisite example of the old style. Rescued and restored by Carlos, its architect owner, it won the Europa Nostra prize; easy to see why. A heavy door leads from the street to a galleried inner courtyard, where slender pilasters, wafer-brick columns, delicate mouldings and pool create serenity and space. The same subtle mastery of effect runs throughout. In one of the blissful bedrooms you lie on your bed and espy the Alhambra from a specially angled bathroom mirror. One top-floor room with astonishing views has been turned into the most romantic of eyries; another has a magnificent *mudéjar* ceiling, stripped of its plaster shroud. Bathrooms are ultra-chic. On a more prosaic note, the eateries of Acera del Darro are a step away – or you may climb the labyrinthine streets to the restaurants of Plaza San Miguel Bajo and rub shoulders with the Granadinos.

rooms	14 twins/doubles. ●
price	€114–€196. Singles €91–€115.
meals	Breakfast €10.
closed	Rarely.
directions	Ask hotel for detailed directions.

María Jesús Candenas & Carlos Sánchez

tel	+34 958 221100
fax	+34 958 215796
email	info@hotelcasamorisca.com
web	www.hotelcasamorisca.com

Map 24 Entry 312

Casa del Capitel Nazarí

Cuesta Aceituneros 6, 18010 Granada

At the heart of this restored 16th-century *palazete* is a superb Granadino patio. Half a dozen slender marble columns, two of which are Roman, surround the pebble-mosaic; there's also an exquisite Nasrid carved capital from which the hotel takes its name. Some of the house's original carved wooden ceilings are still in place, too. Look skywards and you'll see the elegant, encircling galleries of the floors above: these lead to the bedrooms. The rooms are small but beautifully finished, and furnished to give a warm and intimate feel. Breakfast is at glass-topped tables in the little dining room; in summer you spill into the courtyard, delightful with plants and wicker chairs. No dinners here, but Mari-Luz, the vivacious manageress, will be delighted to recommend restaurants, tapas bars and Moroccan tea houses. This is one of several of the Albaycín's ancient houses to be converted into a hotel and it is one of the nicest: quiet, stylish, friendly. The position, in Granada's oldest quarter, is superb – 200m from the Plaza Nueva and a 20-minute walk up the wooded Alhambra hill to the palace.

rooms	17 twins/doubles.
price	€85-€91. Singles €68-€72.
meals	Breakfast €9.
closed	Rarely.
directions	N-323 (Bailén-Motril), exit 129 for Centro-Recogidas. On towards centre; follow signs to Parking Plaza Puerta Real (€12 per day). Take taxi to hotel; hotel will reimburse.

	Angela Caracuel Vera
tel	+34 958 215260
fax	+34 958 215806
email	info@hotelcasacapitel.com
web	www.hotelcasacapitel.com

Map 24 Entry 313

Hotel Rural Alicia Carolina

c/Granada 1 (Cruce Colinas), Monachil, 18193 Granada

The modern façade of this roadside hotel belies a homely interior of gleaming terracotta, dark polished wood and shining brass candlesticks. Bedrooms – simple and beautiful with their gleaming floors, lace-covered tables, richly coloured bedspreads and creamy voile – look as though someone pops in to plump up the pillows when the guests are out. Each room has its individual touch, an embroidered cushion, a hand-painted headboard, a pair of antique chairs, a pile of books. And, always, fresh flowers. Choose a second floor attic room for sloping ceilings. Then there are the views... the hotel's plumb-perfect position, outside the village of Monachil, five minutes from Granada, means one side looks towards the city's skyline while the other gazes on the snow-capped peaks of the Sierra Nevada. There's skiing a half-hour drive and plenty of fine walking. In the evening, relax with a drink in the cosy sitting room while Alicia, the young, energetic owner, cooks an authentic Portuguese supper using her grandmother's recipes. Modest, simple, gracious, good value – and in a fantastic spot.

rooms	10: 8 twins/doubles, 1 single, 1 family.
price	€52. Single €39. Family €52; €15 per extra bed. VAT included.
meals	Dinner €10.
closed	First 3 weeks in July.
directions	Granada ring road, exit for Alhambra & Sierra Nevada; then exit 2 for Monachil. At lights, ahead for 700m to crossroads. On right.

	Alicia Higuera & Joaquin Morales
tel	+34 639 203196/+34 958 500393
fax	+34 958 500393
email	info@hotelaliciacarolina.com
web	www.hotelaliciacarolina.com

Map 24 Entry 314

Casa de los Migueletes

c/Benalúa 11 (Plaza Nueva), 18010 Granada

Slip through doors into a quiet courtyard cooled by a fountain and scented with citrus; gaze up to a handsome tier of wooden galleries; catch a glimpse of tiled staircases and inviting archways. Hard to believe you are in the heart of dusty Granada. The 17th-century nobleman's *casa* is as richly atmospheric as the Moorish Albaycín quarter that surrounds it, and has been sympathetically restored. It keeps its grandeur yet is quietly, luxuriously, 21st century. Rooms have beamed ceilings, tiled floors and carved, hand-crafted beds. Polished antiques, plump sofas and rich hangings add to the high-comfort factor while bathrooms spoil with gorgeous soaps, masses of towels and classy tiles. Some rooms overlook the Alhambra, one has a domed bathroom, another is in a tower. Pull out all the stops and choose the four-poster suite in the old chapel. Traditional Andalucían breakfasts are taken in the glowing, brick-arched cellar. Manageress Ingunn makes you feel like family and has an enviable knowledge of Granada's best tapas bars and restaurants: ask for the owners' guide.

rooms	25: 24 twins/doubles, 1 suite.
price	€120-199. Suite €349.
meals	Breakfast €9.50.
closed	Rarely.
directions	Granda 'circunvalacion', exit 129 for Centro-Recogidas. Right for Palacio de Congresos. In square park in underground car park Plaza Puerta Real (special rates for hotel guests) & take taxi to hotel. Taxi fare deducted. from bill. Check web site for more detailed directions.

	Karl Otto Skogland & Ana Raczkowski
tel	+34 958 210700
fax	+34 958 210702
email	info@casamigueletes.com
web	www.casamigueletes.com

Map 24 Entry 315

El Ladrón de Agua
Carrera del Darro 13, 18010 Granada

Captivated by a visit to Granada in 1924, the poet (later Nobel prize-winner) Juan Ramón Jiménez wrote *Olvidas*, a spiritual journey inspired by the water found throughout the city. Raúl, the sympathetic young manager of El Ladrón, hopes his beautiful, unusual hotel will be a source of inspiration too. The place fuses poetry, water, architecture, luxury and friendliness in an irresistible blend. A vast new painting in the hall pays tribute to the poet but the most memorable part of the 16th-century building is its central patio. Slender columns of Tuscan marble support a graceful gallery and the fountain has been sculpted from a block of sombre marble. In the high-ceilinged bedrooms nothing has been stinted or forgotten: sumptuous beds, oriental rugs on terracotta floors, lovely writing desks... Each room has been named after a character or poem connected to Jiménez. Eight look across to the Alhambra hill; those at the front of the hotel are above the busy thoroughfare of the Carrera del Darro. You're right in the middle of old Granada, a short walk from Sacro Monte and the Alhambra itself.

rooms	15 twins/doubles.
price	€99–€195.
meals	Breakfast €9. Half-board €26 extra p.p.
closed	Rarely.
directions	In Granada head for city centre & Plaza Nueva. Here drive up Carrera del Darro (parallel to River Darro). Hotel 50m from Plaza Nueva. Best to park in any central car park & take a taxi.

	Raúl Lozano Ruiz
tel	+34 958 215040
fax	+34 958 224345
email	info@ladrondeagua.com
web	www.ladrondeagua.com

Map 24 Entry 316

Catedral Suites

Plaza de las Pasiegas s/n, 18001 Granada

This elegant townhouse, two steps from Granada's glorious cathedral, reveals an interior of unexpected contemporary cool. Its nine suites are light, roomy, uncluttered and have a subtle designer touch. Floors are pale, fabrics are taupe and cream, lighting is modern and spare. The furniture is minimal but well-chosen – large beds, smooth red sofas, solid wooden chests. Bathrooms are designer-cool with chrome fittings, gleaming white tiles and washbasins set into glass. After a dusty day exploring the Alhambra Palace, the Arabian quarter, the lace market and the lively Bib Rambla plaza, how relaxing to return to this. At once you will feel restored and ready to hit the streets again. The small kitchens are adequately kitted for breakfasts or a quick pasta supper – but why bother, when all around are restaurants and bars? Directly below is the buzzy modern café-bar Pasiegas, with its imaginative tapas, superb cheeses and great choice of wines. In the summer, eat out on the square and be dazzled by the cathedral's fantastical façade. Bang in the middle of Granada, these suites are hard to beat.

rooms	9 self-catering suites for 4.
price	€80–€127 for 2; €125–€174 for 4.
meals	Breakfast at Hotel Reina Cristina €7.50 (see entry 309).
closed	Rarely.
directions	Check in at Hotel Reina Cristina. Staff will park your car after dropping off luggage.

	María Gómez
tel	+34 958 535130
fax	+34 958 255728
email	reservas@catedral-suites.com
web	www.catedral-suites.com

Map 24 Entry 317

Casa Los Naranjos

Barranco de los Naranjos 10, 18010 Sacromonte, Granada

Drop off to sleep in a whitewashed cave, wake to views of the Alhambra – what could be more alluring? The Sacromonte Hill is the most evocative and peaceful quarter of Granada, famous for its caves. These at Casa Los Naranjos have been turned into two modern apartments full of atmosphere, light and airy with terracotta floors, gallery-white walls, stripped beech doors and furnishings sleek and simple. Bedrooms have arched ceilings (of course), snowy bed linen and modest cupboards and shelves. Bathrooms are brilliant white, kitchens come with double sinks, living areas are warm with Moroccan wall hangings and rugs. Leafy plants are dotted throughout. Edith, a sprightly Austrian and a linguist, has lived here for 20 years. She is your perfect guide to Granada. The Albayzin quarter, cathedral and plazas are within walking distance – just as long as you don't mind the hills. Edith also advises on the best *tablaos* in town. And you'll love eating in, on your shared sun-trappd terrace with sensational views across the Durro to the Generalife and Alhambra. *Parking nearby, €6 per day.*

rooms	2 apartments for 2-4.
price	€320 per week for 2, €390-€520 for 2-4. VAT included. Minimum stay 2 nights.
meals	Self-catering.
closed	Rarely.
directions	Park in any city centre car park & take taxi along Camino de Sacromonte as far as María de la Canastera. Just past here, up steps, round to left, pass drinking fountain; house on right.

	Edith Schodl
tel	+34 958 225127
fax	+34 958 225127
email	info@granada-apartments.com
web	www.granada-apartments.com

Map 24 Entry 318

La Almunia del Valle

Camino de la Umbría s/n, 18193 Monachil, Granada

Secluded terraces, soothing fountains, little channels ferrying water to every part of the grounds... In the Moorish period, *una almunia* was a summer residence and there's a distinctly Moorish feel to this hillside garden. The farmhouse, once lived in by a German artist, stands in its own orchards, its crisp white lines softened by an abundance of chestnuts, olives and figs. The interiors have been touched by a masterly hand in a mix of period and modern – traditional slate floors and contemporary art, leather chairs and woven hangings – plus some arresting colours and masses of books. Bedrooms smell deliciously of cherrywood and are lavishly equipped... bright kilims, Casablanca fans and unexpected detail add interest to the understated elegance. From the vast sitting room, painted a warm rose, you step out onto the wide terrace and take in the dramatic sweep of mountains and the Monachil valley below. You're 20 minutes from Granada but it all feels rural, remote and tranquil. Terrific food, too, and a small but good selection of house wines. Perfect for sybarites. *A Rusticae hotel.*

rooms	9 twins/doubles.
price	€98–€114.
meals	Dinner €30.
closed	22 December–2 January.
directions	Follow signs for Alhambra & Sierra Nevada on Ronda Sur ring road. Exit 2 for Monachil. On following signs for Monachil & Casco Antiguo. Through hamlet; follow signs along narrow road to La Almunia.

José Manuel Plana & Patricia Merino

tel	+34 958 308010
fax	+34 958 308010
email	laalmunia@infonegocio.com
web	www.laalmuniadelvalle.com

Map 24 Entry 319

Alojamiento Rural El Molino

Avenida González Robles 16, 18400 Órgiva, Granada

Wander round the weekly market to see how colourful and creative this multi-ethnic community is. Órgiva is the New Age capital of Andalucía and you are in the heart of it. It may all seem a touch frenetic but behind the heavy grille lies an enclosed walled patio and another world. Esteban is a young and relaxed host, who ran this old olive mill as a bar before turning it into a *turismo rural*. Terracotta floors, massive beams, a potted palm – there's an Andalucían feel. In the vast and lofty bedrooms – those at the back the quietest – is a mix of simple wooden furniture and the odd antique; one wardrobe was once a confessional. Breakfast is an excellent spread, served, for much of the year, on the patio by the fig tree. Bliss in the heat of the day to float in the small, jacuzzi-style pool under an azure Andalucían sky. This lush, exuberant area, put on the map by Chris Stewart's *Driving Over Lemons*, has some great walks: take advantage of the GR7 long-distance footpath that traverses the southern flank of the Sierra Nevada, or explore the remoter villages of the Alpujarra.

rooms	5 twins/doubles.
price	€54. VAT included.
meals	Evening meals on request.
closed	Rarely.
directions	From Málaga, N-340 for Motril; N-323 for Granada. Exit Lanjarón; N-322 to Órgiva. El Molino on right just before 1st set of lights. Best to park past El Molino, to right, next to Pizzeria Almazara.

	Esteban Palenciano Simón
tel	+34 646 616628
email	elmolino@casaruralelmolino.com
web	www.casaruralelmolino.com

Map 24 Entry 320

Hotel de Mecina Fondales

c/La Fuente 2, 18414 Mecina Fondales, Granada

The walking here is wonderful and this small modern hotel a comfortable place to return to after a day of trail-bashing. It looks out across the lush Guadalfeo valley; read more about the area – and its people – in Chris Stewart's *Driving Over Lemons*. In spite of its large reception area, the hotel has a cosy feel. The dining room is especially inviting, with its dark chestnut beams, patterned curtains and ladderback chairs. Pizza is on the menu – but if you fancy something authentic, try the *plato alujarreño*; this Spanish fry-up has several local variants but will certainly include 'poor-man's potatoes' and sweet green peppers. Victor the owner is keen to promote traditional dishes and local wines. Bedrooms are medium to large, squeaky clean and as smart as can be, with fridge, kettle and central heating; a winter stay would be a cosy one. For views, ask for a room looking south to the valley. The hamlet sits high on the Sierra Nevada, a cluster of whitewashed houses with the flat slate roofs and rounded chimney stacks typical of the area.

rooms	21 twins/doubles.
price	€70–€100 Singles €50.
meals	Breakfast €6. Lunch/dinner €12–€15, €20–€25 à la carte.
closed	Rarely.
directions	N-323 for Motril; C-333 through Lanjarón. Before Órgiva, Pampaneira road to Pitres. 1km before village, right for Mecina. At entrance of village, right.

	Victor Fernández
tel	+34 958 766254
fax	+34 958 766255
email	victor@hoteldemecina.com
web	www.ocioteca.com/hoteldemecina

Map 25 Entry 321

Los Tinaos de la Alpujarra

c/Parras s/n, 18412 Bubión, Granada

These simple, 12-year-old apartments have been built on terraces in local style: slate walls, flat-topped roofs, rounded chimney stacks, rough plaster – and pink potted geraniums in brilliant contrast to white walls. What lifts them into the 'special' bracket is the beauty of their position, close to the village church and looking out over terraced groves of cherry, pear and apple all the way to the Contraviesa Sierra... on a clear day you can make out passing ships on the Mediterranean. Each house has an open-plan sitting, dining and kitchen area giving onto a small terrace – perfect for meals and sundowners. There are open hearths and central heating, workaday pine furniture, smallish bedrooms and bathrooms, and locally woven fabrics to add a dash of colour. At the lower end of this village you shouldn't hear a thing, apart from the murmur of the river and the tolling of the church bells. Wood is supplied in winter for a small charge and Isabel and José, who own the café-bar opposite (breakfasts and snacks), happily advise on where to eat and what to do.

rooms	12 apartments for 6.
price	Apartment for 2, €59; for 4 €78; for 6 €102. VAT included.
meals	Self-catering includes breakfast. Snacks in café.
closed	Rarely.
directions	From Granada N-323 for Motril. Exit V Benaudalla. Here to Órgiva; there; right to Bubión. Enter; left into c/Lavadero. 25m 1st (sharp) left; at small fountain right.

	Isabel Puga Salguero
tel	+34 958 763217
fax	+34 958 763192
email	info@lostinaos.com
web	www.lostinaos.com

Map 25 Entry 322

Alquería de Morayma

Ctra. A-348 Cádiar-Torvizcón, 18440 Cádiar, Granada

Mariano and his family built this fascinating hamlet-hotel in the local vernacular, successfully recreating the rambling feel of an Alpujarran village. The main farmstead and the individual houses (one in the old chapel) are set amid olive groves, vineyards and kitchen garden – all organic. Your immensely likeable host has a commitment to the organic life – and hopes that guests will leave La Morayma with a deeper understanding of the traditions of mountain village life. Inside: antique brass bedsteads, Alpujarra bed covers, marble-topped dressers, good paintings, and photographs of the old farming days. Each room differs from the next, each feels warm and cared-for. Food is important here, a celebration of all things local, from delicious olive oil to charcuterie to the semolina cakes (*migas*) typical of this area. There are two restaurants, and wine from Morayma's bodega. See olives being milled during the the winter, or join in with the grape harvest or the sausage-making! The walking is wonderful – Mariano knows these hills well. *Reiki and relaxation courses available.*

rooms	13 + 5: 13 twins/doubles. 5 apartments for 4.
price	€54–€59. Singles €43-€47. Apartments €63.
meals	Breakfast €2.40. Lunch/dinner set menu €12-€15.
closed	Rarely.
directions	From Granada N-323 south for Motril, then A-348 via Lanjarón, Órgiva & Torvizcón. 2km before Cádiar, signed to left.

	Mariano Cruz Fajardo
tel	+34 958 343221
fax	+34 958 343221
email	alqueria@alqueriamorayma.com
web	www.alqueriamorayma.com

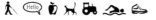

Map 25 Entry 323

Sierra y Mar

c/Albaycín 3, 18414 Ferreirola, Granada

Take the blue door to paradise: enter a sunny, shady, flowery, leafy-walled garden – a world apart. Mention breakfast: a minor feast shared with others under the spreading mulberry tree. This is a gorgeous place run by two delightful northerners (Italian and Danish) who know and love Andalucía; they are relaxed, intelligent and 'green'. The ancient labyrinthine house has been extended with total respect for its origins, and is furnished with old rural pieces and natural materials for curtains and bedcovers, all in simple, wholesome taste. Each room has its own shower or bath, and there's central heating for winter. José and Inger organise walking tours: do make time for the half-day circular hike that begins and ends at the house. There's a well-equipped kitchen for guests, and a great family-run restaurant you can walk to; also, a couple of vegetarian restaurants nearby. The atmosphere is easy, the village is beautiful (you are in the heart of it) and your hosts know the Alpujarras like few others. Wholly special B&B – book well in advance. *Minimum stay two nights.*

rooms	9 twins/doubles.
price	€52. Singles €32. VAT included.
meals	Breakfast included. Kitchen for guests.Restaurant 1 mile away.
closed	Rarely.
directions	From Málaga, on E-15; before Motril, N-323 for Granada. Cross small bridge after Vélez Benaudalla for Órgiva. Park in square, by fountain.

	Inger Norgaard & Giuseppe Heiss
tel	+34 958 766171
fax	+34 958 857367
email	reservas@sierraymar.com
web	www.sierraymar.com

Map 25 Entry 324

Las Terrazas de la Alpujarra

Plaza del Sol 7, 18412 Bubión, Granada

You are high up in the Alpujarra – so high that on a clear day you can see down to the coast, across the Mediterranean and all the way to Africa. Las Terrazas, as the name implies, stands on a terraced hillside on the southern edge of Bubión. Enter the quietest inn in Spain: this is the only place – monasteries and churches aside – where we have ever seen 'Silencio Por Favor' signs on the walls! You breakfast in the modest lounge; unusually, for a simple place like this, the menu includes cheese and charcuterie. No other meals are served but there are plenty of good little restaurants and bars in the village. Bedrooms have terracotta floors, locally-woven blankets, framed photographs on the walls – small, nothing fancy and remarkably good value. Ask for one at the top with a view, or for one with a terrace. You can self-cater here, too – Paco's House nearby or the House of the Mill would be perfect for a vast party of hikers. Your hosts, the kindest of folk, have several mountain bikes and will happily help you plan your expeditions – on wheel or on foot.

rooms	20 + 5: 20 doubles. 3 apartments for 6. 2 houses for 20.
price	€24. Apt €37–€72. Houses €120–€180.
meals	Restaurants in village.
closed	7 January–7 February.
directions	Granada N-323 for Motril; C-333 through Lanjarón; just before Órgiva road to Pampaneira, left to Bubión. In village on left.

Francisco Puga Salguero

tel	+34 958 763034
fax	+34 958 763252
email	info@terrazasalpujarra.com
web	www.terrazasalpujarra.com

Map 25 Entry 325

Hotel La Fragua
c/San Antonio 4, 18417 Trévelez, Granada

Just to the south of the highest peak in the Sierra Nevada, this is one of the prettiest villages of the Alpujarra. Climb (steeply) up to its middle and find La Fragua, made up of two old village houses by the town hall. In one building is the friendly little bar; above, an eagle's nest of a pine-clad restaurant with a terrific view across the roofs – sit and gaze between courses. The food reflects the hostelry: simple and authentic. The locally-cured ham is utterly delicious and the puddings a treat. A few yards along the narrow street is the second house; this one holds your rooms. New terracotta floors, old beamed ceilings, comfy beds, no frills, perfect for walkers. Up above is a roof terrace with tables and another heavenly view. And there's a new annexe, right on the edge of the village, where the rooms are somewhat plusher – worth the extra euros. Your host, Antonio, knows walkers and their ways and will gladly help you plan your hikes. From May on, Trévelez attracts the trippers; come hiking – or riding – out of season, and return to wood-burning stoves.

rooms	24 twins/doubles.
price	€35. Singles €25.
meals	Breakfast €2.80. Lunch/dinner €12, €12–€15 à la carte. VAT included.
closed	10 January–10 February.
directions	Granada N-323 for Motril; C-333 through Lanjarón; just before Órgiva take road to Trévelez. There ask for 'barrio medio'; park in Plaza Las Pulgas. Next to Town Hall.

	Antonio y Miguel Espinosa González
tel	+34 958 858626
fax	+34 958 858614
email	reservas@hotellafragua.com
web	www.hotellafragua.com

Map 25 Entry 326

Casa Rural El Paraje de Matamoros

Ctra. Granada-Bérchules km6, 18451 Bérchules, Granada

A long, long track cuts through groves of almonds, past chestnuts, olives and oak trees and brings you to this old farmhouse high above Bérchules. From the terrace in front – originally the threshing circle – are the most glorious views. And all around, superb walking country; one of the reasons Anita and Walter chose to settle here was so they could indulge their passion for walking. They're Dutch but completely at home in their adopted country – Anita spent about 12 years exploring Spain by bike and knows it intimately. This is a new venture for them: the farm covers about 20 hectares and the house was semi-derelict when they bought it; they've done a lot of the restoration themselves. The simply furnished bedrooms (two sharing a bathroom) are attractively austere but provide everything you need – and the underfloor heating is a superb plus in the long Alpujarran winter. Downstairs is a small bar and restaurant, and the food is a treat. Walter, a terrific cook, uses good, fresh produce and serves local wines. He and Anita are the kindest, friendliest hosts and the area is blissfully tourist-free.

rooms	5 + 1: 5 twins/doubles. 1 apartment.
price	€35-€40. Apartment €45.
meals	Dinner €12.50.
closed	Rarely.
directions	From Málaga, east on N-340. Pass Motril, then left to Albuñol. Just after Albuñol, right on GR-433 to Cádiar, towards Mecina; left to Bérchules. Here left for Juviles; after 2km right at sign.

	Anita Beijer & Walter Michels
tel	+34 626 186035
email	info@elparaje.com
web	www.elparaje.com

Map 25 Entry 327

Hotel Los Bérchules

Ctra. de Granada 20, 18451 Bérchules, Granada

All that a walker could hope for: cosy, inexpensive, with good food and wine and a wonderful welcome from Wendy and son Alejandro. The hotel sits just beneath the village of Bérchules, 1,322m above sea level – about as high as Ben Nevis… Things are on a human scale here: a small, new-pine-clad lounge bar with a brick hearth and a collection of walking guides; a beamed dining room full of good things. Choose between à la carte and the great value *menú del día*; if you like rabbit, try Alejandro's paella. Guest bedrooms are sober and clean, pleasingly furnished with bright Alpujarra-weave curtains and blankets, with their own balcony-terraces and central heating for the cooler months. The best views are from those at the front. The long-distance footpath that runs the length of the southern flank of the Sierra Nevada passes right by; Wendy knows every route, and will run you to and from your hikes. A heated pool is on its way – and don't be put off by the façade: this is a very special place.

rooms	13 + 1: 10 twins, 3 singles. 1 apartment for 4.
price	€41–€49. Singles €30–€36. Apartment €70. VAT included.
meals	Breakfast €3.50. Lunch/dinner €10–€20.
closed	Rarely.
directions	Málaga, E on N-340. Pass Motril, left to Albuñol. Just after Albuñol, right on GR-433 to Cádiar, then Mecina; left to Bérchules. On left at village entrance.

	Alejandro Tamborero Gibson
tel	+34 958 852530
fax	+34 958 769000
email	hot.berchules@interbook.net
web	www.hotelberchules.com

Map 25 Entry 328

El Rincón de Yegen

Camino de Gerald Brennan, 18460 Yegen, Granada

Yegen is the village where Gerald Brennan came to live in the 1920s: his *South from Granada* is essential reading. Getting here is easier than in Brennan's day – and, although the 21st century has caught up with the villages of the Alpujarra, there is still beauty here in great measure. This small village inn, set just back from the road (some noise) fits well with its older neighbours – local slate, beam and bamboo are everywhere. Masses of shade-giving greenery means it's darkish inside, but the beamy dining room is inviting. Agustín, a trained cook, reworks local dishes in a light way, and the food is great value. The onion and goat's cheese tart makes a heavenly starter… and there's partridge, braised lamb with grapes, raspberry fool. Bedrooms are at the back of the restaurant, built high to catch the views from the hotel's 3,500-foot perch – they are large, with loads of space, new pine, stripey bedspreads, white walls, shining floors (warm underfoot in winter). It's as clean and as cared for as can be. If you prefer the independence of self-catering, the cottages have all you need.

rooms	4 + 3: 4 twins/doubles. 3 self-catering cottages for 4.
price	€40. Singles €30. Cottage €400 p.w. VAT inc.
meals	Breakfast €4.25. Lunch/dinner €12 set menu; €15-€25 à la carte. Not Tuesday.
closed	First two weeks in February.
directions	Málaga N-340 Almería. Exit & Albuñol; via Cádiar & Mecina Bombarón to Yegen. Signed left in village.

	Agustín Martín Rodríguez
tel	+34 958 851270
fax	+34 958 851270
email	elrincondeyegen@telefonica.net

Map 25 Entry 329

Casa Rural Las Chimeneas
c/Amargura 6, 18493 Mairena, Granada

Modest Mairena has barely changed since the advent of tourism – a gem of a village at the eastern end of Sierra Nevada. David and Emma are keen walkers and the majority of their guests come to explore the little-trodden paths that radiate from the village. The old house has been restored with particular sensitivity and you feel it the moment you enter. The guests' sitting/dining room is a light, lofty, serene space; four rocking chairs gather around a wood-burning stove, rush matting warms new stone floors, there are plants, books and views across the terraced hillsides. A plant-filled terrace with a tiny plunge pool shares the same view – with tantalizing glimpses of North Africa on a clear day. Guest bedrooms are as special, artistically furnished with antique dressers and beds (and modern mattresses!). Bathrooms, too, are a delight – uncluttered, stylish, homespun – as are the self-catering studios nearby. Dinner and breakfast are enjoyed at one table: the spirit of Las Chimeneas is relaxed and friendly. A perfect place for a long, restful stay.

rooms	7 + 3: 7 twins/doubles. 3 self-catering studios.
price	€65. Singles €45. Studios €50–€90 (€300–€500 p.w.). VAT inc.
meals	Packed lunch €5. Dinner €20. VAT inc.
closed	Rarely.
directions	From Laroles, 2nd right into Mairena by willows. Park in square; down narrow street at south-east corner; 10m to house.

	David & Emma Illsley
tel	+34 958 760352
fax	+34 958 760004
email	info@alpujarra-tours.com
web	www.alpujarra-tours.com

Map 25 Entry 330

Los Omeyas

c/Encarnación 17, 14003 Córdoba

You couldn't hope to find a better positioned hotel than Los Omeyas, in a plexus of mystic alleys, two steps from the great Mezquita in the old Jewish quarter of Cordoba which is one of Andalucía's most alluring city sites. The building is in harmony with its much older neighbours; the whitewashed façade, wrought-iron balconies and shutters are classic Córdoban. Inside is authentic, too, with a small, marbled, glass-roofed courtyard that gives onto bedrooms on two levels. The architecture is pleasing and almost theatrical – there are Mezquita-style arches in reception and the cafeteria-bar, too – but sound insulation is poor and some guests have commented on the echo-chamber effect. In summer, when bedroom windows need to be open, light sleepers may be better off in one of the newer rooms at the top. Throughout, expect simple wooden furniture on white marble floors, fitted wardrobes, air conditioning, phones and TVs, modest bathrooms. A small, functional hotel in the heart of old Córdoba, with very friendly staff.

rooms	40 twins/doubles.
price	€53–€65. Singles €35–€41.
meals	Breakfast €3.50. Lunch/dinner €9–€15 set menu.
closed	Rarely.
directions	Entering Córdoba follow signs for centre, then Mezquita. In a street just off north-east corner of Mezquita. Hotel has own car park; staff will accompany you to park.

	Juan de la Rubia Villalba
tel	+34 957 492267
fax	+34 957 491659
email	reservas@hotel-losomeyas.com
web	www.hotel-losomeyas.com

Map 18 Entry 331

Hotel Zuhayra

c/Mirador 10, 14870 Zuheros, Córdoba

The Zuhayra's monolithic exterior may have you wondering. But do visit this small village at the wild heart of the Subbetica Park: quintessentially Andalucían, its houses hug the hillside beneath the castle. Up above, the mighty mountains; below, mile upon mile of olives – and you are given a bottle of olive oil when you leave. Two delightful, gentle-mannered brothers and their wives manage the hotel. The downstairs café-bar is vast and utilitarian but on the first floor is a smaller room where you can tuck into local delicacies such as partridge, *clavillina* (thick stew served with a fried egg) and *remojón* (potato, onion and pepper salad with oranges). Delicious bread is locally made. Bedrooms are functional: modern pine, coordinated fabrics, hot-air heating, comfy beds. Bathrooms are spotless, all with baths; second-floor rooms get the best views. Walkers love it here and footpaths radiate from the village. There are cave paintings at The Cave of the Bats down the road, you can hire a bike and head off along the *via verde*, and Córdoba is an hour's drive.

rooms	18 twins/doubles.
price	€43–€54.
meals	Lunch/dinner €12; €16–€20 à la carte.
closed	Rarely.
directions	Málaga for Córdoba; passing Lucena, A-340 on right to Cabra; cont. 4km; A-318 to Dona Mencia; pass town on left; right for Zuheros. In same street as Castillo 200m down hill (use castle carpark).

	Juan Carlos Ábalos Guerrero
tel	+34 957 694693
fax	+34 957 694702
email	hotelzuhayra@zercahoteles.com
web	www.zercahoteles.com

Map 18 Entry 332

Hotel Huerta de las Palomas

Ctra. Priego-Zagrilla km3.5, 14800 Priego de Córdoba, Córdoba

Cascades of wrought-iron chandeliers, columned archways and a lofty central hall evoke the gracious style of a traditional cortijo. Yet this rural hotel, wrapped among olive groves, was built last year. Authentic grandeur cleverly combines with 21st-century comforts (large bathrooms, outdoor jacuzzi, gym) and not a trick has been missed – the garden's water feature even plays music. Bedrooms are understatedly stylish with warm pastel shades, wrought-iron bedheads, sleek dark furniture and shuttered windows. Bathrooms are rich in marble and ceramic tiling with plenty of multi-starred extras. You may want to dress up for dinner, the dining room is so prettily elegant; the menu is Andalucían with a modern twist. You could spend the whole day relaxing around the pool and gardens but it would be a shame not to make the most of where you are. Córdoba and Granada are an hour away, and the fabulous baroque architecture of Priego de Córdoba is just down the road. And there's the Subbetica National Park. A tranquil, warm, well-planned hotel, and surprisingly intimate for its size.

rooms	34: 30 twins/doubles, 4 suites.
price	€73-€100. Suites €100-€150.
meals	Lunch/dinner €20; €30-€35 à la carte.
closed	Rarely.
directions	From Málaga N-331 for Antequera, then Lucena. Right onto A-340 to Priego de Córdoba. On entering Priego left on CP-99 for Zagrilla. Hotel on left after 3.5km.

	Salvador Ábalos
tel	+34 957 720305
fax	+34 957 720007
email	huertadelaspalomas@zercahoteles.com
web	www.zercahoteles.com

Map 24 Entry 333

Cortijo La Haza

Adelantado 119, 14978 Iznajar, Córdoba

An old farmhouse lost in the olive belt that stretches from here north and eastwards across almost half of Andalucía. If you like olive groves (it helps) and little-known corners of Spain, stay here – and use it as a base for your visit to the glories of Granada and Córdoba, easily reachable by car. Tim and Keith, quiet and friendly, left teaching and catering (experts, then, at keeping an eye on several things at once!) to set up their delightful, five-bedroom hotel. Word is spreading. The renovation is brand new, but the 'rustic' feel of a 250-year-old Andalucían cortijo has been beautifully preserved: walls have a rough render, old country pieces have been restored. Beamed bedrooms have Egyptian cotton sheets on wrought-iron bedsteads; bath and shower rooms are en suite. The sitting room and dining rooms are deliciously cosy with log-burning stoves, but in summer you spill into the white-walled courtyard. Food is honestly priced, and draws on Keith's long experience as a chef, with vegetarians well catered for. Quiet, remote, friendly... and a pool with a spectacular view.

rooms	5 twins/doubles.
price	€70. Singles €60.
meals	Dinner €20.
closed	Rarely.
directions	From Málaga airport, A-7 for Málaga. A-45 & A-359 for Granada. After 24km, exit 1 onto A-333 for Iznajar. After km55 marker, left on CV-174 for 100m, left by small school for 2.6km. Signed to right.

	Tim Holt & Keith Tennyson
tel	+34 605187546 (mob)
email	info@cortijolahaza.com
web	www.cortijolahaza.com

Map 24 Entry 334

Palacio de la Rambla
Plaza del Marques 1, 23400 Úbeda, Jaén

The old towns of Úbeda and Baeza are often missed as travellers dash between Madrid and the coast, yet they are two of the brightest jewels in the crown of Spanish architecture. At the heart of old Úbeda, the exquisite Palacio de la Rambla dates from the Renaissance and has never left the Orozco family. You enter through an ornate Corinthian-columned portal into the cloistered patio; opulently colonnaded on two levels, smothered in ivy and wonderfully cool on a sweltering day. Lounge, dining room and bedrooms are large to massive and a perfect match for their setting: antique beds, chests, trunks, lamps, pretty washstands, claw-foot tubs, religious momentos, family portraits, and native terracotta softened by *estera* matting. Young, bubbly, glamorous staff will serve you one of the best breakfasts in this book: eggs, toast with olive oil, baskets of fruit, cheese, charcuterie, homemade cakes and jams. Palacio de la Rambla has a long tradition of regal welcoming; King Alfonso XIII stayed here when he was in town. A delectable, peaceful retreat. *A Rusticae hotel.*

rooms	8: 7 twins/doubles, 1 suite.
price	€100–€120.
meals	Restaurants nearby.
closed	15 July–15 August.
directions	From Madrid south on N-IV. At km292 marker, N-322 to Úbeda. There, follow 'Centro Ciudad' until Palacio is in front of you, between c/Ancha & c/Rastro, opposite cafetería La Paloma.

	Elena & Cristina Meneses de Orozco
tel	+34 953 750196
fax	+34 953 750267
email	palaciodelarambla@terra.es
web	www.palaciodelarambla.com

Map 19 Entry 335

La Finca Mercedes

Ctra. de la Sierra km1, 23476 La Iruela, Jaén

La Iruela's crowning glory is the castle fortress built by the Templars; make it to the top for an amazing view. La Finca Mercedes is just outside the village, a simple modern roadside restaurant with rooms. It takes its name from its bright and charming owner, ably helped by her two young daughters. Although you are just next to the road there is little passing traffic; ask for a bedroom at the back, for peace *and* glorious views, across the olive groves and far beyond. In bitter winter the dining room is as cosy as a Cotswold pub, when a fire burns in the corner hearth throughout the day. Decorative flourishes include old copper saucepans, dried flowers, hunting trophies and piano; the food is simple, regional, flavoursome and good value. So too are the bedrooms, a standard size with stained pine furniture and good bathrooms (full-size baths!). There's a garden with a pool, and six new bedrooms at the family's stone farmhouse, Cortijo Berfalá, a five-minute walk down a steep road. Brilliant for walkers, and people on a budget. *Advance bookings preferred.*

rooms	9: 7 twins/doubles, 1 single, 1 suite. Cortijo: 6 twins/doubles.
price	€36-€39. Singles €24-€27. Suite €39-€42.
meals	Breakfast €3.30. Lunch/dinner €12.60 set menu; €18 à la carte.
closed	Rarely.
directions	From Cazorla into village centre; at large square, left for La Iruela. Follow road for 1km round bottom of La I.; Finca just to left. Do not confuse with hotel next door!

	Mercedes Castillo Matilla
tel	+34 953 721087
email	info@lafincamercedes.com
web	www.lafincamercedes.com

Map 19 Entry 336

Molino La Farraga

c/Camino de la Hoz s/n, Apartado de Correos 1, 23470 Cazorla, Jaén

As gorgeous a setting as you could hope to find: a deeply verdant river valley just beneath the rocky crests of the Cazorla mountains. This 200-year-old mill's gardens are an ode to water – it is everywhere, in ponds, channels, races and falls. The gardens were planted by an English botanist, nurtured for years by an amiable American and now tended by friendly new owners Paco and Encarnación. Once you've negotiated the very steep path up, you can revel in simple comfort and buckets of caring in this cool valley retreat. The architecture is an organic, interlocking puzzle of stairways, corners, niches and turns, and the bedrooms are all country-simple, all different: some have fireplaces, some a small terrace; they have knick-knacks, dried flowers, rugs on tiled floors – no stylist's dream, but they are super-clean. The price of your room includes a good Spanish breakfast, dinner is excellent value and the pool is heavenly. Lots of guests are walkers, and there are plenty of maps in the hall. *Non-Spanish-speakers please call 00 34 667 716843.*

rooms	8: 7 doubles, 1 suite.
price	€64–€69. Singles €34. Suite €100–€107. VAT included.
meals	Dinner €10.
closed	15 December–15 February.
directions	In Cazorla, signs for Ruinas de Santa María. Pass between ruined church & restaurant towards 'Castillo'. Park on left by last weeping willow; cross bridge and walk 70m to La Farraga.

tel	+34 953 721249
fax	+34 953 721249
email	farraga@teleline.es
web	www.molinolafarraga.com

Map 19 Entry 337

La Joya del Cabo de Gata
Paraje La Joya, 04149 Aguamarga, Almería

She calls it her "miracle in the desert". Charo Garcia discovered the landscape of Almería, the dry river beds and dunes, the dazzling white dwellings, the tough vegetation… and was captivated. So she built two farmhouses and imported a Bedouin tent, added a terrace shaded by parasols of scrub and heather, a small pool for midnight swims, an open-air shower in a grotto… now her dream appears in glossy magazines. The farmhouses, run on solar energy and recycled water, are ancient yet modern: whitewashed walls, muslin drapes, rustic floors, stainless steel hobs, TVs and DVDs, and terraces that face east and north. The *haymah*, set among olive trees and palms, has an ecological stove for winter (just a few chilly days), ventilation for summer, a vast bed, a perfectly equipped kitchen and colourful Arabic décor. Breakfasts, based on "respect for the environment", are served on the communal terrace. Coves, inlets and empty beaches await, there's Garrucha for sea food, Mojacar for its hippy beach, Nijar for pottery. Rides on horses, ponies and camels can be arranged. *Uninspected at time of going to press.*

rooms	2 apartments for 2-4; 1 Bedouin tent for 2.
price	€120-€190 for 2; €210-€320 for 4. Tent €80-€140. VAT included.
meals	Self-catering.
closed	7-30 January.
directions	A-7/E-15, exit 494 for Carboneras. After 3.5km right following signs to Aguamarga. Paraje La Joya just before Aguamarga.

	Charo García
tel	+34 619 159587
email	reservas@lajoyadelcabodegata.com
web	www.lajoyadelcabodegata.com

Map 25 Entry 338

Hotel Family

c/La Lomilla s/n, 04149 Agua Amarga, Almería

Gentle-mannered Michele and René came to Agua Amarga on French leave;
seduced by what was then a remote fishing village, they dreamed of moving here.
They have given this little place their all, and run it with much energy, helped by
their son and his wife – hence the name. A bumpy track takes you to the
whitewashed *hostal*, restaurant and palm-backed pool – there's an exotic, southern
feel. You are in a quiet part of the village, yards from one of the area's most
gorgeous beaches. Rooms are simply furnished, the nicest and newest on the first
floor, air-conditioned, well-equipped and with their own balconies. Those at the
front have sea views. Come for Michele's food: huge portions and excellent value.
Breakfasts are a feast of yogurts, fruits, tortillas and good toast for homemade
jam. Stay at least two nights and discover the Cabo de Gata National Park: the
walking is wonderful and it holds some of Spain's most beautiful beaches. Agua
Amarga is more developed than it was, but remains an enchanting spot –
particularly out of season.

rooms	9 twins/doubles.
price	€45–€100. Singles €40–€95.
meals	Lunch/dinner with wine €16; lunch weekends only.
closed	1 November–15 December.
directions	From N-344 exit 494 Venta & Carboneras. On for Carboneras; right for Agua Amarga. Signed to right in village as you arrive.

	Marc Bellavoir
tel	+34 950 138014
fax	+34 950 138070
email	riovall@teleline.es

Map 25 Entry 339

Finca Listonero
Cortijo Grande, 04639 Turre, Almería

Lovers of desert landscapes, their aridity and sense of eternity, will be rewarded here. For the sybaritic, this pink-washed, extended farmhouse has all the luxuries. David and Graeme, cultured Anglo-Australians, have lavished care on their conversion: the theatrical dining and drawing rooms, the fern-filled atrium, the antiques and the *objets* impose grandeur on lowly origins – and bougainvillea and oleander defy the sierra with every flower. Each plush and pampering guest room has a different hue; bathrooms and air conditioning are new; and double doors open onto a shared, covered patio stuffed full of sofas, paintings and plants. Breakfast is an easy-going occasion while dinner – book in advance, and don't expect to eat until late – is a serious matter. Dishes are a mix of regional and international, vegetables are from the garden, fish from the port, there are English steamed puddings, good wines and barbecues by the pool. Walking for the hardy in the cooler months, the beaches for summer, riding all year round. No sound – just the chirruping of a thousand cicadas.

rooms	5 twins/doubles.
price	€80–€90. Singles €60–€70.
meals	Dinner €30–€35.
closed	Christmas & New Year.
directions	From N-340/E-7 exit 520 for Turre & Mojácar. 3km on, right through entrance to Cortijo Grande. Finca on right after 3.5 km, signed.

	Graeme Gibson & David Rice
tel	+34 950 479094
fax	+34 950 479094
email	listonero@wanadoo.es
web	www.fincalistonero.com

Map 25 Entry 340

Hostal Mirador del Castillo

Mojácar Pueblo, 04638 Mojácar, Almería

Its slogan is *el punto mas alto* ('the highest point') and that it most certainly is! There was once a fortified castle up here; it was rebuilt in 1960 as a private home and now houses the cultural events of the Foundation FAMA. This wedding-cake-white interpretation of a Moorish fortification may not be to everyone's taste, but don't be put off: this is a sensational spot. You get all-round views of the village, the valley, the mountains and the sea… and there's an enchanting walled garden, too. The bedrooms, three en suite, are well and simply furnished and the whole atmosphere of the place relaxed and happy. For late breakfasts (11am on), light meals and matchless views there's a café/bar, while regular chamber music concerts and jazz in the garden add to the cultural feel. Come for multi-levelled B&B – or make up a party of friends and rent the entire house… perfect for 10, with its Andalucían garden with pool, and vast salon with grand piano and Moroccan-style open fire. *Reservations for whole house required three months in advance.*

rooms	5 twins/doubles.
price	€48-€76. House for 10: €1,930 (four nights). VAT included.
meals	Breakfast €6. Lunch/dinner €14. VAT included. Café closed Wed afternoon & Thurs out of season.
closed	Rarely.
directions	Almería-Murcia E-15; exit 520 Mojácar via Turre. Continue to junc.; right. At top bear left past bar into square; 1st left. Park at top; climb stairs to entrance.

	Juan Cecilio Cano
tel	+34 950 473022
email	info@elcastillomojacar.com
web	www.elcastillomojacar.com

Map 25 Entry 341

Hotel Tikar

Ctra Garrucha - Vera s/n, 04630 Garrucha, Almería

Don't worry that the Tikar is a few blocks from the busy beach and next to a main road – wait and see what's inside. This is not just a hotel, but an art gallery and restaurant too – run with warmth and charm by Beatriz and Sean. The jolly colour scheme – ochre, white and blue – is offset by dark parquet and teak, and modern paintings (for sale) that hang on every wall. The sitting room is cosy with modern sofas, small bar and woodburning stove; bedrooms are large and extremely comfortable. Children are welcomed and well catered for, too; Beatriz and Sean have two young sons of their own. Relax on the rooftop terrace, watch the sea, take a dip in the modest pool. And do eat in: the hotel's trump card is its restaurant, which has a devoted local following. The food is an inventive mix of Californian (vegetables, light sauces, seafood) and traditional Spanish. Plenty of vegetarian dishes too, and a list of over 75 interesting wines – Sean knows his stuff. Garrucha, not the prettiest of fishing ports, has nevertheless an authentic Spanish feel and the lively afternoon fish market is well worth witnessing.

rooms	6 twins/doubles.
price	€57–€130.
meals	Lunch €15 set menu.
	Dinner €19.50 set menu.
closed	15 December–15 January.
directions	From N-340/E-15, exit 534 for Garrucha. Pass Vera & continue round outskirts of Garrucha. Straight on at r'bout. Hotel on right.

	Beatriz Gallego & Sean McMahon
tel	+34 950 617131
fax	+34 950 617132
email	hoteltikar@hoteltikar.com
web	www.hoteltikar.com

Map 25 Entry 342

Las Almendras

Bda. Los Herreras s/n, 04271 Lubrín, Almería

You approach down the proverbial long and winding road, past marble quarries and through barren land… just as you begin to wonder whether the drive is worth it, into view comes the restored Andalucían goat farm, 100 years old and charming. In the garden: a vine-draped terrace for summer dining and a mountain-water plunge pool, tomatoes and herbs popping up among the flowers, bird- and cicada-song in the air. Apricot and lemon trees surround the barbecue area; olive and almond groves stretch beyond. In the cottage for guests you share a sitting room with books and woodburner, a gallery kitchen for coffee and tea, an honesty bar and a fridge of cool drinks. Bedrooms are white-raftered and sweetly furnished; the Blue Room has a double bed perfectly positioned for mountain-gazing. If you love good food, come here: herbs from the garden and eggs from the neighbour, spicy tangines and village-reared ham, almond tart with citrus and sherry… breakfasts may be "full Spanglish". The little-known Sierra de los Filabres waits to be unravelled; let your friendly hosts advise.

rooms	4 twins/doubles.
price	€60. Singles €45. VAT included.
meals	Lunch €8. Dinner €18.
closed	Rarely.
directions	From Almería, N-340 for Huercal Overa. Left at Sorbas for Lubrín on Ruta Valle del Fonte. Pass Lubrín to La Rambla Aljibe; left for Albanchez, through Los Herreras. 50m past sign, left for house.

	Oliver & Helen Robinson
tel	+34 950 528587
email	lasalmendras@terra.es
web	www.lasalmendras.com

Map 25 Entry 343

balearics & canary islands

Les Terrasses

Ctra. de Santa Eularia km1, Apartado 1235, 07800 Ibiza

Françoise Pialoux has crafted, planted and furnished a remarkable vision in this hidden corner of Ibiza. She is an immensely likeable, vivacious woman and her character infuses every corner of her exquisite terraced hotel. The old farmstead (a bus ride from Ibiza) stands alone on a knoll surrounded by Ibizan lushery and bamboo-fringed terraces; every room gets one. Steps lead to secret corners, shaded hammocks and expansive views, there's a state-of-the-art tennis court and two delicious pools. In the sitting room are deep sofas, books, a piano. The bedrooms are on different levels, some in the main house, others outside, perfectly private and secluded. No two are the same. Expect pure colours, white embroidered bedspreads, open hearths, Moroccan tiles, candelabras, heavenly bathrooms. Choose where and when you'd like to breakfast – by one of the pools, in the house or in your room. And stay for dinner; Tuesdays is couscous night and people come from everywhere. A chic, bohemian retreat; there's no more tranquil place to unwind. Be sure to book in advance.

rooms	9: 8 twins/doubles, 1 suite.
price	€155–€255. Singles €110–€150. Suite €210–€270.
meals	Lunch €20. Dinner €30.
closed	15 November–February.
directions	From Ibiza for Santa Eularia; after 9km on right, at blue-painted rock, right; up track, farm on left.

	Françoise Pialoux
tel	+34 971 332643
fax	+34 971 338978
email	lesterrasses@interbook.net
web	www.lesterrasses.net

Map 26 Entry 344

Es Passarell

2a Vuelta No. 117, 07200 Felanitx, Mallorca

Es Passarell is testimony to the boundless energy of María Dolores ('Lola') who saw in these old stones a vision of better things. Now you approach the isolated farm through swathes of palm, vine, honeysuckle, geranium, almond, citrus and fig. You're one of the family here: cats, dogs, frogs, and Lola – relaxed and happy to speak English. The rambling house is great for families, with a 'nursery' in the video room should parents be planning the occasional escape. You choose between self-catering and B&B here: apartments are simple, with an extra sofabed in the sitting room and a private terrace; B&B rooms are big, cool and mostly on the ground floor, the newest with white walls, the oldest with sloping rafters. There are bright rugs and cushions, lace drapes, dried flowers, intimate terraces and, everywhere, that delicious whiff of linseed used to treat beam and tile. New is a Moroccan tented area in the garden, sensibly set right by the pool. Breakfast is buffet and big, there are gourmet dinners twice-weekly, and the cellar is stocked with delicious and generously discounted wines. *A Rusticae hotel*

rooms	6 + 6: 6 twins/doubles. 6 self-catering apartments for 3.
price	€65–€110. Apartments €75–€135.
meals	Lunch/dinner €12; à la carte €25.
closed	Rarely.
directions	From Llucmajor to Porreres; here, towards Felanitx. Between km2 & km3 markers, at sharp bend, right; after 2.5km, house on right, signed.

	María Dolores Suberviola Alberdi
tel	+34 971 183091
fax	+34 971 183336
email	info@espassarell.net
web	www.espassarell.net

Map 26 Entry 345

Son Mercadal

Camino de Son Pau s/n, Apartado de Correos 52, 07260 Porreres, Mallorca

If you are looking for a blissfully comfortable bed, kind hosts, delicious food and a secluded setting, head here. The family derive great pleasure from welcoming guests to their rambling, beautifully restored farmhouse, whose every last corner is a delight. The house is a 'painting', as the Spanish would say, a measured still life of things old and rustic. José's son Toni is responsible for the decoration and his artistic eye has created a warm and harmonious mood. Most of the country antique pieces were already in the family: the grandfather clock, piano, old washstands, a complete Art Deco bedroom set, the engravings of Mallorca. And the food is of the best the island has to offer: Toni is keen for you to try the local specialities. Breakfast on the vine-shaded terrace on local sausage, cheeses, eggs from the farm, wonderful bread and Mama's watermelon jam; at dinner, on *tumbet* (the local meat-and-veg delicacy) and some of the island's very best wines. Much of what graces your table is straight from the farm, there are prize-winning horses in the stable and a large and lovely pool.

rooms	7 twins/doubles.
price	€99. Singles €75.
meals	Lunch/dinner €21, on request.
closed	Rarely.
directions	From Palma towards Santyani. Here, on far side of town, left to Porreres. Follow signs for Campos. After approx. 1.5km left at sign Son Mercadal & Son Pau. 2km of track to house; tucked away on right.

	José Roig Ripoll
tel	+34 971 181300
fax	+34 971 181300
email	son.mercadal@todoesp.es
web	www.son-mercadal.com

Map 26 Entry 346

Leon de Sineu

Carrer dels Bous 129, 07510 Sineu, Mallorca

Mellow Sineu is one of the oldest small towns of Mallorca, in the middle of the island. People have been coming to the farmers' market since 1214 – and still do (it's on Wednesdays). The bars and restaurants are another draw. The Leon is fresh, clean and welcoming, with a lovely symmetrical façade and a gorgeous cobbled garden on many levels. A large arch spans the entrance hall, beyond which is the Winter Room, a covered terrace where one can sit and admire the garden. The bedrooms, opening off a balustraded staircase of almost Parisian wrought-iron splendour, are a charming mix of dark antique beds and fresh white walls, the prettiest under the rafters. Hospitable Senora Gálmez Arbona manages to recreate the atmosphere of a Mallorcan home, and the food is something he is proud of: the Leon has one of the best restaurants in town. Breakfasts, on that lovely terrace or in the stylish vaulted dining room, are traditional Mallorcan – cheese, salami, pâté, eggs, fruit, cake. Just the thing before you squeeze into your bikini and head for the cool pool – or the beach.

rooms	8: 6 twins/doubles, 1 single, 1 suite.
price	€115–€200. Singles €90. Suite €162. VAT included.
meals	Lunch €27 à la carte. Dinner €20 set menu; €27 à la carte. VAT included.
closed	3 November–3 December.
directions	Head for town centre. Hotel signed.

	Francisca Gálmez Arbona
tel	+34 971 520211
fax	+34 971 855058
email	reservas@hotel-leondesineu.com
web	www.hotel-leondesineu.com

Map 26 Entry 347

Son Porró

Diseminados Poligono 3, Parcela 223, 07144 Costitx, Mallorca

You are at the heart of the Plá – all ancient farmhouses and equally ancient fig and almond groves. Son Porró's stone walls look old, too; the house, however, is new. It owes its existence to Pilar Sánchez, who greets you (in Spanish!) as she would an old friend: nothing is too much trouble and when guests arrive unavoidably late she'll cook a meal at midnight. Her bedrooms are very comfortable and roomy, one with huge views, the nicest off the pretty cobbled courtyard at the back; all come with modern bathrooms, satellite TV, minibar and bowls of apricots or cherries. Two apartments with kitchenettes are in the stone-built outhouses that lie just beyond the lovely pool. In Son Porró's vast lounge the bright Mallorcan *lenguas*-weave of the curtains adds zest; reddish-brown leather sofas are more sombre. What makes this place special are Pilar's lunches, dinners and barbecues – on that patio in summer, at the polished dining table in winter. She tailors her cooking to suit her guests and uses ingredients from the local markets. And friends of hers can take you out on a guided walk or ride.

rooms	6 + 2: 1 twin/double, 5 suites. 2 apartments for 4.
price	€96–€120. Suites €126–€150. Apartments from €210. VAT inc.
meals	Lunch/dinner €15.
closed	Rarely.
directions	From Palma towards Alcudía on m'way. Exit for Inca & at 2nd r'bout follow signs for Sineu. Son Porró signed on right after 9km. Down narrow bumpy road for about 1km.

	Pilar Sánchez Escribano
tel	+34 971 182013
fax	+34 971 182012

Map 26 Entry 348

Torrent Fals

Ctra. Sta. María-Sencelles km4.5, Aptdo Correos 39, 07320 Santa Maria, Mallorca

What a position! Flanked by the Trammontana mountain range, this low, golden, 15th-century farmhouse is surrounded by vineyards and plains. The views are phenomenal – especially if you get the suite with the roof terrace – and inside is just as alluring. In three years Pedro and his English wife Victoria have transformed this once-desolate ruin. Throughout, the effect is one of airy spaces and understated elegance. In the striking, uniquely-shaped sitting room (once the wine cellar), the walls are creamy stone and the high ceiling is striped with beams. Shapely arches lead from uncluttered bedrooms to delectable marble bathrooms. Cool chic and latest mod cons notwithstanding, the place has a real feeling of warmth and comfort, much enhanced by Pedro's friendliness and energy. He's receptionist, gardener and cook: duck and fish are a house special and the fruit and veg are grown on his brother's allotment. He can even be found hard at work cleaning the swimming pool – vast and magnificent, and designed to allow water to escape in a tantalising trickle at either end. *A Rusticae hotel.*

rooms	8: 2 twins/doubles, 6 suites.
price	€140. Suite €160. VAT included.
meals	Dinner €25, on request.
closed	Rarely.
directions	From Palma PM-27 for Inca/Alcudía. Right on PM-303 before Santa María for Sencelles. Torrent Fals on left short way up track, before Biniali. Look out for signpost.

	Pedro Cañellas Llabrés
tel	+34 971 144584
fax	+34 971 144191
email	pjcanellas@terra.es
web	www.torrentfals.com

Map 26 Entry 349

Scott's Hotel

Plaza de la Iglesia 12, 07350 Binissalem, Mallorca

Your English and cosmopolitan hosts have created a glamorous, intimate, English hotel out of a grand seignorial townhouse in the centre of old Binissalem; you'll be blissfully comfortable. Enormous beds were handmade in England, goosedown pillows were brought over from Germany, and bedspreads and Percale sheets from New York. "Pretty came second," says George, but pretty Scott's most certainly is and a night here is an experience to remember. Suites have any number of exquisite decorative touches and the feel is fresh, light and elegant; here an 18th-century Japanese print, there a grandfather clock, perhaps a Bokhara rug or a chaise longue. All are large and luxurious, at the front overlooking the church square, at the back the lovely patio-courtyard. Breakfast out here till late, and dine in the hotel's bistro, a seven-minute walk: candles, damask, fresh flowers, Gershwin tinkling in the background and simple but sumptuous food. You get your own front door key, an honesty bar and a small indoor pool: more lavish private house than hotel.

rooms	17: 11 twin/doubles, 6 suites.
price	€175-€205. Singles €131-€154. Suites €235-€330.
meals	Dinner €23, €32 à la carte.
closed	Rarely.
directions	From airport for Palma, PM-27 (Via de Cintura) for Inca. Exit km17 for Binissalem. Next to church; discreet brass plaque by entrance.

	George Scott
tel	+34 971 870100
fax	+34 971 870267
email	stay@scottshotel.com
web	www.scottshotel.com

Map 26 Entry 350

Scott's Galilea

Costa Den Mandons 3, 07195 Galilea, Mallorca

From your private terrace, you look down over the tiled roofs of lovely Galilea, across a green valley and on to the sea. Mallorca's most heavenly views? Possibly. Certainly these are some of the island's most heavenly holiday homes – designed in 1978 as an artists colony. Perfected since, each studio suite and house has a deliciously rustic-chic feel. Whitewashed walls and splashes of colour, integrated stone bookcases (with books), open fireplaces, ultra-stylish bathrooms. The handmade beds are blissful, "the best that money can buy" – super-big, dressed in crisp linen with goosedown pillows and copious cushions; insomniacs will succumb. And there's no such thing as oversleeping here: breakfast is served until noon. As for other meals, you could prepare your own. On the other hand, why bother? A chef appears three times a week to cook dinner, and there are barbecues on Sundays. A tapas bar is within walking distance, or you could have a single-dish meal delivered from Scott's Bistro. Two acres of garden and a dreamy pool... privacy and tranquillity reign. *Children over 12 welcome.*

rooms	2 houses for 2; 1 house for 4; 6 studios for 2.
price	€250-€270 for 2; €300-€330 for 4; studio €175-€205.
meals	Self-catering. Breakfast included. Dinner served three times p.w. in season. Restaurants nearby.
closed	Rarely.
directions	Airport-Palma; exit right onto 'V de cintura' for 'Puigpuynent' to Galilea. Follow signs to top, ignore dead end on right, down steep path on left.

	George Scott
tel	+34 971 870100
fax	+34 971 870267
email	stay@scottsgalilea.com
web	www.scottsgalilea.com

Map 26 Entry 351

Hotel Salvia

c/de la Palma No. 18, 07100 Sóller, Mallorca

Siobhan and Brian, planning to buy a boat in Palma, fell in love with a hotel in Sóller. Now the 200-year-old townhouse, its gardens brimming with banana trees and bougainvillea, has become a cool and luxurious haven. There's elegant rusticity in the thick silk drapes, cobbled entrance hall, Irish vases stuffed with flowers, pretty chandeliers – and the bedrooms are palatial. One suite has an ornate Mallorquin bed and 20ft-high doors to the bathroom (antique mirrors, original tiled floor); another is seductively pink; all are different in layout and colour, are deeply peaceful and have valley views. The whole gorgeous place is overseen by funny, friendly, stylish Siobhan. Experience magic as you settle down to delectable tapas (once weekly, from your chef-hostess) on the vine-strewn, wicker-chaired terrace... jazz in the background, candles on the steps; there are barbecues on summer Sundays. The pool is dreamy, its fridge deliciously stocked. Sweet Sóller, the Valley of Gold to the Moors, huddles among orange groves not far from the sea – and there's a wonderful, rickety old train to Palma.

rooms	6: 2 twins/doubles, 4 suites.
price	€235-€260. Suites €290-€330.
meals	Tapas €35. Barbecue (3 courses) €50.
closed	January-February.
directions	From airport 'Vía circular' west; then Sóller. After Sóller tunnel right at 1st r'bout; over tram tracks. Right into San Niclau; next left & 1st right into c/Pala Noguera. 2nd right into c/de la Palma at bottom.

	Siobhan & Brian Kearney
tel	+34 971 634936
fax	+34 971 638285
email	info@hotelsalvia.com
web	www.hotelsalvia.com

Map 26 Entry 352

Hotel Agroturismo Ca's Xorc

Carretera de Deiá km56.1, 07100 Sóller, Mallorca

Spectacularly positioned high in the mountains — not the place for nervous drivers! The narrow track is entertainingly switchbacked and steep, but once you've arrived you'll not want to leave. Here, with views down to the sea, you're cocooned in luxury and peace, and looked after by friendly, impeccably trained staff. The bedrooms are serene, simple and beautiful, the views stunning. If you're in a deluxe room, you'll have your own private terrace where you can sit and watch the sun subside into the sea between twin mountain peaks. Ca's Xorc was originally two fincas, the earlier 300 years old, the other a mere half that age. The Ploenzkes have transformed it. The once-bare gardens are now lush and exotic, with terraces and lawns, a Moroccan-style gazebo, an aviary of flamboyant parrots and a bridge arching over a swimming pool that appears to spill into the valley below. Despite all this splendour (Ca's Xorc attracts the rich and famous), the owners strive to be eco-friendly and grow their own fruit, veg and herbs. You'll be warmly welcomed by the striking, multi-lingual Britta.

rooms	12 twins/doubles.
price	€160–€290. VAT included.
meals	Lunch €60. Dinner €65.
closed	Mid-November–mid-February.
directions	From airport on Vía Cintura for Andratx; exit for Sóller. After tunnel and village take road for Deiá on the left. At km marker 56.1; left and after 800m you'll see the car park on left.

	Britta Ploenzke
tel	+34 971 638280
fax	+34 971 632949
email	stay@casxorc.com
web	www.casxorc.com

Map 26 Entry 353

Son Canals

Apartamento 3F, Son Canals, Deià, Mallorca

Come for one of the most magical villages in the Baleriacs, perched between the mountains and the deep blue sea. Robert Graves was one of the first to discover its beauty; artists, writers and musicians followed, now one of its restaurants has a Michelin star. In this attractively renovated red-stone building are two excellent holiday homes – owned by David, friendly and helpful, who lives nearby. The beamed one-floor apartment has a terrace, the duplex has two – and a little garden. Otherwise the spaces are much the same: open-plan living areas, well-equipped kitchens, double and twin bedrooms, luxurious bathrooms, and views – what more could you desire? Décor is fresh and modern, there are white walls, blue sofas and yellow cushions, patterned curtains and tiled floors, music and TV. Walkers and birdwatchers come in spring, autumn, winter; sun-lovers from May to September. Choose between snorkelling and swimming in the pine-fringed cove with pebbled beach, a bus ride to elegant Palma, and wild coastal walks to Soller with the treat of tram and bus home. *Uninspected at time of going to press.*

rooms	2 apartments for 4.
price	€400–€900 per week.
meals	Self-catering.
closed	Rarely.
directions	From Soller, through Deià (Deya); just outside village, 50m after last entrance to Residencia Hotel; entrance gate on left.

	David Hare
tel	+34 971 639438
email	info@deyamallorca.com
web	www.deyamallorca.com

Map 26 Entry 354

Fornalutx Petit Hotel

c/Alba 22, 07109 Fornalutx, Mallorca

Whether the nuns who lived here until the 1920s chose this spot for its setting we'll never know – but this is its trump card. Fornalutx is said to be the loveliest village in Spain and this peaceful hotel has inspirational views. (Pay more for a room with a view – it's worth it.) In the tranquil garden, stretch out with a book in the shade of the citrus trees – source of the wondrous orange juice squeezed and served at breakfast by Isabel and her helpers. A delicious small pool and jacuzzi provide cool in high summer, and there's a sauna. Indoors, a series of bright, appealing rooms with a rustic-minimalist feel. Large, high-ceilinged bedrooms are simply furnished, colourful abstracts by local artists brightening the cool colours of the walls, while a breakfast room in the cavernous cellar makes a charming wet-weather alternative to the alfresco version on the terrace. The cobbled cul-de-sac street outside (traffic is virtually non-existent) is your departure point for the beautiful town of Soller just down the valley, and the pretty resort of Puerto de Soller lies a few miles beyond.

rooms	8: 6 twins/doubles, 2 suites.
price	€129–€139. Singles €77. Suites €181–€226.
meals	Good restaurants nearby.
closed	Rarely.
directions	From airport ring road west; exit for Puerto de Soller. After Bunyola through tunnel. At Soller towards Fornalutx. There, park in public car park after shops; head down towards river; c/Alba on right.

	Patricio Roig Monjo
tel	+34 971 631997
fax	+34 971 635026
email	info@fornalutxpetithotel.com
web	www.fornalutxpetithotel.com

Map 26 Entry 355

Ca'n Reus

Carrer de l'Auba 26, 07109 Fornalutx, Mallorca

Few villages in southern Europe have quite such a heart-stopping natural setting. Fornalutx is in the middle of Mallorca's rumpled spine, sandwiched between the craggy loveliness of the Puig Major and the Puig del'Ofre. Artists, sculptors and writers discovered the village long ago yet the place has kept its charm. Light, elegant C'an Reus was built in faux-Parisian style by a returning emigrant – with none of the ostentatiousness that some of the *casas de Indianos* are wont to display. The entrance hall is stunning and the bedrooms are to die for, with their original floors, 19th-century Mallorquin beds, crisp white bedcovers and simply mesmerising views. Owner Sue Guthrie has breathed new life into the whole gorgeous place, and introduced a delightful mix of Englishness and exoticism: deckchairs in the garden, candles up the stairs, perfect towels from John Lewis. At breakfast, local cheeses and sausages, homemade marmalades and tarts as you gaze on more loveliness from the steeply terraced garden – and sociable dinners cooked once a week by Sue. It's friendly, peaceful, special.

rooms	8 twins/doubles.
price	€110–€150. VAT included.
meals	Dinner available €30; Mondays or Thursdays to coincide with local restaurant's closure.
closed	Rarely.
directions	Round Palma on ring-road; exit for Soller. Through (toll) tunnel, round Soller for Puerto de Soller. At 2nd r'bout, right at signs for Fornalutx. Park in village & walk; C'an Reus in lowest street.

	Susan Guthrie
tel	+34 971 631174
fax	+34 971 631174
email	info@canreushotel.com
web	www.canreushotel.com

Map 26 Entry 356

Finca Es Castell
c/Binibona s/n, 07314 Caimari, Mallorca

One of the oldest fincas on the island has become one of the loveliest hotels. These 750 acres once yielded olive oil; today a hammock sways between the olives and a lazy pool beckons. The rambling farmhouse has been in the family for ever – along with a small mountain behind (let Paola's puppy be your guide). Now it is rented to this young English couple and has been infused with new life. A huge old olive press, a 12th-century fireplace, ancient beams: old and modern meet in a glowing restoration. New are the chunky terracotta floors, the chestnut tables twinkling with night lights, the curly wrought-iron terrace chairs, the pretty beds, the fresh bathrooms, the paintings on whitewashed walls. The inner courtyard is rustically dotted with pots and overflows with green. You can't help but warm to this lovely place, and the setting is sensational: watch the sun dipping down over the Tramuntana mountain ranges as you dine (well) on one of three terraces. The old finca is surrounded by palms, pines, olives – and a grassed area where classes are sometimes held (best to check). Mallorcan heaven.

rooms	12 twins/doubles.
price	€124-€200.
meals	Dinner €30. Not Wednesday.
closed	January
directions	From airport for Palma; exit 3 for Viá Cintura; exit for Inca. There, towards Lluc & Selva. After Selva, road on right for Es Castell; on for 3km. At entrance of Finca-Hotel Binibona, right; 0.5km.

	Paola Cassini & James Hiscock
tel	+34 971 875154
fax	+34 971 875154
email	es-castell@terra.es
web	www.fincaescastell.com

Map 26 Entry 357

Can Furiós

Camí Vell de Binibona 11, 07314 Binibona-Caimari, Mallorca

A year ago Can Furiós was one of the most upmarket of Mallorca's country house hotels. Then Adrian and Susy swept in with an impeccable new broom and turned it into an even better place to stay. It is in the hamlet of Binibona – no shops, six small hotels – on the stunning, sheltered, eastern flank of the Tramuntana Sierra. Impossible to believe that a decade ago the building was in ruins... now terraced gardens with palm, olive and citrus trees wrap themselves luxuriously round both pool and smartly renovated 16th-century house. There's a lovely sociable terrace for pre-dinner drinks – and dinners, served at formally dressed tables in the old farm's almond press, are delectable, fresh seafood being the house speciality. The bedrooms are in the main house and the suites in the farmworkers' cottages: all are cosy, traditional and very comfortable, with oriental rugs on tiled floors, best English mattresses and patterned drapes. Extra touches include white bathrobes and Crabtree & Evelyn soaps – and torches for jasmine-scented strolls after dark. Adrian and Susy have thought of everything.

rooms	7: 3 twins/doubles, 4 suites.
price	€150–€200. Suites €180–€280.
meals	Lunch €10–€14 set menu. Dinner €37.
closed	14 December–14 February.
directions	From Palma, PM-27 m'way N to Inca. There, follow signs to Selva & Binibona. Final couple of km on small country roads. Can Furiós on square in Binibona.

	Adrian & Susy Bertorelli
tel	+34 971 515751
fax	+34 971 875366
email	info@can-furios.com
web	www.can-furios.com

Map 26 Entry 358

Posada de Lluc

Roser Vell 11, 07460 Pollensa, Mallorca

Pollensa, as old as the Middle Ages, is a charming town, long a favourite of painters; 21st-century galleries are mushrooming in the old town, and art furnishes many of this hotel's walls. The Posada has an interesting history. Built for a medieval nobleman it became a sanctuary for monks in 1459 – a handy place to decamp to after visiting the monastery at Lluc; today it is a more prosperous retreat. The two-year-old hotel stands in a quiet, narrow street, so don't expect lavish views or acres of land. But do expect space: behind that inconspicuous façade lie an unexpectedly large, airy, cobbled entrance hall, eight immaculate bedrooms and a super new pool. Furniture is antique Mallorquin, sofas are modern, chandeliers come from the glass factory in Campanet, and all is modesty and elegance, down the chess set (do play). Joana ensures you get the best local produce at breakfast and is always happy to advise. The bedrooms are large, peaceful (particularly the poolside ones), uncluttered and cool, with beams, stone floors and white or open-stone walls. A perfect, small-town hotel.

rooms	8 twins/doubles.
price	€95–€140.
meals	Restaurants nearby.
closed	December & January.
directions	From airport for Palma; m'way for Inca & Alcudia. 20km after Inca left exit to Pollensa. After 11km left into Pollensa. Follow road left up Carrer Roser Vell.

	Joana Vives Cánaves
tel	+34 971 535220
fax	+34 971 535222
email	info@posadalluc.com
web	www.posadalluc.com

Map 26 Entry 359

Son Siurana

Ctra. Palma-Alcudia km45, 07400 Alcudía, Mallorca

The family has been here for 200 years and the latest two generations have given the estate a new lease of life. Although you are close to Pollensa Port and Alcudía, this is a deep retreat, surrounded by fig and almond groves and sheep-grazed pastures. The main house is a long, low and graceful stone building, its doors and windows highlighted by light and elegant *marés*, or surrounds. Life in summer centres around a large terrace with woodburning stove that looks onto a luxurious pool sculpted in among the rocks. Beyond, ancient pines, lakes and a vegetable and herb garden that supplies Siurana's kitchen: guests can pick their favourite vegetables for the twice-weekly dinners. You stay in one of eight stylish self-catering cottages which have been slotted into the farm's outbuildings. The beautiful rooms have hand-painted tiles, terracotta or wooden floors, good modern furniture and delicious antiques – design mag photographers have flocked to write about the place. Breakfast is served in the main house, on the terrace or in your cottage. Sensational. *A Rusticae hotel.*

rooms	1 + 8: 1 suite. 5 self-catering cottages for 2; 1 cottage for 4; 2 apartments for 4.
price	Suite €105-€148. Cottages/apartments €114-€238.
meals	Breakfast €10. Lunch €10. Dinner €25-€30 (Tuesday & Thursday only).
closed	Rarely.
directions	From Palma towards Alcudía. Left for Son Siurana opposite km45 marker.

	Montse Roselló
tel	+34 971 549662
fax	+34 971 549788
email	info@sonsiurana.com
web	www.sonsiurana.com

Map 26 Entry 360

Agroturismo Finca Son Pons

Ctra Búger-Sa Pobla, 07311 Búger, Mallorca

This pink and cream farmhouse is several centuries old, set deep in a vast country estate and surrounded by woodland – an impressive, lone palm tree, dwarfing the rough stone walls, stands guard. Sit on the wide terrace edged with stone water troughs, or in a wicker chair by the 16th-century well, and savour the silence. Behind the house is a big garden, with well-kept lawns and plenty of shady patios – perfect for watching the wildlife. Rabbits hop across the grass and exotic birds from the nearby nature reserve drop by. There's a large modern pool, too, beside a bougainvillea-swathed patio. The house is equally appealing inside, with stone walls, beams and lots of old Mallorquin furniture. The big bedrooms are all different, full of intriguing features and original artwork. Your hosts are an immensely friendly, multilingual French family. Toni and his son do the cooking which is excellent – a super breakfast, and dinner on request a couple of times a week. They'll even do you a packed lunch if you want to spend the day exploring the countryside on foot or on horseback. And the beaches are 12 minutes away.

rooms	6: 1 twin/double, 5 suites.
price	€45. Suites €62-€85.
meals	Dinner €21, on request. VAT inc.
closed	Rarely.
directions	From Palma towards Alcudía; here follow signs for Búger. From centre of Búger take road to Sa Pobla (also signposted to Son Pons). Hotel 1.3km further on left.

	Inés Siquier & Christophe Bedos
tel	+34 649 453776
fax	+34 971 50 91 65
email	finca@sonpons.com
web	www.sonpons.com

Map 26 Entry 361

Fínca Son Gener

Ctra. Vieja Son Servera-Artà km3, Apartado de Correos 136, 07550 Son Servera, Mallorca

Not a family hotel, nor a place for the gregarious, but an architect-owned paradise on the brow of an olive-groved hill. The once-dilapidated farm buildings have become an understatedly elegant small hotel, miles from the bronzing crowds. Impeccable lawns frame the house with its gently luminous *maré* facade; there are palms, roses, bougainvillea and exotic trees. The interior is a celebration of light and form: old rafters, limestone floors, neutral natural colours and carefully selected sofas, plants and flowers. Art ranges from striking abstact-modern to rich mock-renaissance. It is calming and uplifting, with each lofty bedroom a cool haven in summer, and as snug as toast in winter. Ground-floor rooms overlook the courtyard, upstairs ones get the views; all have fine Mallorquin linen and private terraces. Some rooms have a more rustic mood, and their own fireplaces. The gym, spa and saltwater swimming pools, one out, one in, share the same purity of style – and you breakfast and dine on one of many patios, each lovelier than the last. Exclusive and exquisite.

rooms	10 suites.
price	€250. VAT included.
meals	Lunchtime snacks. Dinner €35. VAT included. Restaurant closed Tuesday.
closed	1 December–15 January.
directions	From Palma to Manacor. There on for Artá. Through Sant Llorenc; 2km before Artá right on 403-1. Signed on left after 3km.

	Aina Pastor
tel	+34 971 183612
fax	+34 971 183591
email	hotel@songener.com
web	www.songener.com

Map 26 Entry 362

Alcaufar Vell Hotel de Agroturismo

Ctra. de Cala Alcaufar km8, 07710 Sant Lluís, Menorca

The house is old, its 14th-century Moorish tower added to down the centuries, along with the grandiose 1773 façade. Six generations of the family have lived here and much of the beautiful furniture remains. An entry in the guest book reads: "We came for one night and then booked for four, we stayed for eleven... need we say more?". There is a lot of heart in this family home, run by María Angeles and son Jaume in the finest Spanish tradition of *mi casa es tu casa*. You get three sitting rooms, one with a vast inglenook... and books, agricultural implements and a serenely Spanish, uncluttered feel. The dining room is grander with blue and white stucco and Art Nouveau floor tiles. Outside, a beautiful pool set in manicured lawns, and a roof terrace that gazes over 160 acres of wild olive trees. Feast at breakfast on fruit and honey from the farm, local sausage and bread from a wood-fired oven, as you catch a glimpse of the sparkling sea (white beaches a 10-minute drive). At dinner relish the best of Menorcan. Then retire to lofty bedrooms and great big bathrooms – enchanting like all the rest.

rooms	12: 4 twins/doubles, 8 suites.
price	€126–€198. VAT included.
meals	Dinner €25. VAT included.
closed	December-mid-March
directions	From airport towards Maó, then to Sant Lluís. Just before Sant Lluís turn for Cala Alcaufar. Pass turning for Punta Prima, then 2nd turning to right. Signed.

	Jaume de Febrer & Maria Angeles de Olives
tel	+34 971 151874
fax	+34 971 151492
email	hotel@alcaufarvell.com
web	www.alcaufarvell.com

Map 26 Entry 363

Hotel Rural Biniarroca

Camí Vell 57, 07710 Sant Lluís, Menorca

Biniarroca once was a working farm; now it is a place of luxurious beauty.
Sheelagh, a designer, once ran a guest house on the island, Lindsay is a painter
whose light-filled creations grace antique-filled rooms. Together they have created
something very special on this flat tract of land that leads down to Menorca's
southern coast. A solitary palm stands sentinel over the cobbled courtyard; to one
side is an elegant pool. Plumbago and bougainvillea festoon the façade of the old
farmhouse; the oleander- and tamarisk-strewn gardens and shaded terraces are
enchanting. Bedrooms are stylish and beautiful, with generous beds, antiques, oil
paintings and optional extras including internet access. Those in the old stables
have their own private terraces and a second pool. The restaurant is another draw
and the food sophisticated mediterranean: fish ocean-fresh, vegetables organic and
home-grown. Breakfasts are as delicious as you would expect: a cornucopia of
cheeses, breads, fruits, pastries. Peace reigns – apart from the cockerel's crow.
Impossible to imagine a more stylish or tranquil place – perfect for couples.

rooms	18 twins/doubles.
price	€120–€225. Singles €75. VAT inc.
meals	Light lunches €10. Dinner €40 à la carte. Restaurant closed Sundays.
closed	November–March.
directions	From airport towards Maó, then to Sant Lluís. Here, follow signs for Alcaufar; 1st left for Es Castell. Biniarroca signed on left after 2km.

	Lindsay Mullen & Sheelagh Ratliffe
tel	+34 971 150059
fax	+34 971 151250
email	hotel@biniarroca.com
web	www.biniarroca.com

Map 26 Entry 364

Hotel Rural Las Calas

c/El Arenal 36, La Lechuza-Vega de San Mateo, 35320 Las Palmas, Gran Canaria

Hide away in the hills, below the peaks of Gran Canaria. This is a relaxed and relaxing little hotel (friendly dogs, an easy feel), converted from a century-old building. Abundant wood, stone walls, warm colours and traditional Canarian furnishings are tempered by splashes of restrained modernism; the predominating peace may be broken by the laughter of friends popping in for one of owner Magüi's parties. The generously sized rooms, each with its own personality, open onto a courtyard garden – just the spot for browsing your pick of the hotel's library. If you get restless, scrump some fruit from the orchard – with Magüi's permission, of course; she turns most of it into delectable jam. When evening comes, you could dine in on some typical Canarian cuisine – around the canopied table much of the year. Beyond the hotel lie the protected natural havens of the Cumbre and Pino Santo. Explore on horseback; there's an equestrian centre nearby. Vega de San Mateo is the nearest small town with a colourful cattle fair and farmers' market at the weekends, an ethnographic museum and a pretty church.

rooms	7: 6 twins/doubles, 1 suite.
price	€76–€98; single €60–€74; suite €96–€118
meals	Half-board €20 extra p.p. Dinner available.
closed	Rarely.
directions	Airport-Tafira; after Santa Brigida, Vega de San Mateo; follow sign at end of village for Tejeda; cont. to lane on left, signed La Lechuza; pass football field on left, & turn down lane (opp. main road); signed.

	Raul Ortega
tel	+34 928 661436
fax	+34 928 660753
email	reserva@hotelrurallascalas.com
web	www.hotelrurallascalas.com

Map 22 Entry 365

Hotel Rural El Patio

Finca Malpaís 11, El Guincho, 38450 Garachico, Tenerife

Much comfort, a fabulous setting and not a sound, other than the dawn chorus and the distant swish of waves breaking on the shore. El Patio sits in one of the oldest and lushest banana plantations in Tenerife. Rustically elegant bedrooms, each opening out onto a balcony, are housed in three separate buildings, each with a fascinating history. The listed 16th-century mansion and its 25-acre estate have been in the Ponte family for 500 years, and signs of the past are delightfully present: a 1565 chapel at the entrance to the estate, a 400-year-old dragon tree on the exuberant patio. But time has not stood still, and now you have a heated swimming pool, a solarium, a fitness room, a tennis court and even a golf-practice area for your pleasure. A Canarian aristocrat, Baltasar Ponte Machado is a plain-speaking man who has strict rules – rules designed to make you feel at home. He gives you keys to the bar – just help yourself and settle up when you leave – and to the front door, so you may come and go as you please.

rooms	26 twins/doubles.
price	€64–€111.
meals	Dinner from €15.
closed	17 May–23 July.
directions	From the airport on motorway towards Puerto de la Cruz & Icod de los Viños. Hotel 4km after Icod towards Garachico.

	Baltasar Ponte Machado
tel	+34 922 133280
fax	+34 922 830089
email	reservas@hotelpatio.com
web	www.hotelpatio.com

Map 22 Entry 366

Hotel Rural La Quinta Roja

Glorieta de San Francisco S/N, 38450 Garachico, Tenerife

If you have never ventured beyond the coastal resorts of Tenerife, Garachico is a treat. Its baroque architecture includes palaces, convents, churches – and this mansion, built for the Marquis of La Quinta Roja, Lord Bailiff of Tenerife. If you're interested in the history of the building and the region, Paloma knows it all. The 17th-century exterior may seem forbidding, and, disconcertingly, you enter via a shop selling local products. But, once inside, visions of a grand lifestyle are instantly realised. Hand-carved wood on a monumental scale, a vast wraparound gallery, oak planked floors, ancient stone and, in the middle of it all, a richly planted courtyard patio with original marble fountain. The building has been effectively and sympathetically converted, wood being the dominant feature. Bedrooms vary in size but all are comfortable and well furnished in modern style. Some were once used as grain stores for the Marquis's cattle – hard to imagine now. If you feel like being pampered, visit the spa: treatments are free. And so are the mountain bikes – explore!

rooms	20: 16 doubles, 4 suites.
price	€90-€180.
meals	Restaurants in village.
closed	Rarely.
directions	From Tenerife airport towards Puerto de la Cruz, Icod de los Viños & Garachico.

	Paloma Moriana
tel	+34 922 133377
fax	+34 922 133360
email	hotelquintaroja@quintaroja.com
web	www.quintaroja.com

Map 22 Entry 367

Hotel San Roque

Esteban de Ponte 32, 38450 Garachico, Tenerife

The brochure will lure you straight to the Isla Baja: 'secret Tenerife'. The 17th-century mansion has been transformed into a peaceful, exclusive, family-run hotel – the first to open in Garachico. Wood and steel, geometric shapes and earthy colours have been introduced with a flourish. It is bold yet subtle, and lavish. An immaculately dressed bed floating on a sea of dark-polished parquet, a new Deco rug, heavy linen curtains, contemporary art. Each room is different, each good-looking, with big old rafters and a passing nod to 1930s design. At every turn the eye is drawn to something striking, such as the soaring steel sculpture in the courtyard – a chic outdoor space with original wraparound wooden balcony transformed by terracotta walls, white armchairs and potted aspidistras. Puritans will be unsettled for there are far too many opportunities for decadence: sauna, pool, music, tennis, Canarian cuisine, breakfast as late as you want. Garachico is ancient and intimate, enveloped by mountains and sea. There is everything, and nothing, to do. *Golfing discounts available. A Rusticae hotel.*

rooms	20: 16 doubles, 4 suites.
price	€175-€228. Suite €259-€312.
meals	Light lunch €10. Dinner €25.
closed	Rarely.
directions	From southern airport m'way past Santa Cruz, La Laguna & Puerto de la Cruz. On past San Juan de la Rambla & Icod de los Viños to Garachico. Here, 4th left into cobbled street; 1st left. On right.

	Dominique Carayón Sabater
tel	+34 922 133435
fax	+34 922 133406
email	info@hotelsanroque.com
web	www.hotelsanroque.com

Map 22 Entry 368

Useful vocabulary

Before arriving

Do you have a room free tonight?
¿Tiene una habitación libre para hoy?

How much does it cost?
¿Cuánto cuesta?

Do you have any wedding or conference parties booked?
¿Tienen alguna boda, comuniones o conferencia esos días?

We'll be arriving at about 7pm.
Vamos a llegar sobre las siete.

We're lost.
Estamos perdidos.

We'll be arriving late.
Vamos a llegar tarde.

Do you have animals?
¿Tienen animales?

I'm allergic to cats/dogs.
Soy alérgico/a a los gatos/los perros.

We'd like to have dinner.
Nos gustaría cenar.

On arrival

Hello! I'm Mr/Mrs Sawday.
¡Hola! Soy el señor/la señora Sawday.

We found your name in this book.
Le hemos encontrado en este libro.

Where can we leave the car?
¿Dónde podemos dejar el coche?

Could you help us with our bags?
¿Podría ayudarnos con las maletas?

Could I put this food/drink in your fridge?
¿Podría dejar esta comida/bebida en su nevera?

Could I heat up a baby's bottle?
¿Podría calentar este biberón?

Can you put an extra bed in our room?
¿Es posible darnos una cama supletoria?

Things you need/that go wrong

Do you have an extra pillow/blanket?
¿Podría dejarnos otra almohada/manta?

A light bulb needs replacing.
Hay que cambiar una bombilla.

The heating isn't on.
No está encendida la calefacción.

Can you show us how the AC works?
¿Como funciona el aire, por favor?

Photos Jose Navarro

Do you have an aspirin?
¿Tendría una aspirina?

Could you turn the volume down?
¿Podría bajar un poco el volumen?

How the house/hotel works
When does breakfast begin?
¿A partir de qué hora dan el desayuno?

We'd like to order some drinks.
Querríamos tomar algo.

Can the children play in the garden?
¿Pueden jugar fuera los niños?

Can we leave the children with you?
¿Podemos dejar los niños con vosotros?

We have a problem with the plumbing.
Tenemos un problema de fontanería.

Can we eat breakfast in our room?
¿Podría/mos desayunar en nuestra habitación?

Do you have a quieter room?
¿Tiene una habitación más tranquila?

Local information
Where can we get some petrol?
¿Dónde hay una gasolinera?

Where can I hang these wet clothes?
¿Dónde puedo colgar esta ropa mojada?

Where can we find a garage to fix our car?
¿Dónde hay un taller de coches?

Where can I dry these wet boots?
¿Dónde puedo secar estas botas?

How far is the nearest shop?
¿Dónde está la tienda más cercana?

Could we have some soap, please?
¿Podría darnos jabón, por favor?

Could we have some hot water please?
¿Podría darnos agua caliente, por favor?

We need a doctor.
Necesitamos un médico.

Useful vocabulary

This is a wonderful place.
Este lugar es maravilloso.

Eating in/or out
What is today's set menu?
¿Qué tienen hoy de menú?

What do you recommmend?
¿Qué recomienda?

What vegetarian dishes do you have?
¿Qué platos vegetarianos tienen?

We'd like to see the wine list.
Nos gustaría ver la carta de vinos, por favor.

Do you have some salt/pepper?
¿Me podría traer sal/pimienta, por favor?

Where is the nearest chemist's?
¿Dónde está la farmacia más cercana?

Can you recommend a good restaurant? (to me/to us)
¿Podría recomendarme/nos un buen restaurante?

Where is the nearest cash dispenser?
¿Dónde hay un cajero automático?

On leaving

What time must we vacate our room?
¿A qué hora tenemos que dejar libre nuestra habitación?

We'd like to pay the bill.
Querríamos pagar la cuenta por favor.

Photo Jose Navarro

Where is there a good tapas bar?
¿Dónde hay un bar que sirva buenas tapas?

Please keep the change.
Quedese con la vuelta.

Where are the toilets?
¿Dónde están los servicios?

It was a delicious meal.
Estaba muy rica la comida.

I'd like a white/black coffee.
Un café con leche/un café solo.

We'd like some tea, please.
Quisiéramos tomar un té, por favor.

Suggested reading

• *The Face of Spain* and *South from Granada* by Gerald Brennan
Fascinating perspectives on 1930s' Spain.

• *Death in the Afternoon* by Ernest Hemingway
Touches on the Spanish passion for bullfighting.

• *The Seville Communion* by Arturo Pérez-Reverte
Ignore the swear words – the prose is superb.

• *Driving over Lemons* by Chris Stewart
An Englishman in Andalucía: on its way to becoming a classic.

• *El Manuscrito Carmesí* by Antonio Gala
Set in the Andalucía of La Alhambra times - a novel of character.

• *Roads to Santiago* by Cees Noteboom
A modern day pilgrimage through Spain.

• *Don Quixote Delusions; Travels in Castilian Spain* by Miranda France
"A fascinating romp through the Spanish psyche."

• *As I Walked Out One Midsummer Morning* by Laurie Lee
Irresistible account of his walk across Spain at the time of the Spanish Civil War.

• *Viaje a la Alcarria* by Camilo José Cela
Travel literature – quirky and funny.

• *A Stranger in Spain* by H V Morton
Classic travel guide through untouched Spain.

• *Duende* by Jason Webster
An entertaining account of an Englishman's attempt to infiltrate the flamenco scene.

• *Spain* by Jan Morris
Still a bestseller, after 30 years.

• *El Jardin de las Dudas* by Fernando Savater
A much-acclaimed novel by this professor of ethics.

• *Culture Shock: Spain* by Marie Louise Graff
A must if you intend living here, even for a short time.

• *Xenophobes Guide to the Spanish* by Drew Launay
Mostly accurate and very funny.

• *Blindness* by José Saramago
Winner of the 1998 Nobel Prize for Literature.

• *The Last Jew* by Noah Gordon
An action-packed novel set in the time of the Spanish Inquisition.

A short selection compiled by Jose Navarro.

shops, others into cafés or restaurants, yet others into hotels, the La Parade del Compte (entry 97) in Aragon being one (surprisingly luxurious) example. At the old stations of Puerto Serrano and Olvera on the Vía Verde de la Sierra, a couple of simple hotels have been created, so you can leave your car at one end and cycle both ways over one or two days.

The *Vías Verdes* project was launched in 1993, its aim to rejuvenate a total of 7,600 kilometres of abandoned line (some private industrial but most authority-owned). More than €50m has been invested to date. Where trains once passed, pushchairs, wheelchairs, horses and bikes now proceed - every means of non-motorised transport is welcome. It's a novel resource for active tourism in Spain, and has an attractively ecological slant.

Discover the hidden corners of Spain. *Vías Verdes* or Greenways - are breathing new life and new jobs into many of the rural communities – and, slowly but increasingly, drawing crowds away from the hectic coastal resorts into the countryside. Now visitors and locals alike can cycle, ride or stroll along 1,300 kilometres (and growing) of disused, narrow-gauge railway lines – 67 at the last count.

It's not just the tracks that have been given a new lease of life but the stations too. Some have metamorphosed into bike-hire

In spite of Spain's rugged landscape, the *vías* run mostly on the flat: unscary terrain for children and the elderly. The fascinating *Carrilet Vía Verde* (102km), which crosses a volcanic region in the foothills of the Pyrenees, includes the ancient city of Gerona, touches the Costa Brava, and draws 120,000 visitors a year, many from the city of Barcelona. But you'll often

Photo Fundación de los Ferrocarriles Españoles

find the tracks are virtually people-free. Dig out the binoculars as you pass through stunning nature reserves; dwell on the history as you cross viaducts 100 years old (one designed by Gustave Eiffel). No need to be spooked by the cool, dark tunnels – they're reassuringly illuminated by solar power as you enter. Stay at the charming Etxatoa (entry 65) in the Navarra and cycle the length of the *Vía Verde Plazaola*: it has no fewer than 14 tunnels along its 12km track.

Vías Verdes Day

Walking and cycling en masse on the second Sunday in May.

Greenways Magic Tour

A two-week whistlestop tour of Spain (May and October) by bus, train and bike along 350km of diversely beautiful track, with visits to Merida, Seville, Granada, Barcelona, Bilbao, Gerona and Oviedo, and accommodation, included.

Guía de Vías Verdes is a two-volume Spanish guide (€17), including maps, pictures, railway connections, bike hire etc. Worth it if you're planning a cycling or walking holiday based around the *Vías Verdes*.

www.viasverdes.com
Tel: 00 34 911 511065.

Photo Jose Navarro

IGN maps

1:2,5000, 1:50,000, 1:100,000 are the equivalent of OS maps, although nowhere near as accurate and user-friendly as their British counterparts. Best to order them from Stanfords before you go.

Editorial Alpina

www.editorialalpina.com
Classic walking maps of mountainous areas of Spain. Not the most accurate maps in the world but very user-friendly and they keep the spirit of adventure alive.

Spanish food

The bar tradition of tapas is popular across Spain – with subtle differences between the regions. Grilled mushrooms with prawns, a slice of baguette topped with Manchego cheese or Serrano ham, a mouthful of tortilla... best accompanied by a cold beer or a glass of chilled sherry.

In recent years tapas have also become a major influence in the European restaurant scene, and the small, exquisite platefuls of hot or cold food have become the very essence of modern cooking. At Spain's most controversial restaurant El Bulli, near Barcelona, self-taught pioneer Ferrán Adriá is famous for his sense-tickling arrays of mini gastronomic creations... vanilla-scented whipped potatoes, roast duck with olive oil chocolate bonbons, almond ice cream on swirls of garlic olive oil and balsamic vinegar, even melon caviar. In spite of his experimental approach, Adriá still insists he is as Spanish as paella.

Which brings us to the national dish! Originally farm labourers' food, prepared in the fields after a morning's work (it's still considered a lunchtime dish) paella is often called, simply, *arroz* (rice), and was probably invented in Valencia. The name, generic for 200 or so distinctive rice dishes, comes from the Latin *patella*, meaning pan. Valencia is also famous for its fruits and its desserts.

Photo Jo Boissevain

Spain has a rich gastronomic history, the Roman and Arab civilisations leaving a distinctive culinary mark. And, thanks to the country's climatic diversity, it is possible to grow fresh fruits and vegetables virtually all year round, while vines, olives and tomatoes - essentials of the so-called Mediterranean diet – thrive.

The Spanish diet is one of the healthiest in the world and there are too many treats to mention, from the bean and fish stews of Asturias, to the succulent Rubia Gallega beef of Galicia, the green Gernika peppers of the Basque country, the almond cakes of Santiago, the sherries and brandies of Jerez. All over Spain there are people devoted to good food, and increasing numbers of the world's top-flight chefs are Spanish.

Jo Boissevain

Pimientos de la Abuela
Stuffed peppers
Serves 6

6 green peppers (as round as possible)
2 onions (finely chopped)
Olive oil
Vegetable stock cube
Half a glass of white wine

Filling:
0.5kg minced beef
0.5kg minced pork
1 tablespoon breadcrumbs
2 tablespoons milk
1 egg
Salt and pepper

In a large bowl, mix the beef and pork, breadcrumbs, milk, egg and seasoning.

Wash and unseed the peppers. Add a pinch of salt and fill with the meat mix until compact. Seal the top with some flour.

In a large saucepan, fry the onions on a medium/low heat until transparent. Add the peppers and brown them, stirring often. Add enough water to cover the peppers halfway; then add the wine and stock. Heat to boiling, then lower heat and half cover the pan; cook for 45 minutes, turning occasionally.

If sauce runs out or is too thick, add more water as desired.

Albóndigas de la Tía
Meatballs
Serves 6

Meatballs:
0.5kg minced beef
0.5kg minced pork
1 tablespoon breadcrumbs
2 tablespoons milk
1 egg
Salt and pepper

Sauce:
1 onion finely chopped
1 small leek finely chopped
1 tomato peeled and chopped
1 vegetable stock cube
100g blanched almonds or pine nuts
Half a glass white wine
1 clove of garlic
Fresh parsley

Prepare meat as for the stuffed peppers. Shape into meatballs, roll in flour and fry lightly. Put aside in a big saucepan.

In another pan, fry the onions over a medium heat in olive oil. Add the leek, then the tomato. Add three glasses of water, the stock and the chopped nuts, then the wine and chopped parsley. Cook over a gentle heat for 10-20 minutes. Blend in a blender, adding water if required.

Add sauce to meatballs, and simmer half-covered for 20 minutes, stirring occasionally.

Spanish food

Paella

Serves 4

200g monkfish
250g prawns
250g clams
1 large squid
200g rice (4 cups)
1 clove garlic
Parsley
2-4 strands of saffron
Olive oil (4-5 tablespoons)
Half an onion
1 green pepper finely chopped
1 medium-sized tomato, peeled and chopped
1 vegetable stock cube

Optional: different ingredients can be used, like chicken and peas.

Two hours before starting place the clams in a bowl of salted water so they open a bit; rinse and remove sand. Once ready, boil until they open fully; drain, and keep water for later. Boil the prawns (for 3-4 minutes) and mussels (until they open); drain and keep the water. In a mortar, mash the garlic with the parsley and a few strands of saffron. Put aside.

The *paellera* must be large and shallow, and the flame must cover the entire base of the pan. Fry the onion and pepper in oil over a low/medium heat. When almost done, add the tomato, then the squid (cut into rings or squares) and the monkfish (diced). Add the rice and stir for a few seconds. Then add double (and slightly over) the amount of reserved shellfish stock to rice, ie. at least eight cups. Turn the heat up to boiling point, then simmer. Add the mix from the mortar, washing the last of the precious saffron with a dash of stock, and the crumbled stock cube. Do not stir, but drag a wooden spoon across the paella in the shape of a cross – just once (you can repeat later on).

Cook for 15 minutes, then add the clams, prawns and mussels for a further four minutes, adding hot water and more stock if necessary, and 'cross-mixing' again. Cover with a tea towel and leave to rest for 10 minutes.

Photo Casa del Pinar, entry 194

Torrijas
An Easter treat
Serves 8-10

1 wide baguette
I litre full-fat milk
2 cinnamon sticks
Fine peel of 1/4 of a lemon
0.5kg sugar
Cinnamon powder (to turn sugar brown)
3 eggs
Olive oil

Heat milk with lemon peel, cinnamon sticks and 5-6 tablespoons sugar. Stir. Once boiling, remove from heat and put aside. In a bowl, mix the rest of the sugar with the cinnamon powder, and put aside.

Slice bread into 2cm slices and place on a platter. Remove lemon and cinnamon sticks from milk and slowly spoon the lukewarm milk over the bread, letting it soak (but not float!). If the milk is added too quickly the bread may crumble. Beat the eggs and dip the bread slices into them. Pour enough oil into a frying pan to half-cover the bread; once oil is bubbling, fry bread until golden, on both sides. Remove bread from frying pan, allow oil to drain, place on a platter and sprinkle both sides with the dry sugar/cinnamon mix. Cool – and consume!

Thanks to Emilio Serrano, Almudena Adan, Pilar Serrano and Eduardo Ramos for these recipes.

Photo Jose Navarro

Historic sites and museums

Camino de Santiago, Galicia
Europe's most renowned pilgrimage, whose six routes pass through France, Spain and Portugal to converge on the cathedral of Santiago de Compostela
http://www.caminosantiago.com/

Guggenheim Museum, Bilbao, Basque country
Frank Gehry's modern masterpiece and museum of contemporary art
www.guggenheim-bilbao.es

Wine Culture Museum, Briones, La Rioja
One of the world's few museum dedicated to one particular wine (rioja!)

Dali Museum, Figueras, Catalonia
http://www.salvador-dali.org/

Photo Jo Boissevain

Sagrada Familia Church, Barcelona
The pinnacle of Antoni Gaudi's creativity, started in 1882, still under construction
www.gaudi2002.bcn.es/english/

Parc Güell, Barcelona
Gaudi's 1900 'paradise in the city', originally conceived as a residential estate

Royal Palace. Madrid
Full of treasures inside and out, with immaculate gardens.
www.patrimonionacional.es/en/preal/preal.htm

Prado Museum, Madrid
www.museoprado.mcu.es

Reina Sofia National Art Centre, Madrid www.museoreinasofia.mcu.es

Thyssen-Bornemisza Museum, Madrid www.museothyssen.org

Toledo, Castilla-La Mancha
Mudéjar-rich Toledo has been designated a World Heritage Site
www.toledoweb.org/En/Default.htm

Acueducto de Segovia, Castilla-Léon
Superb example of 1AD engineering, built without cement or mortar

Segovia Alcázar, Castilla-Léon
Impregnable 13th-century fortress – the inspiration behind Disneyland's castle

Burgos Cathedral, Castilla-Léon
Superb gothic cathedral in the old capital of Castile

Universidad de Salamanca, Castilla-Léon **Spain's most ancient university, founded in 1218**

Roman Theatre, Mérida, Extremadura
A superbly preserved ruin, and a fine venue for recitals

La Alhambra, Granada, Andalucia
Spain's most luscious assemblage of palace buildings, courtyards, fountains and gardens, dating from the 9th-century www.alhambra.org/

The Generalife, Granada, Andalucia
Vast 14th-century royal orchard and country residence of the sultan

The Albaycin quarter, Granada, Andalucia
Charming Old Town, teeming with Spanish bars and Arabic tea houses

Mezquita de Cordoba, Andalucia
Eighth-century mosque: one of the most beautiful examples of Muslim art in Spain

Picasso Museum, Malaga, Andalucia
www.museopicassomalaga.org

Seville Cathedral, Andalucia
The third largest cathedral in the Christian world; fine views from the Giralda tower

Balearic Isles
Palma Cathedral, Mallorca
Immense waterfront cathedral in Mallorca's elegant capital

Ciutadella of Minorca
The old capital of the island, renowned for its megalithic structures, or taulas
www.menorca-net.co.uk

Useful contacts
Spanish Tourist Board
www.tourspain.es
An excellent site, covering culture, food, nature, sports, children, beaches and more.
Federación Española de Montaña
www.fedme.es
They have a superb index of short (PR) pathways and long (GR) hiking routes, organised by counties. The site is in Spanish, but it's easy to navigate.
P&O Ferries
www.poferries.com
Brittany Ferries
www.brittany-ferries.com
Spanish airports
www.aena.es
Spanish railways
www.renfe.es
Spanish coach company
www.enatcar.es
British Embassy
www.ukinspain.com/english/
Emergency tel 112

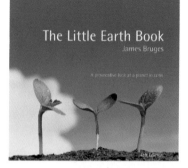

The Little Earth Book
Edition 4, £6.99
By James Bruges

A little book that has proved both hugely popular – and provocative. This new edition has chapters on Islam, Climate Change and The Tyranny of Corporations.

The Little Food Book
Edition 1, £6.99
By Craig Sams, Chairman of the Soil Association

An explosive account of the food we eat today. Never have we been at such risk - from our food. This book will help understand what's at stake.

The Little Money Book
Edition 1, £6.99
By David Boyle, an associate of the New Economics Foundation

This pithy, wry little guide will tell you where money comes from, what it means, what it's doing to the planet and what we might be able to do about it.

www.fragile-earth.com

Six Days

Celebrating the triumph of creativity over adversity.

An inspiring and heart-rending story of the making of the stained glass 'Creation' window at Chester Cathedral by a woman battling with debilitating Parkinson's disease.

"Within a few seconds, the tears were running down my cheeks. The window was one of the most beautiful things I had ever seen. It is a tour-de force, playing with light like no other window ..."
Anthropologist Hugh Brody

In 1983, Ros Grimshaw, a distinguished designer, artist and creator of stained glass windows, was diagnosed with Parkinson's disease. Refusing to allow her illness to prevent her from working, Ros became even more adept at her craft, and in 2000 won the commission to design and make the 'Creation' Stained Glass Window for Chester Cathedral.

Six Days traces the evolution of the window from the first sketches to its final, glorious completion as a rare and wonderful tribute to Life itself: for each of the six 'days' of Creation recounted in Genesis, there is a scene below that is relevant to the world of today and tomorrow.

Heart-rending extracts from Ros's diary capture the personal struggle involved. Superb photography captures the luminescence of the stunning stained glass, while the story weaves together essays, poems, and moving contributions from Ros's partner, Patrick Costeloe.

Available from Alastair Sawday Publishing £12.99

Order Form

All these books are available in major bookshops or you may order them direct.
Post and packaging are FREE within the UK.

British Hotels, Inns & Other Places	£13.99
Bed & Breakfast for Garden Lovers	£14.99
Pubs & Inns of England & Wales	£13.99
London	£9.99
British Bed & Breakfast	£14.99
French Bed & Breakfast	£15.99
French Hotels, Châteaux & Inns	£13.99
French Holiday Homes	£11.99
Paris Hotels	£9.99
Ireland	£12.99
Spain	£13.99
Portugal	£8.99
Italy	£12.99
Mountains of Europe	£9.99
Europe with courses & activities	£12.99
India	£10.99
Morocco	£10.99
The Little Earth Book	£6.99
The Little Food Book	£6.99
The Little Money Book	£6.99
Six Days	£12.99

Please make cheques payable to Alastair Sawday Publishing. Total £ _____

Please send cheques to: Alastair Sawday Publishing, The Home Farm Stables,
Barrow Gurney, Bristol BS48 3RW. For credit card orders call 01275 464891
or order directly from our web site www.specialplacestostay.com

Title   First name   Surname

Address

Postcode   Tel

If you do not wish to receive mail from other like-minded companies, please tick here ☐
If you would prefer not to receive information about special offers on our books, please tick here ☐

Report Form

If you have any comments on entries in this guide, please let us have them. If you have a favourite house, hotel, inn or other new discovery, please let us know about it. You can email info@sawdays.co.uk, too.

Existing entry:

Book title: _____

Entry no: _____ Edition no: _____

Report:

_____
_____
_____
_____
_____
_____
_____

Country: **New recommendation:**

Property name: _____

Address: _____
_____
_____
_____

Tel _____
_____

Your name: _____

Address: _____
_____
_____

Tel: _____

Please send completed form to ASP, The Home Farm Stables, Barrow Gurney, Bristol BS48 3RW or go to www.specialplacestostay.com and click on 'contact'. Thank you.

Bilingual booking form

Atencion de:
To:
_____

Date:
_____

Estimado Señor/Estimada Señora,

Le(s) rogamos de hacernos una reserva en nombre de:
Please make the following booking for (name):
_____

Para	noche(s)	Llegando día:		mes	año
For	night(s)	Arriving: day		month	year
		Saliendo día:		mes	año
		Leaving: day		month	year

Necesitamos		habitacíon(es),	:
We would like		rooms, arranged as follows:	

Doble	Con dos camas	
Double bed	Twin beds	
Triple	Individual	
Triple	Single	
Tipo Suite	Apartamento	ou autre
Suite	Apartment	or other

Requeriremos también la cena:	Si	No	Para	persona(s)
We will also be requiring dinner	yes	no	for	person(s)

Les rogamos de enviarnos la confirmacion de esta reserva a la siguiente dirección:
Please could you send us confirmation of our reservation to the address below
(esta misma hoja o una fotocopia de la misma con su firma nos valdrá).
(this form or a photocopy of it with your signature could be used).

Nombre: **Name:**
_____

Dirección: **Address:**
_____

_____

_____

Tel No:	Email:
Fax No:	

Discover your perfect self-catering escape in Britain...

We have launched a brand new self-catering web site covering England, Scotland and Wales. With the same punch and attitude as our printed guides www.special-escapes.co.uk celebrates only those places that we have visited and genuinely like – castles, cottages, bothies and more...

Special Escapes is a shining beacon among the mass of bleak holiday cottage sites cluttering the search engine pages. Each place is described in the style for which Alastair Sawday Publishing is so well known – and since it won't be published in book form, you'll be able to read the full description along with details about amenities and what to see and do locally.

Russell Wilkinson,
Web Site Manager

Quick reference indices

Photos Jose Navarro

266 • 269 • 282 • 283 • 285 • 286
• 288 • 289 • 290 • 293 • 296 •
297 • 299 • 302 • 303 • 307 • 308
• 310 • 314 • 320 • 321 • 322 •
323 • 324 • 325 • 326 • 327 • 328
• 329 • 330 • 331 • 332 • 334 •
336 • 337 • 339 • 341 • 342 • 343
Balearics 345 • 361
Canary Islands 366

Air-conditioning

These places have air conditioning in some or all bedrooms

Asturias & Cantabria 35 • 36 • 54
Basque Country 61 • 64
Navarra - La Rioja 67 • 70
Aragón 72 • 75 • 77
Catalonia 88 • 91 • 99 • 106 • 108
• 111 • 113 • 114 • 115 • 116 • 123
• 126
Castilla-León 130 • 131 • 137 • 139
• 140 • 142 • 143 • 144 • 147 •
149 • 152
Castilla - La Mancha 156 • 157 •
158 • 159 • 160 • 161 • 162 • 163
• 164 • 165 • 169 • 170
Madrid 173
Levante 178 • 179 • 182 • 187 •
190 • 191 • 192 • 193 • 195 • 197
Extremadura 198 • 200 • 201 • 202
• 204 • 209 • 210 • 211
Andalucía 213 • 218 • 219 • 220 •
222 • 223 • 224 • 225 • 226 • 227
• 228 • 231 • 232 • 233 • 238 •
244 • 246 • 247 • 248 • 249 • 250
• 251 • 252 • 253 • 261 • 263 •
266 • 270 • 274 • 275 • 276 • 277

• 278 • 279 • 280 • 281 • 282 •
284 • 285 • 287 • 291 • 293 • 296
• 297 • 298 • 299 • 300 • 308 •
309 • 311 • 312 • 313 • 314 • 315
• 316 • 317 • 320 • 321 • 331 •
332 • 333 • 335 • 336 • 339 • 340
• 342
Balearics 344 • 347 • 349 • 350 •
352 • 353 • 354 • 355 • 356 • 358
• 360 • 361 • 362 • 363 • 364
Canary Islands 366 • 367 • 368

Pazos de Galicia

Galicia 2 • 4 • 5 • 7 • 8 • 13 • 17 •
19 • 20

Rusticae Hotels

Galicia 5 • 11 • 18
Asturias & Cantabria 26 • 28 • 33 •
38 • 42 • 49 • 51 • 54
Basque Country 55
Navarra - La Rioja 67 • 69 • 70
Aragón 72 • 76 • 78 • 85

Quick reference indices

Swimming pool
Pool on the premises; use may be by arrangement.

Index by property name
(both with and without prefixes)

Index by property name
(both with and without prefixes)

Index by property name
(both with and without prefixes)

Index by place name

① Catalonia

Mas Salvanera
17850 Beuda, Gerona

In a blissfully quiet corner of the wooded Pyrenean foothills this solid, semi-fortified farmhouse has been transformed into a small luxury hotel. Your hosts still glow with enthusiasm for the project that changed their lives. The guest bedrooms, in an olive mill next to the main house, are named after signs of the zodiac and are large and elegant. Beneath old, darkening beams are colourful fabrics and antiques, many of which Ramón has restored himself, while Rocío's decorative flair is on show throughout. Bathrooms are generous and lovely. The main building has a pretty old well, vaulted ceilings, open hearths, exposed stone, an authentic country feel; the dining room is up one level, its centrepiece a fine 18-place dining table. Everyone eats together (but no meals in summer) and many of Rocío's recipes are Basque. Paella and rabbit are specialities, rioja is the wine of choice. Breakfasts are big and buffet, taken whenever you like. Outside, a peaceful walled garden and a big sculpted pool beneath the olive trees, great for families. **②**

rooms	9 twins/doubles. **③**
price	€120; half-board €174. **④**
meals	Dinner €27. Restaurant 8km. **⑤**
closed	1-10 January; 1-10 July; 11-19 September. No meals July-Sept. **⑥**
directions	Barcelona A-7 Gerona. Exit 6 for Gerona Norte; C-150 to Banyoles & Besalú. Right on N-260 Figueres; left for Maià de Montcal. Follow signs to Beuda; 1.6km to hotel. **⑦**

	Rocío Niño Ojeda & Ramón Ruscalleda
tel	+34 972 590975
fax	+34 972 590863
email	salvanera@salvanera.com
web	www.salvanera.com

⑨ Map 9 Entry 105 **⑧**

Explanation

1 region

2 write up
Written by us.

3 rooms
Bath/shower rooms may not all be en suite; see introduction.

4 price
The price shown is for two people sharing a room, exclusive of VAT at 7% unless stated. A price range incorporates room/seasonal differences.

5 meals
Prices are per person. Half-board prices may be quoted per room or per person. If breakfast isn't included we give the price, exclusive of VAT at 7%.

6 closed
When given in months, this means for the whole of the named months and the time in between.

7 directions
Use as a guide, check when booking, and travel with a good map.

8 symbols
See the last page of the book for a fuller explanation:

🕭	wheelchair facilities		guests' pets welcome
🕭	easily accessible bedrooms		owners' pets live here
🕭	no smoking anywhere		working farm
🕭	cash only		pool
🕭	good vegetarian dinner options		bikes on the premises
(Hello)	English spoken		tennis on the premises
			information on local walks
			air-conditioning in bedrooms

9 map & entry numbers
Self-catering properties are shown in pink on the map pages.

Britain • France • India • Ireland • Italy • Morocco • Portugal • Spain... all in one place!

On the unfathomable and often unnavigable sea of online accommodation pages, those who have discovered www.specialplacestostay.com have found it to be an island of reliability. Not only will you find a database full of trustworthy, up-to-date information about all of our Special Places to Stay, but also:

- Links to the web sites of all of the places in the series
- Colourful, clickable, interactive maps to help you find the right place
- The opportunity to make most bookings by email – even if you don't have email yourself
- Online purchasing of our books, securely and cheaply
- Regular, exclusive special offers on books
- The latest news about future editions and future titles
- Special offers and news from our owners

The site is constantly evolving and is frequently updated with news and special features that won't appear anywhere else but in our window on the worldwide web.

Russell Wilkinson, Web Site Manager
website@specialplacestostay.com

If you'd like to receive news and updates about our books by email, send a message to
newsletter@specialplacestostay.com